THE LONG-RANGE WAR

Sniping in Vietnam

Peter R. Senich

PALADIN PRESS
BOULDER, COLORADO

Also by Peter R. Senich:

The Complete Book of U.S. Sniping

The German Assault Rifle: 1935–1945

The German Sniper: 1914–1945

U.S. Marine Corps Scout-Sniper: World War II and Korea

The Long-Range War:
Sniping in Vietnam
by Peter R. Senich

Copyright © 1994 by Peter R. Senich

ISBN 0-87364-789-0
Printed in the United States of America

Published by Paladin Press, a division of
Paladin Enterprises, Inc., P.O. Box 1307,
Boulder, Colorado 80306, USA.
(303) 443-7250

Direct inquiries and/or orders to the above address.

All rights reserved. Except for use in a review, no
portion of this book may be reproduced in any form
without the express written permission of the publisher.

Neither the author nor the publisher assumes
any responsibility for the use or misuse of
information contained in this book.

Credit for photos appearing on front and back covers,
dust jacket, and end sheets goes to the U.S. Army.

Contents

Chapter 1 Sniping in Vietnam: The Early Days	1
Chapter 2 Sniper Operations: A Program Takes Hold	27
Chapter 3 Sniper Weapon System: The XM21	55
Chapter 4 The Suppressor and the Sniper Rifle	95
Chapter 5 Auto-Ranging Telescope: The Leatherwood Principle	107
Chapter 6 A Riflescope for the M16	121
Chapter 7 The USAMTU and the Sniper Instructor Groups	139
Chapter 8 Noise Suppression: The Silent War	157
Chapter 9 The Marine Corps Model: The Green Scope	187
Chapter 10 Silencers and Suppressors: The Sionics Legacy	201
Chapter 11 Night Vision Sights: A Definite Edge	221
Chapter 12 The M21: A System in Transition	247

"A sniper is a soldier with special abilities, training, and equipment who is designated to deliver discriminatory and highly accurate rifle fire against enemy targets which, because of range, size, location, fleeting nature, or visibility, cannot be engaged successfully by the average rifleman."

—United States Army
Combat Developments Command
May 1968

Preface and Acknowledgments

Of all the armed conflicts U.S. combat forces have been involved with in this century, the war in South Vietnam marked the first time in American military history that trained snipers, special rifles, telescopic sights, ammunition, and noise suppressors were brought together and employed successfully in a combat environment.

With the realization that the Communist insurgents, the Vietcong (VC), were moving about freely in the areas surrounding the American positions during the early months of the war, the Army and the Marine Corps found themselves faced with a unique dilemma. Even though the 7.62mm M14 service rifle then in use was entirely capable of delivering relatively accurate medium- and long-range fire in the hands of a competent rifleman, the Vietcong were not the least bit intimidated by ordinary rifle fire. As the range increased, the chances of hitting the enemy with aimed shots using conventional rifle sights decreased proportionately.

And while ragged and ill-equipped in many cases, the VC knew full well when they were in danger and when they were not. As a result, individuals and small groups of enemy personnel were frequently observed in full view of the American positions directing mortar and rocket fire or simply going about their business with virtual impunity. Although calling for mortar and artillery fire in return did work to some extent, neither measure could be carried out without providing some advance warning. Consequently, as soon as the firing started, the Vietcong simply disappeared from view. The chances of taking out one or two of the enemy under the circumstances were less than satisfactory, and the entire process proved to be an exercise in futility more often than not.

To many of the "old hands" in the Army and Marine Corps, the solution was obvious: employ skilled riflemen capable of engaging enemy personnel at extended ranges with consistent results in and around the enclaves. There was no other choice; trained snipers armed with telescopic sighted rifles were the answer.

In spite of the fact that the Army and the Marine Corps chose to field vastly different weapon systems for their snipers—the Army favored a match-conditioned version of the semiautomatic service rifle, while the Marine Corps decided on a commercial bolt-action rifle configured to its specifications—the nucleus of both sniper programs comprised a resolute group of accomplished riflemen and competitive marksmen, many of who had been actively involved with their respective rifle teams and marksmanship training units (MTUs) prior to the war in South Vietnam.

Of course, it would take considerable time and effort training and equipping snipers for combat before the results clearly justified the course of action. But when the first Marine marksman, a 3d Marine Division sniper, brought down an unsuspecting enemy soldier with his telescopic sighted rifle in 1965 (3d MarDiv is credited with fielding the first organized sniping program in Vietnam), from that point forward, the everyday life of the Communist forces operating in Southeast Asia became infinitely less secure.

Though months would pass before an effective Army sniper program would take shape, as the buildup of American forces continued through late 1965 and into 1966, many of the units destined for combat duty deployed to South Vietnam with token quantities of telescopic sighted military and commercial rifles.

As the war progressed, there were, in fact, two forms of sniping carried out in Southeast Asia—that which took place as part of, or in conjunction with, the organized Army and Marine Corps programs and that conducted by "riflemen with telescopic sights" (not viewed as "snipers" by themselves or the military) acting independently of any authorized program. There was a great deal more sniping activity in Vietnam than either the Army or Marine Corps was aware of—or cared to acknowledge, for that matter. In addition to the men actually trained and fielded as snipers by the Army, Navy, Marine Corps, and Air Force, an unknown number of combat personnel made effective use of telescope-equipped rifles during the war in Vietnam. Army and Marine snipers kept careful track of their "kills" as a measure of their programs' effectiveness, but there was no way of knowing exactly how many Vietcong and North Vietnamese combatants were rendered *hors de combat* by enterprising American riflemen armed with telescopic sighted rifles of one kind or another.

In any event, whether the men using telescope-equipped rifles were trained as snipers as part of the organized programs or simply acting on their own, the overall U.S. sniping effort in Southeast Asia proved to be an extremely effective means of countering the tactics and activities of the Vietcong.

In many respects, the VC and North Vietnamese Army (NVA) personnel were infinitely more concerned with the prospects of an encounter with an American sniper than a flight of B-52 bombers dropping 750-pound bombs. However, with the exception of the few personal narratives that provide insight on sniping activities in a given area or time frame, the unprecedented use of snipers and sniping equipment during the conflict in Southeast Asia has been largely ignored. Many contemporary works concerning U.S. combat involvement in South Vietnam from 1965 to 1973 mention sniping only in passing. Therefore, I have written this volume dealing with sniping in Vietnam in an effort to focus attention on a small but extremely significant aspect of modern military history.

Even though various aspects of the early Marine Corps sniping

Preface and Acknowledgments

effort have been duly noted in this volume, Marine snipers and their equipment will be thoroughly detailed in the next book in this series. The material presented here deals primarily with the Army sniper program, the circumstances behind the fielding of the sophisticated XM21 sniper rifle, and the Adjustable Ranging Telescope (ART) developed for use in Vietnam. In addition, the origins and the subsequent combat application of sound suppression devices for rifles and special carbines are covered in this volume. Though employed only on a limited basis by snipers and special mission personnel, the unique attachments were characteristic of the unconventional nature of the warfare in Southeast Asia.

This book is the culmination of an information-gathering process that actually began as the war in Vietnam was in full-swing during the late 1960s. The material herein was obtained from official correspondence, reports, ordnance documents, intelligence sources, and the recollections of the military and civilian personnel who were directly involved with the Army and Marine Corps sniping programs during this hectic era.

In preparing this book, I made every effort to provide the reader with as much insight as possible. In this regard, the excerpts from the correspondence and documents generated by the principals involved with the Army sniper program and the XM21 are particularly noteworthy. These afford the reader the unique opportunity to review significant information as it moved between Southeast Asia and the United States during the height of the war and to get the author's perspective as well.

Having obtained much of the material in this book from the officers and men who were part of the sniping effort in Vietnam, I want to extend a special note of appreciation to them for granting me access to their personal archives, for sharing their experiences, and for having the foresight to retain pertinent documents relating to the Army and Marine Corps sniping programs that otherwise would have been lost or destroyed. In addition, my eternal gratitude to the persons and organizations who provided me with information, photographs, and their support. For this help I wish to thank:

Robert I. Landies
Max Crace
Donald G. Barker
Gerald J. Boutin
Mrs. William S. Brophy
Bruce Nelson
Uyless L. Glover
Bill Grube
Rich Urich
William S. Brophy III
Richard H. Thomas
Theo. C. Mataxis
John Foote
James W. Alley
Charles Leatherwood

Herb Rosenbaum
J. David Truby
Robert W. Fisch
Konrad Schreier Jr.
Richard Slack
Colin Doane
Barry Zuckerman
John L. Plaster
William E. Thomas
Charles B. Mawhinney
Maxwell G. Atchisson
Robert Bell
Allan D. Cors
Scott A. Duff
Keith R. Pagel
Jerry Tarble
Herbert J. Woodend
Mitchell E. Mateiko
Archie DiFante
George E. Hijar
Kathleen J. Hoyt
Ludwig P. Gogol
Blair M. Gluba
Daniel T. Whiteman
Fred Martin
William H. Woodin
John W. Scott
Ronald Twiggs
Dan Shepherd
O.P. Seberger Jr.
Sam Bases
Frank W. Hackley
Robert N. Reaume
William H. Woodin
R.H.G. Koster
Brad David
Alston Waylor
Bill Mangels
Geoffrey WerBell
Mitchell L. WerBell IV
Albert W. Hauser
John C. McPherson
Gil Parsons
William J. Ricca
Craig Roberts
Elroy Sanford
Paul M. Senich

George Niewenhous
William D. Harris
John G. Griffiths
Thomas Shannon
Donald Urtz
Joseph T. Ward
Kenneth Kogan
K.L. Smith-Christmas
Dean H. Whitaker
Elliott R. Laine Jr.
Irl Otte
American Rifleman magazine
Leatherneck magazine
Library of Congress
National Archives and Records Service
West Point Museum
U.S. Patent Office
Springfield Armory NHS
Excaliber Enterprises
Redfield, Inc.
Rock Island Arsenal Museum
Brookfield Precision Tool
Marine Corps Gazette
Infantry magazine
Woodin Laboratory
MAC Sales, Inc.
Remington Arms Co., Inc.
Marine Corps Air-Ground Museum
Marine Corps Historical Center
Parsons Riflescope Service
Naval Historical Center, U.S. Navy
Office of the Chief of Military History, U.S. Army
Colt's Manufacturing Co., Inc.
Office of Air Force History, U.S. Air Force

While every contribution to this project, regardless of its size, was both welcome and greatly appreciated, a very special expression of thanks goes to the following gentlemen for rendering assistance far beyond what any author has a right to expect:

Donald G. Thomas
Francis B. Conway
Edward J. Land Jr.
Willis L. Powell
Robert J. Faught
Robert A. Russell
James M. Leatherwood

Although these individuals and organizations deserve proper credit for helping me locate and piece together the vast amount of information this project required, any error in putting this material in its final form properly rests with me.

This book is intended as an instrument of historical reference for the sole purpose of describing and illustrating the activities and equipment of the United States Army and Marine Corps sniper during the Vietnam War.

—Peter R. Senich

Preface and Acknowledgments

WILLIAM S. BROPHY

When William S. Brophy passed away in the spring of 1991, the distinguished hunter, competitive shooter, author, and indefatigable advocate of Army marksmanship had earned the respect and admiration of those in the civilian and military community who knew the importance of maintaining an optimum level of marksmanship training in the United States Army. His life-long accomplishments included serving his country in World War II, Korea, and Vietnam, although Lieutenant Colonel Brophy was best known in recent years for his definitive books on American small arms.

During the Korean War, Brophy launched what some considered "a one-man campaign" to focus attention on the inadequacies of Army sniping equipment by using a commercial Winchester Model 70 target rifle to demonstrate what the right combination of weapon and trained marksman could achieve. As a result of 1,000-plus-yard shooting considered nothing short of phenomenal at the time, he brought about a general concensus that equipment of this type could be maintained under battle conditions if placed in the hands of highly trained marksmen.

Capt. William S. Brophy with Winchester target rifle circa 1952. The .30-caliber (.30-06) Model 70 "Bull Gun" was fitted with a Unertl 10-power, 2-inch objective target telescope for sniping purposes. (Brophy Collection.)

Interestingly, although the contemporary focus of sniping accomplishments with the Model 70 Winchester has been on Marine Corps efforts in South Vietnam, Bill Brophy gave serious meaning to Army use of the Model 70 for sniping purposes. In addition, the innovative ordnance officer was among the first to employ special .50-caliber rifles in combat for sniping at extended ranges.

Though rarely noted, of all the things Colonel Brophy gained recognition for during his long and illustrious career, his efforts to both organize and preserve the vast collection of Model 1903 Springfield rifles at Springfield Armory—at a time when the very existence of this venerable institution was seriously in doubt—deserves proper recognition.

In the course of my research activities, I had the opportunity to observe the results of Colonel Brophy's work at the Armory—which were so remarkable that I was moved to name Bill Brophy "Mr. Springfield" in a later work.

By any measure or standard, Lt. Col. William S. Brophy, USAR (Ret.), was an American of note and a "contributor" without peer.

—P.R.S.

CHAPTER 1

Sniping in Vietnam: The Early Days

The period between the end of the Korean War and full-scale United States military intervention in South Vietnam saw little advancement in sniper training and equipment. Although few within the military would dispute the need for basic marksmanship training, despite the demonstrated benefit of adding to a rifleman's skills by providing him with the means to consistently engage the enemy at extended ranges, sniper operations were virtually nonexistent in the Army and Marine Corps in the years preceding the war in Vietnam (apart from an occasional article appearing in an Army or Marine Corps periodical addressing the "need" for a sniper program and suitable equipment). As a matter of course, studies were conducted and training manuals periodically amended, but, as in the past, sniper training was not compulsory, and the whole concept of sniping was considered little more than a bother to most commanders. Excepting the rare occasion when a sniper program was set up under the aegis of a division or regimental commander with a keen appreciation of individual marksmanship, few snipers were fielded.

Even though the successor to the M1 Garand, the M14 (adopted in 1957), had added a groove and screw recess on the left side of the receiver, ostensibly for mounting night vision equipment and telescopic sights, no telescope mounting was adopted for this weapon. The first notable application of telescopic sights to the M14 took place in 1958, when Lt. Col. Frank Conway (Ret.), while serving as an ordnance captain with the U.S. Army Marksmanship Training Unit (USAMTU), mounted commercial Weaver K-6 scopes on two M14s by means of special bases.

THE LONG-RANGE WAR: SNIPING IN VIETNAM

The USAMTU Capability Study: Sniper Rifles and Telescopic Sights, July 1967

Information gathered from the Marine Corps Sniper Program indicates the average range for kills over a five month period to have been 557 meters. They have made extensive use of externally adjusted scopes [target telescopes] zeroed at 600 yards with adjustments for longer or shorter ranges as required.

He mounted the front base on the M14 barrel with the rear handguard clip removed and the handguard cut to fit. He affixed the rear base to the receiver in place of the conventional sight. In order to compensate for the difference in height between the rear of the receiver and the barrel, he used a "high" Weaver mount in front and a "low" mount at the rear to bring the scope in line with the bore. As such, the rifles were fired by Capt. Richard Wentworth at the Running Deer World Championships held at Moscow with excellent results.

Nevertheless, the task of convincing higher echelons that a sniper system was necessary during peacetime remained formidable, although a myriad of concepts and objectives were formulated under or stemmed from the Army's marksmanship training program known as "Trainfire." With no requirements for such equipment, sniping developments not only lagged, but were, in fact, nonexistent. Consequently, when faced with the realization that the Vietcong were moving about freely beyond the range of the average rifleman, and that VC snipers were taking out U.S. combat personnel in various sectors, the military found itself in a familiar posture; that is, without satisfactory sniping equipment available for immediate use. As a result, a flurry of both official and quasi-official efforts to field sniper weapons commenced in earnest, although references such as "supplemental," "expedient," and "improvised" were frequently used to describe Army and Marine Corps sniping equipment at all levels of command during the "early days" in South Vietnam (1965-1966).

Vietnam-era USMC combat photo: "A Marine sniper from G Company, 2nd Battalion, 9th Marines (3d MarDiv) takes aim at Hill 251 during Operation Harvest Moon." The rifle is a Winchester Model 70 with an 8-power Unertl telescopic sight, the principal Marine Corps sniping issue during early combat activity in South Vietnam. (U.S. Marine Corps.)

In addition to an accelerated Marine Corps program intended to "meet or exceed" existing requirements for sniper training and equipment in Southeast Asia, in 1966, Army Weapons Command (USAWECOM) developed a hinged-telescope mount to accommodate the 2.2-power M84 sight. On 19 October 1966, the United States Army Infantry Board (USAIB) was directed to test this mount with the M14 rifle to determine its suitability for

Sniping in Vietnam: The Early Days

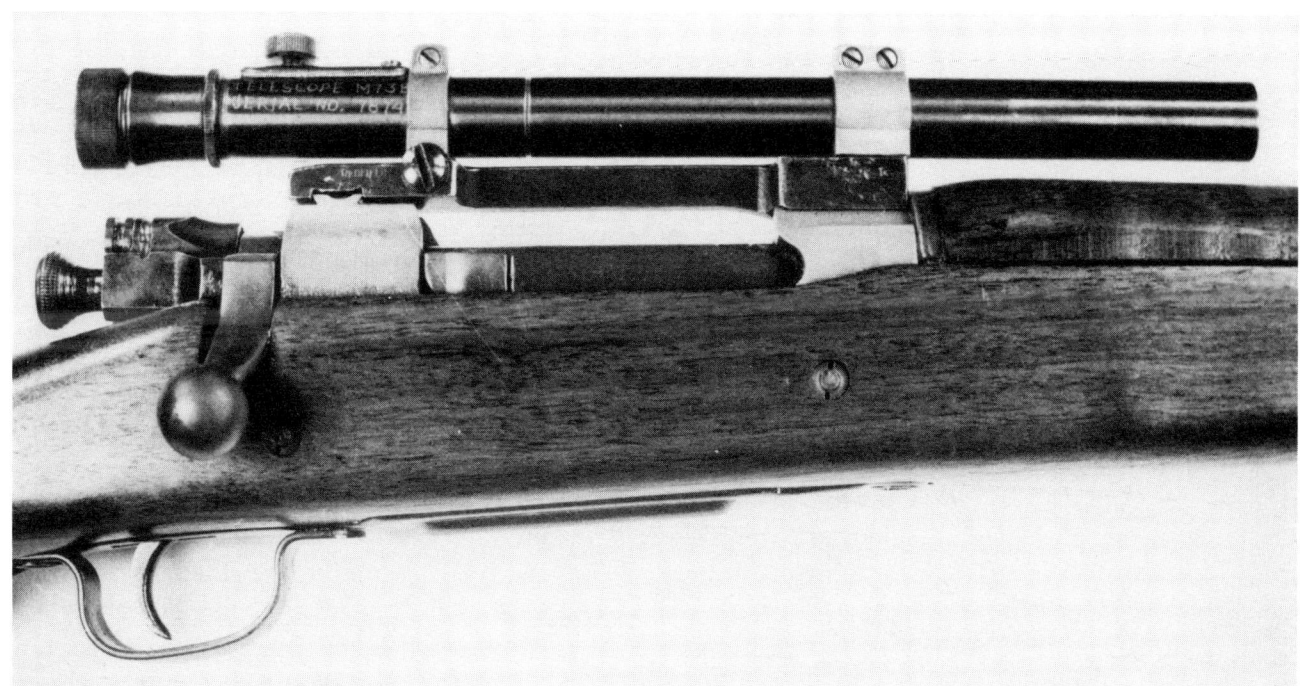

U.S. Rifle, Caliber .30, M1903A4 (Sniper's) with Telescope M73B1 (Weaver 330C). The World War II- and Korean War-era Remington M1903A4 sniper rifle and standard M1903A3 rifles converted for sniping purposes were fielded by U.S. military advisors and combat personnel during early action in South Vietnam. Although M73B1, M81, and M82 telescopes were mounted on the A4 rifle in Korea, the 2.2-power M84 was authorized for use with the Remington sniper rifle when the early scopes became obsolete. The M1903A4 continued to be referenced in technical manuals and ordnance bulletins during the height of U.S. involvement in Southeast Asia. According to Army Ordnance documents, "The M1903A4, M1C and the M1D remained in storage" well into the late 1970s. (Peter R. Senich.)

use in Vietnam. Testing began on 9 May 1967 and was completed on 28 June 1967. All testing was conducted at Ft. Benning, Georgia.

Four 7.62mm M14 rifles with hinged-telescope mounts and M84 telescopes would serve as the test weapons. All rifles except one were "match-conditioned" and met National Match accuracy requirements. Test sights were regular issue M84 telescopes (a straight-tube, conventional telescope with universal focus, 2.2-power magnification, and a field of view of 27 feet at 100 yards) originally designed in 1945 for use as snipers' sighting devices with the .30-caliber M1C and M1D rifles.

There was no difficulty in acclimating the personnel used in this test, since all had an Army Marksmanship Qualification of Expert. However, the initial exercise of aligning the scope with the rifle required more than one hour for each system under ideal range conditions and proved to be beyond the capability of the average soldier in a field environment. Neither the mount nor telescope proved sufficiently durable, with a number of malfunctions and breakages occurring at various times during the testing.

The principal deficiency of the M84 scope rested with the marginal benefit it afforded in seeking and/or engaging targets at extreme ranges due to low magnification. Flakes of internal coating material appeared within the field of view of each sight at various times, distracting the shooter (a condition that was characteristic of the M84 sights). The

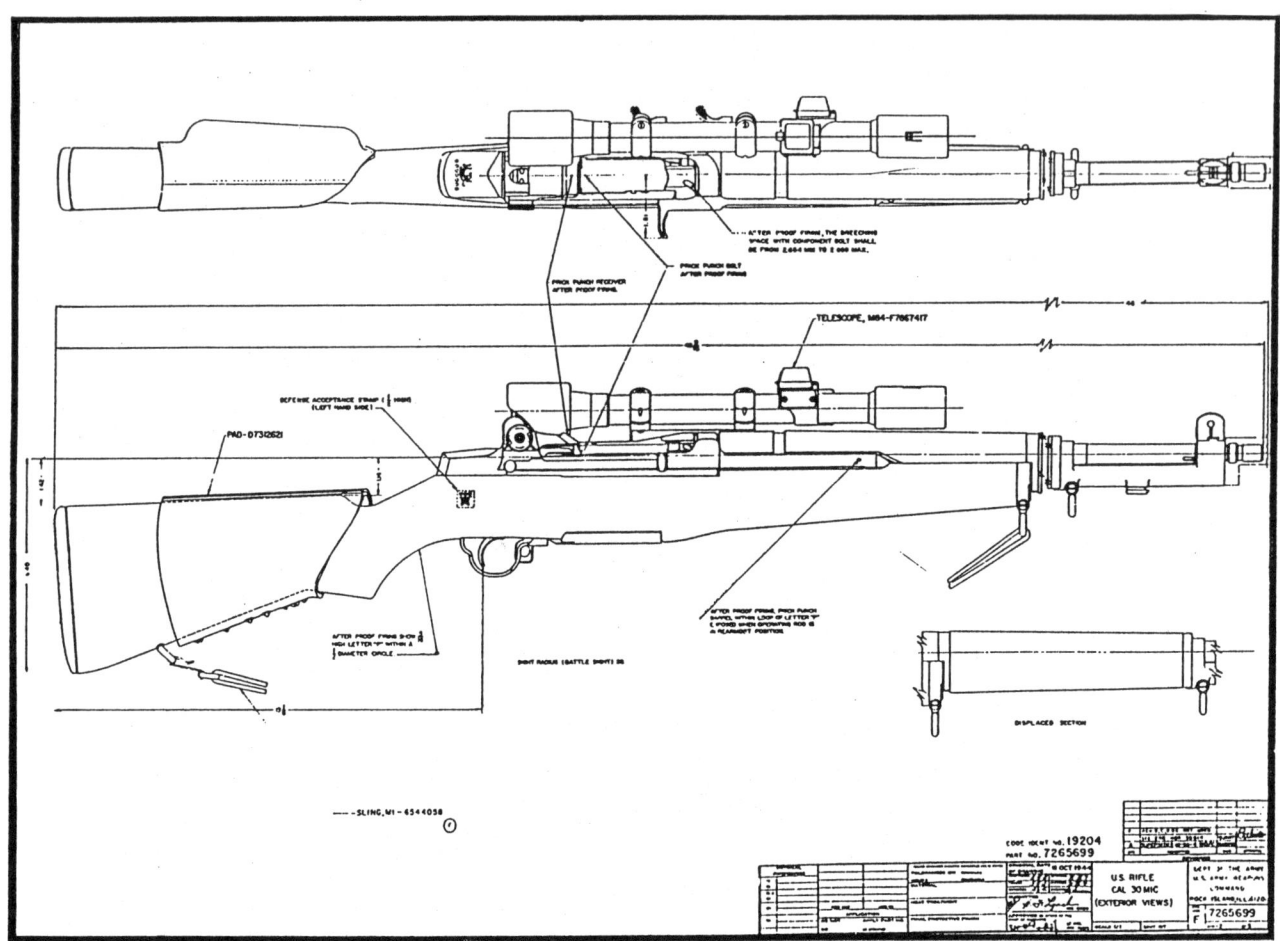

A post-Korean War ordnance drawing (U.S. Army Weapons Command, Rock Island, Illinois) of the "U.S. Rifle, Caliber .30 M1C." Despite reports of both M1C and M1D rifles being drawn from ordnance stores and sent to Southeast Asia during the initial phases of the war, by all accounts, the M1C was rarely encountered in Vietnam. In addition to providing M1 sniper rifles to the ARVN, according to Army Ordnance documents, the Royal Thai Army was known to have received 460 M1D sniper rifles as part of the "assistance" from the United States. (Scott A. Duff.)

scopes also had the tendency to rust excessively under prolonged humid conditions.

Although the maximum effective range of the M84 telescope, as determined by the test, was approximately 800 meters, the objective consensus was that "pure chance" accounted for hits at this range. As a matter of interest, during subsequent combat use in Vietnam, documented hits were recorded out to 800 meters with the M84, but this was rare, and two or three shots were required to get on target.

The Army Weapons Command (AWC) mounts were, in fact, similar to the Pachmayr type tested between 1951 and 1953 by the USAIB, when a swing or hinge mount was necessary to facilitate clip loading of the M1 rifle from above. However, since the M14 was normally loaded by magazine from beneath, the requirement for a telescope mount such as this no longer existed. Based on the results of its testing, the Army Infantry Board concluded the following:

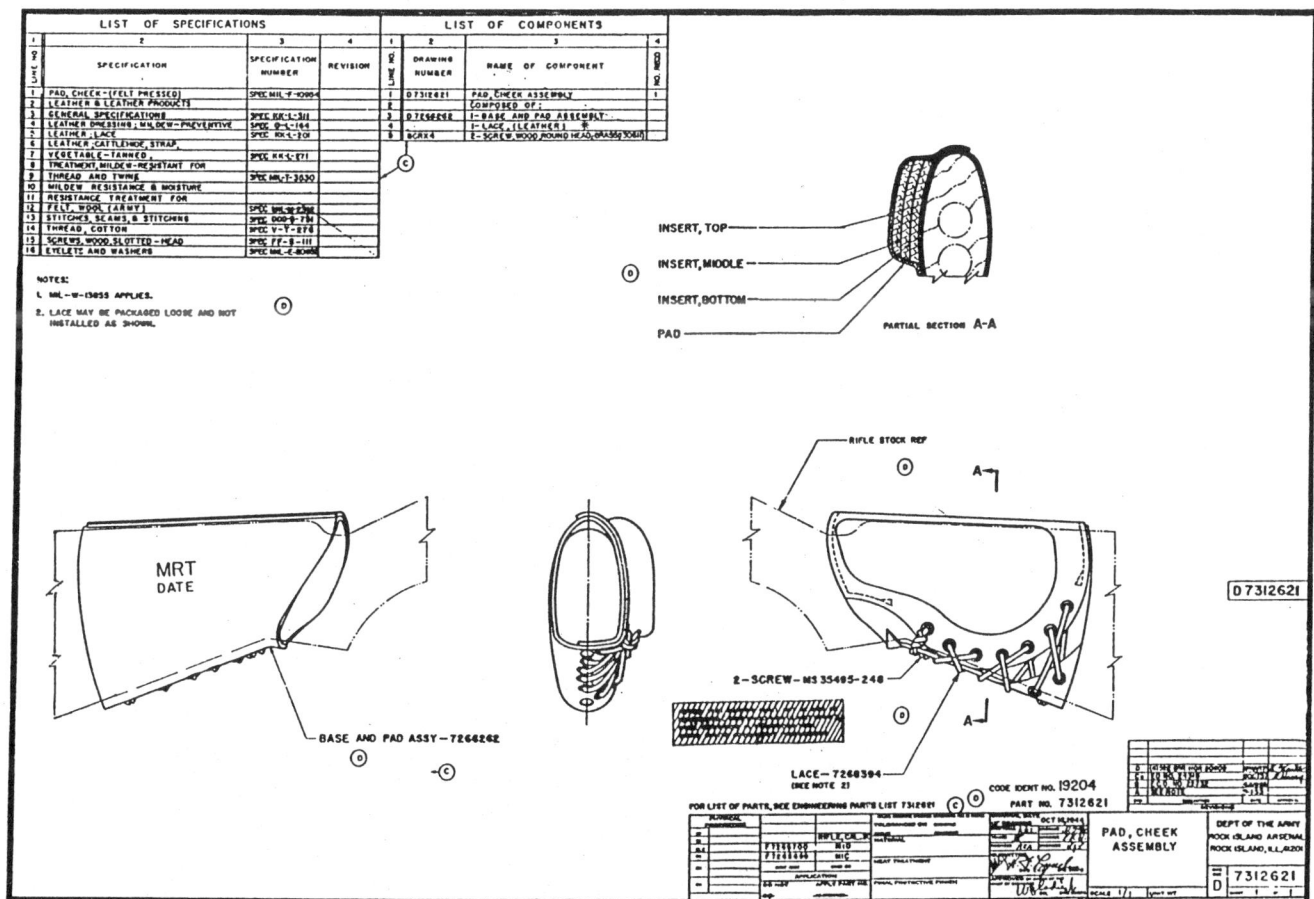

A Department of the Army, Rock Island Arsenal (RIA) ordnance drawing for the "Pad, Cheek Assembly" issued with the M1C and M1D sniper rifles. Though pictured frequently, this unique accessory item is rarely seen in an original ordnance drawing. The leather cheek pad was used to compensate for the offset position of the telescope on the M1 sniping rifles. Though intended for the Garand, the cheek pads were employed with a variety of sniping weapons. (Scott A. Duff.)

(A) The hinged-telescope mount for the M14 rifle will not be suitable for sniper use in Southeast Asia until its deficiencies are corrected.

(B) The Cartridge, 7.62mm, Ball, M80 is not sufficiently accurate for sniping purposes.

(C) The M84 Telescope is unsuitable for use, except under some conditions, and represents the least suitable element of the system furnished for test.

(D) The M14 rifle with National Match accuracy characteristics employing 7.62mm, M118 National Match Ammunition, provides sufficient systems accuracy for sniper purposes.

(E) A variable power telescope or one with a minimum of 4-power magnification is needed in the sniper role.

The Marine Corps used a limited number of 3X-9X variable-power rifle scopes manufactured in Japan (the scopes were trademarked "Marine"; the brand name and Marine Corps use were coincidental in this case) with the Model 70 for early USMC sniping activity beginning in 1965. While hardly an optimum rifle sight, its ranging capability (variable power adjustment) was seen as a "desirable feature" in a field scope. The Japanese hunting sights were purchased on Okinawa as a supplemental measure. The Marine sniper (Donald G. Barker) maintains his vigil following a patrol near Marble Mountain. The Model 70 has a heavy barrel and target stock. According to Marine Corps documents, "The first Model 70 rifles fielded for the 3rd Marine Division sniper program (12 rifles) were Winchester target rifles with heavy barrel and target stock." The rifle was known as a "factory heavy" to many of the Marines. (U.S. Marine Corps.)

Model 1903A4 sniper rifle with the M84 telescope. In addition to the vintage M73B1 and M84 sights, the versatility of the Redfield Junior telescope mounting allowed for the use of contemporary rifle scopes as well. While hardly "issue" equipment, a variety of fixed-power and variable-power commercial telescopic sights (1-inch tube) were reportedly fitted to the M1903A3 and M1903A4 Remington rifles for use in South Vietnam. With many American advisors—and eventually the special mission groups—operating "off the books" with respect to their equipment and activities in particular, the "special small arms" fielded in RVN, especially during the early months of full-scale U.S. combat activity, were, in many cases, a simple matter of "whatever it takes." The rifles and telescopic sights employed for sniping purposes were no exception in this regard. (Peter R. Senich.)

Sniping in Vietnam: The Early Days

In retrospect, the most significant finding of the USAIB evaluation was perhaps the suitability of a match-grade weapon and ammunition for sniping. This, of course, was unprecedented for the Army and actually paved the way for what eventually became the first military application of accurized semiautomatic rifles and match-grade ammunition for combat use (the XM21 system). For the record, however, when the Marine Corps shipped Model 70 Winchester "team rifles" to South Vietnam for sniper use in 1965, it furnished National Match ammunition with this equipment. By so doing, the Marine Corps established a precedent that has carried through to this day—the field use of "match-grade ammunition" for sniping purposes.

At this juncture, however, in order to meet the pressing need for telescopic sights in Vietnam, it was decided that the M84 telescope should be used as an "interim item" until a satisfactory variable ranging telescope could be adopted. Consequently, even though the hinge mount never made it to Vietnam, the M84, despite acknowledged deficiencies, was employed with improvised military and commercial telescope mountings in considerable numbers, particularly during early sniping activity.

In some quarters, including Army Weapons Command, retention of this sight with standard issue M14s and M80 ball ammunition was, for a time, considered adequate for Army snipers. The M84 was available from military stores and presented a practical choice among those having no conception of what effective sniping consisted of at the field level. However, there was still no satisfactory mount to permit use of this sight with the M14—or the M16 for that matter.

As early as 1965, efforts to fill this vacuum included a number of improvisations. Among these, M. Sgt. Robert Walsh, an USAMTU

The Vietnam-era Department of the Army Technical Manual TM 9-1005-205-12 (December 1970) provided instructions for operation and organizational maintenance for "Rifle, Caliber .30, M1903A4 (Sniper's), fitted with the Telescope, M84." (U.S. Army.)

A Vietnam-era (1960s) ordnance illustration of a .30-caliber M1D sniper rifle mounting an M84 telescopic sight. The weapon is fitted with a post-Korean War T37 flash hider in this case. As a matter of interest, even though the M2 "cone-type" and, to a lesser extent, the T37 "prong-type" flash hiders were normally issued with the M1C and M1D rifles, both Army and Marine Corps personnel have indicated that flash hiders, in any form, "were always in short supply in Vietnam." (U.S. Army.)

Springfield Armory M1D sniper rifle, serial no. 3602284, with an "SA 3-53" M1D barrel and early-manufacture M84 telescopic sight (no. 5618). An "original issue" Army sniper rifle, the M1D is part of the West Point Museum Collection. (West Point Collection.)

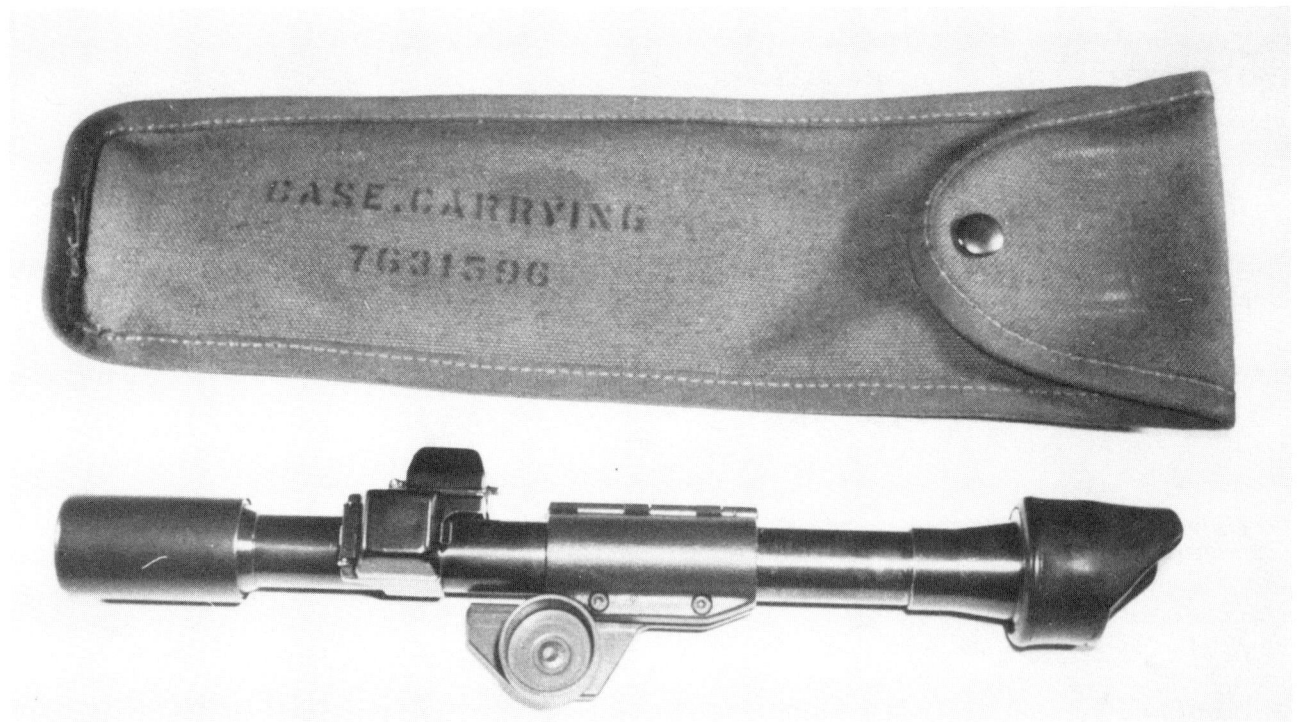

The 2.2-power M84 telescope and M1D mounting with an issue carrying case. The ordnance drawing number for the M84 case was listed as "D7631596" in various technical manuals. The telescope carrying case for the M1 sniper rifle was referenced as a "Small Arms Item." The same case was also authorized for use with the Vietnam-era M1903A4. (Peter R. Senich.)

machinist, fashioned special aluminum mounts to adapt M84 scopes to the M14 for the 11th Air Assault Division following its alert for duty in South Vietnam.

Shortly after this, a similar mount was fabricated at the AMTU at Ft.

Sniping in Vietnam: The Early Days

Marine sniper candidates on the firing line during early training activity in Vietnam. The center rifleman has an M1D with an M84 telescope; the others are sighting Unertl-equipped Model 70 Winchesters. The Marines used 155mm propellant canisters to define the firing areas. With a wide, white band as an aiming point, the same canisters were partially buried at 100-yard intervals out to 1,000 yards. According to personnel then involved, the Marine Corps ranges at Da Nang, Chu Lai, and Phu Bai "were set up using this system." (U.S. Marine Corps.)

An original M1D sniper rifle with the 2.2-power M84 telescopic sight. As ordnance records indicate, both the Army and the Marine Corps assembled M1Ds (rebuilt or converted M1 rifles) at various arsenals and depots on an "as needed basis." A USMC museum piece in this case, the Springfield Armory rifle (serial no. 282929) was fitted with an "SA 1-53" M1D barrel, M2 flash hider, T4 leather cheek pad (MRT 2-52), and M84 telescopic sight (no. 10002). A number of M1 sniper rifles were known to have been assembled at the larger USMC base depots through the years. The conversion of a standard M1 to a sniping rifle was readily accomplished by any competent armorer. When earmarked for sniper use, the weapons were chosen with no regard for their origins. The M1D in particular was based on M1 rifles manufactured by Springfield Armory, Winchester, Harrington & Richardson, and, to a lesser extent, International Harvester. The M1D was included (though few in actual number) among the supplemental sniping equipment fielded by the Marine Corps in South Vietnam. (Peter R. Senich.)

Benning and sent to AWC at Rock Island for its consideration. In this case, use of a Weaver "long-base" enabled virtually any telescope to be used. In addition to using the standard mounting spot on the M14 receiver, this mount also attached to the clip-guide to provide increased rigidity much the same as a bridge-type mounting.

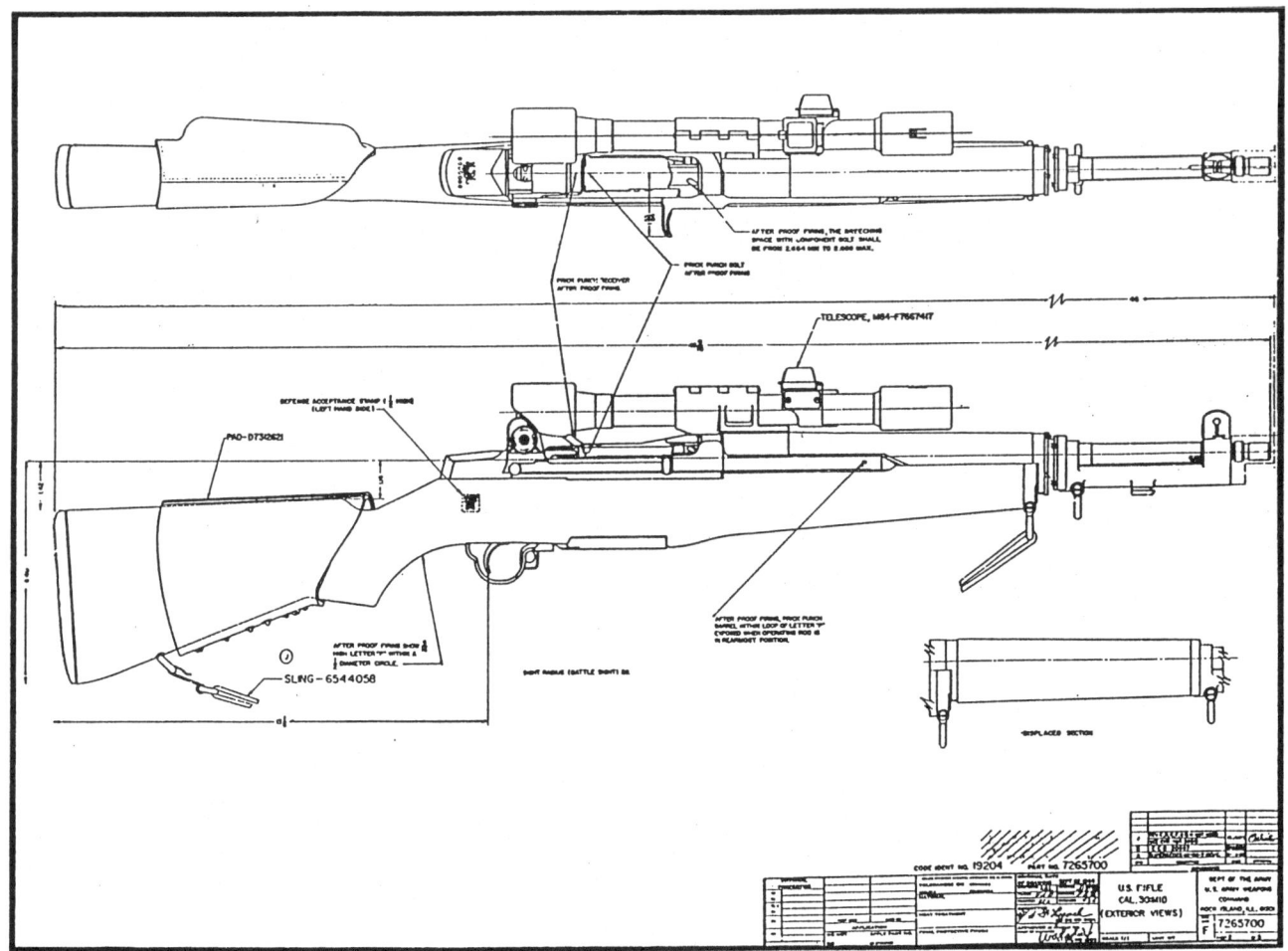

The "U.S. rifle, Caliber .30, M1D" as shown in a U.S. Army Weapons Command ordnance drawing. Although field use of the M1D sniper rifle was hardly extensive, the semiautomatic sniping rifle was exposed to a wide range of combat applications by regular and irregular U.S. and allied forces in Southeast Asia. From an operational standpoint, with as many standard M1 Garand rifles as there were in service with the ARVN, the availability of .30-caliber ammunition (.30-06) cartridge clips and spare parts is said to have posed no problem. (Scott A. Duff.)

At Chu Lai early in 1967, the 196th Infantry Brigade (Light), in addition to establishing one of the first in-country Army sniper schools, fielded a number of effective M14 sniping arms for use by its marksmen.

Sfc. Herbert F. Donnally designed three prototype mounts to mate the M84 to the M14. These were handmade by the ordnance section of the Brigade's 8th Support Battalion.

After the final design was chosen, the 64th Ordnance Section at Cu Chi machined duplicates. Drawing on his experience with the Army rifle teams, Sergeant Donnally "fine-tuned" the M14s and, since the scopes were offset to the left, obtained leather cheek rests originally intended for the M1C and M1D and attached them to the stocks.

Commenting on the use of "modified M14s" for sniping operations in the Central Highlands of South Vietnam, Louis A. Garavaglia, an Army lieutenant with a 4th Infantry Division, Long Range Reconnaissance Patrol company (LRRP), recorded the following information in the January 1968 issue of *American Rifleman*. In an article entitled "Snipers in Vietnam Also

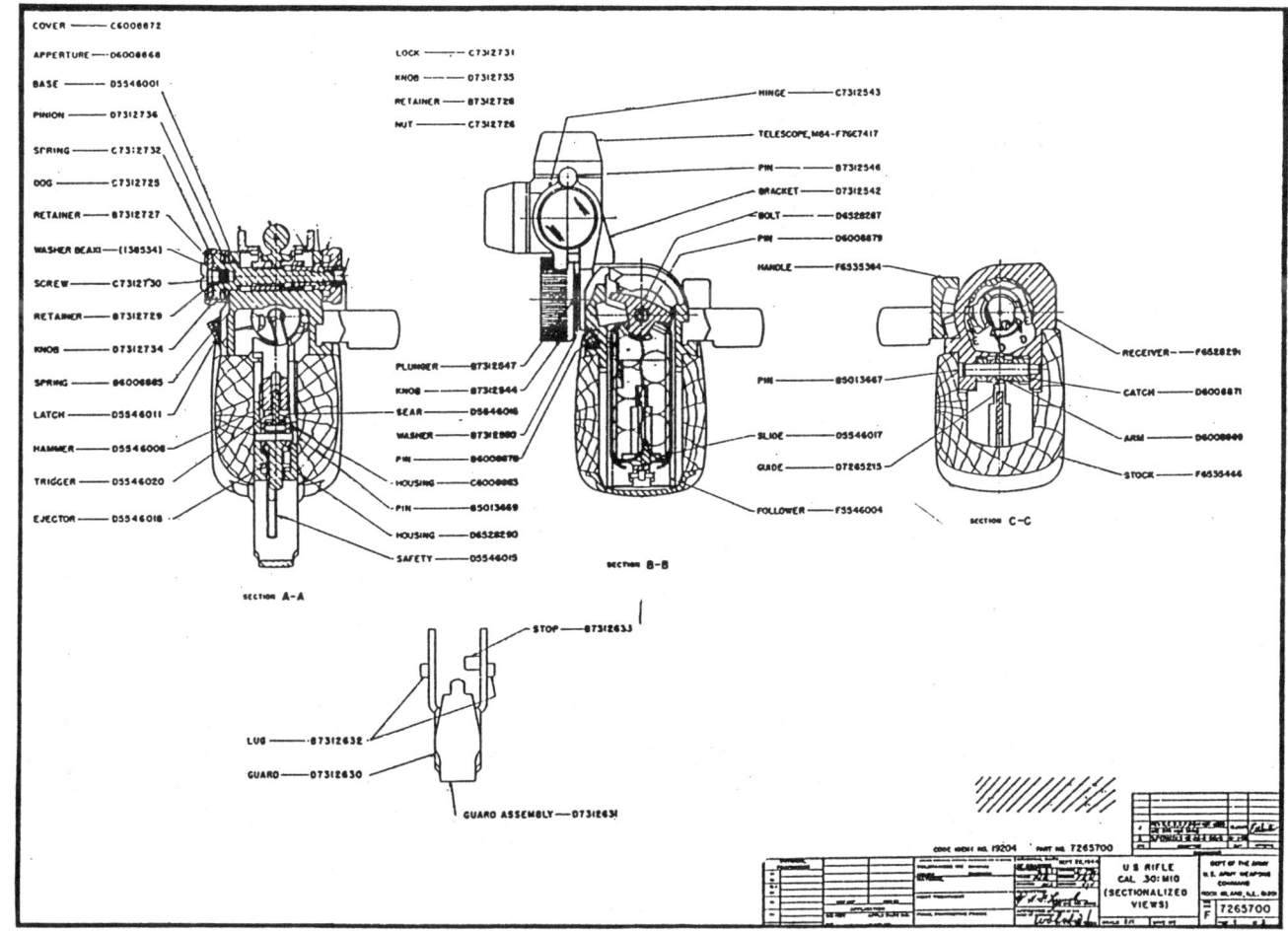

An ordnance drawing of the M1D sniping rifle showing the various components (sectionalized views) and the positioning of the M84 telescope on the left side of the receiver. (Scott A. Duff.)

Need Firepower," Garavaglia described the M14s fielded by his unit:

> The M14s, all made by Harrington & Richardson, were modified as follows:
>
> 1. Selector switches were installed, to provide volume firepower capability.
>
> 2. Straight-line stocks designed for the M14E2 were mounted. With no drop at the comb and an almost vertical pistol grip, these were more comfortable for use with a scope than the standard stock and gave better control of fully-automatic fire.
>
> 3. M84 2.2X scopes were attached by a mount with a heavy coinslotted screw which engages the hole in the left side of the M14 receiver. The scope has a sliding sunshade and detachable rubber eyepiece. Its reticle is a tapering vertical post with horizontal crosshair.

Capt. Robert A. Russell, the Officer in Charge (OIC) of the 3rd Marine Division sniper program, with Marine sniper candidates following a training exercise. The gathering of Model 70 Winchester rifles with Unertl telescopic sights was enough to "raise the pulse rate" of any Winchester aficionado. An unknown quantity of USMC Model 70 target rifles was also furnished to the 1st Marine Division when its sniper program, led by Capt. Edward J. (Jim) Land Jr., shifted into high gear during the latter part of 1966. Securing adequate sniping equipment proved no less of a problem for the 1st Marine Division than it had for its counterparts. The M1D and the Model 70, in both target and sporter form, served 1st MarDiv during early going as well. (U.S. Marine Corps.)

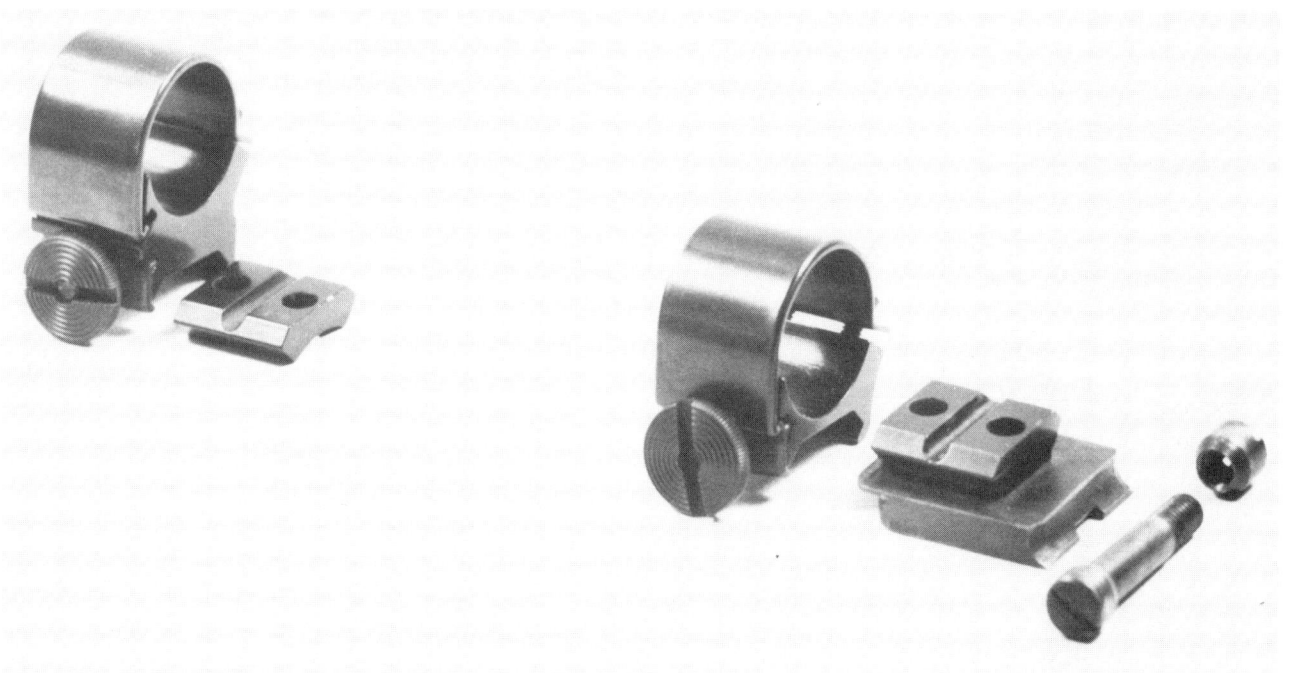

Weaver commercial mounts adapted to the M14 for shooting matches held in Moscow in 1958. A Weaver "high" mount was used in front and a "low" mount at the rear in order to compensate for the difference in height between the receiver and the M14 barrel. Weaver K-6 telescopic sights were mounted directly over the receiver in line with the bore. The measure proved to be one of the first successful attempts to mount rifle scopes on the M14 rifle.(Lt. Col. F.B. Conway, Ret.)

Sniping in Vietnam: The Early Days

In an attempt to satisfy the urgent requirement for a telescope-equipped M14 sniper rifle in 1966, Army Weapons Command (USAWECOM) developed a hinged mount to accommodate the M84 sight. (Gray Collection.)

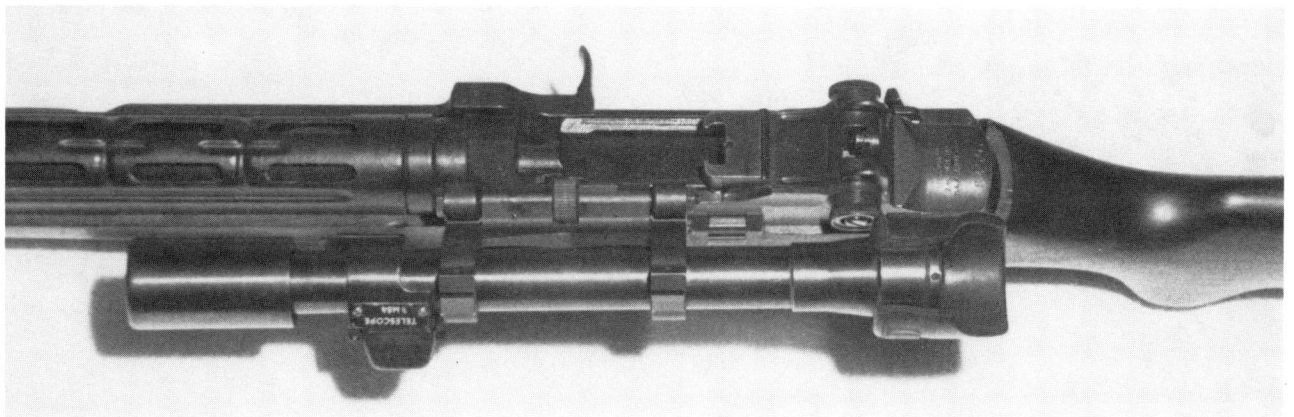

Top view of the AWC hinged-telescope mount with the M84 sight rotated to the left. The lower portion of the rubber eye guard was removed to clear the rear sight. (Gray Collection.)

4. Light clamp-on bipods designed for the M16A1 were substituted for the bipods originally made for the M14. We felt the latter were unnecessarily heavy. The clamp-on bipod snaps neatly onto the M14 gas cylinder just in front of the spindle valve.

With M14s thus modified, seasoned marksmen, firing from the prone position at 700 meters, had no trouble hitting the

Army marksman test-firing an M84-equipped M14 rifle with the AWC hinged telescope mount at Ft. Benning, 1966. (U.S. Army.)

A typical "U.S. Rifle, 7.62mm, M14" fielded during the war in Vietnam. Depending on their intended use, M14 rifles were issued as semiautomatic or selective-fire weapons. The modification limiting the weapon to semiautomatic involved installing a pin-fastened button (selector lock) in place of the "wing switch." After removing the lock (shown), one could change the weapon to selective-fire operation (semi- or full-automatic) in a matter of minutes with the appropriate parts. Even though the match-grade and XM21 sniper rifles sent to Southeast Asia were fitted with the selector lock (semiautomatic fire), many were reportedly altered to provide selective fire during the course of the war. (West Point Collection.)

Army "E" type silhouette targets, which correspond roughly to a man in kneeling position. And this range was far greater than most of those at which hits were later made.

On missions, M14-armed snipers carried nine 20-round magazines loaded 18 rounds to the magazine; 2 of the magazines contained 7.62mm, match-grade ammunition; the remaining 7 were loaded with the 7.62mm "duplex" round. In a firefight, snipers would eject the match-grade, switch to

Sniping in Vietnam: The Early Days

The "groove and screw recess" on the left side of the M14 receiver served as a mounting platform for telescopic sights and night vision equipment. The 20-round magazine was standard. Note the "Defence Acceptance Stamp" (typical) above the trigger guard. (West Point Collection.)

"duplex" and flip the selector switch to full-automatic for volume fire.

In addition to providing information on the type of M14s employed by the unit sniper detachment, Garavaglia offered the reasons behind their choice in this case:

> The detachment was divided into 3-man teams which usually operated at considerable distances from conventional troop units. If spotted and attacked while moving to or from an objective, the team was on its own, its survival depending on being able to deliver ample firepower.
> At first the sniper detachment had no standardized Table of Organization and Equipment and so we had plenty of latitude in our choice of weapons. This let us intensively range test the Winchester 70 and Remington Model 700, the scoped bolt actions used by Marine snipers, and compare them with the M14, M16A1, and 3 versions of the Russian AK-47 Assault Rifle.
> Our area of operations, the Central Highlands, ran the gamut from very dense to very sparse vegetation. The bolt actions would have been ideal for the 800 to 1000 meter shots the latter areas afforded, but they couldn't deliver the volume punch the 3-man teams needed to fight their way out of jungle ambushes.
> The M16A1 functioned well when kept cleaned and lubricated properly, and had the added advantage of lightweight ammunition; the AK-47s scored high in ruggedness and the capacity to function even with deteriorated ammunition. But we finally settled on a modified version of the M14.

The examples cited were indicative of the efforts both stateside and

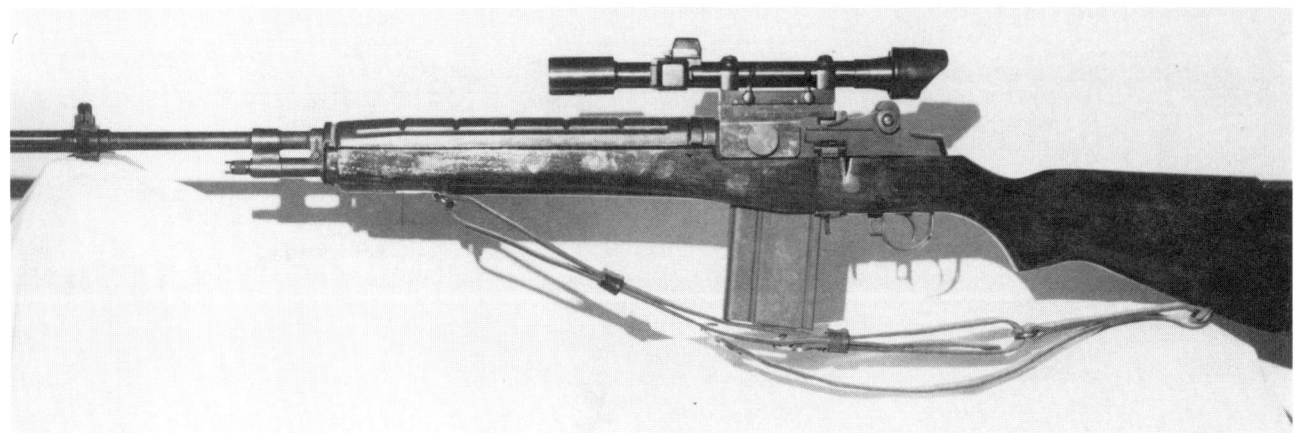

Match-grade M14s with 2.2-power M84 telescopes prepared by Army Weapons Command at Rock Island Arsenal remained in general use in RVN even after the XM21/ART system had been fielded in quantity. The first M84-equipped "match-grade" M14 sniper rifles were shipped to South Vietnam in March 1967. (Lt. Col. F.B. Conway, Ret.)

M84 telescope, Griffin & Howe mount, and the offset receiver bracket developed by Army Weapons Command for use with the Rock Island Arsenal match-grade M14s in Vietnam. The hinged metal covers served as protection for the elevation and windage adjustment turrets. The levers on the telescope mount are in the locked position. The levers were turned to the left (forward) to release the mount. Though the levers were originally designed to rotate nearly 180 degrees to lock the mount on the M1C receiver base, dimensional differences between the Griffin & Howe mount and the AWC/RIA receiver bracket base placed the levers at different "locked" positions. The components were basic, rugged, and durable; the system "worked well" in Vietnam. To the chagrin of the USAMTU, the AWC/RIA match-grade sniper rifle was considered all the Army needed in many quarters of the U.S. Army. (Peter R. Senich.)

in Vietnam to field sniping equipment. By the time the "official" Army and Marine Corps sniper programs finally shifted into high gear, telescopic sights had been fitted to the M14 and the M16 by every means short of hose clamps and electrician's tape.

As a matter of interest, during the height of U.S. combat involvement in Southeast Asia, the principal news magazines ran an occasional wire service photo-illustration of an Army or Marine Corps rifleman armed with an M14 mounting fixed- or variable-power commercial rifle scopes. Although Marine Corps use of the M14 in a sniping capacity is

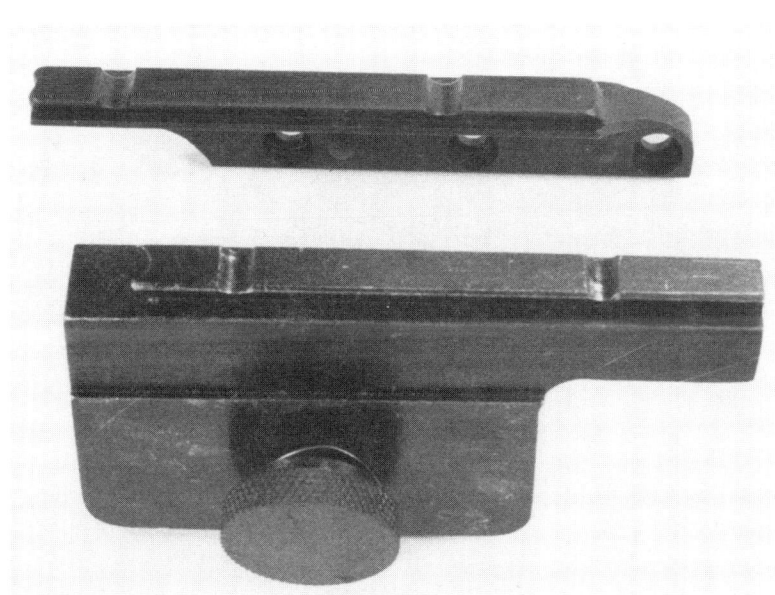

Comparative view of an original World War II M1C receiver base male dovetail with that of the AWC/RIA M14 receiver bracket for the M84 telescope. (Peter R. Senich.)

A close view of a match-grade M14 rifle with the AWC/RIA receiver bracket and M84 telescopic sight. The 2.2-power scope was finished in black oxide and issued with the standard M84 web carrying case. The overall length with rubber eyepiece and extended sun shade was 13.188 inches, with a tube diameter of .870 inch. An identification plate bearing the model designation and serial number was attached to the right side of the turret housing. In addition to match-grade M14 rifles fitted with M84 scopes, separate telescope mounts and receiver brackets for the M14 were sent to Vietnam as well. (Lt. Col. F.B. Conway, Ret.)

rarely mentioned, enterprising Marine marksmen employed a number of "field-expedient" M14 sniper rifles during the war in Vietnam.

Though the M14 was eventually replaced by the M16 for general field use, a considerable number of M14 rifles remained in Marine Corps service during the course of the war. It was not uncommon to see Marine combat personnel armed with an equal mix of M14 and M16 rifles. For many Marines, if an option existed, the M14 was their choice.

In any case, the date of official adoption of the 5.56mm M16 rifle by the Marine Corps was recorded as follows in *The Marines in Vietnam*:

Weapons Command receiver mounting brackets utilized with M84 telescopes were blued-, black oxide-, or parkerized-finished and furnished with a large, knurled mounting screw. A small knob with a screwdriver slot and socket-head screws with washers (recessed hex) were used as well. The back of the mounting was configured to match the "groove and screw recess" on the M14 receiver. (Peter R. Senich.)

A close view of the M84 telescope elevation (top) and windage adjustment turrets with dials set at zero. The turret covers were easily damaged, and many were lost or removed during the course of service in RVN. The 2.2-power M84 telescopic sight saw considerable use during the Vietnam War. (Peter R. Senich.)

1954–1973, published by the History and Museums Division, Headquarters, U.S. Marine Corps (January 1974):

> The decision to equip Marine forces in the Western Pacific with the M16 had been made in March 1966, after consideration of the request by Commander, U.S. Military

```
QUANTITY: (1)
NOMENCLATURE - M-84 TELESCOPE W/E
STOCK NO. F001-6,784,690
SERIAL NO.        34927
PKGD. BY: LIBBEY-OWENS-FORD GLASS COMPANY
DATE PACKED      JAN 30 1953
```

The markings on an original M84 telescope shipping carton for sight No. 34927 as packed by Libby-Owens-Ford (LOF) on 30 January 1953. The heavy cardboard cartons were 17 inches long, 6 inches wide, and 3 inches high, with a sealed foil pouch containing a dehydrating agent. Even though commercial telescopic sight development would attain a highly sophisticated level in the years following the Korean War, the M84 sight was to remain as the principal sniper telescope for both the Army and Marine Corps until the early 1960s, when U.S. military involvement in Southeast Asia emphasized the upgrading of existing sniper equipment. Nevertheless, with a total of "well over 40,000" M84 telescopic sights manufactured before production finally ended, and with the U.S. policy of "surplus disposal" such as it is, the 2.2-power scope will undoubtedly remain in service someplace on this globe for years to come. (Peter R. Senich.)

Assistance Command, made in December 1965, for a lightweight weapon with a high rate of fire to replace the M14. The Marine Corps had been testing other lightweight weapons systems, but the fast-firing, hardhitting M16 was in production, readily available, and the choice of the Army. Therefore, after further testing by the Marine Corps, the rifle—manufactured by Colt—was procured in quantity from the Army at a cost of $121.00 per rifle, and issued to maneuver units in March and April 1967, in time for the heavy fighting at Khe Sanh.

In due course, a satisfactory receiver mounting bracket, developed by Army Weapons Command, emerged as the principal device utilized with the M14/M84 combination, remaining in general service use in a supplementary role even after the sophisticated XM21/ART system had been fielded in quantity.

With a male dovetail virtually identical to the M1C receiver base, the AWC offset receiver bracket made use of the World War II-vintage Griffin & Howe mount assemblies originally manufactured to accommodate M81 and M82 telescopes. While it did serve to adapt the M84 to the M14, this mounting was in fact nothing more than an extension of the state of the art as it existed in 1945.

Army Weapons Command eventually prepared match-grade M14s

Members of a 101st Airborne Division sniper team following a mission in Vietnam. The men (left) are armed with match-grade M14s mounting M84 telescopes. Note the trooper in the background with forefinger extended; a sign that his snipers are number one! (U.S. Army.)

utilizing this mounting with the M84 for sniper use in RVN. While these were reported to be "somewhat less accurate" than the M14s accurized in accordance with the USAMTU rebuild procedures eventually adopted (XM21), a fair share of Vietcong and North Vietnamese Army personnel were rendered *hors de combat* with this sniping variant.

Predating the expanded official use of the M14 in a sniping capacity, Korean War vintage .30-caliber (.30-06) M1C and M1D rifles were drawn from ordnance stores primarily for use by indigenous forces in Southeast Asia.

In addition to the initial general use of the M1 Garand by the Royal Thai Army (RTA) and the South Vietnamese Army (ARVN), an unspecified quantity of M1C and M1D sniping rifles were among the military hardware furnished to Thailand and the Republic of South Vietnam as part of the overall "military advice and assistance plan" practiced by the United States in Southeast Asia.

Although M1 sniper rifles were also available for use by the

Sniping in Vietnam: The Early Days

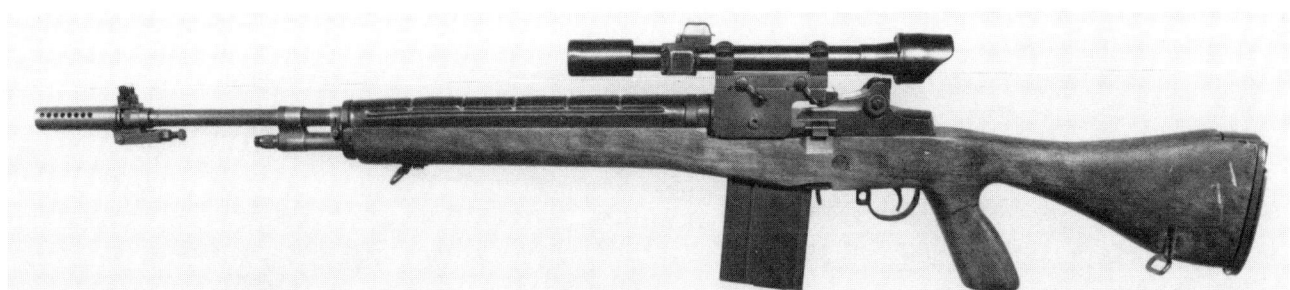

An excellent example of a "combat improvisation" in Vietnam. An M84-equipped standard M14 rifle adapted for sniping purposes by an enterprising 1st Cavalry Division company commander (1970). (West Point Collection.)

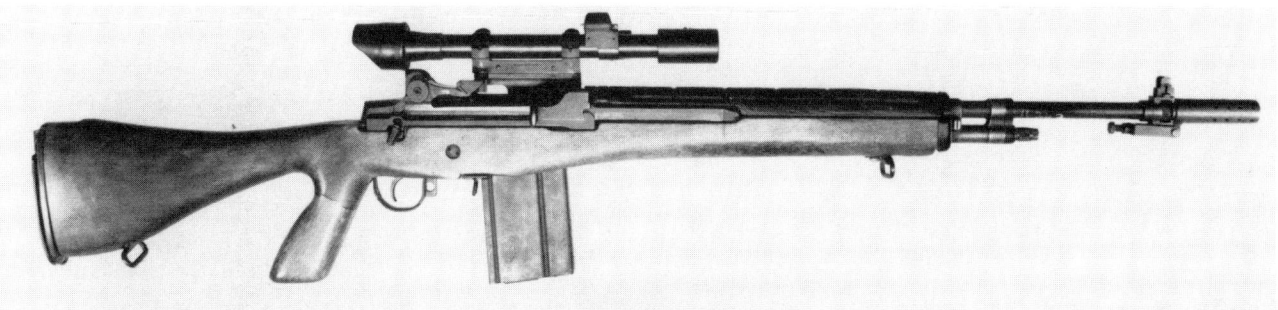

An alternate view of the improvised M14 sniper rifle. Note the "straight-line" M14E2 stock with pistol grip and the muzzle stabilizer (the recoil brake or compensator fastened over the standard M14 flash hider). When developed originally, the stock and the muzzle stabilizer were intended to make the M14 rifle "more manageable" during automatic fire. (West Point Collection.)

Civilian Irregular Defence Group (CIDG), the Special Forces-trained native village and tribal security/reaction forces. As difficult as it was for a man of Oriental stature to handle a standard M1 rifle efficiently, the hefty sniper version proved no less of a problem for the average South Vietnamese or Thai soldier. This factor and the lack of suitable training made the M1 sniper rifles all but useless under the circumstances.

The Army and Marine Corps employed the M1D mounting the M84 telescope in standard (as issued) and "armorer-prepared" (glass-bedded and accurized) form, though few in actual number, as "supplemental sniping equipment" during early combat activity in South Vietnam. Although many of the M1D sniper rifles fielded by American forces were originally intended for the South Vietnamese, by all accounts a number of Army units in particular deployed to Vietnam with M1D rifles among their equipment.

In retrospect, in advance of full-scale U.S. involvement in the Republic of South Vietnam (RVN), many of the American military advisors tasked with "enhancing the combat capabilities" of the "friendly forces" in Southeast Asia were known to include telescopic sighted rifles among the wide range of small arms categorized as "personal defence weapons." Commercial sporting rifles, "well-traveled" M1903A4, M1C and M1D sniper rifles mounting "World War II era rifle scopes," and various examples of foreign military sniping hardware, including the British No. 4 Mk I (T)

A close left view of the M14 rifle with the M84 telescopic sight, Griffin & Howe mount assembly and AWC receiver mounting bracket. In this case, a socket head screw was used to attach the mount to the rifle. Though this arrangement was effective, the wrench needed to tighten or loosen the mount was easily misplaced in a combat environment. (West Point Collection.)

sniper rifle, were all represented during "the early days" in South Vietnam.

So far as the Marine Corps was concerned, however, Headquarters, United States Marine Corps (HQMC) arrived at an early conclusion (based on its early major combat involvement beginning in 1965) that trained snipers and efficient sniping equipment would be essential in South Vietnam.

The Marine presence and subsequent buildup in South Vietnam was officially defined by the Marine Corps as follows:

> In 1965, the Marines were the first of the U.S. Armed Services to deploy large ground combat units to South Vietnam. By the end of the year, more than 38,000 Marines made up the III Marine Amphibious Force (III MAF) under the command of Major General Lewis W. Walt. III MAF was part of the United States Military Assistance Command, Vietnam (USMACV), commanded by General William C. Westmoreland . . . The American command's mission in Vietnam was to assist the Republic of Vietnam (RVN) in its war against the Communist insurgents, the Viet Cong, who were being provided with leadership, reinforcements, and supplies from the north by the Democratic Republic of Vietnam (DRVN).

In due course, the U.S. Marine Corps, 3d Marine Division, would be officially credited with establishing the first sniper program in the

Sniping in Vietnam: The Early Days

Republic of Vietnam. Though variously referenced as having started during "mid-1965" or "early fall [1965]," by the end of the same year, Marine snipers were already exacting their toll on the Vietcong.

According to the "Chronology of Significant Events" recorded in *U.S. Marines in Vietnam: The Landing and the Buildup 1965*, the second volume in a series of chronological histories published by the History and Museums Division, Headquarters, U.S. Marine Corps (written by Jack Shulimson and Charles M. Johnson, USMC, June 1978):

> 14 Oct.—The CG, I Corps approved extension of the Chu Lai TAOR. A USMC sniper team was formed in the Hue-Phu Bai TAOR. The team used Winchester Model 70 rifles with 8-Unertl telescopic sights and killed two Viet Cong at a range of more than 700 yards in the first exercise of the new tactic. Later, M1D rifles with telescopic sights were utilized.
>
> 23 Nov.—By this date there were approximately 20 scout-sniper teams of four men each positioned throughout the III MAF area. On 23 November a team at Phu Bai killed two VC and wounded one at a range of 1000 meters.
>
> III MAF developed and modified techniques and tactics for the employment of small Marine units. The Marines experimented with specially trained and equipped sniper teams. Fifty of the best marksmen were selected from each of the regiments. These troops were divided into four-man teams and equipped with Winchester Model 70 rifles and telescopic sights. After training, the teams rejoined their regiments. During November and December, 20-30 teams operated in the Marine TAORs daily.

Though quoted frequently, the following is one of the more concise accounts of initial Marine Corps sniper deployment, provided by Frank G. McGuire in his article "Snipers—Specialists in Warfare" in the July 1967 issue of *American Rifleman*:

> As related by General Wallace M. Greene, Jr., Commandant of the Marine Corps, in his address to the NRA Annual Members meeting, the Marines in Vietnam "... are equipped with binoculars for wide sweeps of their target area—and with Remington Model 700 bolt action rifles. The rifle mounts a Redfield 3X9 power scope, and fires a 7.62mm cartridge."
>
> Although this is becoming the standard equipment with many sniper teams, a large number of Winchester Model 70 rifles are also used, as well as Unertl 8X telescopic sights. The original Model 70s, which started out as the sole specialized armament of the 3rd Marine snipers, were from the 3d Marine Division rifle team. When these turned out to be too few, more Model 70s were shipped out with heavy barrels and sporter stocks. The 8X telescopic sight was chosen in WWII when it was teamed up with the '03 rifle. The scopes now used in

A close right view of the 1st Cavalry Division improvised M14 sniper rifle. A National Match (NM) sight assembly was used; the barrel and action are "standard M14 components." Note the full- and semiautomatic selector (wing switch) in place directly above the trigger. (West Point Collection.)

Vietnam are the same scopes on newer rifles. Some of the snipers now in Vietnam were not yet born when the telescopic sights they use were employed in a different war.

"In the early 1940s," says a Marine Corps spokesman, "we were advised that a Unertl 8X scope on the Winchester Model 70 was the best sniping combination, but the '03 was available in quantity, so we used it."

Later, efforts were made to get a suitable match rifle for Marine Corps rifle teams that would meet the NRA's weight limitations for such equipment in competition. The late Brig. Gen. George O. Van Orden, USMC (Ret.), head of Evaluators, Ltd., went to Winchester and had some Model 70s made up with a heavy barrel on a sporter stock. This rifle met the weight requirements (since changed by NRA) and also happened to be the same configuration which Van Orden had recommended for sniper use in the early 1940s. It was this configuration of the Model 70 which S/SGT Don L. Smith, USMC, used in 1953 to win the National Match Rifle championship at Camp Perry.

The rifle team of the 3d Marine Division had been using the Model 70 with the heavy barrel and the heavy Marksman stock, in view of the changed weight limitations. When the need arose for more Model 70s the rifles procured by Brig. Gen. Van Orden, including Smith's championship-winning rifle, were shipped out as supplemental equipment to Vietnam.

In addition to these two batches of Model 70s, some MlD service rifles with M84 side-mounted telescopic sights and lace-on cheekpads were shipped to the Marines.

Sniping in Vietnam: The Early Days

Describing the early Marine Corps sniping issue in greater detail, the October 1966 issue of *Guns & Ammo,* in an uncredited article (no byline) entitled "The Snipers of Da Nang," stated in part:

> Two types of rifles are presently being employed by the Marine sniper platoon; they are the Model 70 Winchester (.30-06) and the M1D (.30 caliber).
>
> The Unertl 8X sniperscope and the 3x9 "Marine Scope" (manufactured in Japan) are used on the Model 70 Winchester rifles. The M1D rifle is equipped with the M84 scope, designed especially for the rifle.
>
> All Model 70 Winchester rifles are equipped with target barrels; however, some have sporter stocks while others have target stocks. The sporter stocks are favored most because they are lighter and easy to carry. The M1D rifle is equipped with a standard military stock.
>
> All rifles presently in use by the sniper platoon have been glass-bedded by a Marine Rifle Team Equipment (RTE) Armorer since arriving in Vietnam. The rifles have also been accurized by an RTE armorer.
>
> The rifles presently in use by the sniper team were once maintained by the Marksmanship Training Unit at Marine Corps Schools, Quantico, Va., and have been used in rifle matches, including the National Matches at Camp Perry.
>
> Ammunition used by the snipers for both target and actual work is the standard match Lake City load. It is not handloaded.

NOTE: In their efforts to publicize and place information directly into the "media pipeline," military personnel wrote articles for the express purpose of drawing both public and official attention to the success of one operation or another in Vietnam. On different occasions, magazine articles dealing with early Marine Corps sniping activity appeared in stateside periodicals without bylines or under pseudonyms. The *Guns & Ammo* article quoted above was written by a Marine correspondent.

Even though the Marine Corps eventually replaced the Winchester Model 70 and the M1D with the 7.62mm Remington M700 (M40) bolt-action sniper rifle (adopted 7 April 1966), the Model 70 and M1D remained in service in Vietnam for an extended period.

The Army, on the other hand, chose to base its sniper issue on the highly refined version of the M14, ultimately referred to as the XM21. In addition to the XM21, however, both standard and match-grade M14s mounting the M84 telescopic sight remained in service as well. In one form or another, the M14 is recognized as having been the principal U.S. sniper rifle during the war in Vietnam.

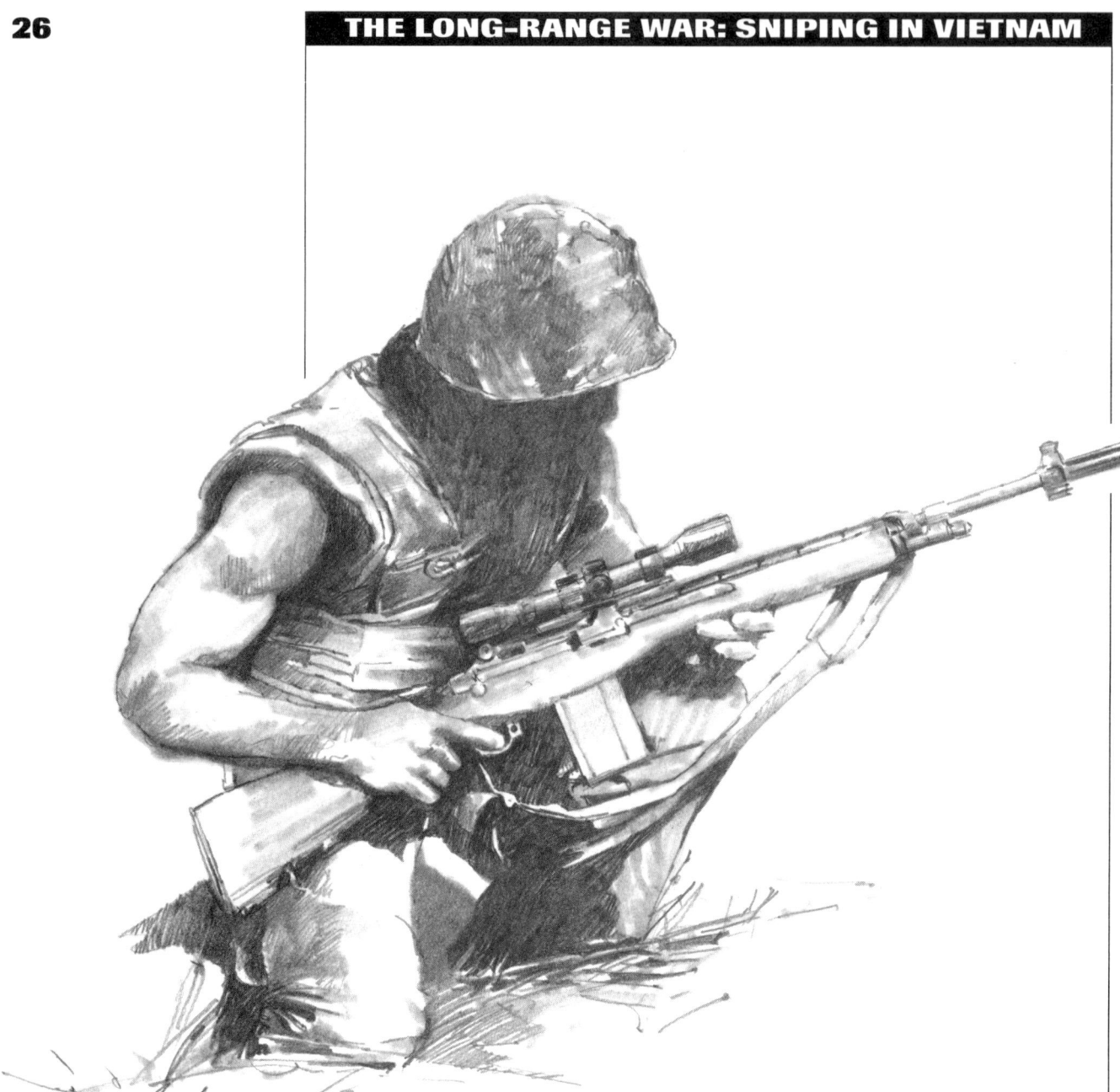

Even though M14 rifles were not a viable part of the Marine Corps sniper program, telescopic sighted M14s were occasionally employed by Marine snipers and riflemen. In this case, the M14 is fitted with a commercial variable-power scope in an improvised mounting. (Max Crace.)

CHAPTER 2

Sniper Operations: A Program Takes Hold

As unprepared as the Army was for sniping operations following the initial deployment of combat forces to Southeast Asia, the ingenuity and resourcefulness of many officers and men provided a resolute group of Army marksmen with the means to conduct some semblance of sniping activity during the early months of the war.

By some estimates, from late 1965 through 1966, Army sniping activities in South Vietnam were conducted almost entirely with "improvised equipment." And while individual riflemen were limited to procuring telescopic sights and mounts as best they could, some units were responding to the shortage of sniping equipment by purchasing commercial hunting rifles and scopes for combat use in Vietnam. A surprising number of Winchester and Remington sporting and target rifles were fielded by Army personnel as a result.

Although some within the military viewed this activity with considerable reservation, the very nature of the war in Vietnam gave rise to any number of unorthodox situations and activities. As one officer summarized it, "By the time the last American combat forces left Southeast Asia, an unprecedented number of Army regulations had either been totally ignored or adhered to selectively." The procurement and the early use of sniper equipment was no exception.

A handful of accomplished riflemen proved early on that a reasonably effective sniping campaign could be waged on a limited, localized basis. But in order for sniping to impact the Communist forces as envisioned at some levels of Army command, it would be necessary to field suitable equipment and implement sniper training as part of an overall program on as wide a scale as possible. However, apart from the independent actions of Army riflemen functioning as "riflemen with telescopic sights," initial small unit sniper activity was conducted on a "trial and error" basis along the same lines as the early Marine Corps efforts.

As circumstances and conditions warranted, experienced Army instructors and competition riflemen, many of who were especially skilled at long-range shooting, gave volunteers a "crash course" in sniping. Apart from the differences in rifles and telescopic sights then in use, the basic precepts remained the same.

According to a veteran Army instructor, "Sure, this was basic, but if you could get them off on the right foot, common sense and field experience usually turned a decent marksman into a good sniper." At this juncture, there was no training syllabus or formal course of instruction, just a handful of motivated riflemen doing the best they could with what they had.

In retrospect, however, according to Army personnel then involved, the greatest difficulty associated with fielding Army snipers at that time stemmed from the lack of proper equipment. The availability of suitable sniper equipment proved to be as vexing a problem for the Army as it was for the Marine Corps.

Although official plans for unified sniper training would follow in due course, by the end of 1966, the main thrust of Army efforts, as pertaining to sniping, was directed toward filling the requests for telescopic sights in South Vietnam. Although the Army had committed to developing an adjustable ranging telescope based on the "Leatherwood Principle," it went ahead with the decision to draw from existing stores of the 2.2-power M84 telescopic sight.

According to information attributed to the U.S. Army Combat Developments Command (USACDC):

> During the period May to December 1966, the Infantry Agency conducted a re-evaluation of the requirement for a sniper capability in units armed with the M14 and M16 weapons. This re-evaluation action established that a need exists for a sniper capability.
> Results of the re-evaluation determined that the M84 Telescope should be used as an interim item until a satisfactory variable power, ranging telescope could be adopted.

When it came to conducting business at this level, the procurement of telescopic sights for Army field use was infinitely more complicated than simply reallocating "parachute money" (maintenance funds) for purchasing rifles and/or scopes in Hawaii or Japan.

Although most of the Army combat forces destined for action in Vietnam had deployed to Southeast Asia by the end of 1966, so far as it is known, the first major shipment of authorized sniping equipment did not take place until 125 M84-equipped match-grade M14 rifles and 384 Colt/Realist scopes (for M16 rifles) were sent to Vietnam in March 1967.

Sniper Operations: A Program Takes Hold

By the end of the same year, Rock Island Arsenal (Army Weapons Command) had shipped additional telescopic sights and mounts for use with the M14 and M16A1 rifles.

NOTE: According to ordnance documents generated at Rock Island Arsenal, 364 Colt/Realist telescopes, 100 Weaver rings and bases (modified), and 425 M1C mounts and "prototype bases" were sent to South Vietnam during 1967 as well. The Colt scopes and Weaver mounting hardware were intended for the M16A1, the other items for the M14. Even though "352" M84 telescopes were also listed, a portion of these were earmarked for use with the Weaver rings and bases on the M16A1 rifle. The 3-power Colt/Realist scope was essentially a self-contained unit and simply attached to the M16 carrying handle without a separate mount. The M84 was rarely used with the M16 in Southeast Asia.

Even though an increase in the availability of telescopic sights and mounting hardware helped to alleviate the equipment shortage, the efficient field use of snipers was no less of a problem in South Vietnam than it had been in Korea, or during World War II for that matter.

Maj. Willis L. Powell and Brig. Gen. James S. Timothy, Assistant Division Commander, on the firing line at Bearcat, October 1968. The general is receiving a "hands-on briefing" on the sniper rifles from the USAMTU. Note the camouflage material wrapped around both ends of the telescope and ART carrying case in the background. (U.S. Army.)

Despite the emergence of some rather sophisticated sniper training programs at division and brigade levels, with few exceptions, men trained as snipers simply went back to their units and only functioned in this capacity as part of their units' operations. There were no special measure designed to take advantage of their training and equipment.

When viewed on an overall basis, by mid-1967, the combined effect of Army sniping activity in South Vietnam was disproportionate to the effort and expense the program had entailed. Although some had feared the entire program would culminate in just another exercise in futility as similar efforts had in past conflicts, according to individuals close to the project, the "turning point" finally came, though indirectly,

Once accepted into the 9th Infantry Division sniper school, students brought a Starlight Scope and mount when reporting for training. A precision M14 rifle and Adjustable Ranging Telescope were issued and retained for subsequent operations; the student's name was taped to the stock. The sniper candidate is sighting an accurized M14, one of the original USAMTU sniper rifles sent to Vietnam in 1968. (U.S. Army.)

as a result of the 1967 Army Concept Team In Vietnam (ACTIV) evaluations of Army sniper operations and equipment in Vietnam.

In addition to generating "pertinent information" on the state of the in-country sniper training and the equipment employed by the various commands, the ACTIV had focused official attention on the "AMTU match-conditioned M14 rifle and the self-ranging Leatherwood scope."

USAMTU personnel were reportedly disappointed to learn their rifles had been evaluated with inconclusive results (according to ACTIV "Trip Reports," the rifles were tested by various units in the hands of both experienced and relatively inexperienced riflemen over an extended period under varying conditions and circumstances), and some still choose to debate the issue. But ACTIV had fielded the "USAMTU prepared" match-grade rifles (10) to begin with and, in so doing, exposed both the rifle and the adjustable ranging telescope to various commands

Sniper Operations: A Program Takes Hold

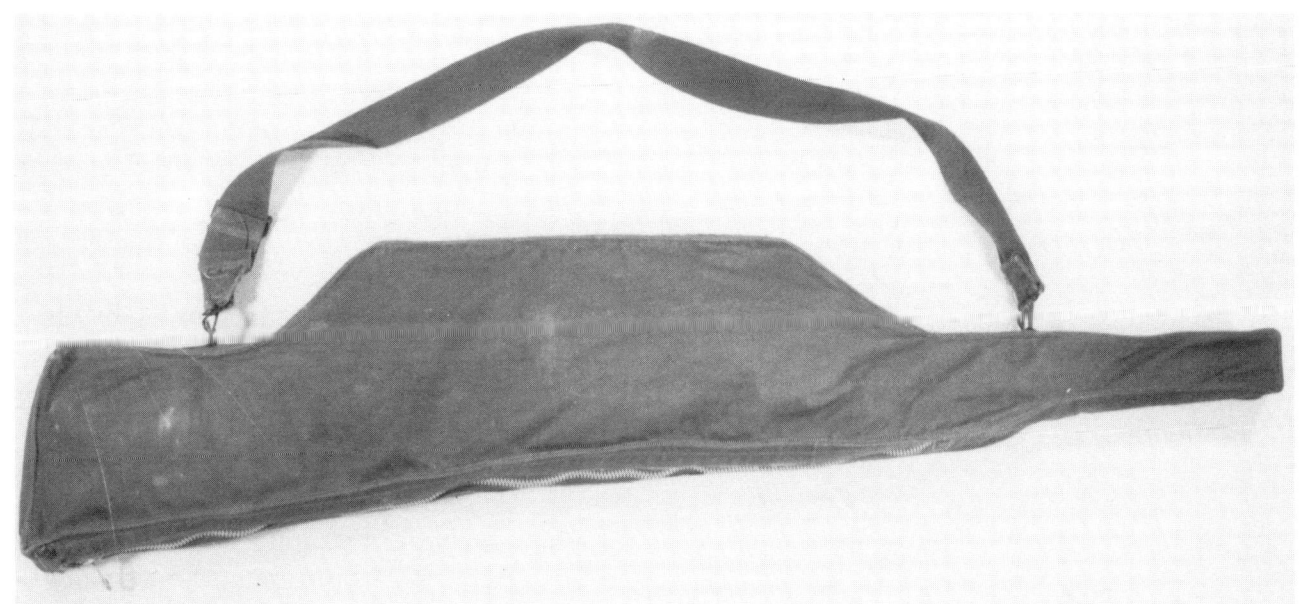

Rifle carrying case provided by the USAMTU for Maj. Willis L. Powell for use in RVN. The canvas case (olive drab) went to South Vietnam with Major Powell without a rifle (June 1968). An M14 was match-conditioned in-country and fitted with a commercial 4X-12X variable-power Redfield sight during the early stages of the 9th Infantry Division sniper training program. There were no ART-equipped sniper rifles in Southeast Asia before the accurized M14 rifles reached the 9th Division in October 1968. (Peter R. Senich.)

(including the 9th Infantry Division). Thus, experts believe, this action was indirectly responsible for division commander Maj. General Julian J. Ewell's requesting USAMTU assistance in developing a program for training and equipping 9th Infantry Division snipers.

Though speculative, perhaps, without the extent of ACTIV involvement in this case, it is doubtful if the USAMTU version of the optimum Army sniper rifle would have made it to South Vietnam when it did ... if at all!

Army Weapons Command (AWC) had already placed Rock Island Arsenal match-grade M14 sniper rifles in RVN for

A student sniper on the firing line at Bearcat, the site of the original 9th Infantry Division sniper school in South Vietnam. The AMTU modified mounting screw on the ART mount has large flats for tightening purposes. Though barely visible, the rifle serial number (six-digits) is engraved on the side of the mount. (U.S. Army.)

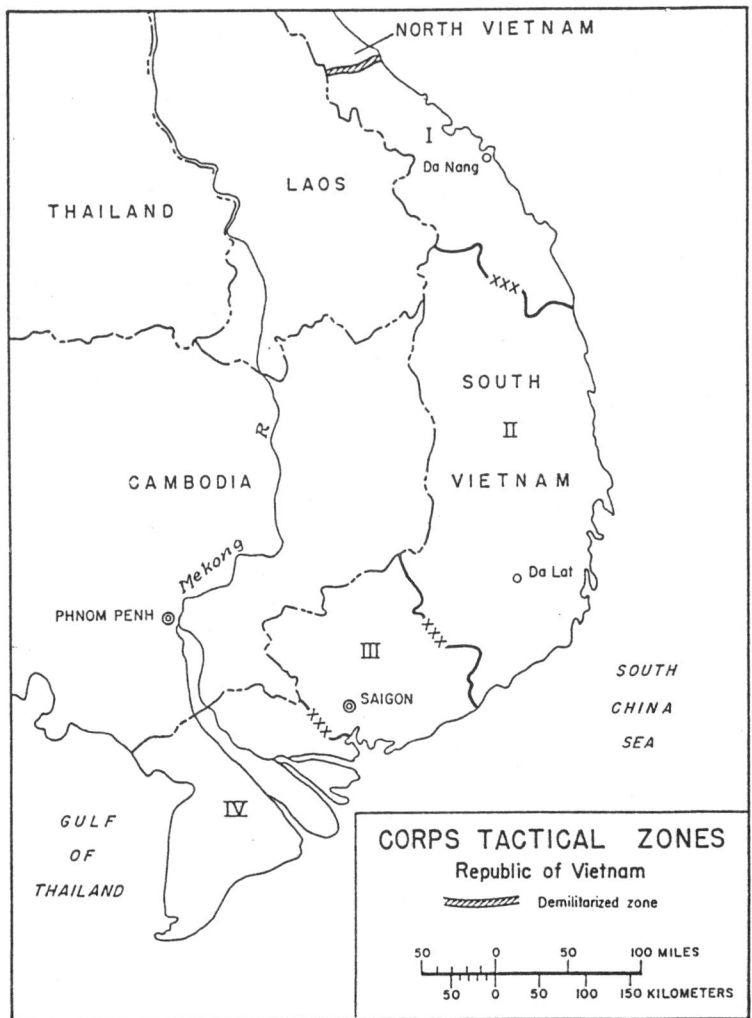

The Corps Tactical Zones (CTZ), Republic of Vietnam. I CTZ was the northern military region, II CTZ the central military region, III CTZ the military region surrounding Saigon, and IV CTZ was the southern military region (Delta) of South Vietnam. (U.S. Army.)

"evaluation purposes" in advance of the AMTU/Leatherwood system. Therefore, with the 2.2-power M84 scope serving as an "interim item" at that point, the attention of Weapons Command was clearly focused on the match-grade rifles and not the vintage telescopic sights.

Given the circumstances, by some estimates the adjustable ranging telescope (ART) would have been mated ultimately with the AWC/RIA match-grade M14 rifle for Army sniper use in Southeast Asia. Thus, rather than simply rendering support for an emerging Army sniper program, the USAMTU became a major player in this case.

The successful field use of the AMTU-accurized M14s in conjunction with the Limited Warfare Laboratory ART system by 9th Infantry Division snipers led to official acceptance of the rifle and sight as the XM21 Sniper Weapon System.

Various forms of sniper training and employment had preceded 9th Infantry Division efforts, and other successful programs would follow. But the imaginative use of the XM21 system in combination with sniper training and tactics developed for the 9th Division area of operations in the Mekong Delta culminated in a sniper program viewed by many in the military as the "high point" of Army sniper operations in Southeast Asia.

Even though a viable sniper program would not materialize until months later, the 9th Infantry Division had recognized a need for snipers shortly after its arrival in RVN (December 1966).

By the following spring, Headquarters had assigned a major as "Project Officer for Sniper Training," and would issue a directive for the purpose of "establishing responsibilities, prerequisites, and administrative procedures for commanders in the development and conduct of the 9th Infantry Division Sniper Program" (17 June 1967).

NOTE: In addition to defining and delegating responsibilities, the directive cites the intended use of "match-ammo," M84-equipped M14 rifles, and M16A1 rifles with "Colt/Realist Scopes" for sniper training

Sniper Operations: A Program Takes Hold

and field use. Of further interest in this case is an obvious reference to the scarcity of equipment: "The number of trained snipers will be determined by available sniper equipment."

In an effort to promulgate the merits of the XM21 system and his unit's sniper program on an Army-wide scale Maj. Robert G. Hilchey wrote a detailed report entitled "Sniper Training and Employment in the 9th Infantry Division" (March 1969). This served to enlighten and assist other combat units intent on establishing sniper operations in Vietnam. As a historical document, the "Hilchey Report," which immediately follows, provides valuable insight on the workings of one of the most successful operations of the entire war.

Ninth Infantry Division sniper candidate on the firing line at Bearcat, RVN (November 1968). Note the open boxes of match ammunition opposite. (U.S. Army.)

A photograph of a box of 7.62mm, M118 match ammunition (20 cartridges) taken at the 9th Division Sniper School (October 1968). According to Army and Marine Corps snipers, the availability of match-grade rifle ammunition "was never a problem" in Vietnam. The experienced riflemen often referred to the special cartridges as "Camp Perry ammunition." (U.S. Army.)

The Overseas Weekly,
Pacific Edition,
7 December 1968

"Most of the kids we get in here are pretty green as far as marksmanship is concerned," said MSG Alfred B. Falcon, NCOIC of the 9th Inf. Div.'s new sniper school. "Spraying the jungle with an M16 is a far cry from hitting a target at over 700 meters with one bullet on the first try.

"It's a good program," Falcon continued. "The guys train on highly accurate match-grade M14 rifles and fire match-grade ammunition. All but two of the instructors are members of the 'President's Hundred,' the top 100 rifle shooters in the United States."

SNIPER TRAINING AND EMPLOYMENT IN THE 9TH INFANTRY DIVISION

by

Major Robert G. Hilchey
Asst G-3
9th Infantry Division

9TH INFANTRY DIVISION SNIPER PROGRAM

I. INTRODUCTION:

The sniper program in the 9th Infantry Division has developed into a valuable asset for the division. This paper will provide interested commanders with an outline of how the program was initiated, the equipment required and the areas in which command emphasis was needed. The paper addresses formation of the school, range facilities, training highlights, employment techniques and a brief discussion of problem areas that occurred in the program. A complete program of instruction for the entire eighteen day course is available from this division for unit commanders planning to establish a sniper school.

II. ESTABLISHMENT OF THE SCHOOL:

A team of one Major and eight NCOs joined the 9th Division in June 1968, from the Army Marksmanship Training Unit (AMTU) at Fort Benning. Each team member had extensive experience in competitive shooting. One member was an experienced gunsmith familiar with M14 accurizing techniques.

A sniper training facility was constructed to accommodate 30 students. The facility included a 15 point firing range and adjacent classroom. The range was built with target facilities at 150, 300, 600 and 900 meters. A moving target was built on the 300 meter butt in addition to the fixed targets at that position.

III. TRAINING:

Students accepted into the sniper program are selected from volunteers. Those who are selected must have 20/20 vision, have qualified as expert riflemen and be well motivated soldiers. Experience in competitive marksmanship is preferred but is not mandatory.

The training includes basic firing positions, and the integrated acts of shooting: trigger squeeze, breath control, sight alignment, and sight picture.

Students are taught the techniques of estimating lead and engaging moving targets. Instruction is provided on the methods for estimating wind over extreme ranges so that a firer can offset his point of aim to place the bullet on target.

Students learn the methods of zeroing their weapons equipped with the adjustable ranging telescopic sight (ART), starlight scope and the fixed power M84 telescopic sight. Night firing is included in the course and each student learns to engage targets with his starlight scope at ranges of 150, 300, and 600 meters.

In addition to the marksmanship training, students are schooled in adjustment of artillery fire, day/night land navigation, and map reading. Each of these subjects is important to the sniper. He frequently must select his position from a situation map and then travel to that location at night. It is essential that he select the optimum position, know his position in relationship to friendly units and is able to navigate to his pre-selected position.

The ability to accurately adjust artillery fire is important to a sniper. He frequently must adjust illuminating rounds and do it skillfully so that illumination is placed on target in such a manner as to illuminate the target and not compromise the sniper's position or an adjacent friendly unit.

Qualification firing is conducted during the last two days of the course. Silhouette targets are engaged at 150, 300, 600 and 900 meters. Eight targets are engaged by each man during two qualifying courses. Ten points are awarded for a first round hit, five points are given for a second round hit. A maximum score is 160 points. A minimum qualifying score is 130.

Experience gained from the first five classes shows that about 50% of the students successfully complete the course.

IV. EQUIPMENT:

The snipers of the 9th Division are equipped with National Match Grade M14 rifles. Fifty-four of these rifles have been accurized by the Marksmanship Training Unit at Fort Benning. These rifles are glass bedded into impregnated stocks which are impervious to water. The rifles are carefully tuned to provide a high degree of accuracy. The remaining 74 rifles are National Match Grade weapons prepared by the Army Weapons Command. These rifles are somewhat less accurate than the AMTU weapons but are sufficiently accurate for sniper activity.

The 54 AMTU accurized weapons are equipped with a 3-9 variable power adjustable ranging telescope sight (ART). The telescope is mounted in conjunction with a ballistic cam. The

---

Correspondence:
Major Powell
to Colonel Bayard,
14 December 1968

Class #3 graduated on the 13th of December. The class started with 28 students, and 15 successfully completed the course. The Honor Graduate was a student returnee from the first class. He did a real fine job on his second try, and was promoted to Sergeant for his efforts. When this class gets back from R&R, we will have 42 snipers operating in the field. Class #4 will begin on 17 December. Hopefully, we will reach our goal of 54 by the end of this class.

—Maj. Willis L. Powell
Commandant, Sniper School,
9th Infantry Division

> **Correspondence: Major Powell to Colonel Bayard, 16 February 1969**
>
> General Abrams and General Hines (USARPAC CG) came down for a briefing last week and we had all of the II Field Force units represented at a Sniper Program seminar we conducted here at Dong Tam.
>
> At the present time, we are teaching 30 students from the 101st Abn to help them get a program started. They are rushing to put a school together and build a range so they can teach their own troops soon. They have 226 NM M14s with M84 scopes and they are chomping at the bit.
>
> We now have 74 additional new NM M14s with the same M84 scopes.
>
> —Maj. Willis L. Powell
> Commandant, Sniper School,
> 9th Infantry Division

sight reticle includes a pair of stadia lines. By varying the power of the telescope until the stadia lines define a 30 inch area on the target, the ballistic cam raises the sight to the proper elevation for that distance. Errors due to range estimation are virtually eliminated with this system.

The 74 National Match Grade M14s prepared by Army Weapons Command are equipped with the M84 telescope. These sights are a fixed 2.2 power telescope with a post reticle. Using the M84 the sniper must accurately estimate the gun target range and either hold over the target or adjust the elevating mechanism on the sight to the estimated range.

The AN/PVS-2 Starlight Scope has proven more effective for sniper use than the AN/PVS-1. Focusing is improved on the AN/PVS-2, and the windage/elevation controls are more reliable than on the latter sight. The sight reticle in the AN/PVS-2 better lends itself to engagement of long range targets. Students bring a starlight scope and mount to the sniper school when they report for training. The sight is mounted on the rifle and zeroed during training. The sniper retains that scope/rifle combination during subsequent operations. This procedure assures retention of zero even though the sight is dismounted during daylight operations and remounted for night operations.

The ammunition used in sniper training and combat is 7.62mm National Match Grade.

V. <u>ORGANIZATION:</u>

Six snipers are assigned to each battalion headquarters and headquarters company and four at each brigade headquarters. It has been found essential that sniper employment be planned and controlled no lower than battalion level.

VI. <u>METHODS OF EMPLOYMENT:</u>

a. Ambush Patrols:

Placing snipers with ambush patrols has been the most successful method of employment. Two techniques are used extensively: (1) The sniper team accompanies a platoon on an ambush; (2) The sniper team, with a security element of five to eight men, establishes an ambush/sniper position.

   1. When employed with a platoon ambush, the sniper team remains close to the platoon command post. When an element of the platoon observes enemy activity, the snipers are alerted to that location. The snipers engage selectively at night with the starlight scope or with the ART scope during daylight. If

Sniper Operations: A Program Takes Hold

there is but one Viet Cong in the area, he is taken under fire by a sniper. In this way the ambush position and location of automatic weapons are not compromised. When a group of Viet Cong approach the killing zone, the snipers engage the Viet Cong leaders and radio operators while the platoon fires into the general kill zone. Another technique which has been successful in an ambush is that of having the snipers fire tracers to mark the flanks of an enemy force which has approached the position in an area other than the specified kill zone. Snipers are also used to engage Viet Cong who probe the ambush site, attempting to incite the ambush to fire prematurely, thus disclosing automatic weapons positions and detonating its claymores.

    2. The second successful method of employment has been that of placing a sniper team and a five to eight man security element in a carefully selected sniper/ambush position. The general area is selected by the battalion commander who considers the enemy activity in the area and the advice of the sniper team. The team is moved to a company forward position where it is joined by the security element. The security element is equipped with M16s, an M79, and an AN/PRC-25 radio. The sniper/ambush position is occupied just prior to dark. The location is selected to provide maximum range of fires and is located within a reasonable distance from a friendly unit. The snipers maintain a continuous surveillance of the area. Eye fatigue at night is minimized by having the snipers alternate use of the starlight scope throughout the night. The M79 is an especially useful weapon at a sniper/ambush position. Viet Cong frequently have been observed in a treeline or vegetated area in which a shot was not possible due to low light level. By directing M79 fire into the area, the Viet Cong, on several occasions, have been forced to move and expose themselves to sniper fire.

  b. Stay-Behinds:

    Snipers, having a long range capability, are extremely effective in engaging Viet Cong who follow a unit as it moves from one location to another. A sniper team with a 5-8 man security element is selected to provide long-range observation of the route over which the unit has traveled. Snipers with their telescope sights are able to engage Viet Cong at ranges out to 900 meters. At extreme ranges, the Viet Cong frequently are not cautious about their cover and concealment. Thus, they present excellent targets for the sniper team.

  c. Off-Set:

    1. A xenon search light has been used to covertly illuminate an area with pink light. The starlight scope is sensitive to a portion of the infrared band that is pink and

---

Correspondence: Major Powell to Colonel Bayard, 18 March 1969

    I've been on a couple of the "night-hunter" missions with the choppers and gunships. With the moon in a bright phase or flare ship support, it is possible to detect and mark sampans infiltrating down from the Cambodian border. Once the target is marked by a sniper using tracers, the gunships engage, and the only thing left afloat is a few chips scattered around. I have also gone out with a couple of the units on ambush patrols. The methods of employment are sound, and if the targets present themselves a body-count is usually recorded. The snipers aren't missing many shots and we continually stress re-zeroing the scopes whenever possible.

    —Maj. Willis L. Powell
Commandant, Sniper School,
9th Infantry Division

**Correspondence:
Major General Ewell to
Woolnough, CG, CONARC,
1 April 1969**

We arranged for a team from the Army Marksmanship Training Unit (AMTU) at Ft. Benning to join the division and set up the sniper school. The team, under Major Willis Powell, has done a remarkable job. The accurized M14s prepared by the AMTU and the Limited Warfare Laboratory adjustable range telescope sights (ART) are an outstanding combination. The most significant weapon/sight combination, however, is the accurized M14 and the Starlight Scope. Our experience is that most sniper kills are made at night with the latter combination.

—Maj. Gen. Julian J. Ewell,
USA Commanding

near the visible light portion of the spectrum. By using a pink filter on a xenon search light, an area can be illuminated with invisible light that registers in the starlight scope. This phenomena has been used successfully in two types of sniper activity; berm security and ambush operations.

    2. Successful ambushes have been conducted by placing a searchlight-equipped 1/4-ton vehicle 1200 to 1500 meters from a road intersection. Snipers equipped with starlight scopes were placed 300 meters from the intersection. Maintaining radio contact with the searchlight operator, the snipers controlled the covert illumination to the intersection and surrounding areas. When Viet Cong appeared in the kill zone they were easily engaged by the sniper team. It has been found that by off setting the sniper teams from the searchlight and placing the searchlight and 1/4-ton vehicle in a position remote from the ambush site, the enemy in the kill zone were not alerted by the noise of the running vehicle engine.

    3. The pink light/sniper combination has been successfully employed in base camp security operations. The searchlight, mounted on a 1/2 ton vehicle, responds to radio equipped sniper teams in position either on the berm or on ambush positions outside the berm. The background noise of a fixed base camp effectively conceals the noise of the engine and activity of the searchlight crew. In forward base camps, the searchlight remains in the center of the base camp and, by swinging its beam through 360 degrees, covertly illuminates avenues of approach into the position. With this method it is again essential that the sniper teams maintain radio contact with the searchlight crew. The pink light is particularly useful during the dark of the moon period.

    d. Counter Sniper:

Sniper teams are effective in countering Viet Cong sniper activity. Each team, equipped with its telescopic sight and M49 Spotting Scope, searches the area of suspected sniper activity. The optical equipment permits a detailed search of distant areas. A recent example is that of a unit which, after having been fired on by a Viet Cong sniper from long range, deployed its sniper team. The team searched the tree line with its optical equipment and the Viet Cong sniper was discovered in a tree at 720 meters. While one team member judged the wind using the M49 spotting scope, the other man fired one round, killing the Viet Cong sniper.

    e. Night Hunter Operations:

Night Hunter Operations have made extensive use of snipers to mark targets. A sniper team is placed in the lead helicopter. They observe the ground with starlight scope-mounted rifles. When the enemy is sighted, the snipers engage with tracers. The gun ships, following at a higher altitude, then engage the targets. Artillery HE and illumination are adjusted on target as necessary.

VII. PROBLEM AREAS:

The following problem areas have been encountered in training and employment. The problem areas are discussed here to provide guidance to units initiating a sniper program.

    a. When sniper teams are employed for prolonged periods with units other than units of assignment, there is a tendency for the snipers to be overlooked when promotions are considered, when Rest and Recuperation leave is scheduled and other personnel affairs.

    b. The personal interest of battalion and company commanders is essential in selecting candidates for the sniper school. Men have been "volunteered" for the course when they not only expressed no interest in the program but had a very short time remaining in country. The selection and training of only well motivated and interested men is essential to the program.

    c. Commanders must take an active interest in employing snipers. Without command interest, sniper teams will be employed poorly and the results of the sniper program will be meager. There have been examples of snipers being positioned in dense vegetation with limited fields of fire while riflemen in the same unit were located in positions with wide fields of fire. In those units in which the commander imaginatively employed his snipers the results have been significantly greater than in units which the commanders were less interested in the program.

    d. A sniper, with his optical equipment, frequently is able to see the immediate reaction of a Viet Cong as he is hit by a bullet. In some cases, a sniper who has been well motivated will suddenly lose interest in sniping after witnessing a kill. This can be detected only by careful and regular debriefing of both members of the sniper team.

VIII. STATISTICAL DATA:

    a. The snipers were first assigned to maneuver battalions on 7 November 1968 and obtained their first kill on 10 November 1968. To date (10 March 1969), the fifty-four snipers employed in the division have had 135 contacts and accumulated a total of 211 confirmed enemy kills, or 1.56 kills per contact.

Correspondence: Major Powell to Colonel Bayard, 6 April 1969

Since my last letter the kills have really started to increase. In March we had 116 contacts and made 211 kills. The most significant part of the total kills for March is that 70 were in the daytime. This is more daytime kills than we have ever had. Also, the majority of the 70 kills were with M14s with M84 scopes. The division total is now 254 contacts/433 kills. In April so far we have 20 contacts/37 kills.

The reference in the pamphlet on "Sniper Training and Employment," 9th Infantry Division, concerning the accuracy of the NM rifles, was included to point out that kills could be made up to the range capability of the M84 scope, and that rifle and scope accuracy was sufficient for the majority of targets we engaged. I test-fired one match grade rifle prepared by AWC and it grouped 7 inches at 300 meters. The longest kill we have on record with the M84 scope is 800 meters, and it took 3 shots to get on target. This is a rare case and I know the ART scope would have done the same thing with one shot. I strongly recommend that snipers be armed with the more accurate MTU accurized M14 w/ART, and I feel USARV was convinced this was the only way to go. First class all the way.

—Maj. Willis L. Powell
Commandant, Sniper School,
9th Infantry Division

Correspondence: Major Powell to Colonel Bayard, 6 April 1969

I visited the 1st Marine Division Sniper School and was disappointed in the set-up. They run a five day in-country refresher course and zero exercises on an "as needed" basis. Their rifles (Remington Model 700) are in bad shape, and they are having trouble getting new ones. I demonstrated our rifle and scope and recommended they switch to it in the future. I pointed out the advantages, 20 round magazine, night capability with the Starlight, superior scope, in the supply system, etc., etc. Also shot a demonstration on moving targets for them. They have a moving target at 300 meters that travels about 30 meters on each pass, and they fire one shot on each pass. I put seven out of seven shots in the heart area of the target on one pass, and all I can say is they are hard to convince. They are still sold on the bolt action with the Accu-Range scope. They zero point of aim/point of impact at 500 meters, and hold over or under for targets that are not at 500 meters. They claim kills up to 1400 meters, and one at 1800 meters with this method. I'm not knocking their program, they have good results to date. I just think they could do better with our rifle and scope.

—Maj. Willis L. Powell
Commandant, Sniper School,
9th Infantry Division

(continued on page 41)

b. The light conditions under which the kills were made:

1. Daylight	16
2. Night with Ambient Light	185
3. Night with Pink Light	10

c. Number of kills per sniper:

SNIPERS	CONFIRMED KILLS
18	0
27	1-4
7	5-9
1	12
1	92

d. The following data reflect sniper results during the period 1 January 1969 through 10 March 1969.

(1) Number of rounds expended per kill:

249 Rounds Fired
182 Confirmed Kills   = 1.37 Rounds Per Kill

(2) Kills in relation to time of day:

KILLS	TIME OF DAY
7	0600-1800
89	1800-2100
68	2100-2400
18	0001-0600

(3) Kills in relation to range:

KILLS	RANGE IN METERS
15	0-100
31	101-200
40	201-300
41	301-400
25	401-500
18	501-600
11	601-700
1	701-800
0	801-900

NOTE: Though few in actual number, noise suppressors had figured prominently in early sniper operations in the Mekong Delta. Rather than provide the Vietcong with useful information, however, the Hilchey Report omitted the mention of suppressors and subsonic ammunition at the request of Major General Ewell. As a point of interest, according to correspondence from the 9th Infantry Division to the USAMTU, by 13 March 1969, a graduate of the division sniper school, S.Sgt. Adelbert F. Waldron, had accounted for "92 confirmed kills." From this total, 40 were reportedly made with a "noise suppressor."

Lieutenant General Ewell provided a brief summary of the 9th Division sniper program in "Impressions of a Division Commander in Vietnam" (a U.S. Army document circulated within the Army, 17 September 1969):

> The most effective single program we had was the sniper program. This took a whole year to get off the ground from scratch but we ended up with 80 snipers who would kill (or capture) from 200 to 300 enemy a month. Not only did we get this direct return but they also encouraged the other men to shoot well. Snipers, like everything else, are highly sensitive to tactics and techniques so one has to handle them well. The flat open Delta terrain was ideal for snipers. Other divisions are now trying snipers in other areas, so we shall see how they work on a broader basis. Snipers had been tried before in the theater with tepid results, but we insisted that the entire program be exactly right, demanded results and got them.

NOTE: For the sake of clarification, Julian J. Ewell commanded the 9th Infantry Division with the rank of major general from February 1968 until April 1969, when Maj. Gen. Harris W. Hollis assumed command.

For the record, although a number of officers and men both stateside and in-country were responsible for the success of the program, Brig. Gen. James S. Timothy, though rarely acknowledged, has been credited officially with "getting the sniper program off the ground" during the early organizational phases in RVN.

The peak of 9th Infantry Division sniping operations came during April 1969, when the highest level of "kills" was recorded.

Maj. Willis L. Powell, commandant, 9th Infantry Division Sniper School, noted the results of this activity in a letter of information to Col. Robert F. Bayard, commanding officer, USAMTU, Ft. Benning, Georgia (30 April 1969). The correspondence stated the following (in part):

> We have trained cadre for the 1st, 1st Air Cav, 25th, 3/82nd Abn, and 199th LIB, and snipers for the 101st Abn Division. These units are supposed to start a sniper school of their own.
>
> General Hollis took over the 9th Division from General Ewell, and he is solidly behind the sniper program. The 9th Division is leading all others in the VC elimination category. This month the snipers have made an impressive kill record. The total for April is 346, with 248 night kills and 98 daylight kills. The longest kill in daytime was 820 meters and at night 3

NOTE: However suited for combat the Marine Corps sniper rifle may have been (Remington Model 700 [M40], Redfield 3X-9X variable-power Accu-Range scope), by late 1967, unsatisfactory field reports citing one problem or another began filtering back to HQMC in Washington. The rigors of sustained combat use in Vietnam were revealing flaws in the system that did not turn up when the rifle and sight were evaluated originally.

Apart from remedial measures intended to sustain the system in RVN, the USMC "Scout-Sniper Rifle" was about to enter a period of transition that would extend well beyond Marine Corps combat involvement in Southeast Asia. Despite the problems, the Marine Corps remained committed to the bolt-action sniper rifle.

VC KIA at 700 meters. The Division total is 499 contacts with 749 kills, as of 2400 hrs, 30 April.

Our daytime kills are coming up now. Some of the units are inserting small groups (4-8 men) with 2 snipers into an area that is 100% VC territory. They are engaging small groups of VC (1-10 men) that are walking around not knowing the sniper groups are close by. These insertions are usually put in the day (a.m.) following a large unit sweep operation of the area. On these large unit sweeps, normally the only people seen are women and children. Then the next day when the small group is put in the same area, they see men walking all over the place. A light fire team is kept on stand-by to bail out the small killer team if they get tangled up with something bigger than they can handle. Also, we're getting more daylight kills because the commanders are employing the snipers better on daylight operations. It doesn't take long for word to get around when a new twist is tried with good results. The moon phase has a lot to do with our night kills. Naturally the bigger the moon, the better we can see and the count goes up.

In the time remaining, the number of recorded kills leveled off to approximately 200 per month, until sniper operations were phased out as the U.S. military prepared to leave South Vietnam. The majority of the 9th Infantry Division returned to the United States during August 1969.

The division redeployed to Hawaii as part of the first increment of the U.S. withdrawal but left the 3d Brigade in Vietnam. The 3d Brigade (separate) served under the command of the 25th Infantry Division until it departed Vietnam. Even though the sniper program ended as a result, some of the personnel tasked with training 9th Infantry Division snipers with time remaining in RVN were reassigned to other combat units where their work continued.

Army sniper candidates carefully squeezing off each round in preparation for "working the Mekong Delta." The 9th Infantry Division sniper program served as the pilot project for Army sniper operations in Southeast Asia. In one way or another, the experience gained was adapted by other combat units during the course of the war. (U.S. Army.)

Sniper Operations: A Program Takes Hold

Army personnel "working the range" at the 9th Infantry Division Sniper School (Bearcat, RVN). Note the weapons carried by the troopers. Even under the best circumstances, the threat of Vietcong infiltration was always present. (U.S. Army.)

Qualification firing at 150, 300, 600, and 900 meters was conducted during the last two days of the 9th Division sniper course. Those failing to qualify were washed out with no exceptions. Note the M49 spotting scope in the foreground. The instructor (left) is Sfc. James L. Tuck, a member of the sniper school cadre. (U.S. Army.)

Correspondence:
Major Chittester to
Colonel Bayard,
12 June 1969

The kill count went to 1000 at 111500 June 1969. SP4 Tropeano, CO C, 4th BN, 39th INF, made the shot.

—Maj. Gary R. Chittester
Commandant, Sniper School,
9th Infantry Division

THE LONG-RANGE WAR: SNIPING IN VIETNAM

The "first class" of Army snipers graduated by the 9th Infantry Division sniper program in South Vietnam (Bearcat, November 1968). Maj. Gen. Julian J. Ewell, Brig. Gen. James S. Timothy, and Maj. Willis L. Powell are pictured with the group. The sniper school later moved from Bearcat (near Saigon) when Division headquarters relocated to Dong Tam, west of My Tho City. (U.S. Army.)

Certificate awarded to 9th Infantry Division marksmen following satisfactory completion of their 18-day sniper training. So demanding were the requirements that only 50 percent of the candidates completed the first five classes. The original certificate (shown) was designed at Ft. Benning. The USAMTU form was later replaced with a three-color version made in Vietnam. (U.S. Army.)

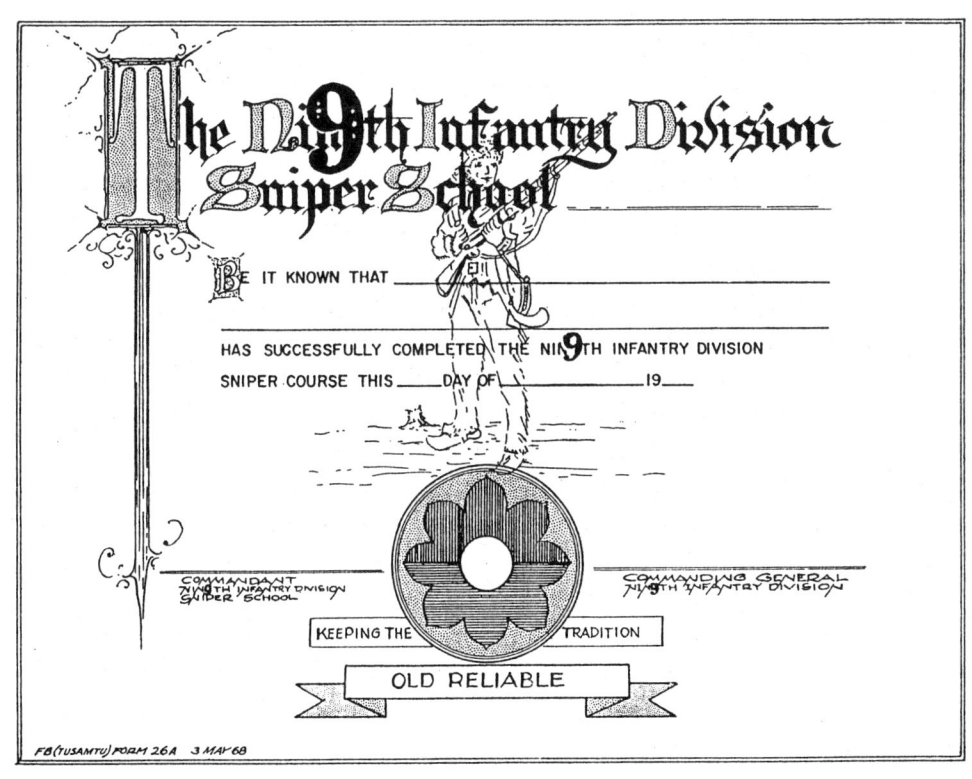

Sniper Operations: A Program Takes Hold

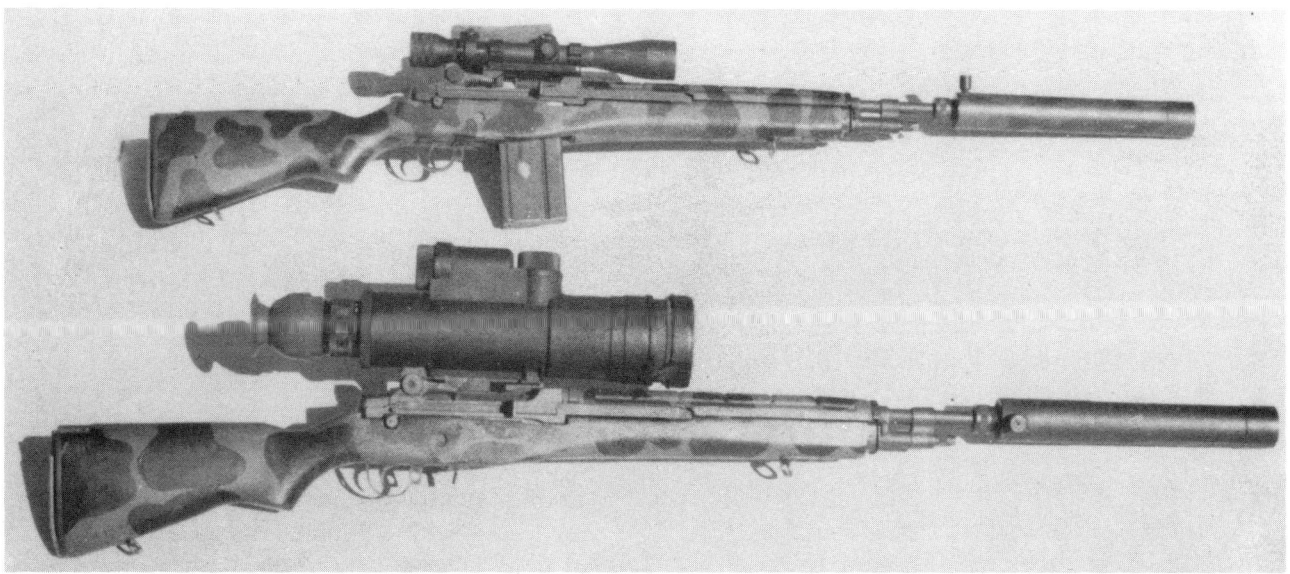

With a day and night capability, the Vietnam-era XM21 mounting the ART or the Starlight Scope in combination with the Sionics M14SS-1 Suppressor wrought havoc among VC and NVA combat personnel in Southeast Asia. The rifle stocks were "pattern-painted" to facilitate their concealment. Both rifles are fitted with suppressors; the night vision sight is an AN/PVS-2 model. (U.S. Army.)

An XM21-equipped Army sniper moves across a dike adjacent to a rice paddy. The dark object beneath the left forearm is an ART carrying case attached to the ammunition belt. According to an Army sniper instructor, "To begin with, the men were advised to carry the aluminum cases in the field, and many did. As time passed, however, the carrying cases were rarely taken on a mission." Carrying as little as possible was the rule. In many cases, when it became necessary to remove the scope from the rifle, they were carefully wrapped and strapped to the pack while moving through the bush. (U.S. Army.)

46 THE LONG-RANGE WAR: SNIPING IN VIETNAM

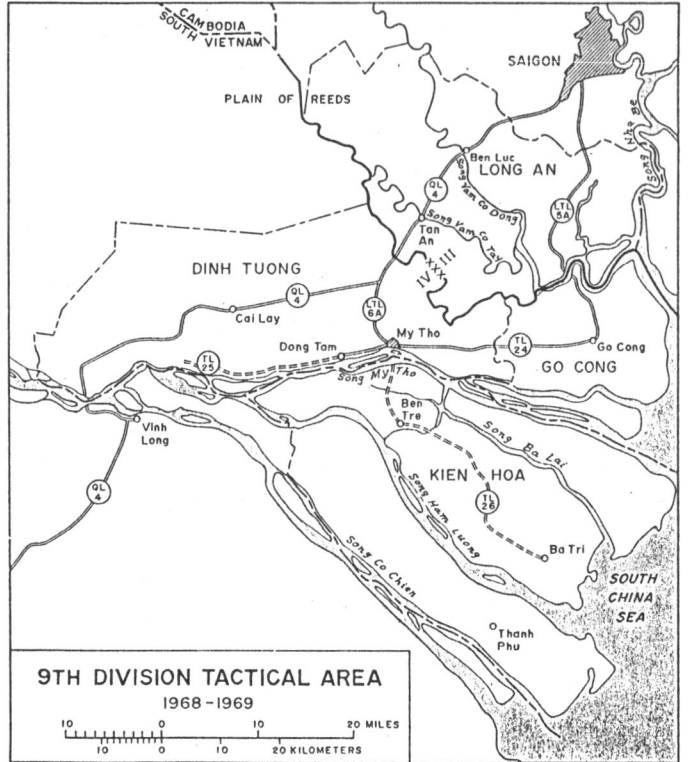

9th Infantry Division Tactical Area 1968–1969, Republic of Vietnam. (U.S. Army.)

An Army sniper sighting "his mark." The rifle is an accurized M14 with an Adjustable Ranging Telescope. The 900-meter capability of the XM21 system made the everyday life of VC and NVA personnel quite hazardous. (U.S. Army.)

Sniper Operations: A Program Takes Hold

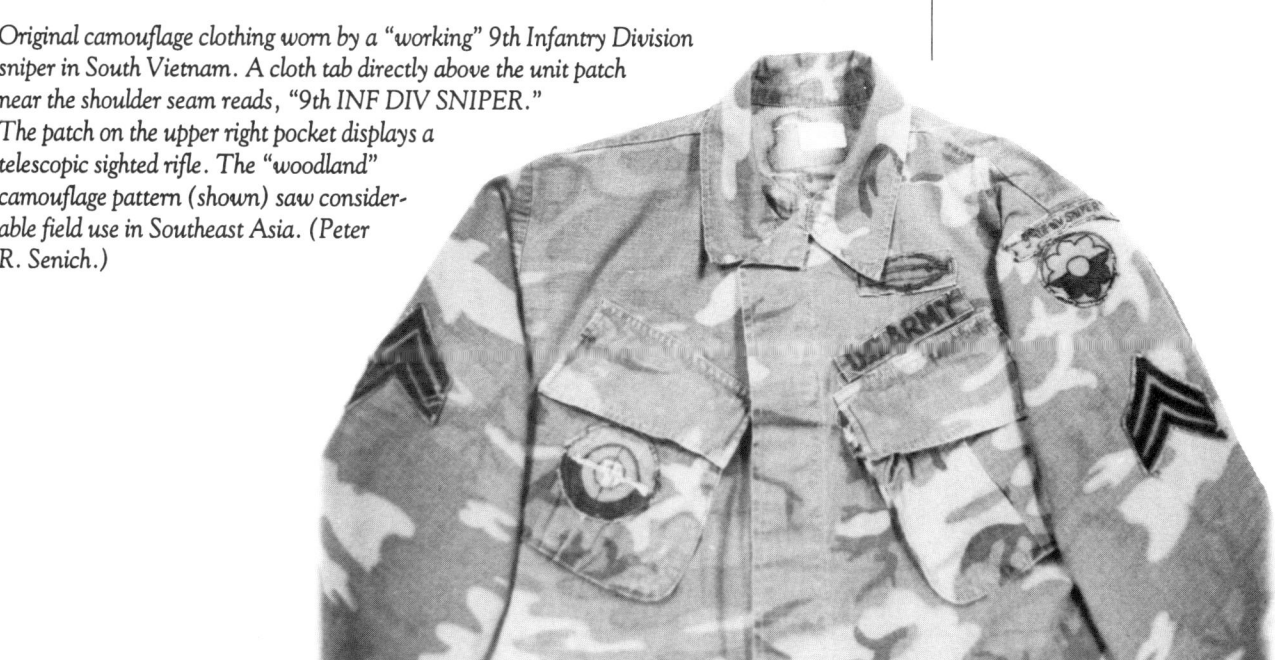

Original camouflage clothing worn by a "working" 9th Infantry Division sniper in South Vietnam. A cloth tab directly above the unit patch near the shoulder seam reads, "9th INF DIV SNIPER." The patch on the upper right pocket displays a telescopic sighted rifle. The "woodland" camouflage pattern (shown) saw considerable field use in Southeast Asia. (Peter R. Senich.)

During the course of field operations in the Mekong Delta, 9th Infantry Division snipers reported directly to company commanders, received a briefing on proposed tactics, picked the platoon and area where they thought they could be most effective, and positioned themselves where targets were likely to appear. (U.S. Army.)

A 9th Infantry Division sniper spotting and firing on the enemy. The extraordinary sequence photograph was taken during operations in the Mekong Delta region. The rifle is an ART-equipped XM21. Note the shooting position and the method of steadying the rifle. The marksman has made the best of a difficult situation in this case. (U.S. Army.)

Sniper Operations: A Program Takes Hold

Sgt. Barry Zuckerman, a sniper with the 9th Infantry Division, is pictured in front of his "hootch" with an XM21 sniper rifle mounting an AN/PVS-2 Starlight Scope and a Sionics M14SS-1 suppressor. Though barely visible as reproduced here, the sign above the doorway reads, "VC Hunting Club." (Barry Zuckerman.)

Ninth Infantry Division sniper on patrol in the Delta region (1969). The rifle is an AMTU accurized M14 with an Adjustable Ranging Telescope. In one form or another, the M14 served as the principal sniper rifle during U.S. combat operations in Southeast Asia. (U.S. Army.)

An Army field photo of 9th Infantry Division marksman, Sfc. Adelbert F. Waldron, taken in South Vietnam (1969). (U.S. Army.)

Sniper Operations: A Program Takes Hold

Fortunate indeed was the marksman who happened to claim a Vietcong tax collector. As one Army sniper related, "VC tax collectors carried large amounts of Vietnamese currency (piasters), tribute from various villages and hamlets. The recovered money was put to good use for off-duty recreation." Although large sums of currency were supposed to be turned in, in one case, a Vietcong officer brought down with an open-sighted XM21 sniper rifle at 150 meters happened to be carrying the piaster equivalent of a few thousand dollars. According to the marksman involved, "We made the most of Saigon for a long, long time." The 500-piaster note is the "last" piece of currency from the memorable occasion. (Zuckerman Collection.)

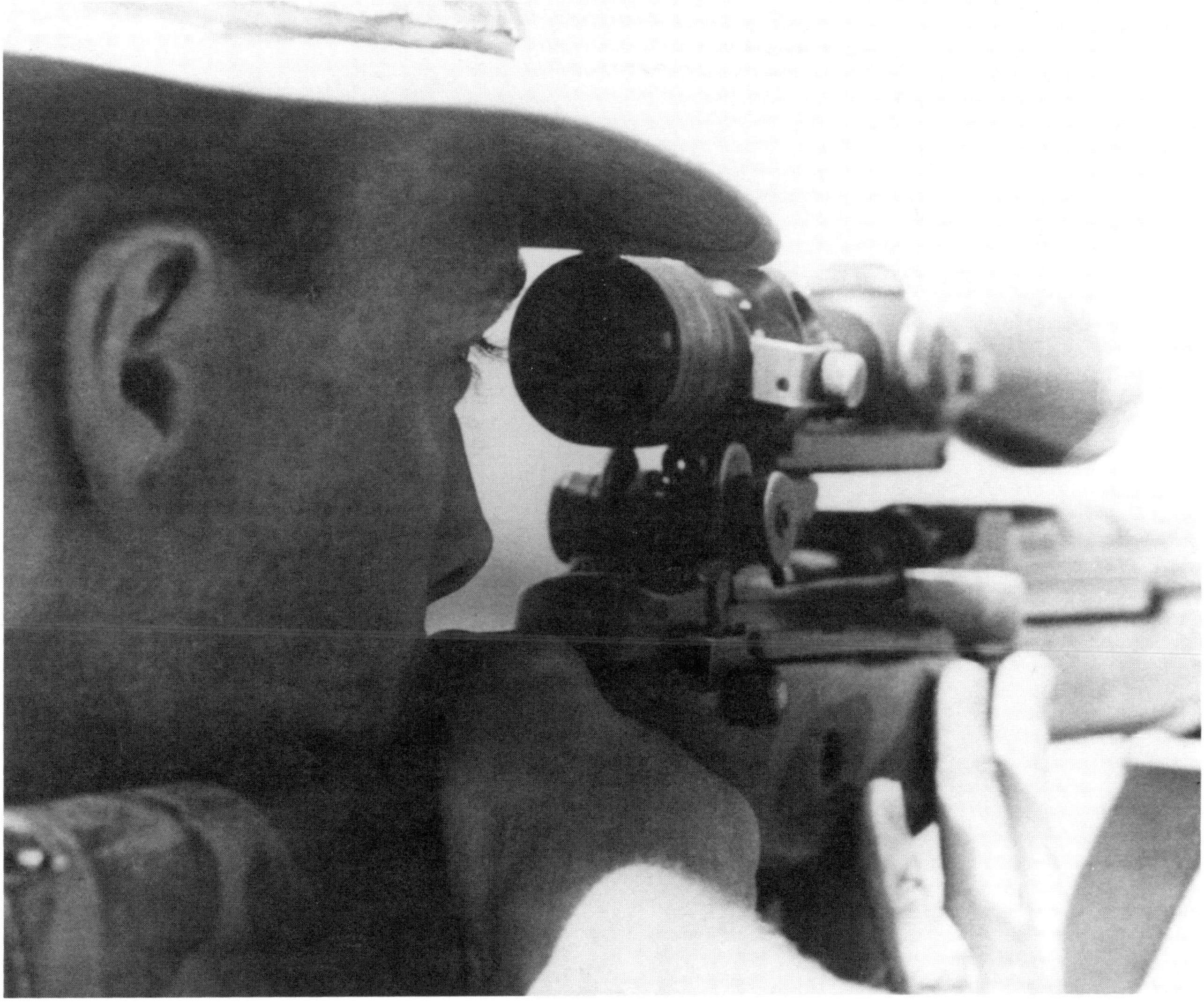

A close view of an Army sniper sighting an Adjustable Ranging Telescope. The power adjusting ring is positioned at 9-power. (U.S. Army.)

A close view of original Vietnam-era 9th Infantry Division unit and "sniper" patches. The cloth tab and the patches were worn by Maj. Willis L. Powell during his tour of duty in RVN. (Peter R. Senich.)

Sniper Operations: A Program Takes Hold

53

A measure of sniper effectiveness was best summarized by Lt. Gen. Julian J. Ewell as follows: "The sniper program of the 9th Infantry Division was one of the most successful programs that we undertook. It took over a year from its inception in the States to its peak performances in Vietnam. It also took plenty of hard work and belief in the concept of our snipers. But more than anything, it restored the faith of the infantryman in his rifle and in his own capabilities." The unique combat photograph was taken near Dong Tam. The marksman pictured, Pfc. R. Brown, was awarded the Silver Star for his sniper duty with the 9th Division in RVN. Ironically, the veteran sniper was killed in an automobile accident following his discharge in 1970. (U.S. Army.)

THE LONG-RANGE WAR: SNIPING IN VIETNAM

An Army infantryman shown with an M16 mounting a 3-power Colt/Realist telescopic sight during early combat activity in South Vietnam. Though eventually issued by the Army in limited number, many of the "Colt Scopes" found their way overseas when Army combat units began deploying to Southeast Asia. (Max Crace.)

CHAPTER 3

Sniper Weapon System: The XM21

The role of U.S. forces in the Republic of South Vietnam changed from "advisory" to "combat" in early 1965. In addition to an expanding Marine Corps presence, the buildup of Army combat forces began in earnest with the arrival of the 173d Airborne Brigade in May, the 1st Cavalry Division in September, and the lst Infantry Division in October.

In contrast with the fact that the Marine Corps focused official attention on an accelerated sniper training and equipment program in the latter part of 1965, when it came to the Army, research indicates that, except for occasional "requests for assistance" pertaining to sniper training and support during the initial phases of Army combat activity, no organized effort to field snipers in RVN would take shape at the official level until months later.

Even though Army combat strength increased significantly during 1966 with the arrival of the 25th Infantry Division in April, the 4th Infantry Division in August, and the 9th Infantry Division in December, from late 1965 through 1966, Army sniping activity in South Vietnam fell somewhere in between "nonexistent" and "loosely organized," with little effect on the Communist forces.

With telescopic sights in short supply, enterprising units and individuals brought commercial rifle scopes from the United States or procured them from the PX. Although military regulations prohibited bringing personal weapons to Southeast Asia, rifle scopes were not included. Consequently, a number of Army sniping weapons were fielded under these circumstances. Both stateside and in-country, telescopic sights

A 1st Infantry Division sniper team during operations south of Lai Khe, South Vietnam (October 1969). The rifle being sighted is equipped with the AWC telescope mounting and M84 scope. The other M14 has the night vision adapter bracket in place on the receiver. Note the "pattern-painted" rifle stocks and the use of natural vegetation for camouflage purposes. (U.S. Army.)

were mounted to the service rifles by every means possible. By the time the Army had an "official" sniping program in place, a surprising number of skilled Army marksmen had established their own agenda for dealing with the Vietcong in this regard.

The USAIB evaluation of the M14 with a hinged-telescope mount would serve as the foundation for the Vietnam-era Army sniping issue by emphasizing the suitability of a match-grade semiautomatic rifle and match ammunition for sniper use. But it remained for the U.S. Army Marksmanship Training Unit to take the concept one step further by developing an M14 sniper rifle accurized in accordance with specifica-

An original copy of the USAMTU "Standards and Procedures" for match-conditioning the M14 rifle (23 June 1968). The M14 sniper rifles (54) sent to the 9th Infantry Division in late 1968 were fabricated in the AMTU shop at Ft. Benning using the procedures in this manual. With the easing of some requirements (barrel specifications and accuracy) deemed necessary by Army Weapons Command to facilitate the production of sniper rifles at Rock Island Arsenal, the AMTU manual served as the rebuilding standard for the XM21 system. The revised edition was dated 1970 on the front cover. (U.S. Army.)

tions the AMTU had established in support of the program—"a weapon possessing match-grade characteristics, and then some."

As a matter of interest, the concept of employing a highly refined semiautomatic match-grade rifle for sniping purposes met with a fair amount of resistance due to the system being, as some saw it, altogether "too complex" for practical field use. Despite this, however, the USAMTU vision of the optimum sniper rifle would emerge as the principal Army sniping issue during the war in Vietnam.

By the time the last American combat forces left Southeast Asia, at least three types of telescopic sighted M14 rifles saw field use in the hands of Army marksmen: the standard M14 rifles with commercial scopes, improvised mounts, and, in some cases, M84 sights in the receiver mounting bracket developed by Army Weapons Command; the basic match-grade M14 rifles prepared by AWC at Rock Island Arsenal with the M84 telescope in the aforementioned

An XM21 sniper rifle in combat trim. M14s serving as the basis for this system were rebuilt from those made by the various manufacturers (Springfield Armory, Harrington & Richardson, Winchester, and Thompson Ramo Wooldridge), with all regarded equally desirable, except for barrels having chrome bores, which were considered unsatisfactory for precision shooting. "SAK" barrels manufactured at the Saco, Maine, Ordnance Depot were reportedly used with the bulk of the Vietnam-era XM21 rifles under ENSURE No. 240, the XM21 project. Rock Island Arsenal would accurize and target-in the rifles. The AMTU at Ft. Benning was tasked with final acceptance testing and "minor gunsmithing" necessary to accomplish this end. Accepted rifles were sent to the Anniston Army Depot for packing and shipment. Although many of the M14 sniper rifles made use of camouflage, except for the AMTU rifles fielded in 1968, this was usually done on an in-country basis after the weapons reached Vietnam. For the record, however, the majority of the M14 sniper rifles fielded in Southeast Asia did not use camouflaged stocks. (U.S. Army.)

DTM 9-1005-221-10

OPERATOR'S MANUAL

RIFLE, 7.62-MM, XM21, SNIPER
W/ADJUSTABLE RANGING TELESCOPE
AND MOUNT WITH EQUIPMENT
(1005-179-0300)

DRAFT COPY
This publication is not available through AG publication channels

HEADQUARTERS U.S. ARMY WEAPONS COMMAND
ROCK ISLAND, ILLINOIS

The original "Draft Technical Manual" DTM 9-1005-221-10, November 1969, for the ART-equipped XM21 Sniper Weapon System produced at Rock Island Arsenal. An XM21 maintenance and repair manual intended for ordnance support (DTM 9-1005-221-20) was also circulated by Army Weapons Command. (Brophy Collection.)

mounting; and, finally, the USAMTU-inspired XM21 system with the ART.

Though perceived as "an obsolete weapon system" when the war in Southeast Asia began, the "U.S. Rifle, 7.62mm, M14" saw extensive use as a sniping weapon during the Vietnam War, in view of its overall use for Army sniping purposes, the limited Marine field use of M14 sniper rifles categorized as "improvised" (commercial scopes and improvised mounts), and the employment of standard M14 rifles by USMC Scout-Sniper teams for security and "open-sighted sniping."

NOTE: In many cases, Marine snipers were known to establish an arbitrary range at which the second member of the team would "take over" and engage the enemy with semiautomatic or automatic rifle fire in defense of their position. By all accounts, in addition to providing team security, Marine snipers using the M14 with standard sights and, on occasion, the Starlight Scope as well took out any number of VC and NVA personnel.

Although diverse organizations conducted a number of evaluations during the mid-1960s in the quest for a sat-

Sniper Weapon System: The XM21

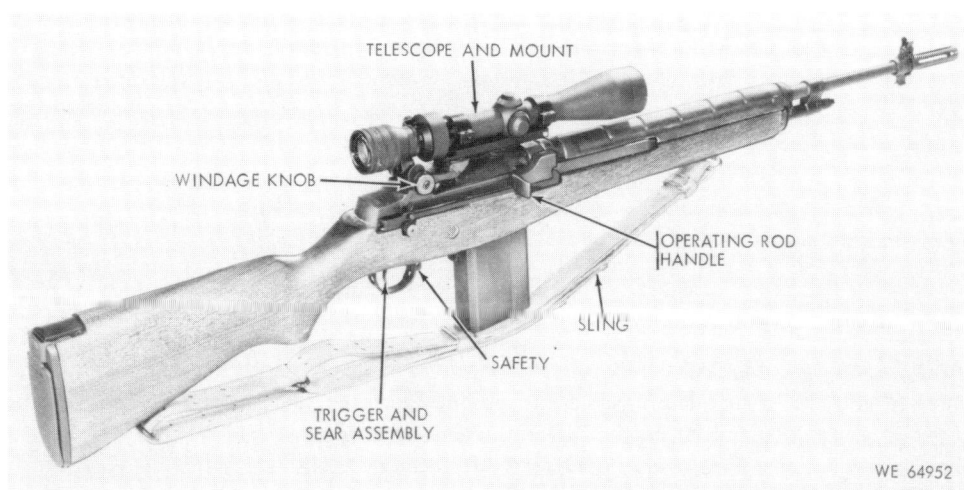

One of the principal weapon illustrations from DTM9-1005-221-10 (Figure 1-1): "Rifle, Sniper, 7.62mm, XM21, w/adjustable ranging telescope and mount, sling, and controls—right rear view." The early AWC manual detailed operating instructions, operator maintenance, and the basic issue items for the Army sniping system. (Brophy Collection.)

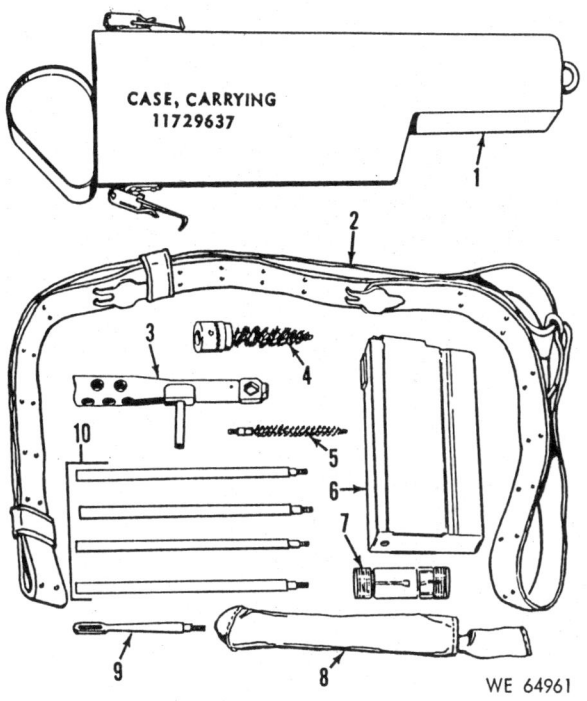

An illustration from DTM 9-1005-221-10, the operator's manual for the XM21 showing the basic items issued with the rifle. In addition to the telescope carrying case, an "NM" leather sling, magazine, and cleaning equipment were furnished as well. (Brophy Collection.)

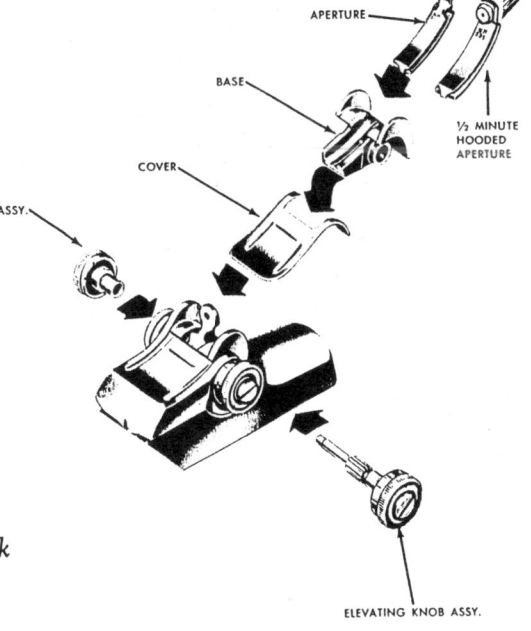

The National Match rear sight assembly employed with the Vietnam-era M14 sniper rifles fielded in Southeast Asia. According to the Army sniper training manual (TC 23-14), "The hooded aperture, rear sight provides 1/2-minute changes in elevation and is available in two peephole diameters . . . the windage knob produces a 1/2-minute change in windage for each click of the knob . . . the front sight has a blade width of .062." (U.S. Army.)

Below Left: The U.S. Army Marksmanship Training Unit, active in development of telescope mountings for the M14, designed and fabricated various aluminum mounts for the M14 for evaluation purposes prior to its involvement with the ART system. The mount is an early AMTU version of a "two-point" M14 telescope base with provision for a clip-guide mounting screw. (Lt. Col. F.B. Conway, Ret.)

Below Right: The original Adjustable Ranging Telescope prototype mount as fabricated by the USAMTU. The aluminum mount was built around an M80 Ball ballistic cam furnished by Franklin Owens of the Limited Warfare Laboratory. (Lt. Col. F.B. Conway, Ret.)

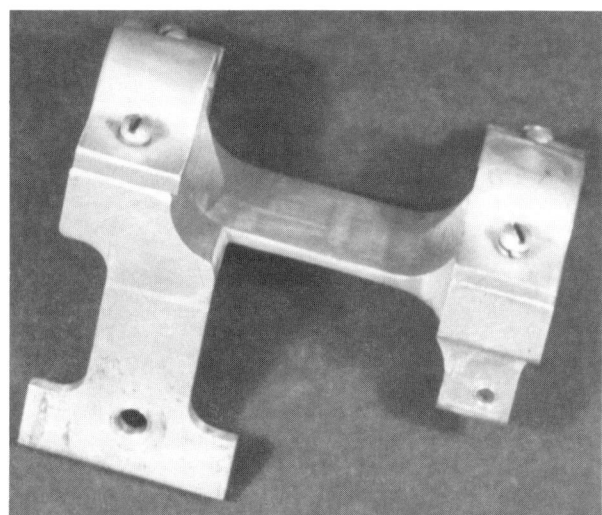

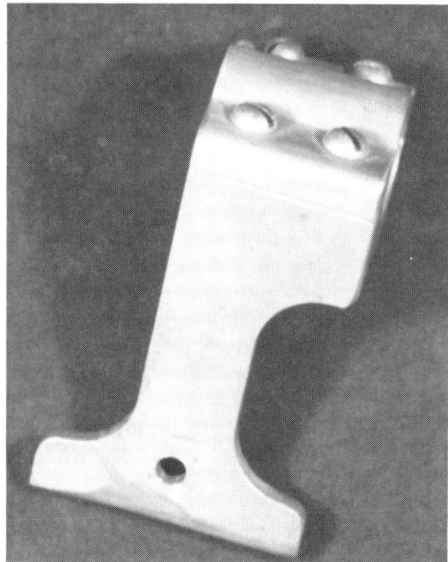

Above: A "single-support" AMTU telescope mounting intended for the M14 rifle. (Lt. Col. F.B. Conway, Ret.)

Right: The Chief of the USAMTU Test & Evaluation Section during the XM21 era, Maj. Ray Orton (Ret.), is shown with the original prototype mount (right). The late M.Sgt. Robert Walsh (opposite) was responsible for the necessary machine work; the sergeant is holding a conventional M14 telescope mounting. (Tom Dunkin.)

One of the original Adjustable Ranging Telescopes, a modified Redfield variable-power sight in a mount fabricated by the Limited Warfare Laboratory Technical Support machine shop at Aberdeen Proving Ground. The commercial Accu-Range sight was reconfigured to ART specifications by altering the reticle and attaching a ballistic cam and a locking device (power ring lock) to the Redfield power selector ring. Except for the "flats" on the telescope mounting screw, a modification recommended by the AMTU, the ART pictured is the same as the "tool room" version evaluated by ACTIV in 1967. (According to AMTU personnel, a socket-head screw and washer were used to secure the LWL mount to the M14 receiver.) The special 7-round magazine was developed by the AMTU for Army sniper use. (Lt. Col. F.B. Conway, Ret.)

isfactory telescope for Army sniper use, the ART fielded by the U.S. Army Limited Warfare Laboratory (LWL) met the necessary requirements for accurate long-range sniping in Southeast Asia. The ART, in conjunction with the M14s accurized according to USAMTU standards (firing M118 National Match Ammunition), provided the Army with the epitome of sniping efficiency—a weapon capable of consistent first-round hits.

The workings of the Adjustable Ranging Telescope, a sophisticated sighting system based on the 3X-9X variable-power Redfield rifle scope introduced in the early 1960s, were summarized in the *Department of the Army Training Circular, TC 23-14, Sniper Training and Employment*, 27 October 1969:

> The ART is a lightweight, commercially procured, three to nine variable power telescopic sight, modified for use with the sniper rifle. This scope has been improved with modified reticle and a ballistic cam mounted on the power adjusting ring.
>
> The modified reticle utilizes vertical and horizontal stadia marks to measure size or actually the angle of an object of known size. The vertical stadia marks subtend thirty inches while viewing at three power. As the telescope incorporates a nonmagnifying reticle (i.e., the stadia mark spacing remains the same regardless of power change), the sniper can then uti-

A close view of the early LWL/ART system. In original form, the aluminum mount consisted of a sideplate and a spring-loaded base assembly. The primary components were held together with a socket-head screw (recessed hex). The scope rings were shaped as they were (a series of flat surfaces, "multi-sided"), to "expedite machining." The ballistic cam and the power ring lock were fastened directly to the original power selector ring. The lock was necessary to keep the ring from moving during repeated firing. Note the scope rings marked to ensure matching and the LWL-applied legend (stamped) on the sideplate (CAL. 7.62-M14). From all indications, the "10 or 12" sights evaluated in Vietnam (1967) had the entire M14 serial number engraved on the left side of the mount (sideplate). The early LWL/ART system made use of the first-generation 3X-9X variable-power Redfield telescopic sights. The factory markings on the turret are representative of this series. The scope has a black gloss commercial finish. (Lt. Col. F.B. Conway, Ret.)

lize the increasing power of the scope to pull any known object of thirty inches, within the scope's capability, toward him until it fits between the stadia lines. This calibration will give a ranging capability from 300 to 900 meters, comparable to the three to nine power capability of the scope. Ranges and/or powers are inscribed on the focusing ring to give a range read-off capability. This method is considered 95 per cent accurate when applied by a trained sniper.

The ballistic cam is affixed to the power adjustment ring and is designed and ground to compensate for the trajectory of 7.62mm, M118 match ammunition. The trajectory of the 7.62mm, M118 match ammunition is much flatter than that of other 7.62mm service ammunition. The cam rests on the cam rest of the scope mount and is held in position by a return spring positioned in the mount.

As the cam is calibrated to the ranging capability of the scope, from 300 to 900 meters, any ranging accomplished is accompanied by an automatic adjustment in elevation of the scope to correct for bullet trajectory. This in effect eliminates the necessity to adjust sights manually for each range.

Sniper Weapon System: The XM21

A Limited Warfare Laboratory ART system with the base-adapter and ballistic cam (M33 Ball) for the Browning machine gun. The original LWL concept called for using the Adjustable Ranging Telescope with the M14 rifle and the .50-caliber machine gun. Although various "experts" believe this was intended to be carried out on an "expedient basis" by simply replacing the ballistic cam, removing the socket-head screw, and exchanging the machine gun base with the M14 sideplate, at this juncture there is nothing to confirm that the original LWL mount assemblies were designed with this purpose in mind. The telescope is a modified Redfield 3X-9X variable-power commercial model. An extremely early variant in this case, this model's power ring lock has not been fitted to the original power selector ring. The telescope base was formed to match the dovetail groove on the Browning sight assembly and attached to the machine gun as shown. (Peter R. Senich.)

The scope mount is of lightweight aluminum construction and designed for low profile mounting of the scope to the rifle utilizing the mounting guide grooves and threaded hole on the left side of the receiver. The mount consists of a side mounting plate and a spring-loaded base with scope mounting rings.

TABULATED DATA

Scope:
Weight (with cam and lock) . . . . 16.05 ounces
Length . . . . 12 3/4 inches
Magnification (variable) . . . . 3 to 9 power
Eye relief . . . . 3 – 3 3/4 inches
Adjustments . . . . Internal (1/2 minute graduations for elevation and windage)
Reticle . . . . Cross hairs (with stadia marks)
Ballistic cam . . . . For M118 match ammunition
Objective diameter . . . . 1.820 inches
Eyepiece diameter . . . . 1.565 inches
Finish . . . . Black matte anodize

Mount:
Weight . . . . 5.95 ounces
Material . . . . Aluminum 7075-T6
Operation . . . . Hand fixed, spring loaded base
Finish . . . . Black matte anodize

A close view of the 7.62mm M80 Ball and M118 Match ammunition ballistic cams developed for the Adjustable Ranging Telescope. The M33 Ball cam (right) was part of the original Limited Warfare Laboratory concept of equipping .50-caliber Browning machine guns with the ART. The aluminum alloy cams were held to the magnification sleeve by one screw and could be changed by the sniper as circumstances warranted. (Lt. Col. F.B. Conway, Ret.)

The second or "transitional model" in the Vietnam ART series, a second-generation Redfield 3X-9X variable-power sight reconfigured by the Limited Warfare Laboratory in 1968. The ballistic cam, power adjusting ring, and ring lock were redesigned to function as a complete unit and replaced the original power selector ring. The mount was then machined from an aluminum alloy (7075-T6) extrusion to form a one-piece mounting. The rifle sights were procured directly from Redfield and modified by the LWL; the ART mounts were procured by an "outside contractor" in this case. Although telescope mounting screws modified by the AMTU were used in place of the LWL circular version, the transitional ART system was fitted to the accurized M14 sniper rifles sent to Vietnam for 9th Infantry Division use in September 1968. The system is detailed in the Installation and Operation Manual for the Adjustable Ranging Telescope (ART) Mounted to the Match Conditioned 7.62mm M14 Rifle (September 1968), the original ART manual circulated by the U.S. Army Limited Warfare Laboratory. The transitional LWL-ART system made use of commercial 3X-9X variable-power telescopic sights. The turret housing bears second-generation Redfield markings, though they are barely visible. The scopes had a black satin commercial finish. Note the circular scope rings and the ring markings. The left side of the mount was stamped "USALWL," with "CAL. 7.62-M14" directly beneath. The ballistic cam was marked with the caliber "7.62mm" and the match cartridge designation "M-118 NM." The mount assembly and related components were given a black-matte finish. As the telescope serial number was obscured when the sight was fitted to the ART mount, various sights from this series have been noted with the factory serial number engraved on the left side of the turret housing. The numbering was applied by the military for identification and tracking purposes. There is no rifle serial number on the mount pictured. Although the total remains unknown, the transitional LWL/ART system was made in limited numbers. With minor changes, the system emerged as the principal sight for Army sniper use in Southeast Asia. (Peter R. Senich.)

As originally fielded, a Redfield "Accu-Range" 3X-9X variable-power sight provided the basis for the Adjustable Ranging Telescope. In addition to the ballistic cam, the heart of the system—the Redfield sight—was further modified by removing its interior range indicator and changing the

Sniper Weapon System: The XM21

With trigger finger poised and ready, an XM21-equipped U.S. Navy sniper maintains a vigil from the deck of a River Patrol Boat (PBR) during a momentary stop on the My Tho River (Mekong Delta). Although Navy marksmen had employed telescopic sighted rifles for various purposes in past conflicts, the war in Vietnam marked the beginning of a formal U.S. Navy sniping effort. (Max Crace.)

The third and final version of the ART fielded during the war in Vietnam, the "production model" of the Adjustable Ranging Telescope manufactured by Redfield with an ART mounting fabricated at Frankford Arsenal. Even though the sights were essentially second-generation 3X-9X variable-power rifle scopes, rather than adapting existing commercial sights, the production version with the ART reticle, ballistic cam, power adjusting ring, and ring lock were made to ART specifications at the Redfield plant in Denver, Colorado. The sights were shipped to Frankford Arsenal, where they were mated with the mount assembly. Except for the military designation on the turret housing "identification plate" (3X-9X AR TEL SER NO 000), black matte finish, and reconfigured side mounting plate (45-degree corners), the telescope and mount were virtually identical to the LWL-ART system described as the "transitional model." The AR TEL shown is serial no. 0510; the mount is numbered (engraved) "6021." At one time or another during the course of XM21/ART production, the last four digits of the rifle serial number were engraved or stamped on the left side or the top of the mount. Although telescopic sights and rifles were usually "number matched" following final acceptance, the practice lost its significance in a combat environment when telescopes were switched, by necessity, from one rifle to another. Nevertheless, with the telescope separated from the rifle for packing and shipping, as they were in this case, the numbering served as a means of pairing the assemblies once they reached their destination, if nothing else. The scope and mount pictured are typical of the Adjustable Ranging Telescopes issued with the XM21 sniper rifle during the Vietnam War. (Peter R. Senich.)

An alternate view of the Redfield "AR TEL" serial no. 0510 with elevation and windage adjustment turret caps removed. The raised mounting ridges were designed to engage the groove and screw recess on the left side of the M14 receiver. The mounting screw retainer ("E" ring) is barely visible; the spring-loaded telescope base is directly above the sideplate. The ballistic cam rested on a nonmagnetic hex bushing threaded into the cam base, an extension at the back of the mount. Production sights were given a black matte (anodized) finish to eliminate reflections. (Peter R. Senich.)

reticle pattern to include marks on the horizontal crosshair subtending 60 inches at 300 meters that could be used for estimating the hold-off for wind. However, the reticle spacing of the horizontal stadia lines remained the same as that of the conventional Accu-Range.

Upon sighting a target, the sniper adjusted the ballistic cam until the correct portion of the target was framed between the horizontal stadia lines (waist to top of head for a target of occidental stature; crotch to top of head for a target of oriental stature), centered on crosshair, and fired.

The ART increased accuracy significantly by eliminating the guesswork of range estimation and "hold-over" shooting that had plagued riflemen through the years. One of the greatest benefits of this system rested with the "self-ranging" feature, which allowed competent riflemen to be effective snipers without extensive training. An indication of the accuracy possible with this system

The Adjustable Ranging Telescope reticle showing the stadia marks. The figure has been superimposed to show how the stadia marks work in conjunction with the crosshairs. (U.S. Army.)

Above: Plastic lens caps (black) furnished with the Vietnam-era 3X-9X variable-power Redfield telescopic sights. The covers were made for Redfield by the E.D. Vissing Co. of Idaho Falls, Idaho. Though intended for commercial use, the caps were issued with the USMC/Redfield sniper sight and the Redfield Adjustable Ranging Telescope fielded by the Army. The covers were connected by a thin cord when issued; the lens cap for the ocular end of the second-generation Redfield sight was slightly larger due to the design changes made by the Redfield firm. Though the caps were reasonably effective, direct sunlight and/or elevated temperatures would soften them, causing them to fall from the tube. (West Point Collection.)

Below: An inside view of the Redfield lens caps showing the markings for the objective (right) and the ocular ends of the telescope. In addition to the soft plastic (pliable) covers, the E.D. Vissing Co. made flip-up lens covers for Redfield. The plastics firm was later absorbed by the Butler Creek Corp. in 1974. The caps shown were issued with an XM21/ART system during the Vietnam War. (West Point Collection.)

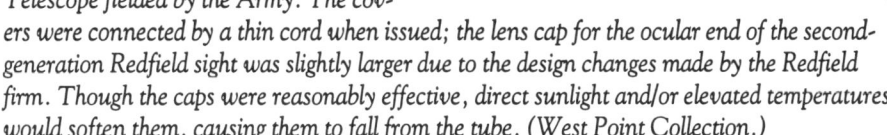

Adjustable Ranging Telescope carrying case developed for Army sniper use in South Vietnam. ART carrying cases were made from .062-inch thick (nominal) 6061-T6 aluminum alloy, coated with olive drab vinyl paint, which had a tendency to peel and weighted in at 18 ounces empty, 40 ounces with scope and mount. The item name ("Case, Carrying") and the ordnance reference number (11729637) appeared on the side of the case. The aluminum container was listed as a "Basic Issue Item." As a matter of interest, even though the objective end of the telescope was intended to be placed into the case with the power ring set at "3" (power), manipulating the power ring one way or the other allowed the scope to go into the case in either direction. (Peter R. Senich.)

An alternate view of the ART carrying case. The 14 5/8-inch-long, 5 1/4-inch-wide case was fitted with a strap and keeper for attachment to the ammunition belt. Soft rubber inserts protected the telescope from shock; a gasket prevented water from entering the case. The earliest published reference to the carrying case appeared in the Limited Warfare Laboratory ART installation and operation manual (September 1968). The first carrying cases categorized as "production" were shipped to Vietnam with the 9th Infantry Division sniper rifles in late 1968. Army Ordnance documents listed Frankford Arsenal as the manufacturer. Though effective for protecting the ART, the aluminum carrying cases were rarely used in combat. (Peter R. Senich.)

was demonstrated by several marksmen of the USAMTU who, during early testing at Ft. Benning, recorded 10-inch groups at 900 meters (2,952 feet) after ranging on a standard "E" silhouette target.

The significance of this sighting principle, originally conceived by James M. Leatherwood in the early 1960s, was quickly recognized by the Army while Leatherwood was stationed at Ft. Benning. Following basic testing, this concept was referred to the Limited Warfare Laboratory at Aberdeen Proving Ground, Maryland, in late 1965. As a result, LWL ini-

An early U.S. Army Limited Warfare Laboratory ART carrying case. Though virtually the same as the production version, this case had no item name and reference number on the side. Instead, Limited Warfare Laboratory (USA/LWL) markings were stenciled on top of the lid to denote the origins and contents of the aluminum case. Though rarely noted, initial LWL efforts to protect and transport the emerging ART system were based on an "aluminum cylinder with a sliding tray." (Peter R. Senich.)

tiated a project to develop a sniper sighting system based on Leatherwood's principle.

NOTE: As then defined, "the Limited War Laboratory was established in 1962 to circumvent the long delay between recognition of a requirement for new materiel and final delivery of the hardware to the soldier in the field." To accomplish this, it "assembled an array of technical, engineering, and scientific talent" who were "given license to 'think for themselves.'"

Although numerous individuals were responsible for bringing the ART to fruition, credit must be given to Franklin Owens (LWL), who did much of the early design work, supervised initial fabrication, and gave the ART its name, as well as to the man responsible for guiding the development of the new telescope, Lt. Col. Vincent Oddi.

Apart from early prototype and subsequent development work the AMTU conducted in support of the LWL at Aberdeen, at one time or another during the evolution of the Adjustable Ranging Telescope based on the "Leatherwood Principle," LWL, Redfield Gun Sight Co., and Frankford Arsenal all fabricated and/or reconfigured to ART specifications the telescopic sights and mount assemblies subjected to Army field use with the XM21 system.

Though rarely defined correctly, three variations of the ART system were eventually fielded for evaluation and combat purposes in Vietnam. The first of these was the LWL "tool room" version originally intended for use with the .50-caliber Browning machine gun as well as the M14. In this case, the LWL-fabricated telescope mounting was based on the two-piece USAMTU prototype version (the mounts were held together with a hex socket head screw and lock washer), with commercial, first-generation Redfield 3X-9X variable-power telescopic

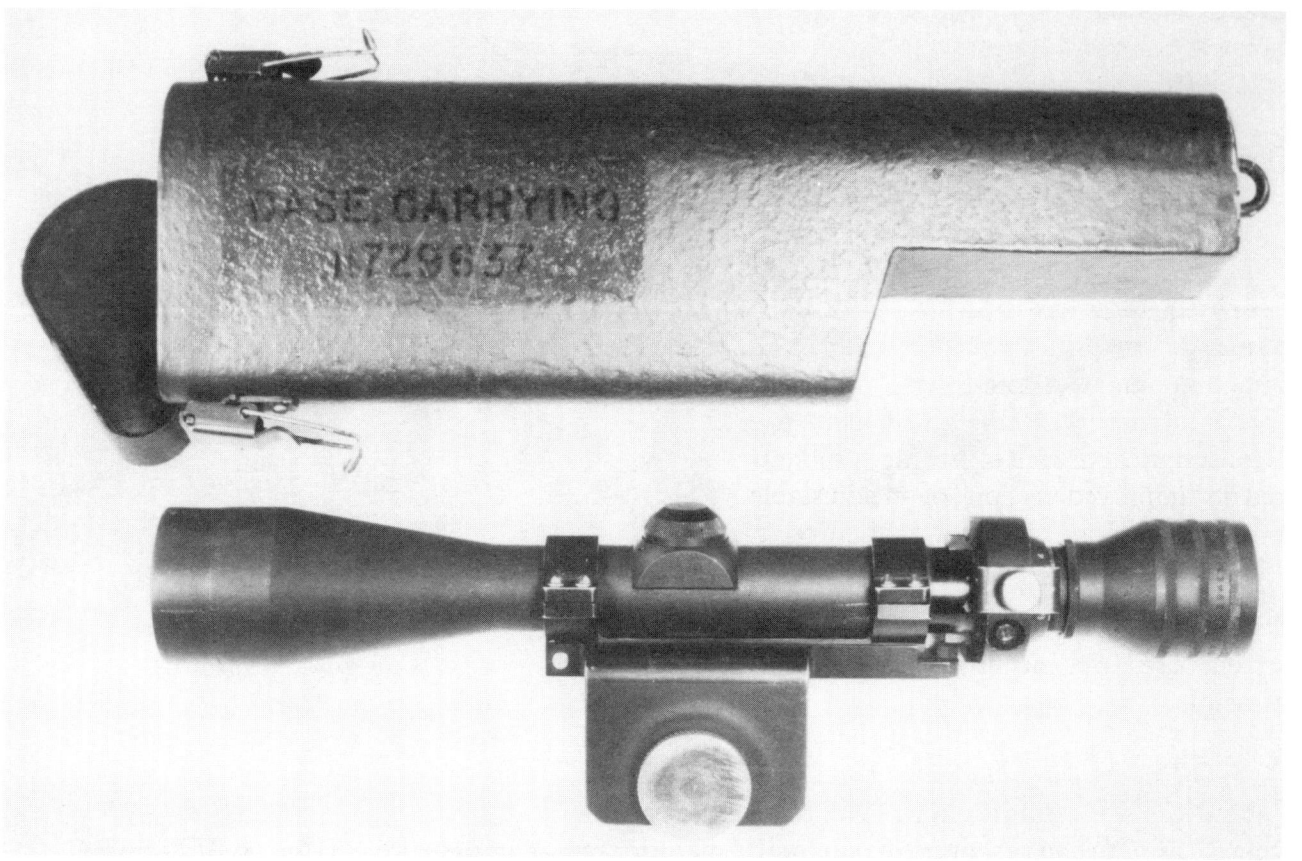

A Vietnam-era variable-power Adjustable Ranging Telescope with an issue carrying case. The Redfield AR TEL is serial no. 1294, the top of the mount is numbered (stamped) "8542." Although production totals ranging between 2,000 and 3,000 have been cited in contemporary offerings, the exact quantity manufactured for the Army during 1969 remains unknown at present. (Peter R. Senich.)

sights converted to ART specifications by the LWL. The second or "transitional model" had the mounts produced by an LWL-directed "outside contractor," with second-generation Redfield 3X-9X variable-power sights reconfigured at the Limited Warfare Laboratory. The third and final variation, the "production model" of the ART scope and mount assembly, consisted of telescope mounts manufactured at Frankford Arsenal with scopes in ART form procured directly from the Redfield Gun Sight Co.

Produced and fielded in quantity, the Redfield ART and the Frankford Arsenal mount represented the culmination of ART system development during the war in Southeast Asia. In conjunction with authorization to produce the USAMTU version of the M14 sniper rifle, according to Army documents, "limited production was authorized by DA Msg 897570, dated 14 February 1969, for Sniper Rifles and Scopes for use in RVN (ENSURE #240)." The Adjustable Ranging Telescope ultimately referenced as the "AR TEL" was covered by the same authority. As Army documents then stated, "In March 1969, Frankford Arsenal received this ENSURE authority (Expediting Non-Standard Urgent Requirement for Equipment No. 240), to procure the modified commercial item from the Redfield Gun

Sight Co. Mounts were manufactured in-house at Frankford Arsenal. Production was completed in October 1969."

Although various commercial publications have cited production totals between 2,000 and 3,000, at this juncture, less than 2,000 of the Redfield/Frankford Arsenal "AR TEL" model are believed to have been manufactured. In any case, however, the exact total produced during 1969 remains unknown at present.

Of further interest in this matter, the Realist optical firm (Realist, Inc.), submitted an "improved version" of an adjustable ranging telescope for Army evaluation in 1970. In response to an unsolicited proposal, Frankford Arsenal awarded Realist Incorporated of Menomonee Falls, Wisconsin, a contract ($1) for development and submission of prototype hardware for U.S. Army evaluation.

As then followed, in accordance with the requirements of AR 70-10, Frankford Arsenal, under letter dated 22 January 1970, requested USATECOM to evaluate the Realist, Inc. telescope through the conduct of Military Potential Tests. A suitable test plan was drawn up by Salvatore M. Adelizzi of Frankford Arsenal (March 1970).

An Army sniper at the edge of a jungle clearing during a quiet moment. The rifle is an XM21 with an Adjustable Ranging Telescope. (Barry Zuckerman.)

The Realist adjustable ranging telescope, a military version of the Realist 3X-9X variable-power "Camputer" scope introduced in 1969, was subsequently tested in comparison with the Redfield ART. Though considered as an "additional source of supply," the Realist model was not adopted by the Army as then submitted.

In retrospect, however, a number of the original "tool room" versions of the ART (10 or 12 scopes) were sent to Southeast Asia for combat evaluation under the auspices of the Army Concept Team in Vietnam, charged with the task of evaluating sniper operations and equipment at the field level. Although the ART mounts and ballistic cams used for these evaluations were fabricated in the LWL Technical Support machine shop, the USAMTU had, in fact, fabricated the original mount for the Redfield self-ranging (Leatherwood) scope, with Master Sergeant Walsh doing the necessary machine work. With the exception of the screws, spring, and pin, the AMTU prototype mount was made of untreated aluminum. Subsequent mounts manufactured under the con-

The three types of telescope mounting screws tested and fielded with the ART system during the course of development. A socket-head screw (left) employed with the early system was recommended for adoption by the USAMTU as the "best method" of securing the mount to the receiver. As an alternative, a circular knob was given large "flats" to provide a better grasp (1.265-inch diameter, .650-inch wide, .175-inch thick with serrations on the flats). In final form, a circular version (1.265-inch diameter, .175-inch thick with a knurled edge) was used with a lock washer and an "E" ring retainer. If the mounting screws were not seated and tightened properly, repeated firing would deform the raised ridges on the back of the sideplate and cause the mount to "rock back and forth" on the receiver. As a result, the issue mounting screw was occasionally "twisted off" at the "E" ring clearance cut (.125-inch diameter) from over-tightening. The method of attaching the ART mount to the M14 was viewed as one of the "weakest parts" of the entire system. (Peter R. Senich.)

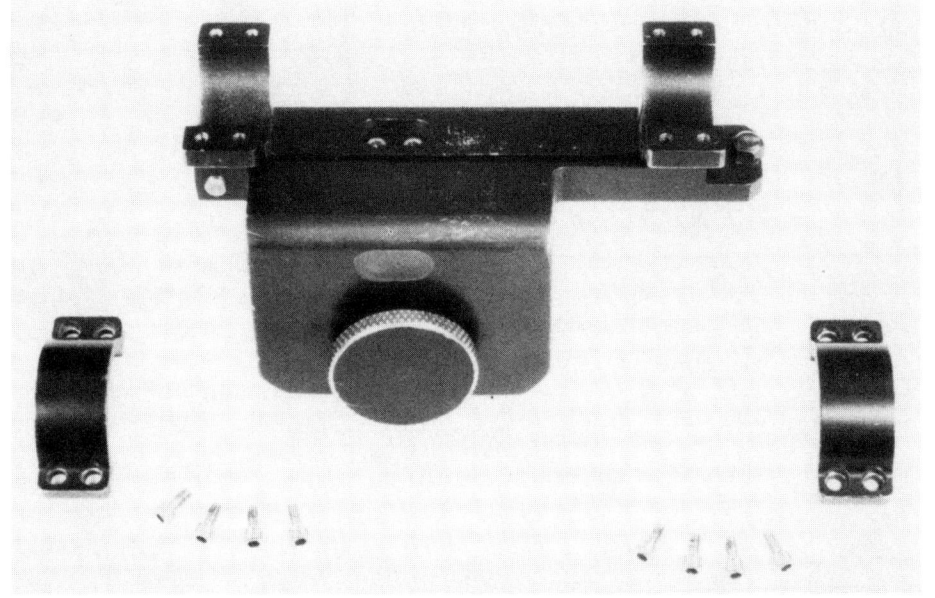

A typical AR TEL (ART) mounting with the sight removed. The scope rings (1 inch) and screws are shown opposite the mount. Although rings were number matched on the LWL development series, the practice ended with the production model. Small "punch" or "scribe" marks were usually placed on the rings to ensure proper replacement when the scope was removed by an armorer or ordnance personnel. Despite problems involving the mount pivot pin and the return spring (the flat spring that enabled the scope base to move up and down in the mount when the cam was turned), by all accounts, the ART mounting system had performed "better than anticipated" in a combat environment. In this case, the original "number" has been removed (milled) from the side of the mount, a post-Vietnam practice when extra ART assemblies or separate mountings were placed in reserve or renumbered for use with another rifle. (Peter R. Senich.)

Sniper Weapon System: The XM21

trol of the LWL were hard-anodized to provide strength and better-wearing surfaces.

According to the "Review of MTU Involvement in Sniper Rifle/Sight/Ammo Program," 18 May 1967, USAMTU support for what eventually became the XM21 system commenced as follows:

> We were contacted by SFC B.H. Willard of the Limited Warfare Laboratory to see if we could accurize ten M14 rifles that were to be equipped with the Leatherwood scope for test in Vietnam.
>
> [NOTE: Even though Jim Leatherwood had limited involvement with the ART system after the LWL took control of the project, the Adjustable Ranging Telescope was frequently referenced as the "Leatherwood Scope" in ordnance documents during the war in Southeast Asia.]
>
> On first contact, we were told that standard issue M14s would be used. However, Sergeant Willard, a competitive shooter and coach, talked his superiors into using National Match rifles. He personally carried these rifles to Ft. Benning, where we worked them over. Basically, this is what was done:
>
> A. The rifles were disassembled down to the basic receiver.
>
> B. Barrels were selected for straightness and uniformity with dimensions to match the lot of ammunition that would be used with them (LC 12049).
>
> C. The barrels were installed with minimum headspace adjustment.
>
> D. The area of contact of the operating rod guide was knurled to make splines to prohibit the guide from rotating on the barrel.
>
> E. The gas cylinder and band were screwed together as an assembly and internally polished to reduce carbon build-up.
>
> F. The piston was polished to reduce carbon build-up.
>
> G. The flash suppressor was reamed out internally to a diameter previously determined to give the best accuracy with National Match ammunition.
>
> H. The mating surfaces between the barrel and suppressor were matched for perfect alignment.
>
> I. Specially treated NM stocks were used after being treated as follows:

Trip Report to 9th Infantry Division, Bear Cat, RVN, 28 June 1967

On the morning of the 28th of June, we went out to the range to begin firing with the ART mounted on the M14 rifle. We set up 30" silhouettes, at a distance of 300 meters. It was fairly hard for the shooters to distinguish where the silhouettes were, because they were painted black, and they blended in with the woods. Also, the sun was shining right in their eyes. Even with these disadvantages, out of the 9 people that fired, 10 rounds each, for a total of 90 rounds, they managed 66 hits, which I thought was very good, considering these soldiers haven't had any type of sniper training, and very little marksmanship training. Besides, none of the men had ever fired a rifle with a telescope mounted on it before.

—Sfc. B.H. Willard
Limited Warfare
Laboratory
Army Concept
Team in Vietnam

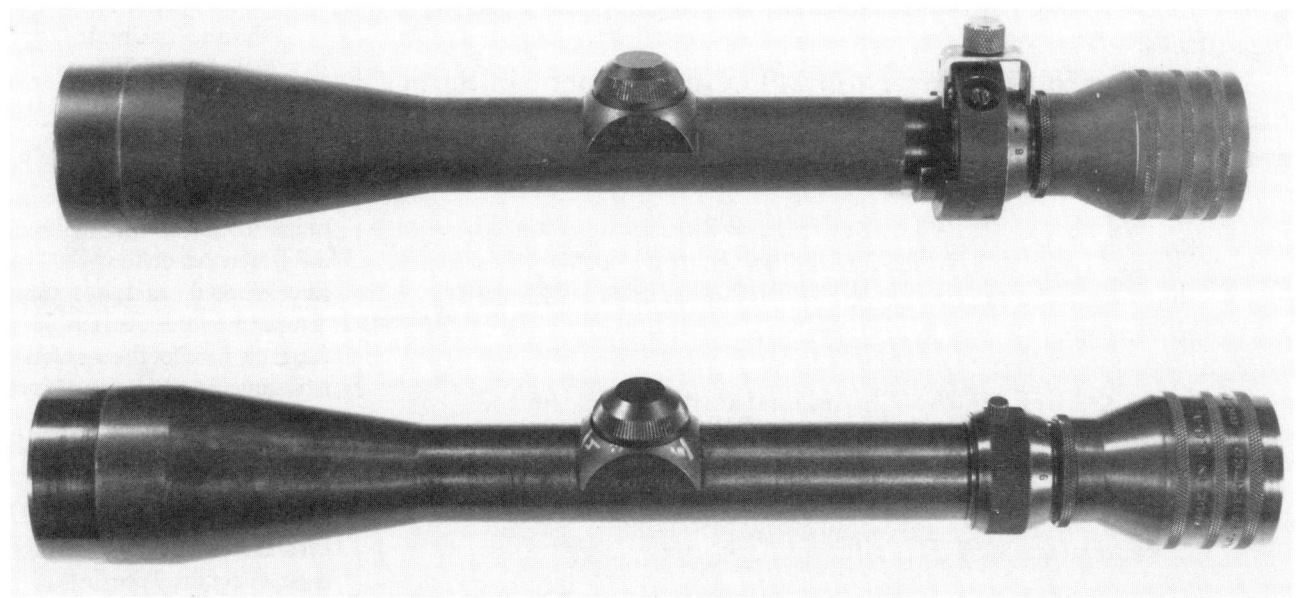

A comparison between a Redfield 3X-9X ART, a production AR TEL model (serial no. 0375), and a commercial Redfield 3X-9X variable-power Accu-Range sight. Both telescopes are second-generation variable-power sights. The ART was issued with an Army XM21, and the Accu-Range model was a Marine Corps replacement sight fitted to an M40 sniper rifle. Except for the finish, reticle, and power selector/adjusting ring assembly, the two rifle scopes are essentially the same. (Peter R. Senich.)

Memo for Record
to USAMTU,
19 February 1968

In a conversation, re: marksmanship in general, with Major Takahashi, he indicated that CG, USARV, has a MTOE change authorizing each Infantry Battalion 24 ea. National Match M14 with M84 telescopes.

—Lt. Col. Jeremiah M. McKenzie
Executive Officer, USAMTU

The stocks are placed in a large container (eight feet in diameter). The lid is toggle-bolted down, the temperature raised to approximately 300 degrees, turning all moisture in the stock to steam. A vacuum pump is turned on and run for about an hour. This removes all moisture. While in the tank at this temperature, an epoxy (by Western Sealant of Conn.) is run inside in a liquid state and held at one-hundred-psi for an additional hour. The pressure is then slowly lowered and the stocks removed. They are then placed in a curing oven where they remain for approximately three days. This sets-up the epoxy while reducing shrinkage to a minimum. The purpose of this treatment is to fill all of the sap pockets and pores with the epoxy, thereby displacing the moisture in the stock. This increases the tensile strength, completely eliminates warpage, and the expansion and contraction of the stock from moisture variations are negligible.

J. Prior to "glassing" the stock, the stock liner was removed and modified to provide one-eighth inch of bedding compound in the recoil areas.

K. The stocks were then fitted to the metal parts in two stages of glass bedding (a type of fiber-glass/epoxy used to obtain a perfect fit between wood and metal). The first stage was to provide a centering of the assembly, as looked at from above. The second stage was to provide a downward pressure (pre-loading) of the front part of the stock to uniformly dampen barrel vibrations and reduce the effect of changes in sling tension.

L. Triggers were adjusted to provide a fine pull (four and one-half to four and three-fourths pounds).

M. The hand guard was cleared of the stock and anchored to the band.

N. The gas cylinder lock was selected to index finger tight at the six o' clock position.

O. A newly manufactured operating spring guide was installed with a cylindrical cross-section to provide smoother functioning, uniform distribution and side pressure on all parts of the operating spring.

P. Certain cams, corners, and bearing surfaces throughout the mechanism were modified to provide smoother operation and uniform return of all moving parts.

These rifles were then tested by the Test Section in our machine rest (cradle) and averaged 5.3 inches vertical by 4.7 inches horizontal with the assigned match ammunition. The ART scopes were mounted and zeroed with all rifles checked to about 700 meters. Due to time limitations and range availability, shooting was not done beyond this range.

In 1968, Lt. Col. F.B. Conway (Ret.) put rebuilding procedures based directly on the aforementioned into manual form. The purpose of this, as specified in the manual, was to accommodate "individual rifle accuracy specialists and organizations within and outside the military services." As the manual further stated:

> The procedures or characteristics specified here are in addition to those of Army Weapons Command for the National Match Rifle and supersede them when requirements are more specific or exacting.

As a matter of interest, these procedures served as the rebuilding standard for the XM21 Sniper Weapon System.

As such, the original 10 mounting the "tool room" ARTs were tested in Vietnam through the latter part of 1967. Although three of the ARTs developed internal fog (common to all sights in Vietnam), and the telescope mounting rings did not appear to be rigid enough, on an overall basis, the ART and the USAMTU accurized M14s performed as well as could be expected.

However, much to the chagrin of those close to the project in the

---

Correspondence: Colonel Bayard to Gen. Robert Taber, 15 January 1969

An Army-wide requirement for the development of a sniper capability was expressed in The US Army Combat Development Command, "Sniper Capability Study," dated May 1968. The weapon recommended in the aforementioned publication is the M14 National Match rebuilt to our specifications (TUSAMTU). The Army Weapons Command has been charged with building a number of these rifles to meet the Vietnam sniper requirement. They appear, to us, to be fighting the problem and are apparently seeking to dilute the specifications. If such is the case, then we will be giving the troops in the field a weapon, inferior to the one field tested by ACTIV and recommended by ACTIV and CDC in turn, which will not be able to do the job at the ranges required.

—Col. Robert F. Bayard
Commanding Officer,
USAMTU

NOTE: The excerpt was drawn from correspondence forwarded to Brig. Gen. Robert C. Taber, assistant chief of staff for force development (ASCFOR) Department of the Army/Pentagon, when it appeared that Army Weapons Command would prefer to field match-grade M14s with the M84 scope rather than the accurized USAMTU version mounting the Adjustable Ranging Telescope.

A right view of the Redfield 3X-9X variable-power ART with the XM21. A fixed-pivot mounting allowed the rear of the scope to move up or down when the sight was being "cammed." Normal eye relief was 3 to 3 1/2 inches. The telescope could not be moved within the mount since it was necessary for the ballistic cam to retain its relationship with the cam base. Even though some problems were encountered with the system, by eliminating the guesswork in range estimation, the Adjustable Ranging Telescope made a significant contribution to the Army sniping effort in Southeast Asia. (U.S. Army.)

States, regular issue M80 ball ammunition was used in place of the match ammo, and in many cases, average riflemen—including those who had never fired a rifle with telescopic sights before—were used for evaluative purposes. Nevertheless, a few riflemen functioning as snipers with units of the 1st and 9th Infantry Divisions recorded a number of first-round hits out to 600 meters with the ART. Prior to this, the same marksmen had rarely engaged targets beyond 400 meters with their M84 equipped M14s and/or M16s mounting Colt/Realist scopes.

However promising and effective the new system was in fact, fielding it in quantity, in an undiluted state, proved to be no small task. For the first time in U.S. history, the Army had a first-class sniping system, and those cognizant of this "dug-in" and prepared for the struggle to have it adopted.

In light of the Army's commitment to the M16 as its principal infantry arm, the M14, out of production since 1964, was destined for obsolescence. As a result, in some quarters the M14 was considered "unsuitable for long-term development" in this capacity, prompting the question as to why it was being "pushed" as the basis for a new sniping arm rather than the M16 or a bolt-action target rifle.

Contrary to most beliefs, however, the M16 did receive due consideration for use as a sniping weapon but could not match the long-range

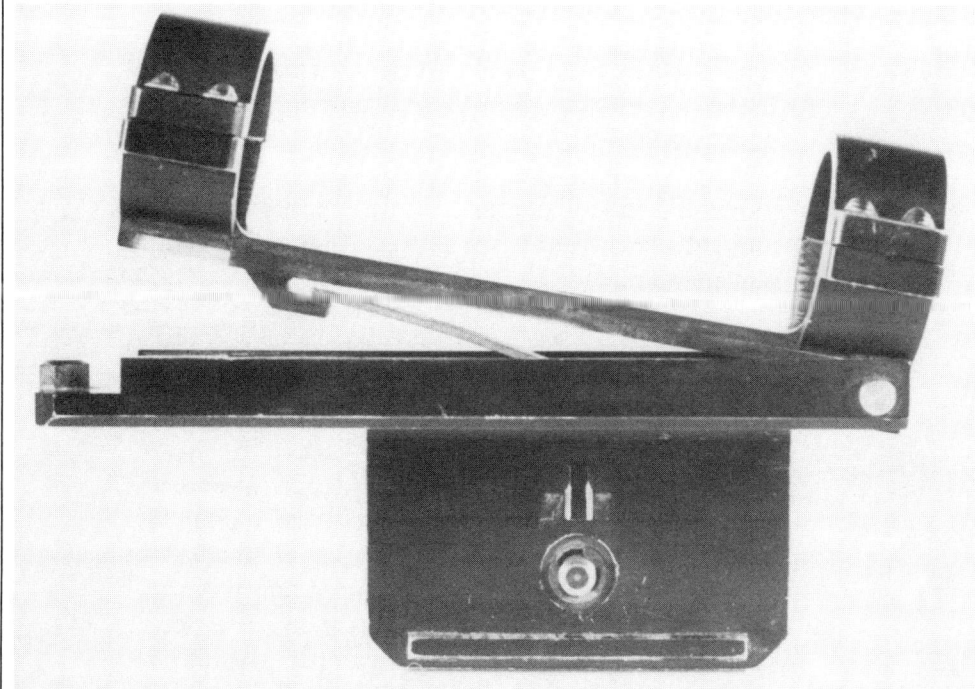

The receiver side of the AR TEL mounting with the scope rings in place and the "spring-loaded base" elevated beyond its normal travel to illustrate how the return spring functioned. Two screws fastened the spring to the mount; a small set screw beneath the front ring kept the pivot pin in place. (Peter R. Senich.)

accuracy of the M14, as proven conclusively when the M16 was subjected to innumerable tests over an extended period. However unsuited the M16 may have been for long-range sniping in Vietnam, the right combination of marksman, rifle, ammunition, and telescope accounted for documented hits at ranges out to 700 meters. Nevertheless, results such as this were far from common, and the effect of the 55-grain 5.56mm bullet on the enemy at extended ranges remained subject to debate.

Of course, a number of organizations supported the use of accurized M14s for sniping, but credit must be given to the various agencies at Ft. Benning among which the USAMTU, under the command of Colonel Bayard, had considered the accurized M14 a prime requisite from the beginning. Their position was based on the results of evaluations conducted with all military and commercial rifles available in the United States, in combination with various types of ammunition and telescopes, during the quest for an efficient sniping system.

The additional reasons were cited by Lieutenant Colonel Conway, the AMTU Shop officer, during the development and subsequent fielding of the XM21 system.

> We realized that it was possible to obtain acceptable accuracy with a manually operated target rifle, and that it was much easier to prepare and glass-bed a target rifle than the machinery of a self-loader. However, if acceptable accuracy could be obtained, the self-loading rifle offered the following advantages:
>
> A. In case of target movement or errors on the part of the sniper, a second shot could be fired immediately.

SUBJECT: Memorandum of Understanding RE: Coordinated Actions (XM21 Sniper Rifles) prepared by Headquarters, U.S. Army Weapons Command, Rock Island Arsenal, 8 October 1969

1. The Army Marksmanship Training Unit (AMTU), Ft. Benning, Georgia has consented to assist USAWECOM in the XM21 Sniper Rifle production program.

2. The following actions to be taken are listed to delineate responsibilities and to eliminate any potential misunderstandings:

   a. Rock Island Arsenal (RIA) will completely accurize and target-in the total quantity of rifles.
   b. RIA will test fire each rifle at 100 yards. This will assure reasonable functioning and accuracy. Rifles which fail to fire to the established accuracy will be examined/re-worked at RIA. The balance will be shipped to Ft. Benning for the final acceptance testing of three (3) consecutive ten (10) shot groups. The acceptance criteria will be as outlined on page one of the AMTU accurizing brochure.
   c. The accurizing work at RIA will be in accordance with a currently "marked-up" AMTU accurizing brochure and future changes thereto. The existing instructions/data changes and additions in the brochure were concurred in by LTC Conway, AMTU, by initials and date.
   d. Following acceptance certifications by Ft.

(continued on page 79)

B. Engaging multiple targets.

C. There was no perceptible movement with a self-loader. Consequently, the possibility of detection was reduced significantly.

D. Both semi and full-automatic fire capability enabled the sniper to defend himself or engage the enemy as circumstances warranted.

E. The M14 possessed both day and night capability, whereas, at that point, no work had been done mounting night vision equipment on bolt-action rifles.

The only real disadvantage of the self-loader, as we saw it, rested with the ejection of brass which could compromise the sniper's position. We considered having sniper ammunition colored dull black, as was done with some dummy rounds. To my knowledge, however, nothing was done in this direction.

As for the M14's accuracy, for example, we analyzed countless score sheets by "All Army" rifle teams and determined that the percentage of first round "V" ring shots at 1000 yards between the M14 and the 30/338 Magnum rifle were not too different. Let me emphasize—when I say M14, I do not mean the regular issue or even the National Match variant prepared by Army Weapons Command, but rather those built to USAMTU specifications.

One point beyond dispute rested with the proven ruggedness of the M14. By this time, the Marine Corps M40 was simply not holding up in the field. These weapons were never intended for the rigors of combat.

There was no question in our minds. We were convinced; accurized M14s were the only way to go. Nevertheless, we had a very difficult time convincing Weapons Command that our system was a good one. We didn't claim to know all the answers, but we were getting accurate results.

Even though the USAMTU could not match the level of influence wielded by Army Weapons Command in matters such as this, its contributions to Army marksmanship had earned the respect of the "front office."

Following the ACTIV field evaluations of the new system, further development and refining of the ART system continued in the States. In late 1967, prior to assuming command of the 9th Infantry Division, Major General Ewell contacted the AMTU requesting its assistance in developing a program for training 9th Division snipers. With the 9th operating in the Mekong Delta, he envisioned an effective utilization of snipers inasmuch as large portions of this region were relatively flat, encompassing large areas of rice paddies.

In response, a sniper instructor team (the first of its type to be used in RVN) comprising eight noncommissioned officers, including a National

Match armorer, and its commander, Major Powell, arrived in Vietnam in June 1968. At this juncture, there were no accurized M14s with the ART in Southeast Asia.

NOTE: The following personnel were selected from the list of volunteers from the USAMTU for assignment to the 9th Division Sniper School:

> M. Sgt. Alfred B. Falcon
> Sfc. Glenn T. Adkison
> Sfc. Albert K. Nainoa
> Sfc. Harry C. Tharp
> Sfc. James L. Tuck
> S.Sgt. William R. Lee
> S.Sgt. Richard D. Rebidue
> S.Sgt. Wayne E. Young

According to Major Powell, a late addition to the staff, Sfc. Arpail Gapol, joined the team in South Vietnam.

Upon arrival, the sniper instructor team set about establishing a suitable training facility from scratch. During this period of organization, the AMTU team served as snipers in order to gain practical experience in actual combat situations. It was reported that during the first month, two members of the team "bagged" 10 VC in a night ambush, engaging the enemy at 500 meters.

The first accurized M14s mounting the Adjustable Ranging Telescope to reach the 9th Division Sniper School (54 rifles) were built and shipped by the USAMTU later that year. According to pertinent documents (2 October 1968), Sergeant Adkison, a member of the USAMTU 9th Infantry Division "Sniper Group in Vietnam," departed Ft. Benning on 25 September 1968, as an escort to the sniper rifles and related equipment shipped to the 9th Division in RVN. The ART scopes and mounts were fitted to the weapons and zeroed prior to shipment; the weapons were also camouflaged. Following a "brief delay" attributed to "aircraft mechanical difficulties," the accurized M14 sniper rifles reached the 9th Infantry Division on 3 October 1968.

NOTE: Although 54 rifles were shipped, according to correspondence from the Limited Warfare Laboratory to Army Weapons Command, a total of sixty-five (65) ART systems was furnished for 9th Infantry Division sniper use in September 1968.

The equipment included thirty 20-power M49 Observation Telescopes and, interestingly, two M14 silencers and 400 rounds of handloaded subsonic cartridges intended for ambush operations conducted at night. As USAMTU documents further stated, "It is believed that with the combination of the silencers and subsonic rounds, there will be absolutely little or no sound when the weapon is fired."

Benning, the acceptance seal will be applied by one of the three (3) WECOM Tech Representatives currently on extended TDY at Ft. Benning.

e. The accepted rifles will then be shipped to Anniston Army Depot for packaging and packing. The rifles will then be either shipped by Anniston or temporarily stored at Anniston, as applicable.

f. AMTU will, at no cost to WECOM, test fire and do any minor gunsmithing necessary to obtain acceptable shot groupings.

g. WECOM will take the requisitioning action to provide AMTU all the M118 ammo required for this program.

h. WECOM will reimburse AMTU, by replacement, any rifle barrels taken from AMTU stocks for this program.

i. AMTU will assure lifetime "mating" of accepted rifle/telescope combinations by marking the appropriate rifle serial number on the mated telescope mount.

j. AMTU will do any accurizing/gunsmithing required on the initial fifty (50) XM21 rifles already shipped to AMTU by WECOM.

k. WECOM will ship to AMTU a minimum of one hundred (100) accurized and targeted-in XM21 rifles every two (2) weeks, beginning 16 October 1969.

   1. AMTU will Acceptance Test a minimum of fifty (50) each XM21 rifles per week.

Correspondence:
Major Chittester to
Limited Warfare Laboratory,
11 October 1969

Enclosed are eight (8) Adjustable Ranging Telescopes (ART) that need to be repaired.

ART F93678: Threads in power adjustment ring stripped. Set screw and lock for power adjustment ring missing. Adjustment caps missing.

ART F94915 and F93770: Internal lens in erector tube loose. Adjustment caps missing.

ART F93776 and F93498: Broken return spring on internal adjustment.

ART F94841 and F93416: Internal moisture.

ART F96114: Collector lens loose.

Generally, the overall performance of this equipment has been outstanding. This equipment has been in continuous use and has received extremely rough handling in rice paddies, swamps and torrential rain.

The problems encountered in the past twelve months are:

1. Return springs in the mounts lose power and become extremely weak in a very short period of time. Replacement springs appear to be of better material. However, the temper of the replacement springs seems to be uneven as three have broken with normal usage.

2. Lock screw that holds the pivot pin in mount works loose. This requires removing the scope from the mount to tighten the set screws. The scope must then be re-zeroed.

(continued on page 81)

NOTE: The M118 match cartridge has a 173-grain bullet with a velocity of 2,550 feet per second (fps). The "hand-loaded" AMTU 7.62mm subsonic ammunition used a 150-grain bullet with a velocity of approximately 950 fps. According to USAMTU information, "The special 7.62mm subsonic ammunition was assembled, loaded, and tested by our Shop," and the "two M14 silencers" were furnished by Sionics, Inc.

The following correspondence from Major Powell to Colonel Bayard (USAMTU), 14 December 1968, provides further insight on the subsonic cartridges:

> I have been experimenting with the M14 noise suppressor and subsonic ammo. Initially, I had trouble with erratic rounds and found the source was in aligning the silencer. This was eliminated by using the new brass bushing.
>
> [NOTE: This was a source of difficulty with early Sionics M14 and M16 suppressors. Efforts to seal and align the suppressor with the barrel at the retaining collar included the interim use of a special brass bushing in this case. Though effective, the use of brass proved "too expensive" for this application. A Teflon bushing was ultimately furnished with the Sionics M14SS-1 system.]
>
> I find the most reliable range for consistent hits is 85 to 125 meters. This creates an aiming problem when using the same scope zeroed for match ammo. I also find that by setting the power of the scope at 7X, it will put you on point of aim at approximately 90 meters with the subsonic ammo. As the range is increased beyond 125 meters, the firer must hold over the target considerably. This will take some trial and error and additional training for the firer to be able to use both types of ammunition in the same rifle.

In a discussion regarding the contemplated use of subsonic ammunition during preparation of this book, Major Powell offered the following:

> A suppressor-equipped M14 sniper rifle firing subsonic ammunition was used for firing demonstrations on several occasions. It was impressive to pop balloons from a concealed position at ranges from 60 to 100 yards with the only noise the spectators could hear made by the balloons popping.

Additional test-firings conducted with modified 7.62mm subsonic ammunition found that, although quiet, it was unacceptable, due in part to its range limitations and marginal accuracy beyond 85 meters. Since high-velocity match-grade ammunition was a prime factor in the XM21 system, it was thought that the ballistic differences between match and subsonic ammunition would create zeroing problems if used alternately. At that point, further consideration of modified ammunition on an issue basis was dropped.

Early in 1969, the USAMTU tested, packaged, and shipped 40 Sionics M14SS-1 noise suppressors to the 9th Infantry Division for combat evaluation on an expanded basis. Early evaluations of the Sionics noise suppressor with the AMTU accurized M14 sniper rifles were recorded as follows:

> Field tests were conducted by the 9th Division Sniper School at Dong Tam in February 1969. The tests consisted of an accuracy test, noise suppression test, and muzzle flash test at night. These tests confirmed that the suppressor would function as designed.
>
> Reports from the field told of numerous contacts indicating that the snipers were able to make multiple kills from one ambush position. The suppressor controlled the muzzle flash and noise so well that at no time did the VC actually pinpoint the direction of the fire or the location of the ambush site. Field and combat test data indicate that the suppressor does the following:
>
> A. Eliminates muzzle flash.
>
> B. Suppresses the muzzle noise considerably and makes it virtually impossible to pinpoint the sniper's position using the "crack" and "thump" method.
>
> C. Accuracy or range is not affected.
>
> D. The added weight is of no consequence when the above advantages are considered.
>
> Based on the successes of the 9th Division snipers in the field with the suppressor equipped rifle, the CG, 9th Division, desired to have at least one suppressor for each two man sniper team. It is recommended that the noise suppressor be furnished as an integral part of the sniper weapons system.

NOTE: The 40 Sionics M14 noise suppressors sent to Vietnam for evaluations came as a result of a "working relationship" between the USAMTU and the Sionics organization. Recalling his involvement, Colonel Conway, USAMTU, added, "The suppressors were not paid for but were sent by Mitch WerBell [Sionics, Inc.] to get them into the hands of our snipers with hopes that they would be paid for later. So far as I know, however, this never happened. In any case, we had M14 suppressors in the field before Army Weapons Command even knew they existed."

Suggest this pin be anchored to the stationary portion of the mount; that it be left at full diameter. This would increase the bearing surface and add to the stability of the mount.

3. Lens covers supplied will not stay on the scope. "Storm Queen" lens covers obtained from commercial sources are more efficient.

4. There is insufficient clearance in the carrying case. The scope cannot be placed in the case with the lens cover mounted.

5. Fasteners on the carrying case lid do not stand up to repeated opening and closure.

—Maj. Gary R. Chittester
Commandant, Sniper School,
25th Infantry Division

NOTE: Though originally involved as the officer-in-charge of the second Sniper Instructor Group assigned to the 9th Infantry Division, Major Chittester served in the same capacity with the 25th Infantry Division when the 9th Division returned to the United States.

The telescopic sights mentioned were part of the "sixty-five (65)" modified by the Limited Warfare Laboratory and sent to Vietnam in September 1968. The entire lot was based on "F" series second-generation Redfield 3X-9X variable-power sights with serial numbers in the low- to mid-90,000s range.

The lens covers that would not stay on the ART scopes were the same type furnished by Redfield with the USMC contract sights.

Although "Storm Queen" lens covers were extremely effective, they were all but impossible to obtain in sufficient quantity.

Even though the original suppressors were, apparently, never paid for, official measures were taken to obtain noise suppressors for Army sniper use in South Vietnam.

A letter from Colonel Bayard, USAMTU to Major General Ewell, 9th Division (25 March 1969), stated the following, in part:

> We have received information from several sources that you desire to procure noise suppressors (silencers). In fact, I received a call from Colonel John S. Wood, Jr., Weapons Division, Directorate of Development, Research, and Engineering, Headquarters, AMC, Washington, stating that he had informally been apprised of your requirement. Colonel Wood advised me that should your requirement be submitted by USARV as an ENSURE item that it would come to his office and that item would be procured immediately. It is our feeling, based on your experiences and our testing program here, that each sniper weapon should be equipped with a silencer. Colonel Wood further stated that if USARV would ask for a <u>specific item</u> by brand name, model number, etc., he feels that this requirement would be immediately filled by AWC.

As then followed, a request that Sionics suppressors be procured through the ENSURE program was forwarded from the 9th Div to USARV, G-4, in April 1969. Although exact quantities remain unknown, Sionics noise suppressors were eventually sent to RVN under separate ENSURE authority.

Following a period of trial and error, during which time the misuse of trained sniper personnel was cited as the greatest problem, the sniper training program employed by the 9th Division yielded extraordinary results and eventually served as the basis for a formal Program of Instruction (POI) for training Army snipers in RVN. Their methods and effectiveness were summarized as follows by Major Powell, Commandant, 9th Division Sniper School, in February 1969:

> Right now we are up to 148 kills and that has probably been upped since 1800 today. Most of the kills are coming at night with the Starlight Scope mounted on the M14, the VC aren't moving much in the daytime, but whenever one of our snipers gets a shot off they rarely miss.
> The equipment is holding up real well, and we've had one-shot kills in daytime up to 800 meters and up to 550-600 meters at night. Most of the employment at night over here is with an ambush patrol. The snipers are given permission to engage one to five man groups and the rest of the ambush element holds their fire until needed. The snipers then maintain surveillance over anybody they knock down and pick off other VC trying to recover weapons, equipment, or the body. This has worked well especially with one battalion . . . Under the present set-up in the division, we will have a total of seventy-two snipers, six per

Standard-issue 20-round M14 magazine (left) and a special 7-round variant developed by the USAMTU for use with the XM21 rifles in Vietnam. The 3-inch-long magazine enabled Army snipers to maintain a lower profile when firing from a prone position. Snipers were advised to use reduced cartridge loading (15 rounds) in the standard magazine to extend the life of the follower spring . . . a practice followed by many combat riflemen. (Lt. Col. F.B. Conway, Ret.)

battalion (equalling sixty), plus four per brigade (equalling twelve). The snipers are employed in pairs, with at least a five to eight man security element along. They are controlled and managed by the Battalion Commander and S-3, and are attached to the companies that have, or are likely to have, the most contacts.

In addition to night ambushes, they have been used on berm, roads, bridges, and firing sites as a security type mission. We have been working in conjunction with the Xenon searchlight with a pink filter. This is a very good combination when the natural light from the moon and stars is at a low level. We also coordinate flares to help out when needed. On daylight missions they are being used in numerous ways, in both elements of a cordon, and searches placed at the back of villages to pick off fleeing VC when the village search is on, and in staying behind elements when units are displacing to a new objective, to pick off VC following them . . .

The primary consideration that must be kept in mind when planning an operation here is to put the snipers in the position with good fields of observation and long fields of fire. The units that are taking a little extra time in the planning phase of an operation are the ones racking up kills with snipers.

Although a number of outstanding feats of combat marksmanship were recorded by Army snipers serving with various commands in Vietnam, Sfc. Adelbert F. Waldron (Ret.), during his tour of duty as a 9th Division sniper, was credited with 113 confirmed kills in a five-month

An experimental XM21 scope base evaluated at Rock Island Arsenal in 1970. Intended to provide greater rigidity for the ART system, the "two-point base" concept was later adopted in modified form. (U.S. Army.)

Correspondence: Colonel Bayard to Army Weapons Command, re: Ft. Benning Participation in the XM21 Sniper Rifle Program, 16 October 1969

Only the last four digits of the rifle serial number will be placed on the telescope mount.

Recommend that Anniston Army Depot be instructed to package in such a way so as to insure that both the rifle and its sight arrive in-country together. It is suggested that eight (8) rifles be packed in the large carton in four (4) boxes and the last box be used to hold the matching eight (8) scopes with mounts and carrying cases (the carton referred to above normally holds five boxes each containing two rifles).

—Col. Robert F. Bayard
Commanding Officer,
USAMTU

period. As a graduate of the 9th Division Sniper School, Sergeant Waldron compiled this impressive score while operating during periods of day and night, armed with the XM21 mounting the ART, Starlight Scope, and noise suppressor in combination as needed.

The following 9th Infantry Division (3d Battalion, 60th Infantry) "after-action report" (4 February 1969) provides an example of Sergeant Waldron's combat activities in South Vietnam:

> Sergeant Waldron and his partner occupied a night ambush position with Company D, 3/60th Infantry on 4 February 1969 approximately three kilometers south of Ben Tre. The area selected for the ambush was at the end of a large rice paddy adjacent to a wooded area. Company D, 3/60th Infantry had conducted a MEDCAP and ICAP in a nearby hamlet during the day, hoping to gain information on Viet Cong movements in the area. At approximately 2105 hours, five Viet Cong moved from the wooded area toward Sergeant Waldron's position and he took the first one in the group under fire, resulting in one Viet Cong killed. The remaining Viet Cong immediately dropped to the ground and did not move for several minutes. A short time later, four Viet Cong stood up and began moving again, apparently not aware of the fact they were being fired upon from the rice paddy. Sergeant Waldron took the four Viet Cong under fire, resulting in four Viet Cong killed. The next contact took place at 2345 hours, when four Viet Cong moved into the rice paddy from the left of Sergeant Waldron's ambush position. The Viet Cong were taken under fire by Sergeant Waldron, resulting in four Viet Cong killed. A total of nine

Sniper Weapon System: The XM21

In October 1970, the Department of the Army approved the Combat Developments Command "Abbreviated Performance Characteristics for a Sniper Rifle System" based on the XM21's characteristics. The Army sniper rifle was type-classified "Standard B" in December 1971 and subsequently adopted as the M21 Sniper Rifle System in 1972. (U.S. Army.)

enemy soldiers were killed during the night at an average range of 400 meters. Sergeant Waldron used a Starlight scope and noise suppressor on his match grade M14 rifle in obtaining these kills.

As a matter of interest, when the number of enemy personnel killed in action (KIA) as a direct result of sniper fire was recorded, while not always the case, it was not supposed to be counted as a "kill" unless the sniper was able to (figuratively speaking) place his foot on the body.

According to a former Army sniper in Vietnam, "I can't speak for the other people, but when it came to keeping track, as I understood it, it wasn't a kill unless I could touch the body. We didn't call them kills; they were simply known as 'step-ons' for obvious reasons."

Though seldom as uncomplicated as that, despite the honesty and integrity of the vast majority of the Army and Marine Corps snipers serving in Southeast Asia, both the number and the manner in which many sniper kills were recorded, or "logged," in a combat environment remains the subject of controversy to this day. In addition, many people have had some difficulty with the accumulation of kills, or rather, the "keeping score" aspect of it all, regardless of the circumstances. As one veteran Marine Corps sniper perhaps put it best, "We certainly didn't paint little flags on our fuselage every time we scored," or as another Marine summed it up, "I didn't shoot women or children, and I didn't shoot anyone that wasn't out to kill me. If someone has a hard time with that, well, tough shit!"

While not disproportionate to those earned by American combat forces at large, a significant number of awards and decorations were earned by Army and Marine Corps snipers during the war in Vietnam.

Lieutenant General Ewell, commenting on the 9th's sniper program in *Sharpening the Combat Edge* following the war (1974), cited another interesting mode of sniper employment in the Delta region:

> One of the unusual night sniper employments resulted

NOTE: As a matter of reader interest, the last four digits of the M14 (XM21) rifle serial number were applied to the ART mount by the AMTU with a "Hermes Engravograph," an engraving machine that transferred letters and numbers from a grooved template to the work surface by means of a pantograph. Unlike the numerals applied with a handheld tool, the engraving was both uniform and consistent in this case.

Information Letter, Re: Support of the XM21 Sniper Rifle, To: ALL PERSONNEL CONCERNED, USAMTU, 11 June 1970

The numbering of the telescope mount base to match the serial number of the rifle was done to simplify identification of matching units. There is no reason at all for not assembling the scope from a disabled rifle on a rifle where the scope has become unserviceable. Only two scope/rifle combinations out of the whole 240 Project would not initially allow sufficient adjustment to establish a zero. Interchanging between other components allowed all units to be used. The error is not in the sight mount, but rather in the mounting area of the receiver, which had rather lax tolerances during manufacture. This was probably due to the fact that no serious consideration was given to telescope sight mounting at that time.

—Lt. Col. Francis B. Conway
Ordnance Officer, USAMTU

---

from the 6th Battalion, 31st Infantry operations from riverine boats along the Mekong River. In this case, the snipers working in pairs positioned themselves on the helicopter landing pad of Tango boats. The Tango boats traveled at speeds of two to four knots moving about one hundred to 150 meters from and parallel to the shore. Often they would anchor for periods of a half-hour before moving to a new location. As the Viet Cong moved along the shoreline, the snipers would make positive identification of the enemy, through detection of a weapon, and would open fire. During the period 12 April to 9 May 1969, snipers of the 6th Battalion, 31st Infantry killed thirty-nine Viet Cong. About 1.7 VC were killed per engagement.

Although many Army and Marine Corps marksmen had plied their trade on or in close proximity to the rivers and waterways in South Vietnam, the 9th Division area of operations in the Mekong Delta provided unique opportunities for employing snipers in conjunction with the Army/Navy Mobile Riverine Force (MRF).

The Mobile Riverine Force and the role of the 9th Infantry Division, a combined operation designed to eliminate the Vietcong's hold on Kien Hoa province, was summarized by Capt. G.O. Hilliard III in *A Distant Challenge*, a compilation of tactics and events in RVN:

> On July 26, 1968, the headquarters of the US 9th Infantry Division moved from Bearcat, near Saigon, to Dong Tam, on the My Tho River, about seven kilometers west of My Tho City. The division's three brigades operated generally in three important provinces around Dong Tam: Long An, Kien Hoa, and Dinh Tuong...
>
> The 2d Brigade, was organized as a riverine brigade of three battalions plus a field artillery battalion, operating from ships and small craft of the U.S. Navy. Kien Hoa Province, with its myriad waterways, was the logical target for this force...
>
> The Mobile Riverine Force provided the allies with a unique operational capability in a unique environment: the Mekong Delta. Its Navy component consisted of four APBs (self-propelled barracks ships), which were 328-feet-long converted LSTs. Each was equipped with a barge moored alongside, from which riverine operations were staged. These four ships also provided mobile billeting facilities for Army and Navy personnel and operations centers manned by both staffs. In essence, they served as base camps for the troops and the smaller boats used in actual watermobile assaults...
>
> There were three general types of small boats used for actual watermobile assaults. The armored troop carriers (ATCs or Tango Boats) functioned as the general purpose carrier of the river assault squadrons and normally carried one rifle platoon each. The assault support patrol boats (ASPBs or Alfa Boats) were fast, highly maneuverable craft for fire support,

Sniper Weapon System: The XM21

A "recon platoon" sniper (196th Infantry Brigade) scanning the area for enemy activity with the ART (Vietnam, February 1970). Many snipers preferred to use their rifle telescopes rather than binoculars or spotting scopes for observation purposes while on patrol. There was no mistaking when a sniper rifle was positioned for scanning rather than sighting a target. (U.S. Army.)

minesweeping, patrolling, and convoy escort on inland waterways... Monitors, or heavies, were fire support boats used mainly during water movement assault landings.

The Navy component of the MRF was commanded by a Navy captain. Navy staff counterparts of the brigade staff worked closely with Army staff members aboard the flagship. The Navy's cooperation and dedication added significantly to the joint efforts in Kien Hoa.

Army snipers, as one might suspect, were not the only marksmen to operate under these circumstances. At the request of the Navy Department, the USAMTU at Ft. Benning rebuilt, tested, and shipped 40 M14 sniping rifles directly to RVN for use on patrol boats by Navy sniper personnel.

NOTE: Although Navy personnel trained as snipers have reported the use of "match-grade M14 rifles with Redfield 3x9 Accurange scopes

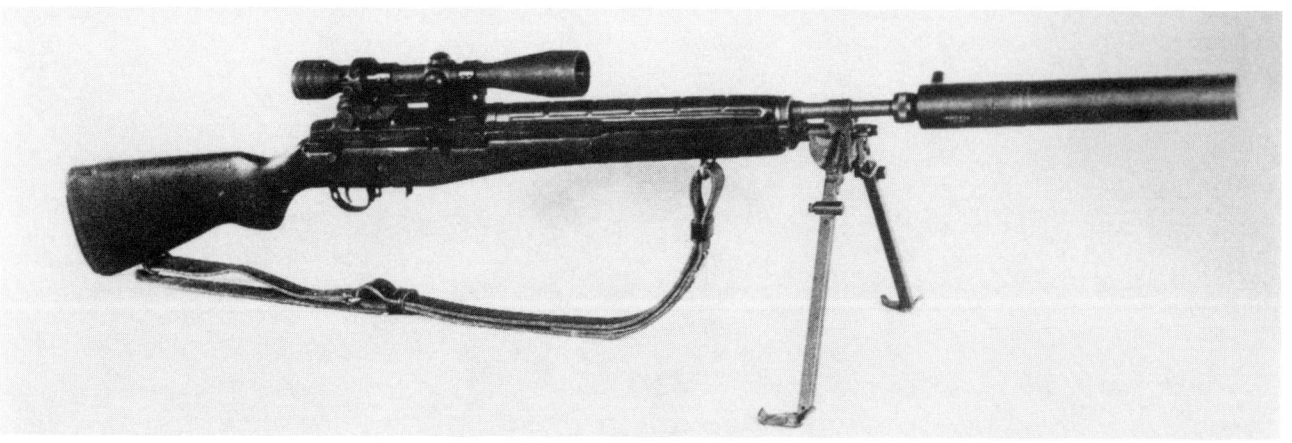

Vietnam-era U.S. Army photograph of an XM21 equipped with a suppressor and a bipod assembly. Even though the noise suppressor and the bipod were not adopted officially, both items were considered an integral part of the system in some quarters of the Army. (U.S. Army.)

and Sionics suppressors" in RVN, according to USAMTU personnel then active (1969), the telescopic sights fitted to the "40" Navy M14s in this case were "conventional, fixed-power rifle scopes."

In addition to the weapons considered "Navy issue," improvised equipment and Army or Marine Corps sniper rifles acquired during the course of waterborne operations in the Delta were used by "crew members" to conduct sniping. For that matter, telescopic sighted rifles were frequently observed on Navy patrol boats throughout South Vietnam. It was commonplace for the smaller boats to possess an assortment of ad hoc weaponry, and sniper rifles were no exception.

Though limited in comparison to the Army and Marine Corps programs, a sniping effort was, in fact, mounted by the U.S. Navy in Vietnam.

From January 1969 until the majority of the 9th Infantry Division was redeployed to the United States in August of the same year, snipers of the 9th accounted for approximately 1,300 enemy KIA with an average of 1.39 rounds expended per kill. It must be pointed out, however, that these results were obtained through combined use of the ART-equipped XM21 and the National Match M14 with the M84 telescope.

The XM21 was finally brought to fruition when, as stated earlier, the Department of the Army authorized "Limited Production for Sniper Rifles and Scopes" (ENSURE No. 240) on 14 February 1969. Col. John S. Wood Jr. Headquarters, AMC, Washington, is credited by those close to the XM21 project as having been the leading proponent in securing the funding necessary for this ENSURE authority.

As then followed, Army Weapons Command was given the responsibility of rebuilding the M14 according to AMTU procedures with the USAMTU functioning as the final inspection agency. Fifty rifles were to be shipped to Ft. Benning on a weekly basis, accuracy tested, fitted with the ART, and sighted in. Not one of the first 100 rifles received from Weapons Command during October 1969 met the necessary accuracy requirements, and they had to be rebuilt by AMTU armorers before acceptance. This rejection rate eventually dropped to approximately 25 to 30 percent per shipment, however. Rework of both the initial and subsequent XM21 rejects from Rock Island Arsenal was directed by M.Sgt. Gerald "Hook" Boutin (Ret.), who was considered by his MTU associates as "one of the best in the business."

After a time, in order to facilitate the rebuilding efforts, Weapons Command requested certain changes in the AMTU procedures, most of which involved a relaxation of barrel specifications. This was effected without compromising weapon accuracy. In response to the question, "Where did the XM21 title originate," Colonel Conway replied, "As I recollect, I received a call from Rock Island inquiring if we had any objection to calling the system the XM21. I replied, 'I don't care what you call it as long as you don't reduce the standards.'"

By Army definition, "XM followed by an Arabic numeral was used to identify an item during its development. Upon acceptance as an adopted type, the letter X was dropped, leaving the letter M followed by an Arabic numeral."

NOTE: Although the exact point at which the Army began referencing the ART-equipped USAMTU accurized M14 rifle as the XM21 remains the subject of debate. By mid-1969, the AMTU version of the accurized M14 had emerged as the XM21 Sniper Weapon System, and the "XM21" designation began to appear in official correspondence and documents. As a matter of interest, the principal Vietnam-era publication dealing with sniper training and equipment, *Department of the Army Training Circular, TC23-14, Sniper Training and Employment* (October 1969), lists the Army sniper rifle as "Sniper Rifle — U.S. Rifle, 7.62-mm, M14, National Match (Accurized)." DTM 9-1005-221-10, the Army Weapons Command Operator's Manual (November 1969) subsequently issued with the M14 sniper rifles accurized in accordance with USAMTU specifications, specifically referenced the system as the "Rifle, 7.62-mm, XM21, Sniper."

A number of difficulties were experienced with the ART system and the accurized M14s during the course of their use in Vietnam, but these were duly rectified over a period of time. The XM21 rifles were in continuous use, subjected to extremely rough handling and adverse weather conditions, but still performed as well as anticipated. By all accounts, one of the greatest problems rested with proper ordnance support, or rather the absence of it.

For lack of a better explanation, considerably more planning had gone into developing and fielding the sophisticated Army sniper rifle than supporting the system in South Vietnam. In addition to parts supply and depot operations, trained National Match armorers ("gunsmiths") were eventually required to render proper field support. In November 1969, the USAMTU stated the following:

Information pertaining to snipers, included in the findings of a USAIS representative during a CONARC liaison visit to South Vietnam (7–22 September 1970)

Snipers and sniping missions have been highly successful; however, credit is not given for many enemy kills due to the distance involved (kills can be made up to 1,000 meters and the body cannot be recovered).

Aberdeen Proving Ground photograph (1972) with caption that reads, "Right side view of an XM21 sniper rifle with telescopic sight." Even though the USAMTU sniper rifle fielded for the ACTIV evaluations in 1967 and the early 9th Infantry Division sniper program in 1968 are often referenced as "XM21 sniper rifles" in post-Vietnam literary offerings, in the interest of historical accuracy, the XM21 designation was used to define the ART-equipped M14 sniper rifles produced at Rock Island Arsenal by Army Weapons Command. (U.S. Army.)

The gunsmith, who is to accompany each sniper instructor team to RVN will be trained by the Shop section of TUSAMTU [variously referenced as the USAMTU, AMTU, or simply, the MTU] and will have the following capabilities:

1. Will be knowledgeable of the complete rebuild procedures as outlined in TUSAMTU manual on the M14 rifle.

2. Capable of installing and headspacing a new barrel.

3. Capable of installing a new stock to include glass bedding.

4. Capable of installing and adjusting all of the remaining component parts of the rifle.

5. Capable of replacing all scope mount parts for the ART system.

6. Capable of instructing on the care and cleaning of the rifle, ART scope, and the silencer.

Even though USAMTU participation in the XM21 program (ENSURE no. 240) was expanded to include "certain responsibilities in support of the XM21 Sniper Rifle presently deployed in Vietnam," and continued during 1969 and 1970 as well, according to an "Information Memorandum" (9 December 1970) circulated by Col. Robert M. Piper, Commanding Officer, USAMTU, to the Sniper Instructor Teams, "The USAMTU has been in the business of providing limited support for the XM21 systems in Vietnam; however, effective 1 January, this support will be provided by Rock Island Arsenal."

While tactical employment of snipers in Vietnam and the results varied greatly, a measure of XM21 and Army sniper effectiveness can be drawn from the following reports from Capt. Virgil L. Umphenour, OIC, 23d Infantry Division (AMERICAL) Sniper School to the U.S. Army Marksmanship Training Unit. The first, spanning a 10-day period, was recorded in May 1970.

Update Information on Sniper Program
AMERICAL Division

1. To date, this division has 57 snipers within combat units.

2. To date, sniper actions are listed below:

Time	Sight	Terrain	Range (meters)	Rds Fired	Kill	Wounded
1630	ART	Trail	450	1	1	—
1900	Star	Trail	500	2	—	1
1930	Star	River	200	2	1	—
1200	ART	Woods	650	1	1	—
1215	ART	Jungle	75	2	1	—
1400	ART	Jungle	45	3	1	—
1715	ART	Hill Top	500	2	1	—
0815	ART	Paddy	900	1	1	—
0515	Star	River	250	1	1	—
0530	Star	Riv. Bank	500	2	—	1
0100	Star	Paddy	100	1	1	—
1415	ART	Trail	700	5	1	—

The second "Update Information on Sniper Program, AMERICAL Division," was dated 12 June 1970. The report reads as follows:

1. To date, this division has 49 snipers within combat units.

2. Sniper actions since last report:

Time	Sight	Terrain	Range (meters)	Rds Fired	Kill	Wounded
1730	ART	Woods	600	5	1	—
1300	ART	Jungle Clrng.	450	3	1	—
0800	ART	Brush	100	1	1	—
0900	ART	Paddy	600	1	1	—
2115	Star	Paddy	100	1	1	—
1600	ART	Trail	600	2	1	—
0730	ART	Brush	600	2	—	—
0850	ART	Paddy	300	1	1	—
1700	ART	Paddy	200	1	1	—
1730	ART	Paddy	650	1	1	—
0600	ART	Treeline	75	1	1	—
1745	ART	Paddy	600	3	2	—
1830	ART	River	700	3	—	2
1745	ART	Paddy	400	3	1	—

NOTE: Captain Umphenour and his instructor team were graduates of the Sniper Instructor Course at Ft. Benning in early 1970. The monthly reports [from all USAMTU-trained instructor groups in RVN] served to keep both the USAIS and the USAMTU apprised of progress and results.

In October 1970 the Department of the Army approved the Combat Developments Command memo, "Abbreviated Performance Characteristics for a Sniper Rifle System," based on the XM21's characteristics. The Army eventually adopted the XM21 as its sniper standard in 1972, at which time it became the M21. Though the rifle was adopted as the "M21 Sniper Rifle System," to the surpise of many, it was, according to Department of the Army information (December 1971), type-classified Standard B for the following reasons:

> . . . because it has to be modified by a gunsmith. This and other problems associated with the noise suppressor, bipod, and extreme weather performance, eliminated the system from Standard A classification. This will satisfy the users and will help the logisticians account for the systems being returned from Southeast Asia. Type classification will allow authorized units to requisition rifles and spare parts.

Interestingly, even though the noise suppressor and the bipod referred to above were not adopted for use with the M21, in many quarters, both items were actually considered part of the system.

As American forces were gradually withdrawn from Southeast Asia, the effect and the extent of Army sniper operations decreased in proportion to the level of the remaining combat activity. By some estimates, the "high-point" of the Army sniper program came during the mid-1970s when both in-country and stateside training and support were said to be nearing "acceptable levels."

NOTE: As a point of interest, the findings of a USAIS representative during a United States Continental Army Command (CONARC) liaison visit to South Vietnam (7–22 September 1970) included the following:

> With the decreased tempo of operations and the NVA and VC's reluctance to engage in large scale operations other than in the northernmost provinces, sniper operations have become a major source of enemy kills. For example, in one division eight-per-cent of all kills since Cambodia are attributed to snipers.

U.S. ground troops ended two months of operations in Cambodia on 30 June 1970.

When the final "peace agreement" was signed on 27 January 1973, the war between North Vietnam and the United States was officially over, but the conflict with South Vietnam would continue until the final week of April 1975 when Saigon fell to the North Vietnamese Army and the Republic of South Vietnam ceased to exist.

By the time the last major contingents of U.S. combat forces had left Vietnam (late 1971/early 1972), 1,400-plus XM21 sniper rifles had reportedly seen combat duty in Southeast Asia (though this is unconfirmed).

Although ENSURE No. 240 authorized production of 1,600 XM21 sniper rifles, the exact number manufactured for Army use in Vietnam has not been disclosed. Despite the fact that this system had clearly demonstrated what a "first-class" sniping weapon could accomplish in a combat environment, following the general stand-down, the Army Sniper Program was relegated to low-priority status once again.

CHAPTER 4

The Suppressor and the Sniper Rifle

During World War II, when silencer use became a necessity, a host of devices were developed and employed for "special operations" by the Office of Strategic Services (OSS), commando units, and agents involved in espionage activities behind enemy lines. Utilized almost exclusively with submachine guns, pistols, and special close-range single-shot weapons, silencers were to prove indispensable for clandestine operations and "quiet killing."

Despite the demonstrated effectiveness of silencers, their use by snipers with telescopic sighted rifles—except in rare instances—was all but nonexistent. However, in view of the extraordinary lack of organized sniping by U.S. combat forces during this period, the exclusion of silencers is not surprising.

In 1950, following a relatively short peace, the weapons and concepts employed during World War II were dusted off and brought forth for the "police action" in South Korea. Although silencers were fielded once again, their use was restricted to clandestine operations on both sides of the 38th parallel.

Despite its vintage, the Model 15 Maxim rifle silencer (1915), one of the most efficient designs of all time, saw limited action with U.S. snipers against select North Korean and Red Chinese targets primarily for "harassment purposes." Aside from isolated use of silencers, however, the Korean War offered little for the advancement of silenced sniping.

Basically, the level of silencer efficiency depends on bullet velocity. If the bullet is subsonic (i.e., muzzle velocity of less than 1,100 fps), and the

Maxim Model 15 silencer fitted to a M1903 Springfield rifle. Even though the Maxim silencer was developed before World War I, the unique design was still viewed as the "standard of comparison" following the Korean War. The U.S. Army became the first military power not only to adopt telescopic rifle sights and silencers but to use them simultaneously as well (1910)—a bold and innovative move during an era of ultraconservative ordnance development. (Thomas Collection.)

Maj. Willis L. Powell, Commanding Officer, 9th Infantry Division Sniper School (December 1968). The rifle is an ART-equipped M14; the Sionics suppressor and one other went to Vietnam with the USAMTU sniper instructor team in mid-1968. An early M14 unit in this case, the pressure relief valve does not have the cap assembly. In this form, a "six-pointed star" emitted from the valve could be seen at a distance of 75 to 100 yards when the weapon was fired at night. Note the Redfield soft plastic lens covers on the ART. The sleeve insignia is a Military Assistance Command, Vietnam (MACV) shoulder patch. (U.S. Army.)

firearm breech is closed tightly, a well-designed silencer can virtually eliminate the noise of the report. A high-velocity bullet, on the other hand, creates its own sonic boom, or crack, after leaving the muzzle of the firearm.

Attempts to mask rifle fire have centered on two concepts—total elimination of muzzle noise and ballistic crack with subsonic ammunition and a reduction of the muzzle blast only, leaving the sonic crack unaltered.

The effect of bullet impact and range limitations of modified ammunition has remained a serious detriment to the consideration of subsonic ammunition for sniping purposes. Although most rifle silencers are designed for the alternate use of standard and subsonic ammunition, the official point of view concerning special cartridges for combat operations has rarely been favorable.

Should any period stand as the "Golden Age of Silencers," it would certainly be the era of U.S. military involvement in Southeast Asia, when a variety of "regular and covertly-regular

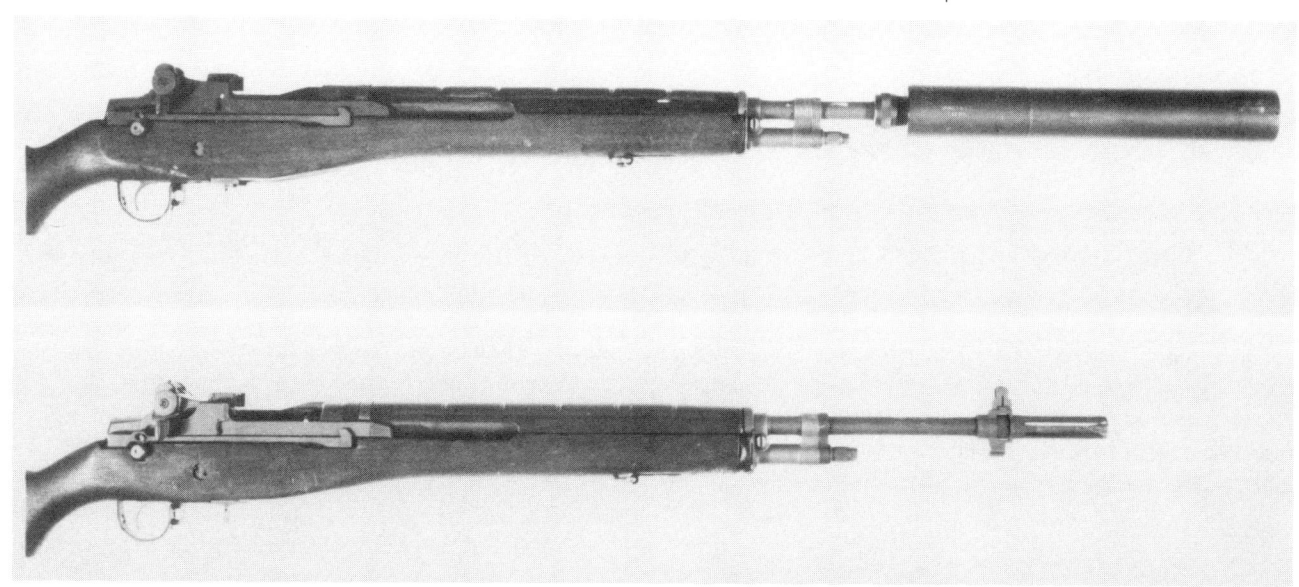

The Vietnam-era Sionics M14SS-1 noise suppressor mounted on an M14 rifle. The standard muzzle area of another M14 provides an effective comparison. Though not adopted officially, noise suppressors were found to increase the confidence and capabilities of U.S. snipers in Southeast Asia. Except for random use by Army and Marine Corps recon personnel, the vast majority of Sionics 7.62mm M14SS-1 suppressors fielded in Vietnam were employed in conjunction with the Army sniper program. (Alley Collection.)

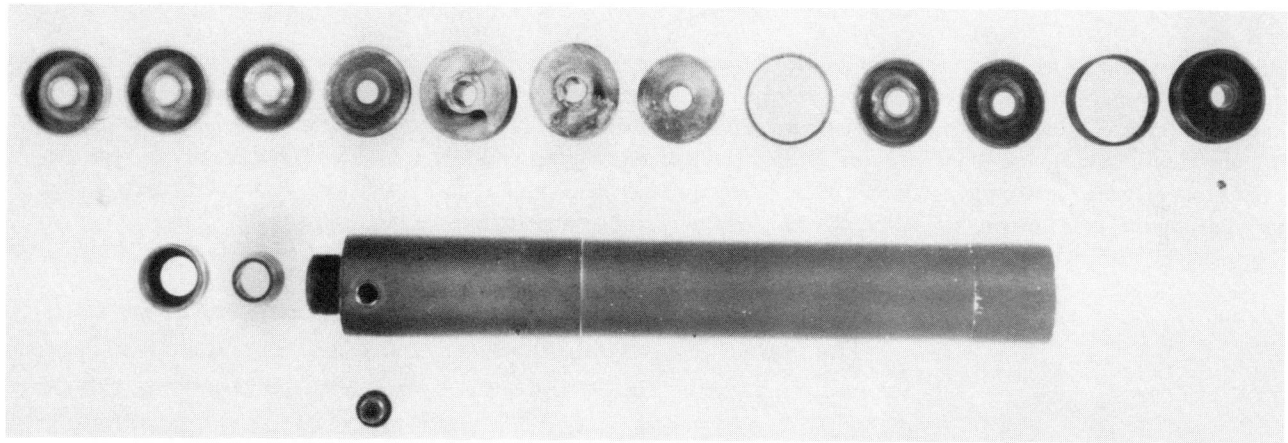

The M14SS-1 Noise and Flash Suppressor shown disassembled with the internal components arranged above the outer casing. The Sionics attachment is 12.75 inches long, extends 9 inches past the muzzle, and has a diameter of 1.665 inches, a bore of .375 inches, and weight of 1 pound, 15 ounces. It is constructed of steel and aluminum and makes use of a brass or Teflon collar bushing. External parts (steel) were black oxide coated; the aluminum casing was black anodized. (Alley Collection.)

U.S. military personnel" utilized silencer-equipped weapons extensively for special operations in Laos, Cambodia, and both North and South Vietnam. In addition, special devices bearing the contemporary name of "noise suppressors" were developed, tested, and found to increase the confidence and capabilities of U.S. sniping personnel, thereby enabling them to create monumental consternation among the VC and NVA.

Although suppressors were tested with the Winchester Model 70 and the Marine Corps Remington M700 (M40) and were issued for field use with the M16, the accurized XM21 fitted with a commercially designed noise suppres-

A Vietnam-era Sionics M14SS-1 7.62mm noise and flash suppressor cutaway. The unaltered side is illustrated in this case. The small indentation on the side of the casing was part of the assembly process. A small recessed hex screw was inserted into the barrel muzzle ring through the casing and then "staked in place" to keep the ring from turning inside the suppressor when the unit was installed on the M14 barrel. The muzzle ring was spot-welded to the steel M16 suppressor tubes and "brazed" in place on the later units. (Collection West.)

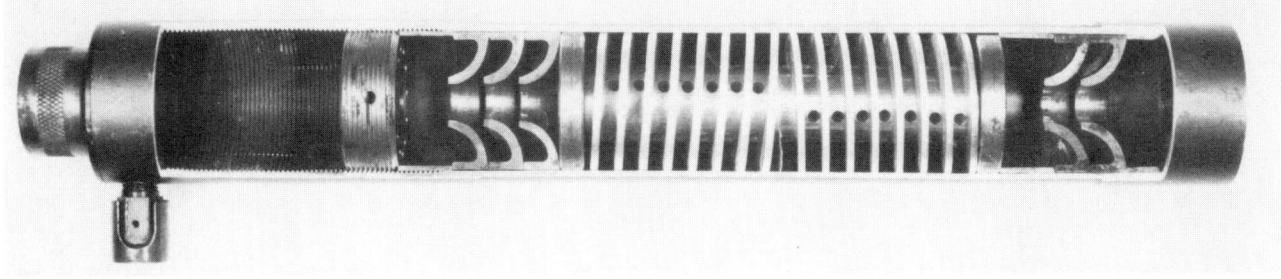

An internal view of the M14SS-1 suppressor showing the principal components. The pressure relief valve (valve assembly) was mounted on the outer casing at the rear chamber. It made no difference which way the valve was pointing when the unit was attached to an M14 barrel. The suppressor casing was enlarged at both ends to accommodate the internal threads. There are no markings on this suppressor. Except for the difference in size, Sionics M14 and M16 suppressor designs were essentially the same. Improvements made to one system were incorporated into the other. Unlike the M16 unit, however, the M14SS-1 suppressor was intended "only" for semiautomatic fire. Surviving examples of Sionics cutaway suppressors are extremely rare. (Collection West.)

sor emerged as the principal instrument of sniper effectiveness in Vietnam.

The brainchild of Atlanta-based Sionics, Inc., the M14SS-1 suppressor made it next to impossible for the VC to locate the firing source at distances greater than 50 to 100 meters ahead of the weapon. Based on early combat use, a select 9th Infantry Division sniper related, "The suppressor is very effective; the VC just seem to mill around even after a couple of them have been dropped."

The purpose and characteristics of the M14SS-1 Noise and Flash Suppressor Assembly were set forth by Sionics, Inc. in the "Operation and Maintenance Manual" as follows:

> The M14SS-1 suppressor is a device designed to deceive persons forward of the firer as to the exact location of the weapon and its operator. It accomplishes this by disguising the signature of origin in two ways. First, it reduces muzzle noise to such an extent that it becomes inaudible a short distance from the weapon—making exact sound location extremely difficult if not impossible; secondly, it suppresses muzzle flash at night making visual location also equally difficult.

The Suppressor and the Sniper Rifle

The business end of the Sionics M14SS-1 noise suppressor. The 6061-T6 aluminum alloy tubing (outer casing) is approximately .090 inches thick. When exposed to the elements for extended periods, the black anodized finish displayed a tendency to change color. Even though a special spanner wrench was required to remove the threaded front insert ("muzzle") to access the internal components, tools were not furnished with the Sionics M14SS-1 and the MAW-A1 suppressors sold to the military. (Collection West.)

Characteristics of M14SS-1

A. The M14SS-1 suppressor has no effect on muzzle velocity and improves the accuracy of the sniper rifle.

B. The M14SS-1 suppressor is a light weight device which may be quickly attached, without tools, to the barrel of a standard, unmodified XM21 Rifle. No assembly alignment is required.

C. The suppressor is designed for use in a semiautomatic mode ONLY to deliver accurate aimed fire, without disclosing the point of origin.

D. The suppressor produces minimum chamber carbonization.

E. Maintenance functions can be easily performed in the field employing standard cleaning equipment issued with the Rifle and one .45 caliber brass brush.

F. No spare or replacement parts are required, other than the bushings, and present tests indicate that the suppressor, properly maintained, will have a service life equal to that of the XM21 barrel.

G. Muzzle jump and recoil are significantly reduced.

H. A gas relief port on the rear chamber of the suppressor permits operation without accelerating the gas blow back system of the XM21. This effectively reduces the gas blow back in the operator's face.

An early 1970 Aberdeen Proving Ground photograph of the markings on a Sionics M14 suppressor ("SIONICS U.S.A. 7.62 MM"). With the addition of a unit serial number, the markings are typical of those applied to the M14SS-1 suppressors furnished to the Army for sniper use in RVN. Generally, however, suppressor markings and serial numbering practice for the Sionics/MAC M14 and M16 units varied during the course of production. (Alley Collection.)

The cover from the original Sionics "Operation and Maintenance Manual" for the M14SS-1 M14 suppressor assembly. A revised edition (December 1969) made specific reference to the "XM21" sniper rifle rather than the M14 National Match Rifle. (Peter R. Senich).

OPERATION AND MAINTENANCE

MANUAL

NOISE AND FLASH SUPPRESSOR ASSEMBLY

M14 SS-1

FOR USE WITH RIFLE, 7.62 MM, M14 NM

sionics

Research and Development
of
SOUND SUPPRESSION – ADVANCED WEAPONRY

1655 PEACHTREE STREET, N.E. / ATLANTA, GEORGIA 30309 / U.S.A. / (404) 873-3672

The Suppressor and the Sniper Rifle

Specifications

A. Total length	12.750 inches
B. Extension beyond muzzle	9.000 inches
C. Diameter	1.665 inches
D. Bore	.375 inches
E. Total weight	1 pound, 15 ounces

The outer casing for the M14 suppressor was 6061-T6 aluminum tubing. The rear retaining collar and internal parts (except for the suppressor rings) were made of 4130 steel. The rings were machined from 6061-T6 aluminum. External steel parts were protected by a black oxide coating; the aluminum parts by black anodizing. A Teflon bushing inserted between the retaining collar and the base of the suppressor served to seal and align the unit on the barrel. There were no moving parts.

Noise suppression and the principal function of the M14SS-1 suppressor were described as follows:

Noise Sources

When the XM21 rifle, or any high velocity weapon, is fired, the resulting noise is produced by two separate sources. Depending on distance and direction from the weapon, the two noises may appear as one or two closely spaced different sounds. These are the muzzle noise and the ballistic crack, or sonic boom produced by the bullet.

    A. The muzzle noise is generated by the blast wave created by the high velocity gases escaping into the atmosphere behind the bullet. This noise is relatively easy to locate as to source, as it emanates from a fixed point.

    B. Ballistic crack results from the supersonic speed of the bullet which compresses the air ahead of it exactly in the same fashion as a supersonic jet creates a sonic boom. The only difference is that the smaller bullet produces a sharp crack rather than a large overpressure wave with its correspondingly louder shock wave. Unlike the muzzle noise which emanates from a fixed point, the ballistic crack radiates backwards in a conical shape similar to a bow wave from a boat, from a point slightly ahead of the moving bullet. Thus the sonic boom created by the supersonic bullet moves at the velocity of the bullet away from the muzzle noise and in the direction of

---

Correspondence: General Ewell to Colonel Bayard, 1 April 1969

We have put in for suppressors for half of our snipers with the thought that one per team would be adequate for night or day work and the other sniper would be a little less loaded down if he had to work quickly in a tight spot. I think your idea of a "Gold Century Rifle" is great. You won't have many takers, but it will be a tremendous incentive.

—Julian J. Ewell
Major General,
USA, Commanding

NOTE: With "100 confirmed kills" by an Army or Marine Corps sniper considered a major accomplishment in Vietnam, in this case, the idea of presenting a "Gold Century Rifle" to every Army sniper reaching this number was considered briefly. So far as it is known, there was only one Army sniper officially credited with 100 or more kills during the Vietnam War.

One of the earliest accounts of U.S. Army use of suppressors in South Vietnam, published in the September 1969 issue of the *Army Journal*, a publication of the Australian army. In addition to providing insight on Mitchell L. WerBell III, the man responsible for the Sionics noise suppressor, Maj. E.S. Holt, Royal Australian Engineers, described the combat use of the suppressor-equipped M14 sniper rifles employed by the 9th Infantry Division in an article entitled, "The Quiet One from Dong Tam." Major Holt began as follows:

> A group of nine Viet Cong were walking along a paddy in the Delta area of South Vietnam. The late afternoon light was softening into early evening haze when both the first and the last Viet Cong stumbled and fell. As the squad waited for the two fallen members to regain their footing two more tumbled from the band. Then one after the other the remainder of the squad fell silently into the rice field. Was it some sort of trick? Or was the squad simultaneously fatigued?
>
> If the Viet Cong had been alive to watch they would have seen two men dressed in camouflage green uniforms rise from sparse cover almost 700 meters distant. They would have seen the two men holding what might at that distance appear to be very longbarrelled rifles. But as the squad members had been efficiently and effectively killed by the suppressed

(continued on page 103)

the target. Location and identification of the initial source of the shock wave is extremely difficult because the moving wave impinges on the ear at nearly ninety degrees to the point of origin. Attention is thus drawn to the direction from which the wave is coming rather than towards the initial source, i.e., the firing position of the weapon itself.

Action of the M14SS-1 Suppressor

A. The M14SS-1 suppressor is effective only in reducing and disguising muzzle noise and has no effect on the muzzle velocity of the bullet. It does not in any way reduce or change the ballistic crack of the bullet.

B. The M14SS-1 suppressor effectively reduces muzzle noise in three ways.

First, the rapidly expanding propellant gases behind the bullet are permitted to flow into the suppressor expansion chambers, which greatly increases the space available in which the gases may expand. As the space into which the gases may flow is enlarged, the gas pressure is reduced.

Secondly, the gases entering the suppressor spiral chamber are directed, by the unique design of the suppressor rings, in a spiral path through the chamber before re-entering the bore and may actually pass through several portions of the suppressor and bore before reaching the muzzle. This greatly increases the distance the gases must travel before being expelled into the atmosphere, which in turn drastically reduces the velocity and the intensity of the accompanying sound wave.

Thirdly, the design and configuration of the suppressor spirals produces a series of reflections of the gas shock waves within the chamber. A large number of sound and pressure waves of various frequencies, wave lengths, and amplitudes are thus produced within the suppressor. Since the direction of the gas flow within the suppressor is alternately in opposite directions, a large percentage of the generated waves eventually get out of phase 180 degrees and thus cancel each other out, producing a sound-nullifying effect and reducing the overall noise spectrum to a minimum auditory factor from a sound loudness viewpoint.

It is believed that a combination of all three of the above sound reducing methods is at least a partial explanation of the extraordinary effectiveness of the M14SS-1 suppressor.

Maj. Willis L. Powell conducting an "equipment briefing" for British army officers, Ft. Benning, Georgia (March 1971). The XM21 rifles are fitted with Sionics M14SS-1 suppressors. The British army, mindful of new sniping techniques and hardware, tested the Leatherwood/Realist Adjustable Ranging Telescope and Sionics noise suppressors with an Enfield Envoy match rifle in 1971. (U.S. Army.)

A principal reason for the success of the Sionics suppressor rested with its innovative "pressure-relief valve," which solved several problems that had plagued the use of such devices on fully automatic and some semiautomatic weapons through the years. According to various military and civilian experts, the Sionics-patented and exclusive gas pressure relief valve solved the following problems: it kept the cyclic rate on fully automatic fire nearly the same rate as that without a suppressor; it prevented the serious problem of excessive gas blowback into the firer's face; it prevented excessive fouling of the action; and, finally, it handled the different pressures, thus eliminating the need to modify the bolt mechanism.

Combined use of the suppressor and Starlight Scope in night operations proved particularly advantageous to snipers for deceptive purposes since the suppressor served to hide muzzle flash as well, thereby making auditory and visual detection equally difficult.

In early use, however, a "six-pointed star" emitted from the pressure-relief valve located at the rear of the suppressor could be observed at a distance of 75 to 100 yards from the firing point. A simple solution entailed placing a cap over the gas-relief port.

The advantages associated with field use of the M14 suppressor were also detailed in the Sionics manual as follows:

M14 rifles of the two man sniper team they saw nothing.

The training of the two man sniper team had enabled it to select and occupy a good but not obvious position; discipline had prevented them from giving away their position; telescopic sights had assisted their naturally good eyesight; and suppressors (sometimes referred to as silencers) had allowed the snipers to retain concealment of their position, achieve and maintain surprise, and to aim and fire without haste at stationary targets.

And in an obvious reference to Maj. Willis L. Powell, he wrote the following:

> In any large group of soldiers there can be found a few who are naturally good shots. At Dong Tam in the Delta there was a quietly spoken American officer who was not only an excellent rifle shot and a good instructor, but was dedicated to his belief that sniper teams could be trained to take the war effectively to the Viet Cong and prevent freedom of movement to the enemy.

(continued on page 104)

Though barely six pages in length, the article by Holt is considered a noteworthy Vietnam-era document pertaining to Army sniper use of noise suppressors. Even though Marine Corps sniping activity received a fair amount of media coverage, the Army program did not, and sniper use of suppressors, in particular, was relatively unknown outside of official Army circles during the war.

As the article concluded:

> The U.S. sniper teams operating so successfully in Vietnam indicate that the art of firing a well aimed shot is not lost. Part of their operational success is due to the use of suppressed M14 rifles which allow snipers to not only operate at the traditional long range of the sniper but also at much closer ranges. The sound and flash suppression of the weapon prevents location of the firer and enables the sniper to fire, re-aim and fire again without fear of immediate retaliation ...
> Meanwhile, back in the Delta, The Quiet One continues to spread the word from Dong Tam.

Use of the M14SS-1 Suppressor for Deception

The M14SS-1 makes it nearly impossible for enemy soldiers to be alerted by the ballistic crack and then by listening for the "thump" of the muzzle blast to locate, by auditory means, the firing source. At a distance greater than approximately 30 meters ahead of the XM21 weapon it is extremely difficult to detect the muzzle noise produced by the XM21 in combination with the M14SS-1 suppressor. Without the suppressor the muzzle blast may be detected up to 1000 meters under isolated field conditions.

Hearing the ballistic crack or sonic boom of the bullet is of little aid in sound location of the weapon and does little in assisting in target acquisition.

Use of the M14SS-1 Suppressor for Night Operations

Night operations result in the added factor of rifle muzzle flash affording the enemy an additional method of target acquisition. This is a problem only partially solved by the issue flash hider for the XM21 rifle, but is eliminated by the M14SS-1 suppressor which effectively hides the flash.

First Round Flash

Traditionally, all large rifle caliber suppressors exhibit a first round flash due to the presence of oxygen in the unit. The M14SS-1 first round flash is comparable with the flash from a standard M14. Additional rounds fired within reasonable limits of time (5 to 10 minutes) will exhibit almost no discernible flash because of the gas residue trapped in the suppressor eliminating the secondary burning of residue propellant or ignitable gas.

Control of First Round Flash

It is recommended that during night operations all possible measures against first round flash be used. There are three methods by which this can be done:

> A. Spray inert gas into the M14SS-1 unit. Spray bug repellent makes an excellent oxygen remover.

> B. Exhale into the gas relief port on the rear chamber of the suppressor for a period of approximately 5 seconds, inducing carbon dioxide to displace the oxygen.

> C. Fire a round in an inconspicuous area and then place tape over the muzzle to retain the propellant gases.

Night operations with the Night Vision Sight, Individual Served Weapon, AN/PVS-2. The M14SS-1 in no way affects the attachment of the night vision sight. It is recommended that for night operations the M14SS-1 suppressor be used in conjunction with the night vision sight for maximum effectiveness in deceiving the enemy.

In night operations it is to the advantage of the sniper to know his position is relatively safe from being compromised when using the suppressor and night vision sight. There seems to be a tremendous psychological impact on the enemy when he is sniped at in darkness and he can not locate the origin of the fire.

As a point of interest, even though the "40" M14SS-1 suppressors sent to Vietnam during early 1969 for 9th Infantry Division combat evaluations had come as a result of a "working relationship" between the USAMTU and the Sionics organization and were obtained without funding, an undisclosed number of Sionics M14 suppressors were eventually procured for the United States Army, Vietnam (USARV) under a separate ENSURE request (ENSURE No. 360.1). Despite tacit acceptance and funding in this case, the Sionics suppressor was not adopted officially.

NOTE: On 20 February 1971, as a result of "redeployments" and "the number of noise suppressors currently on hand," a transmittal from USARV to the Department of the Army concerning "Noise Suppressors for the XM21 Sniper System" requested that "this ENSURE be considered complete."

An Army sniper checks his equipment in preparation for a cross-border incursion into Cambodia ("a trip next door"). The XM21 sniper rifle is fitted with a Sionics M14SS-1 suppressor; the Starlight Scope is an AN/PVS-2 model. Even though the American government took a great deal of heat for ordering large-scale operations in Cambodia in 1970, U.S. military forces, in one form or another, were actively engaged in Laos, Cambodia, and North Vietnam for most of the war. (Max Crace.)

CHAPTER 5

Auto-Ranging Telescope: The Leatherwood Principle

The Adjustable Ranging Telescope fielded for Army sniper use in Southeast Asia was based on a concept James M. Leatherwood developed while attending college in Stephenville, Texas, during the early 1960s. With a fascination for hunting and mathematics, Leatherwood became intrigued with the science of ballistics and the problems associated with trajectory and bullet drop.

Although efforts to field rifle scopes that would compensate for bullet trajectory automatically were nothing new, in this case, a Redfield 3X-9X variable-power rifle sight with its nonmagnifying reticle and Leatherwood's auto-ranging principle were brought together to form an innovative sighting system that would enable a rifleman to aim directly at his target rather than guessing at the amount of hold-over the shot would require.

By adding a unique "cam" to the power selector ring of the Redfield sight and modifying a mount to allow a small amount of vertical movement of the scope, Leatherwood had created the first practical "auto-ranging" telescopic sight.

As then followed, the first of three patents pertaining to Leatherwood's principle, "Adjusting Means for Gun Sighting Scope," was granted on 12 September 1967 (No. 3,340,614). The disclosure for the original patent filed on 19 October 1964 stated the following in part:

> This invention relates to telescopic sights for guns and has for its primary object improved means for automatically adjusting the trajectory of a gun when framing a target through the

The "original" Leatherwood auto-ranging telescope and mount—the forerunner of the Army sniper sighting system (ART) employed in South Vietnam. By adding a camlike device to the power selector ring of a Redfield 3X-9X variable-power sight and modifying a Redfield commercial mount to allow vertical movement of the scope, Jim Leatherwood had created the first practical auto-ranging system. (Peter R. Senich.)

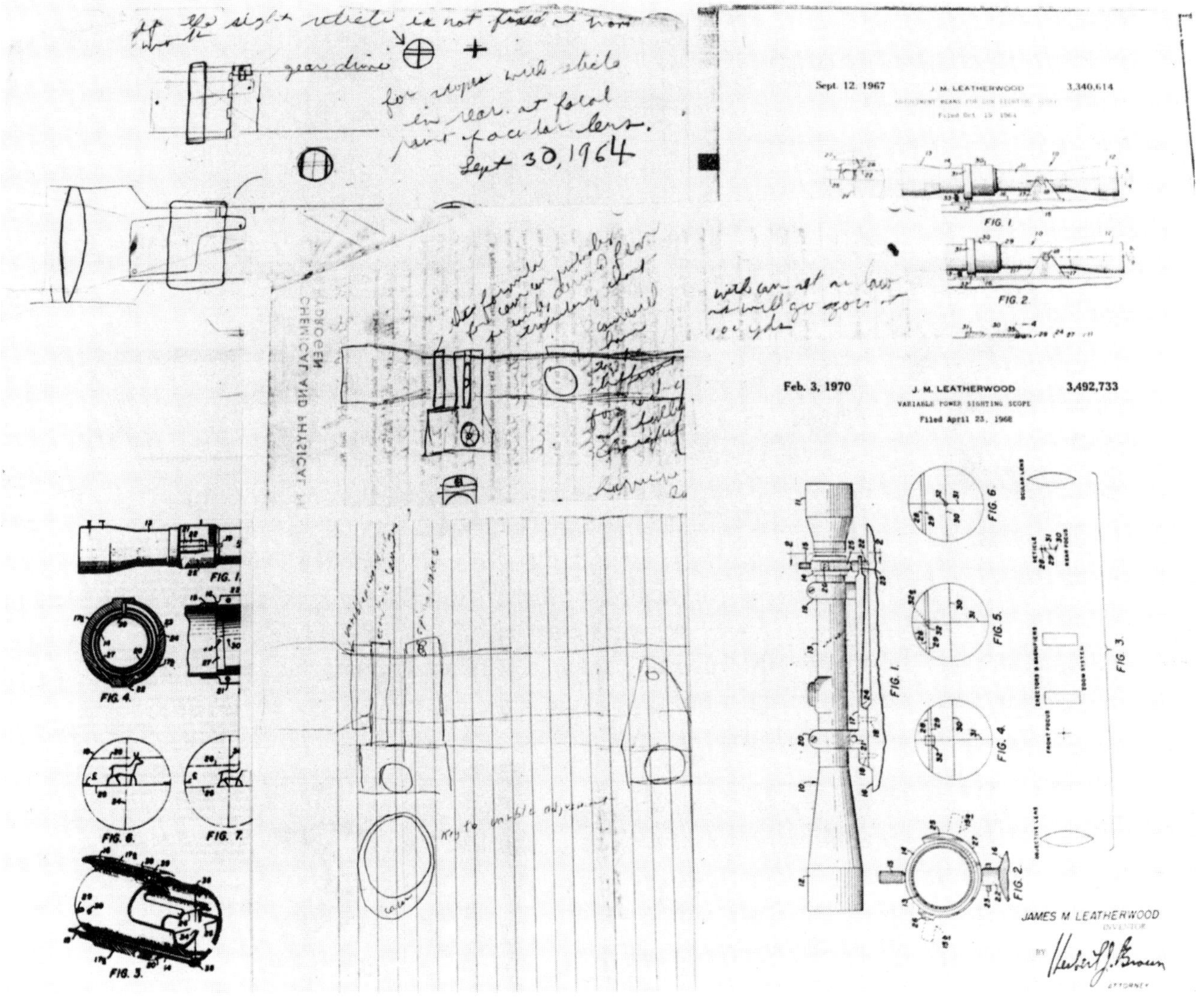

A composite illustration of original development drawings and copies of U.S. patents relating to the Leatherwood auto-ranging principle. (Peter R. Senich.)

Auto-Ranging Telescope: The Leatherwood Principle

The "original prototype mount" used to further the Leatherwood auto-ranging concept. The Redfield telescope mounting was modified to allow a small amount of vertical movement to the rifle scope. The small bushing at the back of the base served as a point of contact for the early "cam." The optical characteristics of the nonmagnifying reticle used with the Redfield variable-power sight allowed the successful application of the external cam principle. (Peter R. Senich.)

Significant parts of the Leatherwood development series, a modified Buehler telescope mount and the reworked Redfield variable-power sight, served as the basis for a patent application filed on 23 April 1968. The patent, for a "Variable Power Sighting Scope" (3,492,733), was granted on 3 February 1970. According to Jim Leatherwood, a similar scope and mount were fitted to a .30-caliber (.30-06) Model 70 Winchester rifle during his tour of duty in Vietnam. (Peter R. Senich.)

A telescope carrying case fabricated by Jim Leatherwood for use with the prototype auto-ranging system. The improvised case was made from an M72 (LAW) rocket launcher tube. The bottom was capped; the hinged lid was fitted with a spring closure. The 14 1/2-inch-long by 2 3/4-inch-diameter case was carried on the ammunition belt. (Peter R. Senich.)

An improvised telescope mounting fashioned from Redfield components, this represents one of Jim Leatherwood's early efforts to develop a sighting system for the M14 rifle. (Lt. Col. F.B. Conway, Ret.)

The first Realist scope to offer the Leatherwood auto-ranging feature, a 6-power fixed-power model (top), was introduced in early 1968 as the "Auto/Range" system. The 3X-9X variable-power "Camputer" series followed in 1969. The Realist version of the military adjustable ranging telescope was based on the Camputer design. (James M. Leatherwood.)

Auto-Ranging Telescope: The Leatherwood Principle

An early military version of the 3X-9X variable-power Realist auto-ranging telescope dating from the late 1960s. Unlike the "fixed-pivot" mounting employed with the AR TEL system, the Leatherwood/Realist design was based on a mount that acted much the same as a large flat-spring. The cam, fastened to the rear of the scope, rested on an extension of the scope rail. As the cam was turned, the angle of elevation of the scope was changed. The aluminum alloy telescope was just over 13 inches in length with a 1-inch tube. Commercial markings appear on the eyepiece; the "3X9" model designation was stamped on the turret housing. The power ring and cam were marked "M118 NM BALL" and numbered 3 to 9 (power). Realist Auto/Range and Camputer models were furnished in a gloss black; military sights were given a dark gray nonglare finish. (Peter R. Senich.)

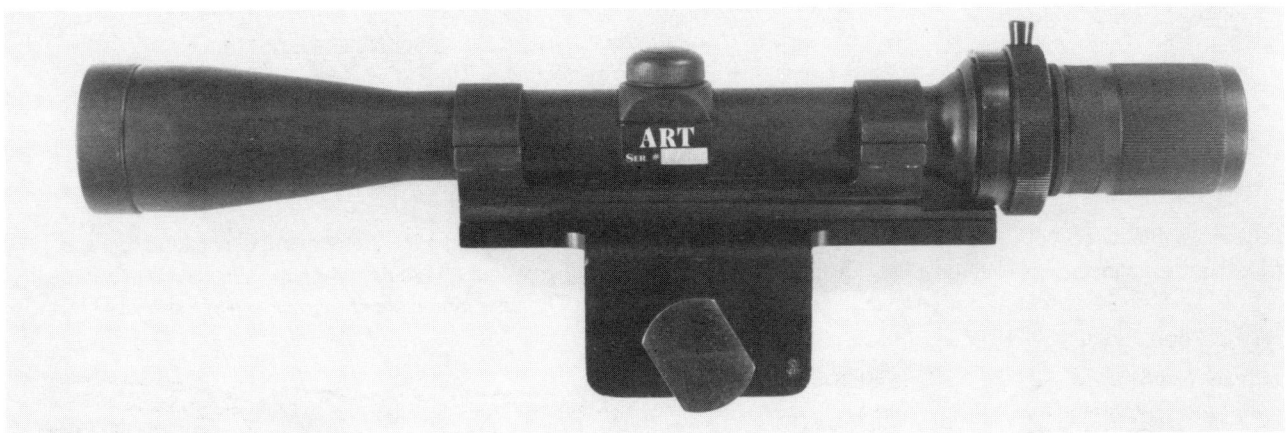

A first-generation Leatherwood/Realist 3X-9X Adjustable Ranging Telescope and mount assembly evaluated by the U.S. Army during the early 1970s. Though tested on more than one occasion, the Realist system was not adopted by the Army during the Vietnam War. Note the configuration of the M14 mount and the mounting screw in this case. (Peter R. Senich.)

sight even though the distance to the target is unknown. Although the invention is adaptable for use on various types of guns, it is particularly useful on hunting rifles because it may be quickly and accurately operated even though the hunter may be under nervous tension at the time of use.

A particular object of the invention is to provide a simplified construction which is adaptable to either fixed focus or variable power scopes.

A further object is to provide a cam operated gun sighting scope which compensates for increased drop of the missile near the end of the trajectory path.

Following graduation with a degree in mathematics, Jim Leatherwood entered the U.S. Army as a second lieutenant. Although Leatherwood had made every effort to interest the major rifle scope manufacturers in his idea, it was the Army, in the midst of its quest for a suitable sniper sight based on a variable-power scope, that entered into a

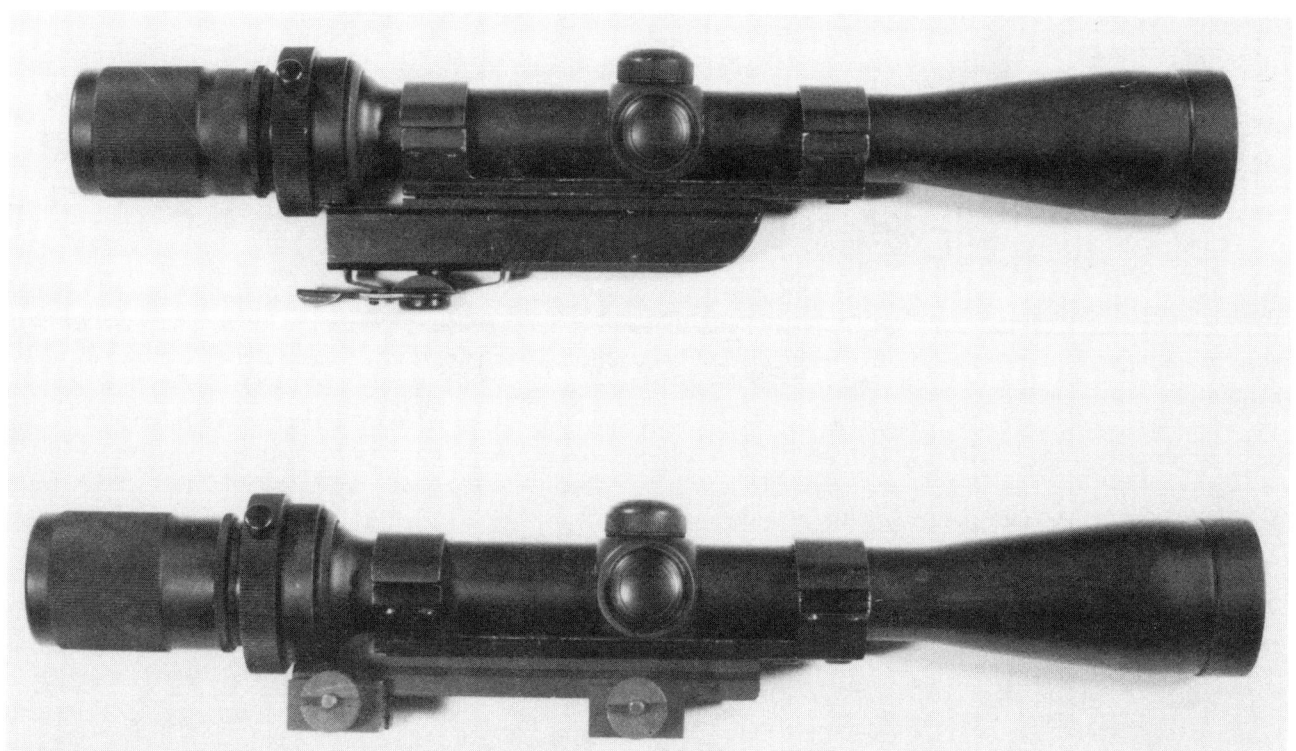

Leatherwood/Realist 3X-9X Adjustable Ranging Telescopes with mountings developed for the Vietnam-era Colt Model 655 and Model 656 experimental M16 sniper rifles. The mounting (top) attached directly to the M16 carrying handle by means of a spring-clip and latch similar to the type used with the 3-power Colt/Realist Scope. The other mount clamped to the top of a special M16 upper receiver. (Peter R. Senich.)

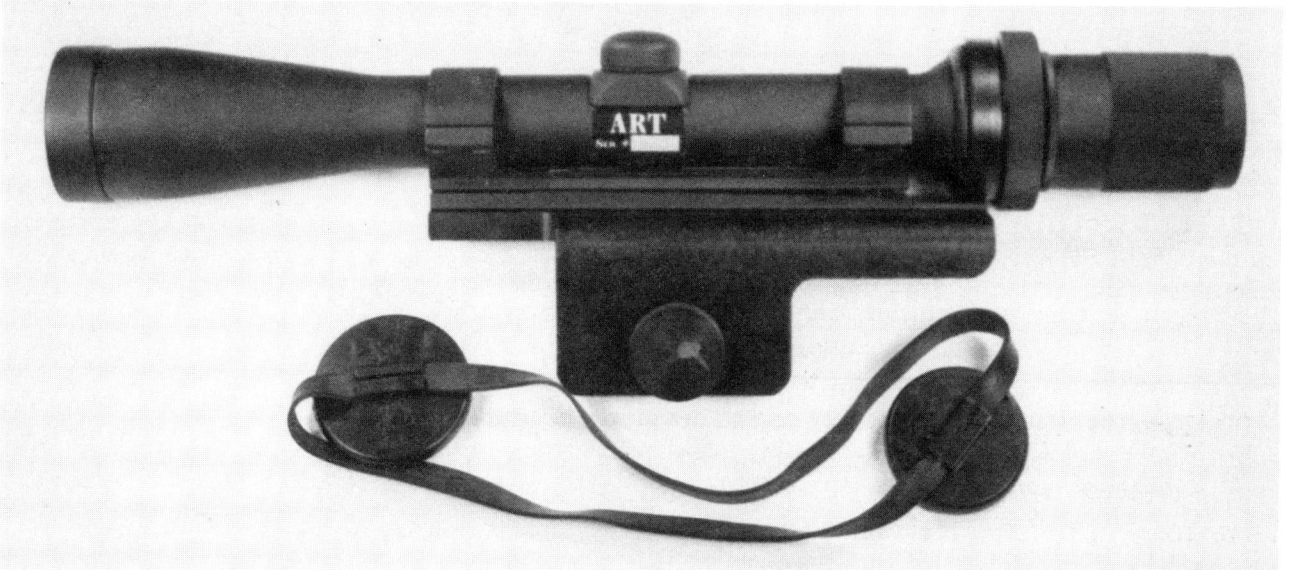

A Leatherwood 3X-9X Adjustable Ranging Telescope with an M14 mounting. The scope is an example of "an early Texas ART" produced and marketed by Leatherwood Bros. during the late 1970s. The lens covers were furnished with the sight. (Peter R. Senich.)

Auto-Ranging Telescope: The Leatherwood Principle

An alternate view of the Leatherwood "Texas ART" with elevation and windage turret caps removed. At one time or another, the Leatherwood/Realist system was referenced as the "ART I" and the "M21" as well. The improved telescope mounting was judged superior to the LWL/ART pivot system, which had a tendency to wear, eventually making it impossible to hold zero. This design withstood 5,000 rounds of continuous fire during tests conducted by the U.S. Navy. (Peter R. Senich.)

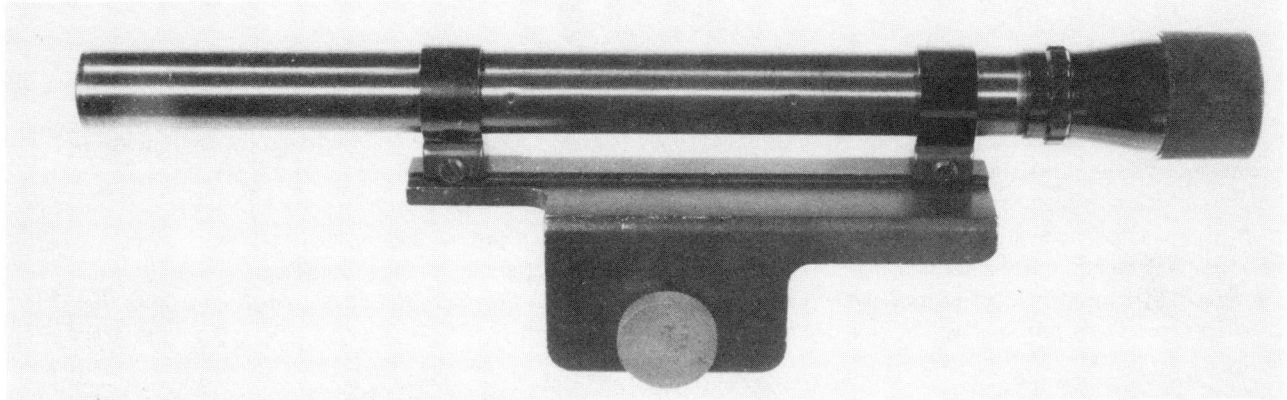

A "Target Acquisition Telescope" and special M14 mounting developed for a joint U.S. Army/Leatherwood/Weaver program in the late 1970s. The unique telescope has no reticle pattern or adjustments. A dovetail was formed on top of the aluminum mount to accommodate Weaver scope rings. The 4-power Weaver sight was intended for training purposes rather than a sniper sight. The scope is 12 5/16 inches long, 7/8 inch in diameter, and has a commercial blue finish. (Peter R. Senich.)

"working agreement" with Leatherwood to develop a military sniper sighting system using his auto-ranging principle.

The Army referred the Leatherwood concept to the Limited Warfare Laboratory in late 1965. A project was initiated, and the first of what became the Adjustable Ranging Telescopes were based on the Redfield 3X-9X variable-power sight, the Leatherwood auto-ranging principle, and a mounting system developed by the LWL at Aberdeen Proving Ground.

As discussed in an earlier chapter, the original tool-room ART series was eventually fielded for combat evaluation by the Army Concept Team In Vietnam (ACTIV) in 1967.

Although some basic testing and development work was conducted

A Leatherwood Bros. 2.5-power telescopic sight tested by the Marine Corps with the M16 rifle in 1977. The fixed-power sight was attached to an M16 military mounting with Weaver-type rings. A "USMC" marking appears on the left side of the turret housing. Realist and, later, Leatherwood telescopic sights were evaluated by the Marine Corps beginning in 1970. (Peter R. Senich.)

A second-generation adjustable ranging telescope described as "one of the original ART II series" with a standard M14 telescope mounting. Although its basic design and operating principles were similar to the earlier models, the ART II displayed a number of new features, including a ranging system with a separate power ring and ballistic cam. A locking thumbscrew on the power ring connected or disconnected the power ring from the ballistic cam. This allowed the sniper to adjust the scope on the target (auto-ranging mode) and then disconnect the thumbscrew to change power (manual mode) without affecting the range adjustment. The ART II was approximately 13 inches in length with a 1-inch main tube. The aluminum alloy sight was given a dull, nonreflective finish. Butler Creek lens covers were furnished with the Leatherwood system. (Peter R. Senich.)

An early-production Leatherwood 3X-9X variable-power ART II dating from the late 1970s, shown with a "Quick-Detachable" (QD) mounting. In this form, the ART II could be removed from a matching base and replaced with no "loss of zero," a feature deemed desirable when the scope was used in conjunction with night vision devices. The early ART II series was stamped "3X9" on the left side of the turret housing and with an "ART" designation (identification plate) on top of the tube. The "Government Model" furnished to the U.S. Army was eventually marked "ART II" as well. (Peter R. Senich.)

Auto-Ranging Telescope: The Leatherwood Principle

A "two-point" Leatherwood M14 telescope mounting developed for use with the Government Model ART II sniper sighting system. Two large mounting screws were used to secure the mount to the rifle. One attached to the left side of the M14 receiver and the other to an altered clip guide in front of the rear sight. In addition to providing increased stability, the mount was designed to compensate for any misalignment between the barrel and receiver. An adjustment incorporated into the rear mounting screw was used for basic windage corrections "only if" the scope would not zero using the internal adjustments. There were two rear mounting screw variations: ART II mounts were furnished with solid rear mounting screw (shown), and a version with a recessed windage adjustment screw. The sight pictured is typical of those furnished to the U.S. Army. (Peter R. Senich.)

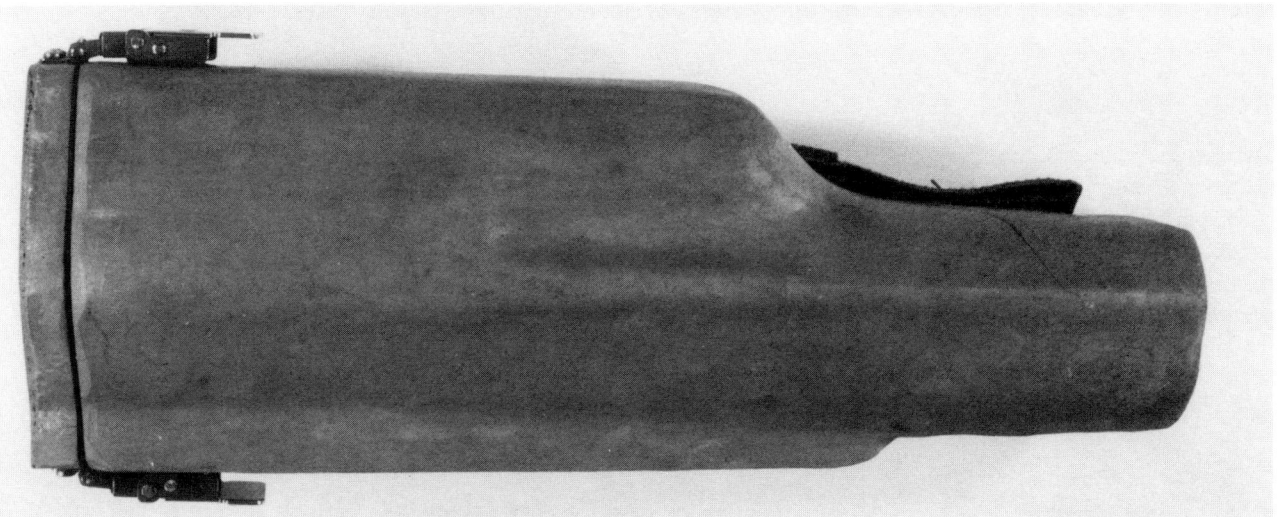

A "standard issue" telescope carrying case intended for the U.S. Army Leatherwood sniper sighting system. The case is made of 1/4-inch-thick laminated fiberglass formed by "heat molding." The rubber sealed cap is secured by two stainless steel latches. The heavy-duty case is 15 inches long and 6 inches wide including both latches. (Peter R. Senich.)

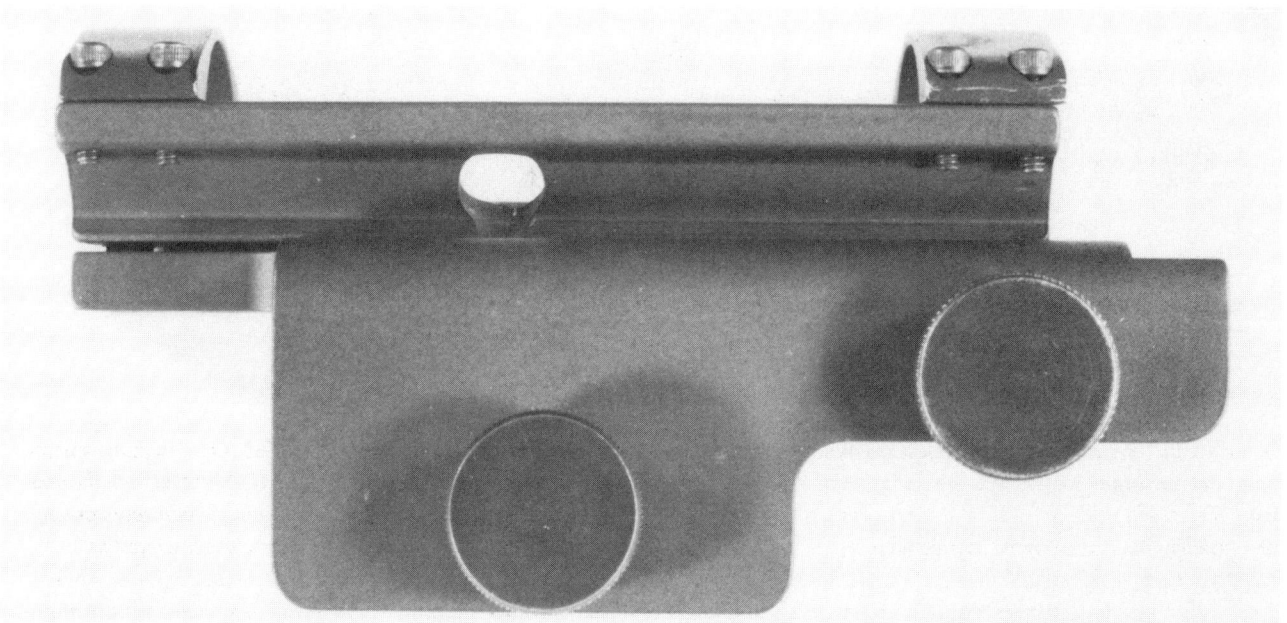

A close view of the "two-point" aluminum telescope mount and ring assembly for the Government Model Leatherwood ART II sniper sighting system. The mount is typical of those furnished to the U.S. Army during the early 1980s. (Peter R. Senich.)

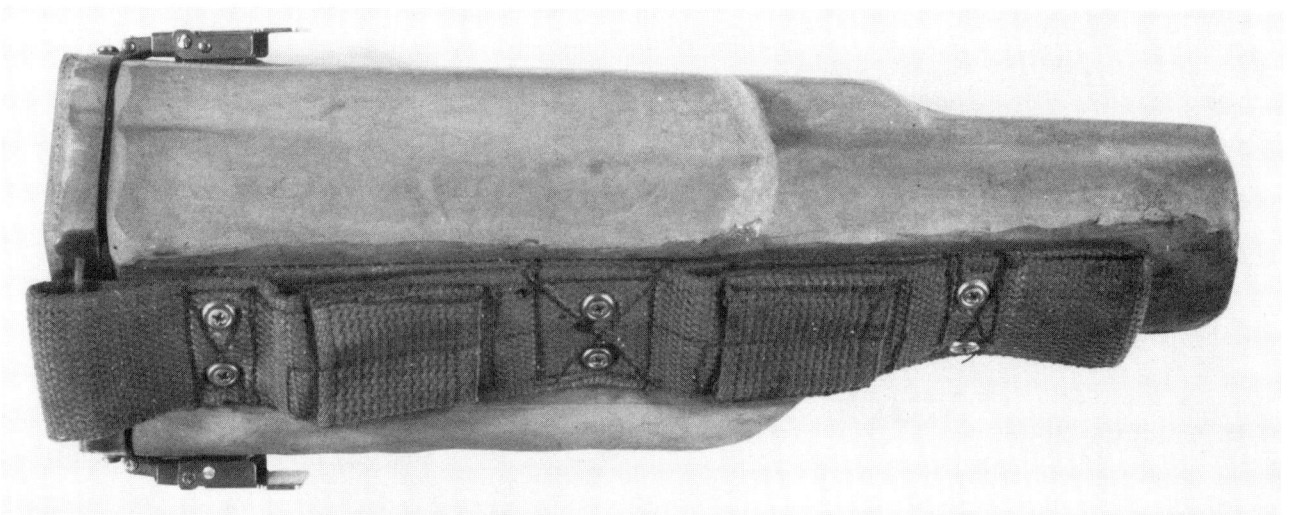

Another view of the ART II carrying case, an extremely durable case some "Airborne" personnel referred to as a "direct descent item" (no parachute necessary). The large web strap served as a hinge and a means of attaching the case to the ammunition belt. The fiberglass case was colored green; an "ART II" designation appears on top of the cap. It would be difficult to imagine a telescope carrying case more rugged than the Leatherwood version. (Peter R. Senich.)

Auto-Ranging Telescope: The Leatherwood Principle

Leatherwood ART/MPC (Military/Police/Civilian) 3X-9X variable-power adjustable ranging telescope dating from the early 1980s. The ART/MPC made use of an "incrementally adjustable range cam" for a variety of cartridges. The ranging system was later incorporated into the "ART II+" series offered by MAC Sales, Inc., the contemporary Leatherwood firm. The "all steel" MPC model was 14 1/16 inches in length with a 1-inch tube diameter. The sight is shown with a quick-detachable mount. (Peter R. Senich.)

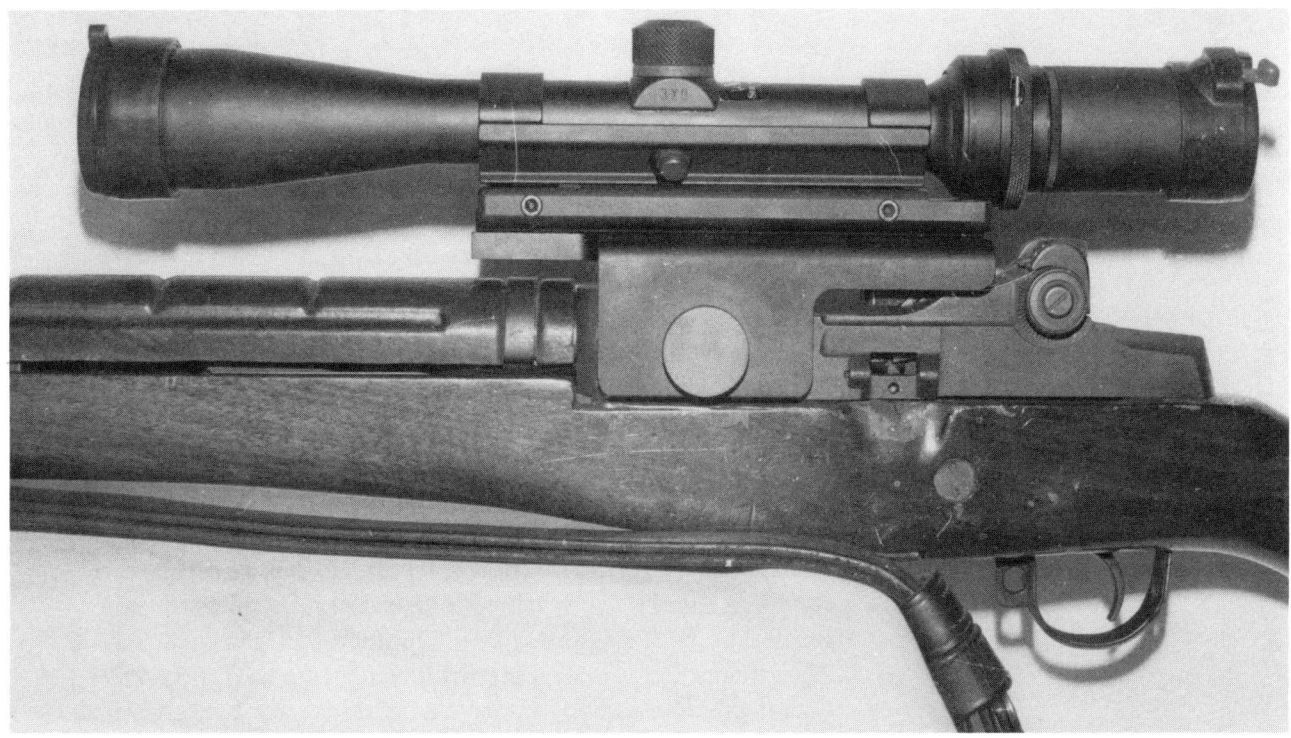

A post-Vietnam Leatherwood 3X-9X Adjustable Ranging Telescope (ART II) with a quick-detachable M14 mount assembly. The sight is an early ART II model. (Charles Leatherwood.)

at Ft. Benning early on, the bulk of the research and development necessary to bring the ART system to an acceptable state was carried out by the Limited Warfare Laboratory.

The Army summarized the benefits of the Adjustable Ranging Telescope as follows:

> One of the greatest advantages of the ART is that it allows a man to be an effective sniper without extensive training in range estimation and ballistics. This permits competent marksmen who are also proficient in other combat skills such as

A view of Charles Leatherwood sighting an ART II-equipped M14 rifle during testing at Stephenville, Texas. (James M. Leatherwood.)

observation, camouflage and concealment, and land navigation to rapidly develop into effective snipers.

[NOTE: With regard to the difficulties associated with training and fielding snipers early on, the officer tasked with establishing the Marine Corps sniping program in South Vietnam in 1965, Maj. Robert A. Russell (Ret.), III Marine Amphibious Force (III MAF), 3d Marine Division, said, "One of the more significant problems we encountered in Vietnam was the individual sniper's inability to estimate range accurately." Even though the Marine Corps eventually selected the Redfield 3X-9X variable-power commercial sight with the Accu-Range range-finding feature for sniper use with this concern in mind, instructing sniper candidates in range estimation and correct "holds and leads" remained an essential part of the USMC sniper training syllabus during the war in Vietnam. Apart from the difficulties affecting the USMC Redfield system at large, the Accu-Range feature did alleviate this problem to some extent.]

Though it is rarely noted, according to pertinent documents, 1st Lieutenant Leatherwood, in addition to his early involvement with the emerging ART system, while assigned to the Weapons Department at the Infantry School (USAIS) at Ft. Benning, received official recognition for "inventions" that included "a subcaliber device for the M72 LAW, improvements on the subcaliber device for the 90mm Recoilless Rifle, and a field expedient mortar sight."

By the time the Army had progressed to actual combat use of the ART, Leatherwood had reached a "business agreement" with Realist,

Auto-Ranging Telescope: The Leatherwood Principle

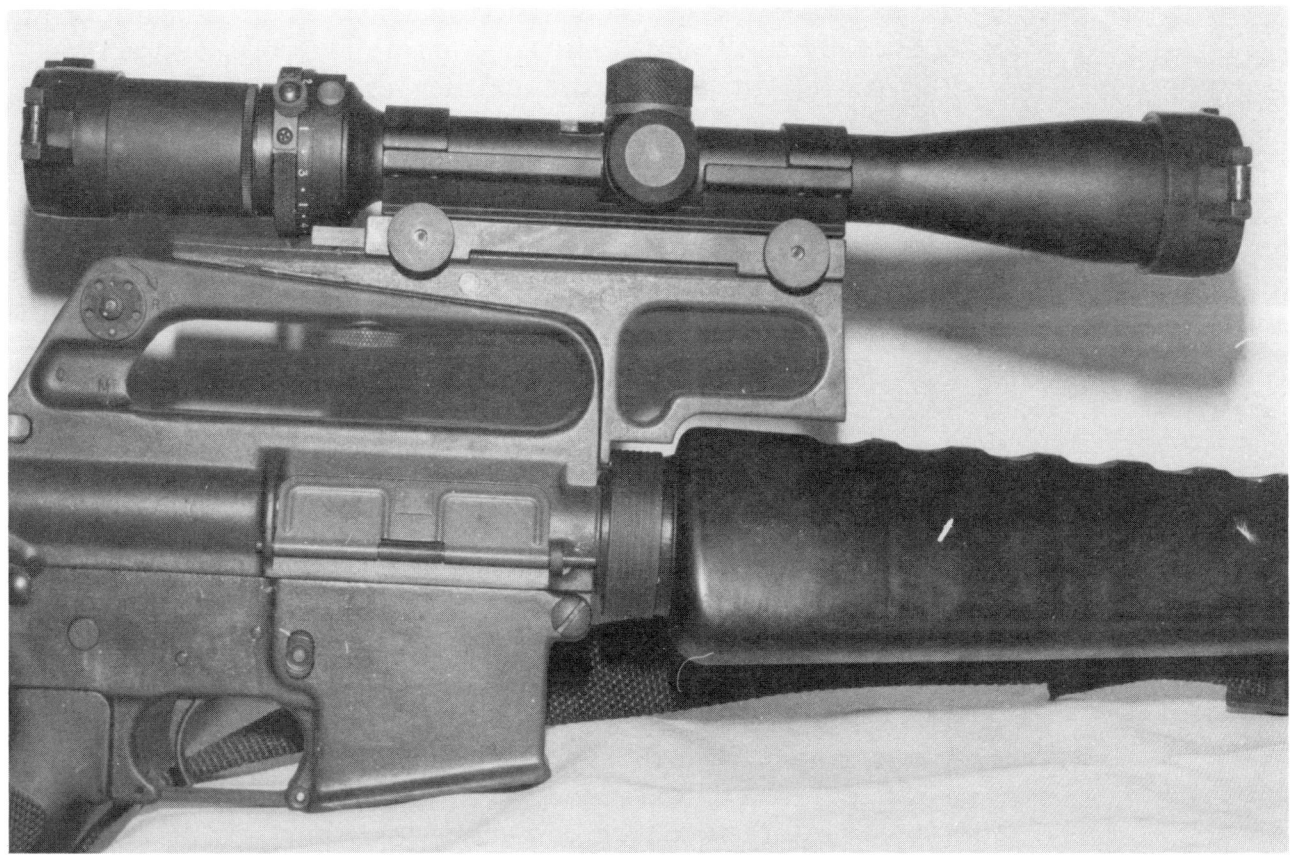

A post-Vietnam 3X-9X Adjustable Ranging Telescope (ART II) with a quick-detachable mounting on a Leatherwood AR15/M16 aluminum base. The "military mounting" extended beyond the carrying handle to provide a balance point for the rifle. The extension also gave extra support to the scope and proper eye relief as well. (Charles Leatherwood.)

Inc., a respected optical firm with more than 60 years of experience producing surveying instruments, to produce and market telescopic rifle sights based on his patent.

NOTE: Although Realist had manufactured and marketed a line of fixed- and variable-power rifle scopes, the arrangement with Leatherwood marked its entry into the auto-ranging field. Until then, one of the most notable rifle sights produced by Realist was universally known as the "Colt/Realist Scope," a compact 3-power telescopic sight made for Colt Industries as a "private label brand" for use with their AR15 and M16 rifles.

The first Realist scope to offer the auto-ranging feature, a fixed-power model (6-power), was introduced in early 1968 as the "Auto/Range" system. A 4-power (fixed-power) version followed, and in 1969 Realist introduced the 1.5X-4.5X and 3X-9X variable-power sights referenced as the "Camputer Scopes" as well.

Following a tour of duty in Vietnam and his subsequent release from the Army as a captain, Leatherwood was actively involved with Realist developing a military version of the 3X-9X variable-power

"Camputer" design. Though the military tested it thoroughly, it did not adopt the Realist Adjustable Ranging Telescope, despite various improvements and optical qualities which military and civilian authorities rated as "excellent."

Although Realist would continue its efforts to replace the Army AR TEL with its sighting system, Leatherwood left the firm in early 1970, joining Mitch WerBell at Sionics, Inc. (later Military Armament Corp., or MAC), where he applied his engineering skills to a wide range of specialized military hardware being generated by the WerBell organization.

With his vision of the auto-ranging telescope unrealized, however, Leatherwood returned to Stephenville, Texas, where he formed his own company, Leatherwood Brothers, for the express purpose of developing an optimum rifle scope for combat use.

The war in Southeast Asia was all but over by this time, and while Realist design efforts culminated in the tacit acceptance of its ART system by both the Army and the Navy, the firm had already decided to divest itself of the rifle scope business and concentrate on its successful line of David White surveying instruments. Realist terminated the manufacture of all telescopic sights and, in 1974, sold the remaining Auto/Range and Camputer scopes and components to the Leatherwood organization, where they were subsequently produced and marketed as the Leatherwood/Realist Scopes.

The Leatherwood firm continued with research and development, however, and by 1978 the second-generation adjustable ranging telescope was nearing production status as the ART II, an auto-ranging system described as "a rifle scope designed to eliminate the deficiencies found in the previous ART systems."

Whether or not the Leatherwood ART was the optimum adjustable ranging telescope remained to be seen. Regardless of whether or not it was ideal, however, the ART II was certainly the only serious contender at that juncture.

The Vietnam-era ART had been in service for 10 years at that point, and the "positive improvements" displayed by the new model prompted the Army to purchase the second-generation Leatherwood ART II as a replacement for the aging Redfield/Frankford Arsenal AR TEL system.

In June 1980, Jim Leatherwood realized one of his original goals: the direct sale of a quantity of Leatherwood-designed auto-ranging rifle telescopes to the U.S. Army. The innovative ART/MPC followed (an auto-ranging scope that required only one cam for a wide variety of rifle cartridges) in 1981, and for a time the Leatherwood line of adjustable ranging telescopes was the sighting system of choice for law enforcement and military applications throughout the world.

Without question, for a relatively small firm and a handful of Texans to have influenced the course of military rifle scope development as long as they have is a feat that can only be described as remarkable.

CHAPTER 6

A Riflescope for the M16

By the time the last American combat forces had been withdrawn from South Vietnam, the 5.56mm, M16A1 rifle manufactured by the Colt Firearms Division, Colt Industries, had emerged as the standard U.S. infantry weapon. Though maligned repeatedly for its marginal reliability and accuracy at extended ranges, the weapon the Vietcong had reportedly dubbed the "Black Rifle" had served as the basic shoulder arm for American, South Vietnamese, Korean, and other allied forces as well.

What started out in Southeast Asia as the AR-15 progressed in form as the M16, the XM16E1, and, finally, the 5.56mm assault rifle became the M16A1 and was type-classified "Standard A" by the U.S. Army on 23 February 1967.

(**NOTE:** In the interest of avoiding any possible confusion, except where noted otherwise, the 5.56mm infantry rifle is simply referenced as the "M16" in this volume.)

From a standpoint of sniper use, contrary to most beliefs, the M16 did receive official consideration as a sniping arm but could not match the consistent long-range accuracy of the M14 rifle. This was proven conclusively by innumerable tests the M16 was subjected to over an extended period by various agencies.

NOTE: In one case, a report by Maj. Ray Orton, Chief of the USAMTU Test & Evaluation Section, concerning M16 accuracy testing (12 August 1969) stated the following, in part:

A 3-power (3X25) Sniper Scope intended for the 7.62mm Armalite AR-10 Rifle manufactured by Artillerie-Inrichtengen (A.I.) of Hemburg-Zaandam (Holland) for a brief period during the early 1960s. Though originally designed for the AR-10 rifle, with minor changes, the unique A.I. sights were produced for an emerging 5.56mm Colt/Armalite AR-15 assault rifle beginning in March 1960. The illustration appeared in the instruction booklet for the AR-10 rifle scope. (R.H.G. Koster.)

A late 1950s instruction booklet for the 3-power A.I. telescopic sight made for the "Dutch AR-10." The sights were manufactured by Artillerie-Inrichtengen in its optical facility (Delft Optics) in Delft, Holland. (R.H.G. Koster.)

„Artillerie-Inrichtingen"
HEMBRUG — ZAANDAM   THE NETHERLANDS

Description of
Sniper Scope 3 x 25
for ArmaLite AR-10 Rifle

A Riflescope for the M16

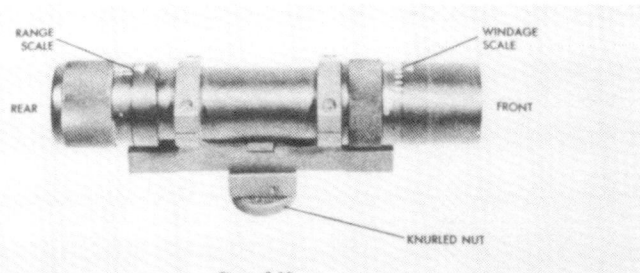

Figure 2-10

Telescopic Sight

The telescopic sight is a 3-power telescope with an inverted post reticle, coated lenses, and internal windage and range adjustments. The sight is shown in figure 2-10.

MOUNTING. To mount the telescope on the rifle, unscrew the knurled nut from the mounting bolt on the telescope. Insert the mounting bolt of the telescope through the hole in the carrying handle of the rifle. Make sure the range adjustment ring of the scope is toward the butt of the rifle. The range adjustment ring has the figures "1" and "2" and is shown in figure 2-8.

Screw the knurled nut on the mounting bolt and tighten securely, making sure that the mounting lug on the bottom of the scope fits securely in the groove in the top of the carrying handle, as shown in figure 2-11. Check the security of mounting by grasping the scope and exerting a firm side-to-side pressure to see that the scope does not loosen. When the telescope is securely mounted, it may then be zeroed to the rifle.

ZEROING. The telescope should be zeroed on a 100 or 200 yard known distance range on a calm day. Before firing, look through the telescope and center the tip of the post reticle in the field of view by turning the windage and range adjustment rings. Figure 2-12 illustrates the inverted post type reticle. Disregard the triangular index marks during the zeroing procedures. Fire the rifle and zero the scope, making sight adjustments with the windage and range adjusting rings. When the scope is zeroed to the rifle, *index* the zero settings.

Figure 2-11

Figure 2-12

AF MANUAL 50-12

The Department of the Air Force manual no. 50-12, Rifle, AR-15 (30 August 1963), the original Air Force training manual for the 5.56mm assault rifle, provided operating details for the A.I. telescopic sight. An early-issue item, the telescope was made in Holland and imported into the United States for use with the AR-15 weapon system. The telescope mounting was furnished by Colt. The Air Force was the first branch of the U.S. armed forces to adopt the AR-15 assault rifle. The initial purchase was approved on 15 May 1962. (U.S. Air Force.)

The M14 rifle shows a superiority over the M16 for accuracy and maintains the necessary accuracy for sniping up to 900 meters range. Previous trajectory tests have shown a decided drop of the 55 grain bullet after passing 300 meters range. If the use of the M16 is contemplated at ranges greater than 300 meters in a sniper role, research should be conducted for a heavier bullet and faster twist barrel combination.

As compared to the M14, however, the M16's integral carrying handle made it possible to attach rather simple telescope mounts over the receiver in line with the bore. As a result, a considerable number of telescopic-sighted M16s were pressed into service in Vietnam well in advance of the match-grade M14s, the highly sophisticated XM21 system, and an organized sniping program.

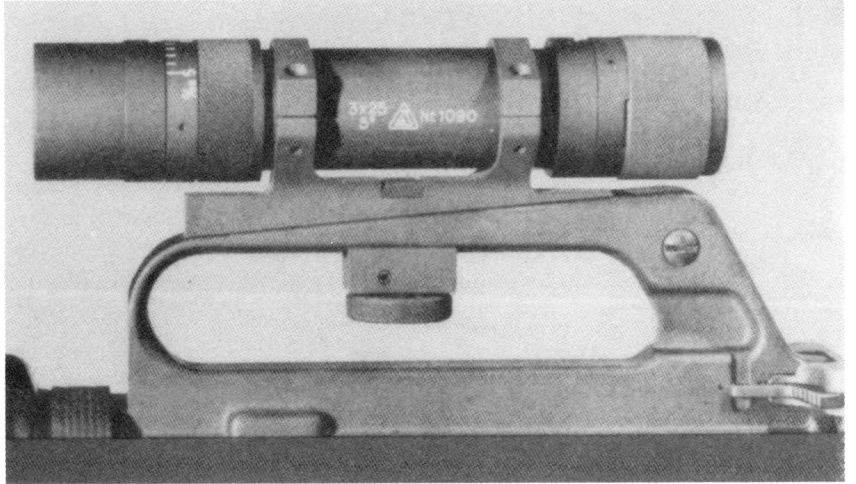

A 3-power (3x25) A.I. telescopic sight (No. 1090) with an AR-15 rifle from a 1964 Colt brochure. According to R.H.G. Koster, a past employee of Artillerie-Inrichtengen and an authority on the Dutch AR-10 rifle, a total of 794 AR-15 sights (1 and 2 range scale numbering) were made for the 5.56mm Colt assault rifle between March 1960 and July 1962. So far as can be determined, there were no sights shipped to the United States after January 1963. (Thomas Collection.)

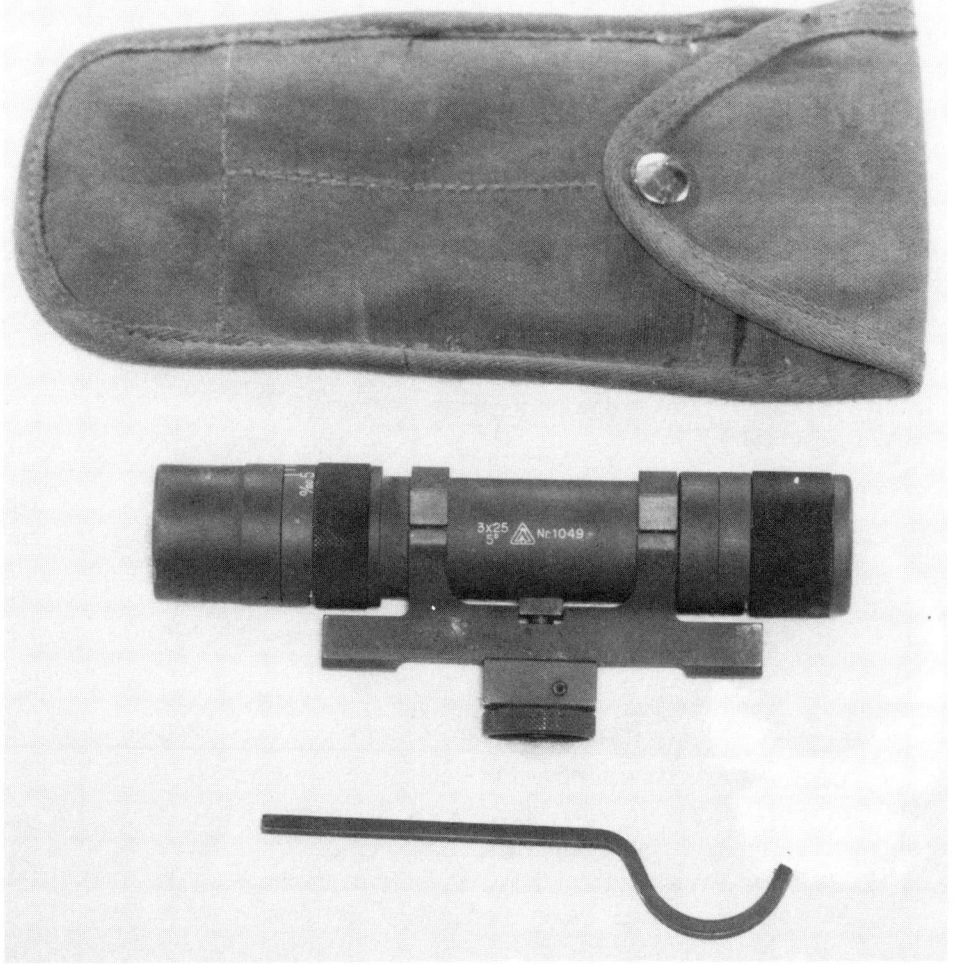

An A.I. telescopic sight, carrying case, and spanner wrench originally issued with an AR-15 assault rifle. The 3-power scope is approximately 7 inches long with a 1.180-inch-diameter main tube. Windage adjustments were made by turning the knurled ring at the front of the scope (left). The elevation ring was located at the opposite end. Although windage graduations remained the same as those of the original A.I. sights, the range scale (elevation) on the AR-15 models was marked 1 and 2 rather than 1 to 7 (100 to 700 meters), as on the AR-10 version. The special wrench was used for indexing the range and windage scales to the adjustment rings after the scope was zeroed to the rifle. The sight has an inverted post reticle; the model designation, an A.I. logo, and the telescope serial number appear on the side of the tube (the number "3X25" indicates 3-power with a 25mm objective lens diameter; the field of view is 5 degrees). The aluminum alloy scope and mount have a black anodized finish. The mount assembly attached directly to the carrying handle of the AR-15 or M16 rifle. Though originally procured for the AR-15 , the 3-power A.I. rifle scopes were also employed with M16 rifles in Southeast Asia. In this case, the sight pictured was fielded by the Marine Corps during the mid-1960s. According to A.I. packing list No. 53950, telescope No. 1049 was among 35 3x25 scopes, with cover and key (carrying case and spanner wrench), shipped to the United States from Holland on 12 September 1962. (Cors Collection.)

A Riflescope for the M16

A close view of an AR-15 telescope mount for the 3-power A.I. telescopic sight. The mount and rings were fabricated from aluminum alloy; the mounting screw and related components are hardened steel. A part number (62215) and both "Colt" and "Armalite" markings appear on the left side of the mount. The mount was used to adapt the "Dutch scope" to the early 5.56mm assault rifle. The A.I. telescope and the Colt mounting were pictured in the original Colt/Armalite AR-15 brochure. (Atchisson Collection.)

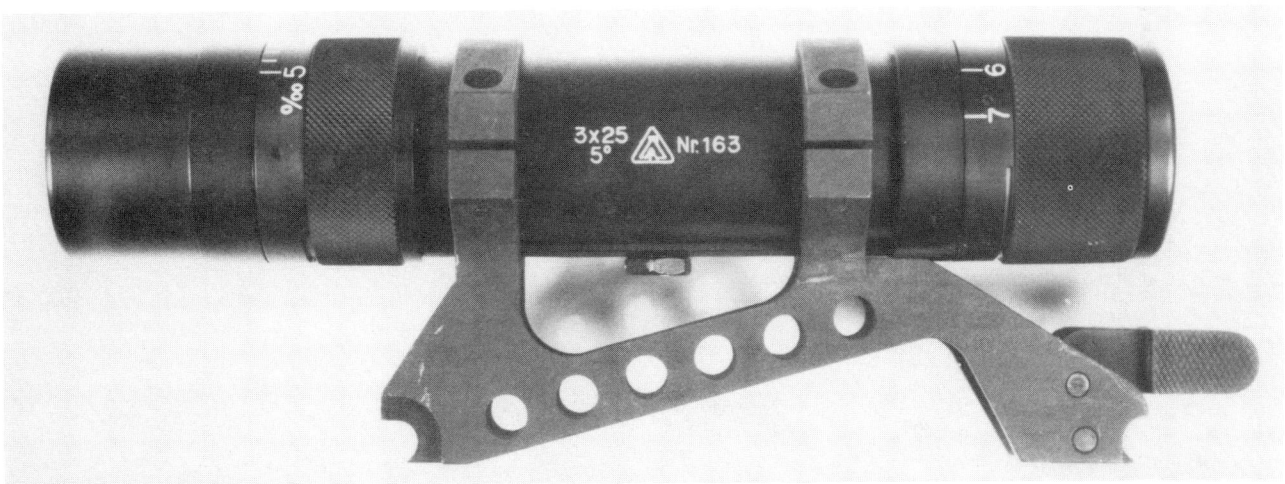

A 3-power A.I. telescopic sight and mounting made by NWM De Kruithoorn N.V., S-Hertogenbosch, Holland, intended for the 5.56mm Stoner 63A1 Assault Rifle. In this case, the telescope and mount ("quick-release adapter") were illustrated in an NWM sales brochure dating from the late 1960s. Though unconfirmed, it is believed that the sight (No. 163) was part of a small lot purchased by NWM from A.I. stock originally made for the AR-10 rifle. Except for minor details, the scope is essentially the same as the AR-15 model, the most notable difference being the range scale numbered 1 through 7. The prototype telescope mount attached to the Stoner assault rifle directly over the rear sight, a spring-latch holding the mount in place. The telescope mount is made of steel, the scope of aluminum alloy. The entire unit has a black matte finish. The mount pictured is the only known example. Despite some combat use of the Stoner 63A assault rifle by the Marine Corps and the 63A1/MK 23 light machine gun by Navy SEAL teams, so far as it is known, telescopic sights were not employed with the Stoner weapon system in Vietnam. (Tarble Collection.)

Nevertheless, with telescopic sights in short supply on an overall basis, especially during the early stages of the war, enterprising units and individuals brought commercial sights from the States or procured them as best they could. Resultantly, an untold number of M16s with rifle scopes were fielded under these or similar circumstances.

An example of this activity was recorded by Robert D. Parrish in his work, *Combat Recon: My Year with the ARVN* (Saint Martin's Press,

A 1965 catalog illustration for the Colt AR-15 Sporter Scope. The replacement for the 3x25 A.I. telescopic sight, the 3-power rifle scope was specifically designed for the AR-15 (M16) by Realist, Inc., of Menomonee Falls, Wisconsin, as a "private label brand" for Colt Industries. Though referenced as a "sporter scope," the compact sight was also pictured in sales literature for the Colt 5.56mm "Military Weapon Systems." The availability of a suitable telescopic sight enhanced the versatility of a weapon system. The Colt/Realist Scope was designed for this purpose. (Thomas Collection.)

USAMTU gunsmith Raymond Behnay, a retired master sergeant, fabricated M16 telescope mounts at his own expense for Army sniper use in Vietnam. The mount was designed to accommodate the 2.2-power M84 telescopic sight using Weaver commercial rings and bases. The blued steel "tip-off" rings clamped securely to the dovetail bases. (Lt. Col. F.B. Conway, Ret.)

A Riflescope for the M16

The Behnay M16 telescope mount with the rings removed. Telescopic sights and mounting hardware in short supply during early combat. An untold number of improvised mounts were sent to Vietnam under similar circumstances. (Lt. Col. F.B. Conway, Ret.)

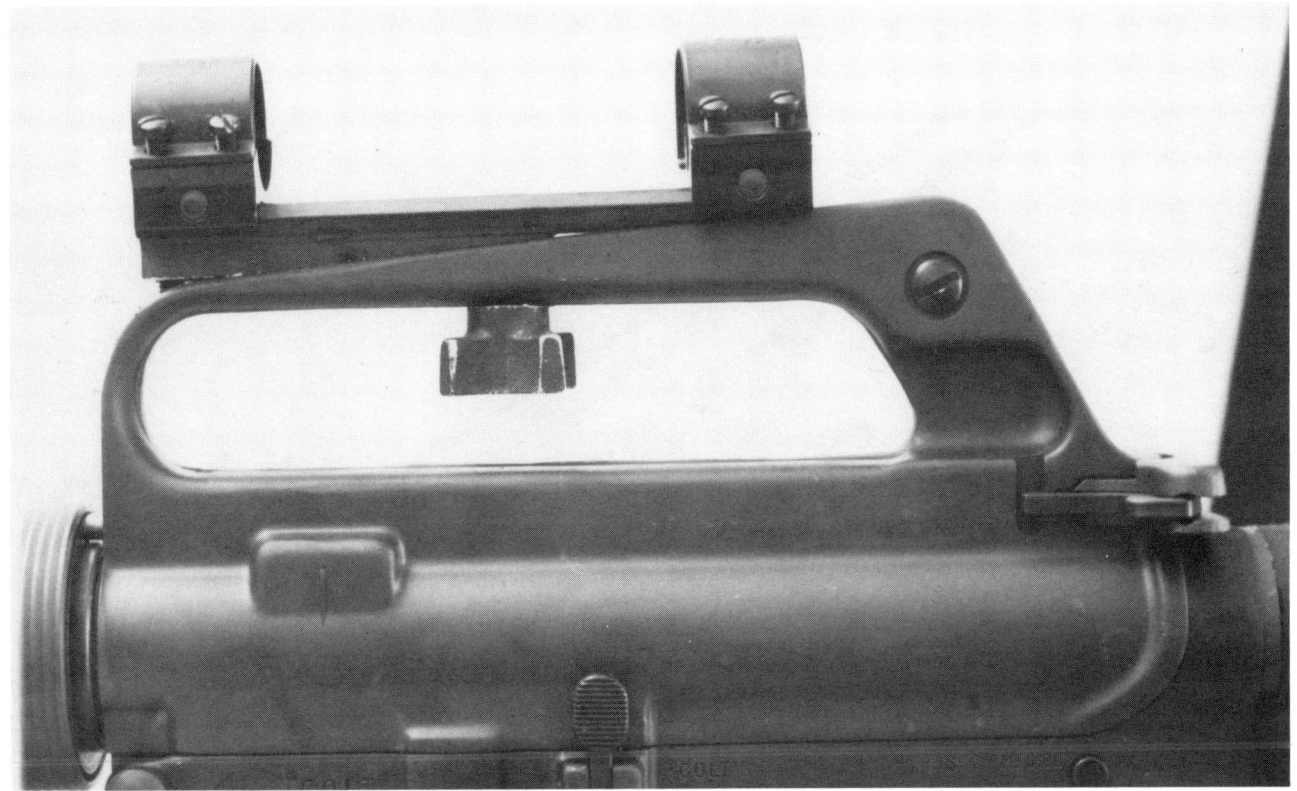

Cook telescope base and Weaver ring set issued in 1967 for mounting the M84 telescope to the M16 rifle. The threaded knob secured the rail to the M16 carrying handle. (Lt. Col. F.B. Conway, Ret.)

1992). An Army lieutenant attached to the Military Assistance Command, Vietnam (MACV) while serving as an advisor to an infantry battalion in the 5th ARVN Division, Parrish was armed with an M16 mounting a 3X-9X variable-power commercial scope and mount he reportedly had purchased from a gunshop in Hawaii. Among the field experiences with the scope-sighted M16 that Parrish made note of was the following:

The Cook M16 mount assembly removed from the rifle. (Lt. Col. F.B. Conway, Ret.)

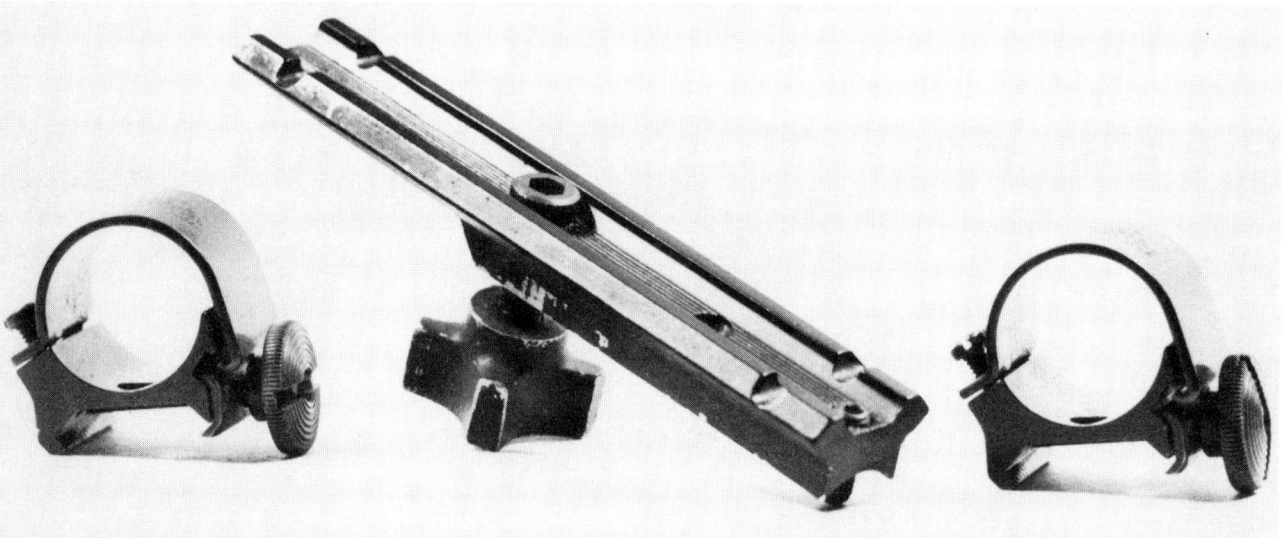

Cook telescope mount with the Weaver scope rings removed from the base. The scope rings were made of steel, the rail of aluminum alloy. In this case, the "quick-detachable" rings allowed the scope to be removed from the rifle with the base remaining. (Lt. Col. F.B. Conway, Ret.)

This was too good to be true. You rarely saw live VC, and to have them running across a 300-meter-wide field in broad daylight was really something. I told the riflemen that I'd take over for a while and carefully laid my M16 on the pile of dirt in front of me. I had just gotten ready when another Charlie broke for a stump. He was about 200 meters away, and I put the scope's cross hairs just a little in front of his chest. I squeezed the trigger and the rifle kicked. When I brought the scope back on target, he was nowhere to be seen, but the cheering from the soldiers told me it was a good kill.

As uncomplicated as it was to mount a rifle scope on the M16

A Riflescope for the M16

A Cook AR-15 Base and Weaver 7/8" Top Mount Ring Set are shown with the original Vietnam-era ordnance packaging. (Lt. Col. F.B. Conway, Ret.)

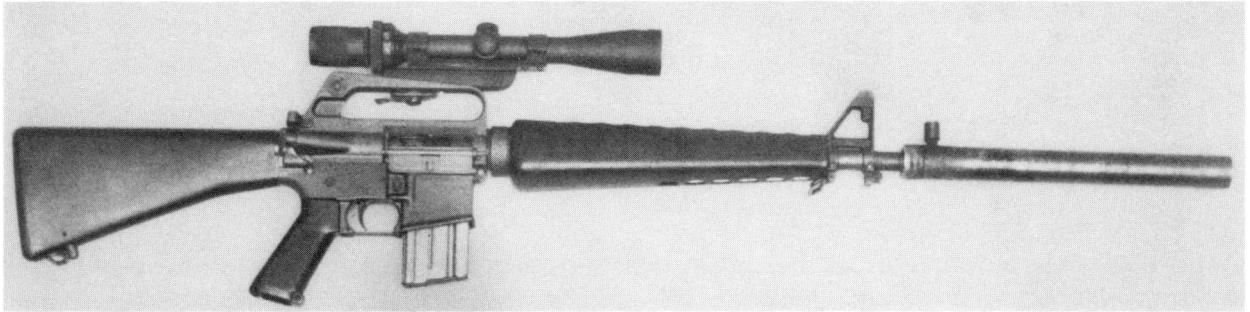

Experimental Colt M16 sniper rifle mounting a Leatherwood/Realist 3X-9X Adjustable Ranging Telescope and Sionics (MAC) MAW-A1 noise suppressor. Colt developed a number of special rifles, including heavy-barrel variants, to evaluate the M16's suitability for sniper use in Southeast Asia. In this case, Colt referenced the weapon as the Model 655 Sniper Rifle. (U.S. Army.)

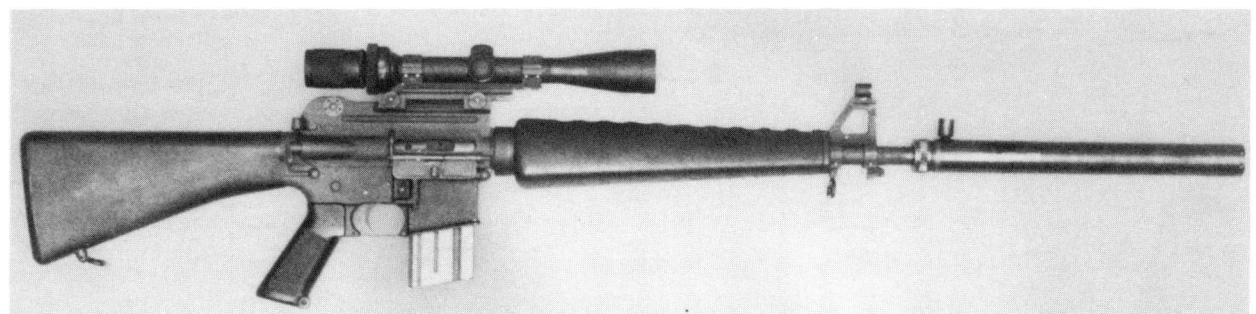

Colt Model 656 Sniper Rifle with Leatherwood/Realist ART and Sionics MAW-A1 suppressor. Note the telescope mounted on a special reconfigured M16 upper receiver. Experimental sniper rifles were often field-tested by experienced combat personnel in Vietnam, the object being to increase the probability of an accurate evaluation. (U.S. Army.)

An M16 telescope mounting developed and manufactured by Military Armament Corp. The die-cast aluminum mount was 7.880 inches long and .680 inch wide. As this is an early version, a Weaver commercial base (scope rail) was attached to the top of the mount. Specifications for the scope mount were detailed on a MAC engineering drawing dated 15 September 1970. (Atchisson Collection.)

Realist 1.5X-4.5X variable-power telescopic sight with an M16 "military mounting" employed by an Army sniper instructor in Vietnam. An auto-ranging version of the Realist "Brushscope" (11 inches long with a 1-inch tube), the sight was originally designed for use in heavy cover. Many of the small variable-power commercial sights were employed in Southeast Asia. Their size, weight, and ranging capabilities made them practical choices for the M16 rifle. (Peter R. Senich.)

(despite its marginal success in a sniping capacity), a surprising variety of telescopic sights were to see combat with this weapon system in Southeast Asia. While the vast majority of these were simply M16s with telescopic sights of one kind or another, in some cases, noise suppressors were employed with this combination as well.

By all accounts, however, of the myriad rifle scopes (fixed-power and variable-power) fielded with the M16 during this era, the 3-power Colt/Realist model appears to have been a popular choice. During the course of the war, the compact sight would see duty in diverse applications, including combat use by the various U.S. "special mission groups."

Though it was never adequately explained, many combat personnel

A Riflescope for the M16

The M16 military mounting extended beyond the carrying handle to provide a balance point for the rifle and extra support for the scope. A design progression in this case, the telescope base and the mount were eventually formed in one piece. The rail was configured for "Weaver-type" rings. The mount was developed and fielded for a Vietnam-era Colt-U.S. Army program. (Lt. Col. F.B. Conway, Ret.)

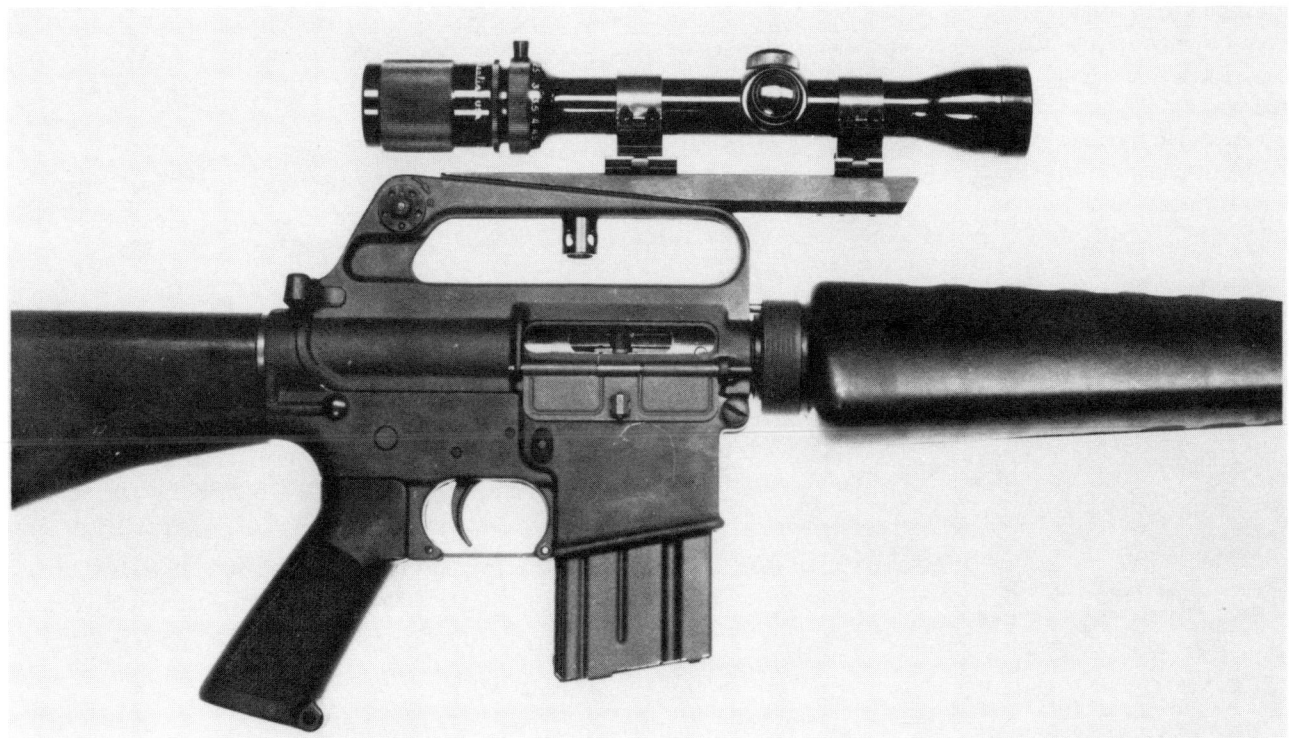

A variant MAC AR-15/M16 telescope mounting intended for military and law enforcement applications. The telescope is a Realist 1.5X-4.5X variable-power Brushscope, a commercial model dating from the late 1960s. Military Armament Corp. offered telescope mountings as an adjunct to its line of specialized hardware. Compare this version of the Realist Brushscope with the auto-ranging model pictured on p. 130. (Thomas Collection.)

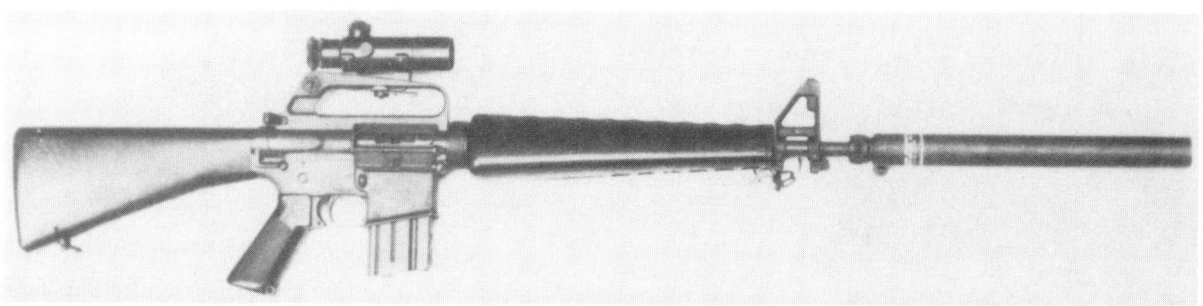

A 5.56mm Colt M16 rifle fitted with a Sionics MAW-A1 noise and flash suppressor and 3-power Colt/Realist telescopic sight. Although M16s equipped with suppressors were employed primarily by recon and special mission personnel, the compact rifle scope saw widespread use in Southeast Asia. (Pattern Room Collection.)

Noted firearms designer Max Atchisson during weapons testing at Ft. Benning, Georgia, circa 1970. The weapon is an experimental M16 rifle fitted with components Atchisson designed and developed. The selective-fire assault rifle fired from the open bolt position and featured a "cyclic rate reducer," a special muzzle brake (variable vector compensator), and a 90-round "Assault Tri-Mag." A standard M16/M16A1 could be readily transformed into a dual-purpose squad automatic weapon (SAW) without alterations or permanent modifications. The Atchisson M16 Commonality System was produced by WAK Inc., of Fairborn, Ohio. (Maxwell G. Atchisson.)

Another view of the Atchisson experimental M16 assault rifle. The telescope is a 3X-9X Leatherwood/Realist ART fitted to an M16 military mount. Though not intended for sniping purposes, according to Max Atchisson, the weapon proved to be "extremely accurate for long-range automatic fire." A special "one-piece night sight" was also offered with the system. (Maxwell G. Atchisson.)

A Riflescope for the M16

Vietnam-era AR-18 5.56mm selective-fire assault rifle with the 3-power compact scope. An accessory item, the telescopic sight attached to a dovetail base on top of the receiver. The workings of the telescope and the mount assembly were detailed in the Armalite instruction manual. Both Colt- and Armalite-marked 3-power sights were reportedly fielded with this system. Though tested by the Air Force and the Army, the AR-18 rifle was not adopted for military use. Note the telescope mounting made for use with the AR-18 rifle. (Thomas Collection.)

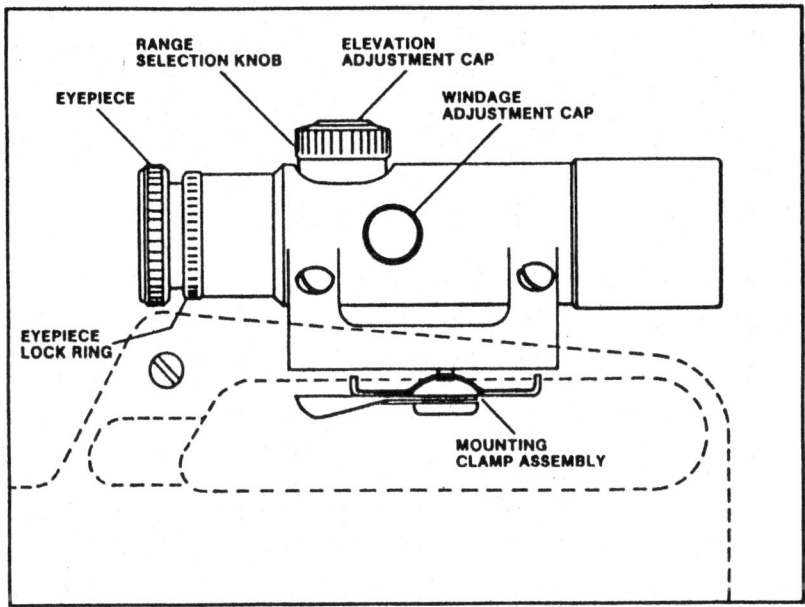

An early illustration for the Colt AR-15 3-power "Sporter Rifle Scope" lists the various components of the sight. (Gary Fellers.)

favored the Colt scope, apparently for no other reason than its diminutive size. Despite its limitations, the Colt telescope was considered "effective enough" in the 200- to 300-meter range.

As a major source of controversy during U.S. involvement in Southeast Asia, the M16 had seemingly endless claims of inconsistent reliability and marginal accuracy leveled against it.

Responding in part, Louis A. Garavaglia gave his impression of the M16 in an article in *American Rifleman* (January 1968) entitled "Snipers in Vietnam Also Need Firepower":

> Despite the derogatory remarks published about the relia-

A post-Vietnam Colt Industries 3-power telescopic sight ("Colt 3X20"). The 6-inch-long aluminum alloy scope has a main tube diameter of 1.380 inch. The elevation adjustment turret is located on top; the windage adjustment is positioned on the right. Early reticle patterns consisted of an inverted post with crosshairs; a duplex reticle was added later. The scope and mount have a black matte finish. The mount assembly attached to an AR-15 or M16 carrying handle with a spring-clip and latch ("mounting clamp assembly"). Lens covers were furnished with the scope. Colt procured the sights when the Realist model was no longer available (out of production). Except for variant markings and the length of the reduced tube diameter directly in front of the eyepiece, the scopes were virtually identical to the original Realist model. The second-generation AR-15/M16 Colt Scope was manufactured in Japan. The compact rifle sight is still available from Colt in a 4x20 version. (Peter R. Senich.)

bility of the M16A1, our sniper teams used these controversial weapons quite successfully on a limited basis.

Even though his unit, a 4th Division Long-Range Recon Patrol Company, made use of M84-equipped M14 rifles for sniping purposes, as Lieutenant Garavaglia continued:

> We found the M16A1 accurate "as issued." The crack shots in my unit could sometimes hit 6" x 6" targets offhand at 200 meters. Not only is this distance greater than that at which most kills were made, it also indicates the weapon can hit more

A Riflescope for the M16

An alternate view (left) of the Colt Industries 3x20 telescopic sight. (Peter R. Senich.)

A comparison between a "2.75X20mm" (so marked) telescopic sight intended for the AR-15/M16 rifle (top) and a scope marketed by Colt Industries ("3X20"). The Colt-marked scope has a duplex reticle pattern; the other has an inverted post with crosshairs. Both sights were made in Japan. Except for the markings and the reticle patterns, the sights are essentially the same. (Gary Fellers.)

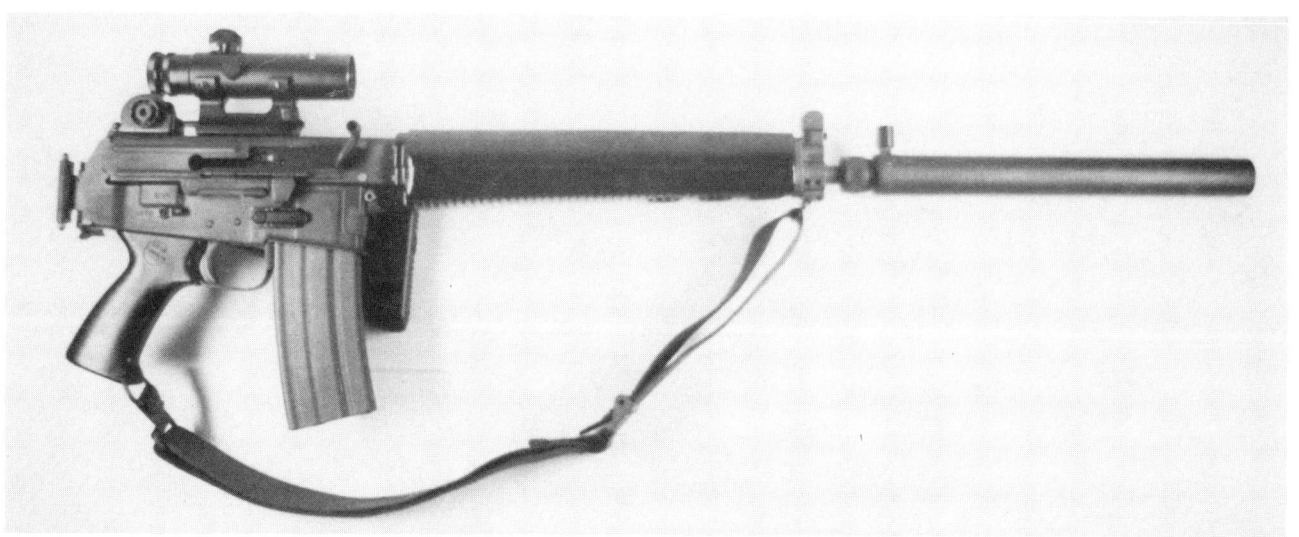

An AR-18 assault rifle with the 3-power scope, Sionics MAW-A1 noise and flash suppressor, and buttstock in the folded position. Considered by many as the "first cousin of the M16," AR-18 rifles saw limited combat exposure in "certain applications." (Thomas Collection.)

Max Atchisson with an Atchisson/M16 9mm Parabellum silenced sniper carbine, an innovative design with the silencer built directly into the M16 forearm. The telescope is a Weaver C-6, 6-power model. Note the heat-resistant padding covering the silencer, 9mm magazine, and sliding buttstock. The unique weapon was offered to the U.S. Army during the mid-1970s. (Maxwell G. Atchisson.)

A Riflescope for the M16

Although most suppressors fielded in Southeast Asia were employed by the special mission groups, regular combat personnel (with the best interest of their units in mind) appropriated equipment of this type whenever possible. In this case, an infantryman makes use of an M16 mounting a Sionics MAW-A1 noise suppressor and a late-war Realist 3X-9X auto-ranging telescope during an extended patrol. (Max Crace.)

closely than most men will hold under combat conditions.

When we used the M16A1s as a substitute sniper rifle, we equipped them with the Colt 3X scope with the upside-down tapered-post reticle. Firing this combination from a supported position, our snipers could consistently hit the Army "E" silhouette targets at 400 meters.

Even though the Army's decision to "go with accurized M14s" for specialized sniper use had been implemented during the late 1960s, considerable efforts to increase the M16's long-range capabilities based on the evaluations of heavy barrels, different cartridge loadings, and bullet weights were to continue through the course of hostilities in Vietnam. Despite such efforts, and excepting limited field tests, the M16 rifles utilized for sniping purposes in Southeast Asia were "as issued."

CHAPTER 7

The USAMTU and the Sniper Instructor Groups

Many veterans of the Army sniping campaign in Southeast Asia have questioned the "post-war focus" on 9th Infantry Division sniper operations, particularly since they encompassed a relatively brief period (approximately 10 to 12 months). But the development and early field use of the USAMTU accurized M14 sniper rifle in conjunction with the ART, the Starlight Scope, and the Sionics noise suppressor were so closely linked to 9th Infantry Division sniper training and employment that, from a historical standpoint alone, the XM21 Army sniper rifle and the 9th Division sniper program literally "grew up together." Thus, drawing attention to one without mentioning the other in any treatise on Army sniping in Vietnam would be shortsighted at best.

By mid-1969, there were few, if any, Army sniper programs operating in-country that hadn't benefited from the efforts of the USAMTU and the sniping experiences of the 9th Infantry Division.

NOTE: In addition to circulating information between combat units on an informal basis early on, by October 1968, the AMTU and the U.S. Army Infantry School (USAIS) based at Ft. Benning, Georgia, had formulated a program of instruction (130 hours in original form) and supporting lesson plans. As they evolved, Department of the Army Training Circular TC 23-14 ("Sniper Training and Employment") and Subject Schedule No. 23-16 ("Sniper Training") were based in part on the training and field experiences of the

Maj. W.L. Powell with Army sniper instructors at Ft. Benning (November 1969). A separate school for training sniper instructors was formed at Ft. Benning following the return of the original instructor group from Vietnam in mid-1969. The rifle is an XM21; note the special AMTU "low-profile" 7-round magazine. Sergeants Adkison (center) and Tharp were members of the original sniper instructor team. (U.S. Army.)

TC 23-14
DEPARTMENT OF THE ARMY TRAINING CIRCULAR

SNIPER TRAINING
AND
EMPLOYMENT

HEADQUARTERS, DEPARTMENT OF THE ARMY
OCTOBER 1969

In addition to circulating sniper training material and information between combat units on an informal basis early on, by October 1968, a program of instruction (POI) and supporting lesson plans had been formulated by the AMTU and the Army Infantry School (USAIS) based at Ft. Benning. As they evolved, Department of the Army Training Circular TC 23-14 ("Sniper Training and Employment"), and subject schedule No. 23-16 ("Sniper Training"), were based in part on the training and field experiences of the USAMTU Sniper Instructor Group attached to the 9th Infantry Division in South Vietnam. The Vietnam-era sniper training manual served the Army until superseded by a revised edition in June 1989. (U.S. Army.)

USAMTU Sniper Instructor Group attached to the 9th Infantry Division in South Vietnam. Of further interest in this case, the USAMTU supplied sniping rifles and accessories used for the illustrations in TC 23-14. In final form, Army Subject Schedule No. 23-16 specified a 118-hour sniper training course of instruction.

So far as the weapon systems were con-

The USAMTU and the Sniper Instructor Groups

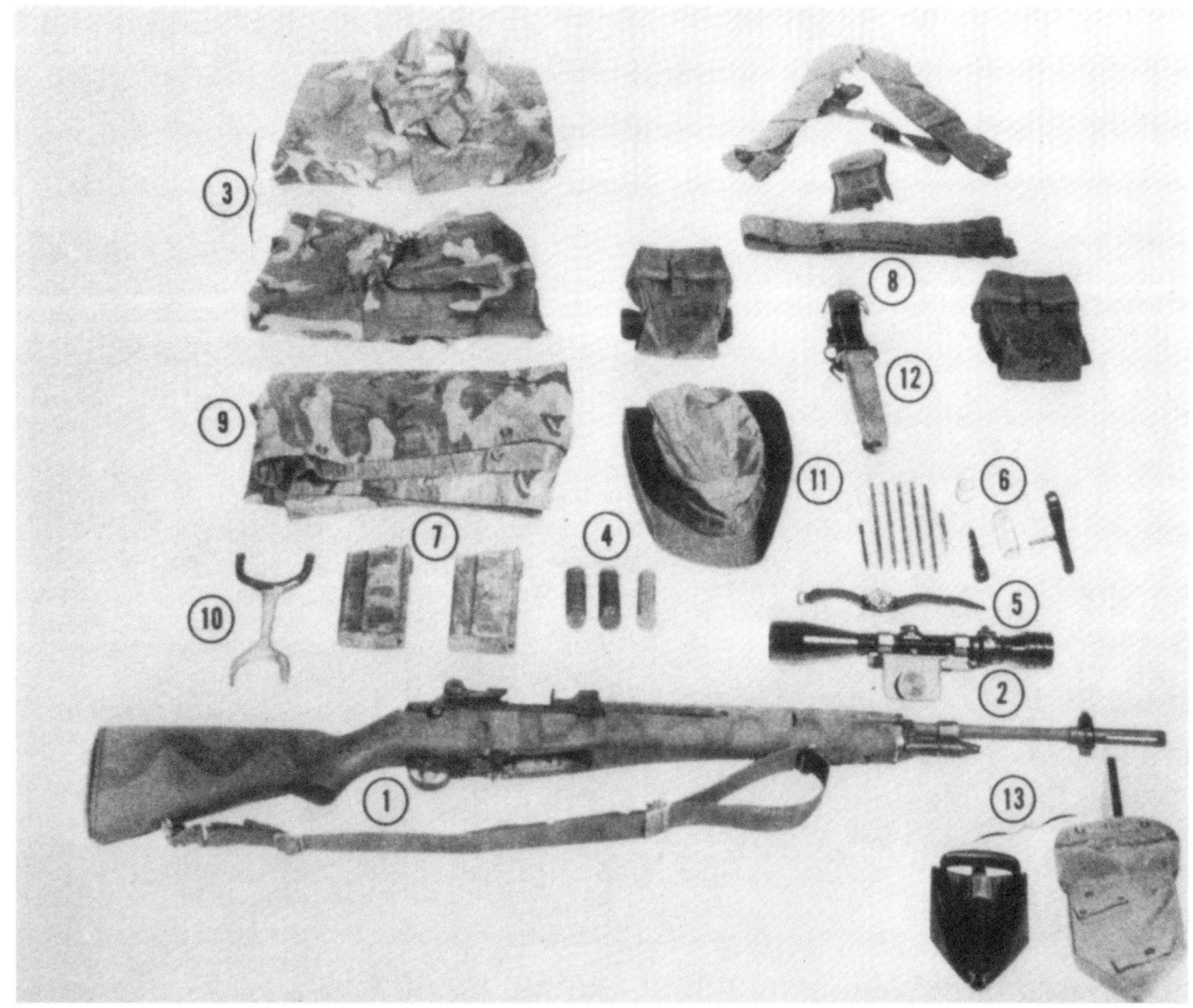

An excerpt from "Sniper Training and Employment" (TC 23-14), October 1969, depicts the individual sniper equipment intended for combat use in RVN. (U.S. Army.)
(1) Sniper rifle; (2) Sniperscope w/ mount (carrying case, protective cover caps not shown); (3) Camouflage clothing; (4) Camouflage sticks; (5) Watch; (6) Cleaning kit; (7) Magazines; (8) Webb equipment; (9) Camouflage poncho; (10) Rifle fork; (11) Hat; (12) Bayonet w/ scabbard; (13) Entrenching tool w/ cover

cerned, even though the AWC/RIA National Match M14 rifles with M84 telescopic sights saw considerable field use in Southeast Asia and, by all accounts, performed "extremely well" in the process, the XM21 would emerge as the "weapon of choice" for those units seriously interested in training and fielding snipers. The Colt/Realist Scopes employed with the M16, though reportedly "still around at the end," were rarely used in conjunction with serious sniper training. When employed within the limits of their design, the 3-power sights were more than adequate.

With proper regards to the officers and men who took their sniper training from, or in conjunction with, the various divisions and separate brigades operating in Southeast Asia from 1965 to 1972, the following

USAMTU personnel at the Ft. Benning shop. The ART- equipped XM21 has been fitted with a pistol grip M14E2 stock assembly. Note the rubber recoil pad and raised comb. In addition to a well-earned reputation as an exceptional armorer, "Hook" Boutin (left) also served with an Army sniper instructor team in South Vietnam. (U.S. Army.)

combat units were known to train and/or field trained snipers in Vietnam at one time or another, in one form or another:

> 1st Cavalry Division (Airmobile)
> 1st Infantry Division
> 4th Infantry Division
> 9th Infantry Division
> 23d Infantry Division (AMERICAL)
> 25th Infantry Division
> 101st Airborne Division (Airmobile)
> 3d Brigade, 82d Airborne Division
> 173d Airborne Brigade
> 196th Infantry Brigade (Light)
> 199th Infantry Brigade (Light)

Apart from the contribution made by the riflemen with telescopic

The USAMTU and the Sniper Instructor Groups

An aluminum "rifle fork" intended to serve as a rifle rest during training and field operations. The "Freeland Rifle Rest" was 8 1/4 inches long, 3 1/2 inches wide, and was made of die-cast aluminum. According to AMTU personnel, the rifle fork would not go into some soils and was very unstable in others. Though pictured in the Army sniper manual (TC 23-14), the unique device was not an issue item (Peter R. Senich).

sights who operated on their own for most part, when it came to combat units fielding men trained as snipers, virtually all of the units tasked with "going nose to nose" with the Vietcong and the North Vietnamese Army had employed snipers to some extent by the time combat operations finally ended.

In addition to providing sniper training for Special Forces, Rangers, LRRPs (later called Long Range Patrols or LRPs), and Military Police, Army sniper instructors had trained snipers for Air Force Combat Control Teams and Combat Security Police as well.

Of further interest in this case, Army instructors reportedly trained a "small number" of Navy personnel and SEAL team members as snipers during the course of combined operations in the Delta region. Though it is difficult to determine the actual extent of this activity, in view of the unique, ongoing Army/Navy operations conducted along the vast network of waterways in the Mekong Delta, such reports are worthy of consideration.

NOTE: The 2d Brigade (9th Infantry Division, Mobile Riverine Force) operated with the U.S. Navy, SEAL teams, and other specialized U.S. and ARVN units during their involvement in the Delta. With few exceptions, the various references to the use of 9th Division snipers on "boats," etc., were drawn from these operations. With proper regards to the Marine Corps, Marine instructors were known to have trained snipers for the Navy as well. Even though the U.S. Navy had been an active participant in match competition in years past, it was not prepared to train and equip snipers adequately at this juncture. Though uncon-

Correspondence:
Major Kendall to
Colonel Bayard,
8 February 1969

Based on your kind offer of 20-40 M14s to start us off, I reported this to the CG. The remaining problem is funds to purchase scopes and mounts. Our G4 called Long Binh and learned that the sniper program was already a hot issue at USARV G3, and four divisions have already jumped on the bandwagon, wanting these rifles based solely on the excellent results obtained from Will Powell's school.

Because of the clamor for rifles, USARV G2 is writing up a TO&E, of sorts, for their issue and employment. They are consolidating the USARV-wide requirements, and ordering the rifles from the U.S.

—Maj. P.W. Kendall
G2 Operations Officer,
4th Infantry Division

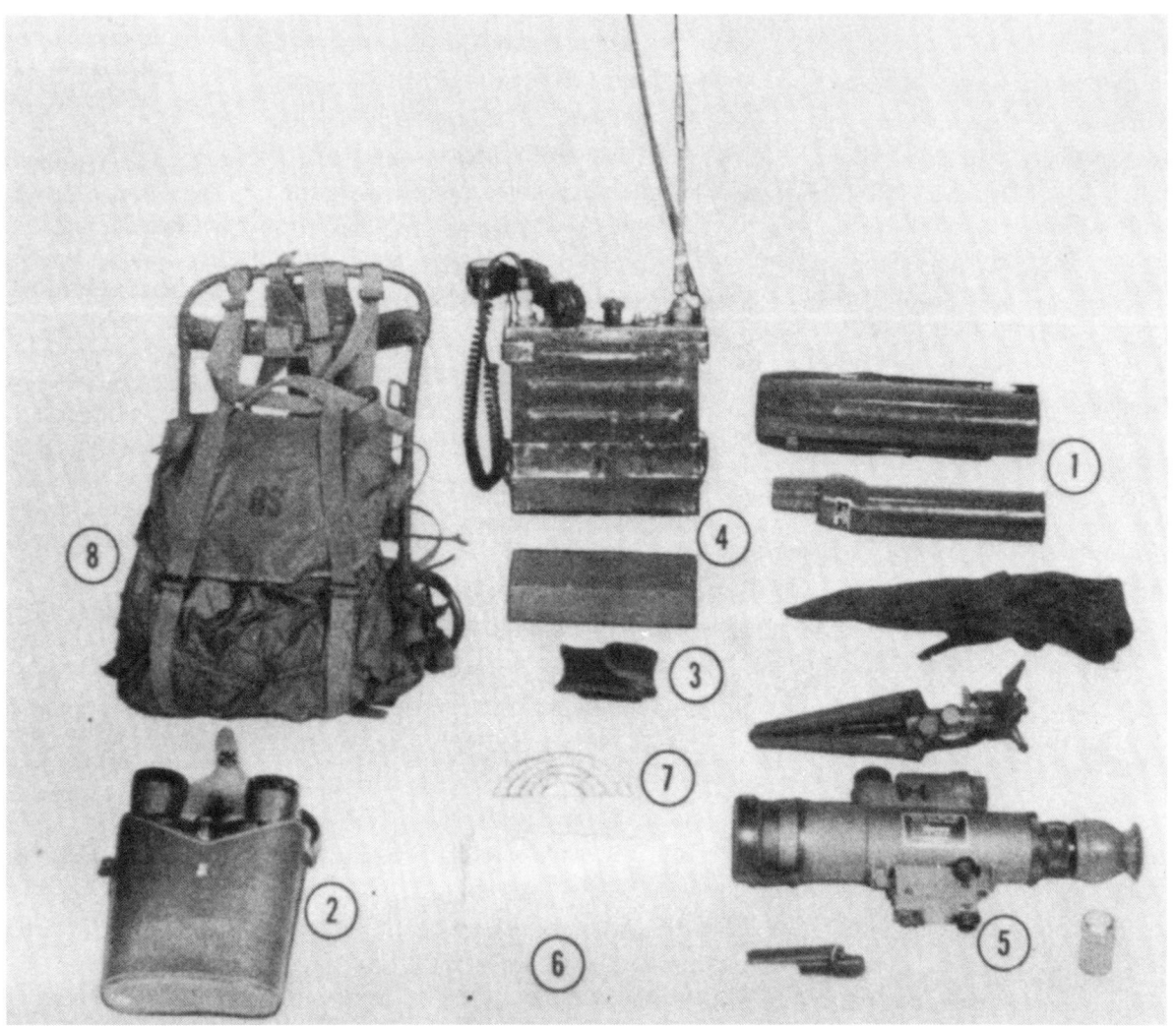

Sniper team equipment illustration from TC 23-14. The binoculars are 7x50 (M19), the observation telescope (M49) is 20-power, and the Starlight Scope is an AN/PVS-2 model. (U.S. Army.)
(1) Observation scope w/ tripod and cases; (2) Binoculars w/ case; (3) Compass w/ pouch; (4) Radio w/ batteries; (5) Night vision sight w/ mount, adaptor bracket and battery; (6) Maps; (7) Sector sketch/range card; (8) Rucksack

firmed at present, Navy marksmen are believed to have employed the bulk of the M14 sniper rifles prepared by the USAMTU in the Mekong Delta.

A residual benefit of the 9th Infantry Division sniper program was the emergence of a specific course for training "instructor groups," which were then posted to various field commands in RVN, where they, in turn, conducted schools for training snipers.

With the original USAMTU Sniper Instructor Group assigned to the 9th Division from June 1968 to June 1969 serving as the "pilot unit" (the second instructor group was commanded by Maj. Gary R. Chittester, and members of the team served in the same capacity with the 25th Infantry Division when the 9th Division returned to the United States), during the closing months of 1969 the Department of

The USAMTU and the Sniper Instructor Groups

An alternative to the aluminum fork, a 10 1/4-inch-long, 3 1/2-inch-wide rifle rest made of .312-inch-diameter mild steel was formed and welded to AMTU specifications. While effective, the steel version of the "rifle fork" was not adopted for Army sniper use. (Peter R. Senich.)

the Army approved a formal program of instruction based on the group's experience. The Sniper Instructor Course was established at Ft. Benning, with Maj. Willis L. Powell serving as the school commandant. The "first class" graduated on 19 December 1969.

In most cases, the teams comprised an officer, seven to eight instructors, and an armorer. The armorer was considered an integral part of the group and was fully capable of rendering proper support for the XM21 system.

Although the war had begun to "wind down" by the time the innovative school finally shifted into high gear, sniper instructor groups trained at "Benning" went on to serve with various commands in South Vietnam before the war ended.

For the sake of clarification, however, while the shortage of potential sniper instructors (personnel with a marksmanship background) serving in Southeast Asia had served as impetus for a stateside course of instruction, qualified personnel were trained as sniper instructors in-country whenever possible.

It is important to note that while all Army sniper instructors had volunteered for this duty and were clearly interested in furthering the Army sniping program in Vietnam, some of the men serving as instructors were not interested in acting as snipers as many did. This, of course, was entirely optional.

By any measure or standard, the U.S. Army Marksmanship Training Unit played a prominent role in the Army Sniper Program during United States military involvement in Southeast Asia. The following information from "The History of the U.S. Army Marksmanship Training Program," generated by Headquarters, USAMTU at the height of the Vietnam War (November 1970), provides insight on the AMTU during this hectic era:

> The United States Army Marksmanship Unit was formed in 1956 at Fort Benning, Georgia. The Unit was given the mission of bringing about an improvement in skill of Army shooters.
> As the nation's largest military service and the major

Correspondence:
Colonel Bayard to
Major General Ewell,
25 March 1969

In as much as the Department of the Army is taking steps to fulfill the sniper weapon and scope requirement in all divisions and separate brigades in Vietnam, I have sold ACSFOR on the requirement of providing instructor teams to each division and separate brigade similar to yours. I feel that the first instructor teams should arrive in Vietnam prior to the first shipment of rifles and scopes.

I am well aware that there are few people in the Army today, knowledgeable in engaging targets beyond 300 meters, and that of this number there are fewer still who also have the ability of imparting their knowledge to others. Therefore, I have sent an officer to Washington to screen the rosters and to come up with a list of marksmen with the required ability. This officer is now attempting to determine the present assignment status of those individuals as well as their availability for assignment to Vietnam.

We proposed to the Department of the Army that a school be established at Fort Benning in which we will take the marksmen mentioned above and train them as instructors and gunsmiths to meet the Vietnam requirement.

—Col. Robert F. Bayard
Commanding Officer,
TUSAMTU

A manual illustration (TC 23-14) of a sniper in camouflage clothing with an ART-equipped M14 and full field gear as envisioned by the Army in 1969. Although circumstances and the situation at hand usually determined the type and amount of equipment a sniper carried into the bush, snipers took no more than necessary to complete the mission and return safely. (U.S. Army.)

ground force, the Army is expected to set the standard of excellence in using small arms. On the national level, the Army must constantly meet the test against rifle teams from the other major services, the National Guard, the Army Reserve, and civilian groups. In these matches the finest marksmen in the country compete, and it takes superior skill to win.

Selection of personnel for the United States Army Marksmanship Training Unit, is based on competitive performance and outstanding soldierly traits. Each year after the National Matches, the most outstanding Army shooters are selected to fill vacancies in the USAMTU. The idea is to feed the Army's top shooters through the Marksmanship Training Unit and return them to units in the field thoroughly polished as marksmen and instructors. There they can impart their shooting skill to other soldiers; they in return discover new talent and prepare the most skillful for later service with Army level competitive teams.

The USAMTU and the Sniper Instructor Groups

A well-used Sniper Firing Data Book employed by an Army marksman in South Vietnam. The small booklets provided an effective means of analyzing the performance of the sniper and his rifle. Entries were made during a training session or following a mission. The "books" were not carried in the bush. (Peter R. Senich.)

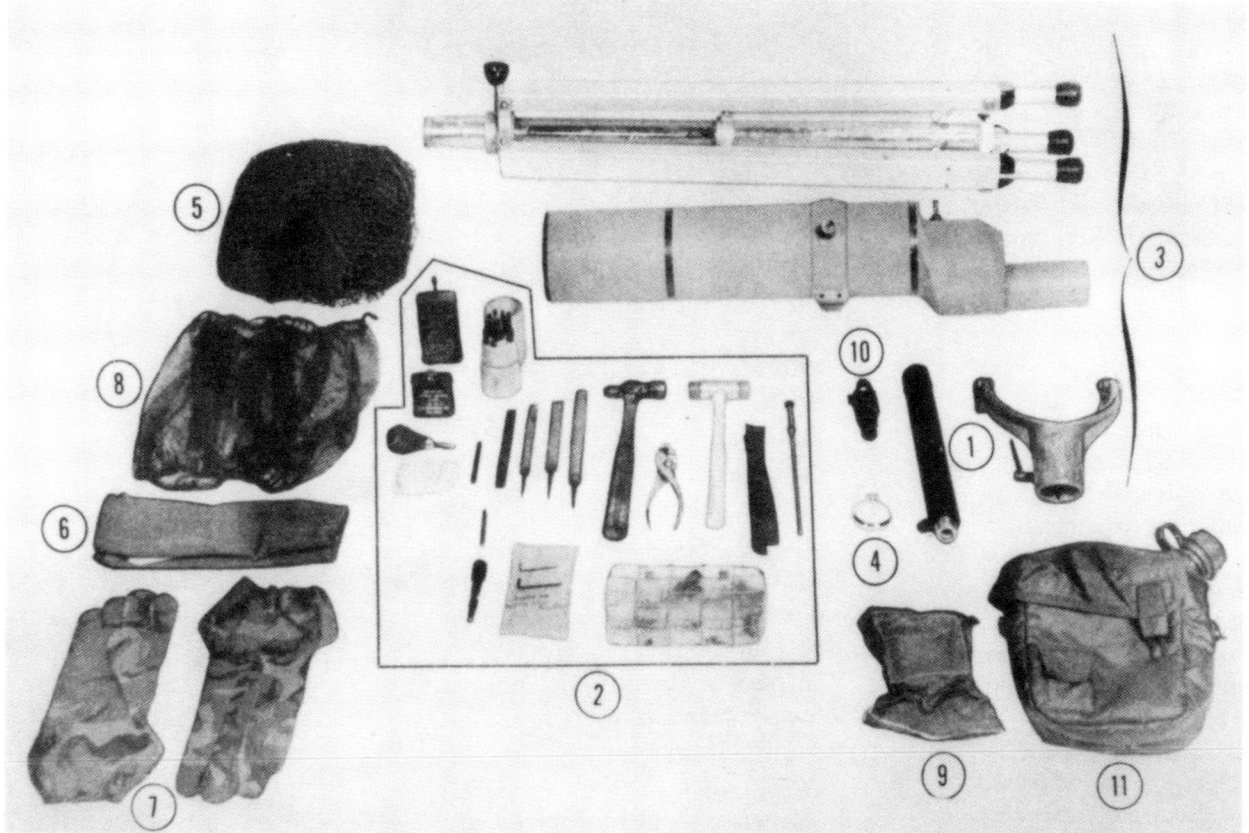

"Special Equipment" illustration from TC 23-14, Sniper Training and Employment. The large 100mm spotting scope, the "standard team scope for most marksmanship units," was rarely available for combat use in Vietnam. The inclusion of the Sionics M14SS-1 "noise suppressor" in this case (item no. 1) marked the first time a device of this type was pictured in a duly authorized sniper training manual. (U.S. Army.)
(1) Noise suppressor; (2) Toolkit; (3) Spotting scope (100-mm) w/ tripod and yoke; (4) Stopwatch; (5) Camouflage net; (6) Camouflage neckerchief; (7) Camouflage gloves; (8) Head net (insect); (9) Dry rations; (10) Gas inertia controller; (11) Two-quart canteen

THE LONG-RANGE WAR: SNIPING IN VIETNAM

A memento of the war in Vietnam: a tropical hat ("boonie hat") with travel-time in Cambodia with a member of 1/50 Scouts (LRRPs) circa 1970. (Zuckerman Collection.)

A "theater-made unit shoulder patch" fielded by the 1st Cavalry Division (Airmobile) in RVN, although many combat units made use of unofficial "sniper patches" during this era. As unpopular as Army and Marine Corps snipers were to the NVA and the Vietcong in particular, many of the specialists simply refused to wear patches or any identification that would connect them with their combat activities. As one Army sniper put it, "It was a lot easier to ditch your rifle if you had to than to try and remove some damn patch." (West Point Collection.)

The United States Army has used snipers in all wars but never had a school for training personnel to meet the skill requirements of sniping. From World War I through the Korean Conflict, the Army authorized a sniper assigned to each rifle squad, and the manner in which the sniper was employed was left to the unit commanders. This use of snipers reflected a lack of command appreciation for the techniques of employment and capabilities of snipers. There was little or no doctrine available for training snipers or guiding commanders in their employment. A specific lesson learned in employment of snipers indicated that a typical rifleman cannot be assigned the sniper mission because "Every marksman is not a sniper, but every sniper is a marksman." There were other skill requirements needed to be an effective sniper, among them being map reading, adjustment of artillery fire, camouflage and concealment, intelligence reporting, etc.

Recommendations after the Korean Conflict included the need for a centralized sniper school. The United States Infantry School was tasked with the mission of organizing a

The USAMTU and the Sniper Instructor Groups

Army Sniper Instructor Group assigned to the 101st Airborne Division in Vietnam (Ft. Benning, 1970). The team was led by Maj. John Foster. (U.S. Army.)

An Army sniper rifle with a known history in this case. The XM21 served a "1st Cav" (1st Cavalry Division) sniper team in South Vietnam. (West Point Collection.)

sniper school coordinated with the USAMTU in 1956. This program reiterated the lesson learned that the best active protection against enemy snipers is a trained sniper. The program was short-lived because of the lack of understanding and appreciation for the value of a sniper throughout the United States Army. In addition, the military attitude then envisioned any future conflict as a nuclear one with defeat or victory decided in hours.

The Vietnam War again revived the need for snipers. Enemy forces demonstrated effective employment of snipers in

Right: A 5th Special Forces NCO, 25th Infantry Division sniper school graduate, and recon team leader with Military Assistance Command Vietnam/Studies and Observation Group (MACV/SOG) assigned to Command and Control South (CCS) at Ban Me Thout is shown with a suppressor-equipped M14 rifle mounting an AN/PVS-1 Starlight Scope. Clandestine operations conducted by MACV/SOG included cross-border raids and intelligence-gathering missions into Laos, Cambodia, and North Vietnam. (Mark Kinsler - John L. Plaster.)

Below: Army Sniper Instructor Group assigned to the 23rd Infantry Division (AMERICAL) following their graduation at Ft. Benning. The team, led by Maj. Lones W. Wigger Jr., was among the last classes sent to Vietnam (1971) and may have been the last. (U.S. Army.)

The USAMTU and the Sniper Instructor Groups   151

The 1st Cavalry Division sniper rifle, an XM21 fitted with a Redfield AR TEL adjustable ranging telescope serial no. 0948. The plastic lens caps are issue items. Note how the stock is "dimpled" below the telescope mount locking screw to facilitate tightening. (West Point Collection.)

An overall view of students and instructors on the firing range at the 23rd Infantry Division (AMERICAL) sniper school, Chu Lai, RVN (September 1971). The weapons are accurized M14s (XM21); the instructors are from Ft. Benning. In addition to the USAMTU assuming certain responsibilities in support of the XM21 system in South Vietnam, sniper instructor groups trained at "Benning" were posted to various field commands in RVN, where they conducted schools for training snipers. (U.S. Army.)

varying tactical conditions. Attempts by U.S. Army elements to engage in countersniping activity were similar to attempts of previous wars; no special equipment or trained personnel and a lack of technique and doctrine for commanders at all levels. In 1968 the Army decided to establish a school for snipers in Vietnam. The USAMTU was given the mission of writing the doctrine, furnishing the skilled marksmen and special equipment, and establishing a school for snipers in the 9th Infantry Division in Vietnam.

The sniper training program was adopted by the U.S. Army and the United States Army Marksmanship Training Unit was given the mission of establishing and conducting a sniper training school at Fort Benning, Georgia. This school was to train instructors to establish sniper training schools in each division in Vietnam and train instructor personnel for replacement of these groups each year. This mission is accomplished by using experienced and skilled shooters throughout the Army, most of which come from the USAMTU and Army area Marksmanship Training Units. These personnel are used because of their knowledge and marksmanship skill, the main factors in determining ability to engage an enemy with a first shot kill at ranges from 200 to 900 meters.

In limited or total warfare the control of the enemy and his territory is still the principal objective, and it is the soldier with his basic weapon who performs this fundamental task.

> Correspondence:
> Major General Pearson to Commanding General, CONARC,
> 4 April 1969
>
> The sniper training program conducted by members of the Army Marksmanship Training Unit (AMTU) attached to the 9th Infantry Division in Vietnam appears to be very successful. Based on the success of this program, it has been recommended that a formal sniper instructor program be established in CONUS to provide sniper instructors to all U.S. Army divisions and separate brigades in USARV. The total training requirement would be 108 enlisted men annually.
>
> Possibly a training program of this nature could be established as a mission for the AMTU at Ft. Benning with minimum additional resource requirements. If such a course is established it will not be an MOS producing course; however, a method will have to be devised to identify graduates.
>
> —Maj. Gen. Willard Pearson, GS
> Director of
> Individual Training,
> Department of the Army

Of further interest in this matter, a review of the December 1969 USAMTU report entitled "Technical Support Rendered to Outside Agencies" offers some measure of AMTU involvement with the ART, the XM21 system, and the Army Sniper Program at large during the war in Vietnam.

<u>USAMTU Support</u>—Army Weapons Command, Rock Island, Illinois

Published a rebuild manual for the National Match rifle to bring it up to TUSAMTU standards. This procedure was suggested as a requirement to field a quality sniper rifle.

Advised AWC at various times on the proper building procedures to properly field a sniping rifle (XM21).

Provided gunsmith support to AWC by conducting a training program for Rock Island personnel on the proper technique of building the XM21 Sniper Rifle.

At present this unit is conducting Test and Evaluation of the XM21 rifle as built by AWC. In the early stages of this program, errors in AWC techniques were noted which necessitated a 100% rebuild by TUSAMTU. However, after providing gunsmith technical support to AWC, the rejection rate of rifles has dropped to an average of only 20%. As of this date, 8 December 1969, this unit has evaluated and shipped to Anniston Ordnance Depot a total of 350 XM21 rifles.

The USAMTU and the Sniper Instructor Groups

Sniper operations were designed to harass, impede, destroy, or prevent movement of individual enemy personnel and units. Despite having taken the Army an inordinate amount of time to mount an effective sniping program in South Vietnam, by the time organized sniping was phased out during 1971 as "responsibility" for the war was turned over to the Vietnamese, Army marksmen had proven the worth of first-class equipment and training. (U.S. Army.)

USAMTU Support—Combat Developments Command—
The Infantry Agency, Fort Benning

USAMTU shooter support was provided CDC, TIA during the period 11–17 July 1967 to assist the Agency in determining the span of ranges over which rifles and sniper fire may be delivered effectively. Special weapons were furnished for obtaining effective sniper fire data. Support consisted of four test personnel of USAMTU firing the Trainfire Record I and II course with iron sights, the M84, and the LWL self-ranging scopes.

Mid-range firing was conducted at ranges of 400-700 meters, using the National Match M14 rifle with LWL scope and the 30/338 Magnum with 14-power Unertl scope.

Correspondence: Major Powell to Colonel Bayard, 30 April 1969

The news of the Sniper Instructor Course to be established at Benning makes us all very happy. I've seen how other divisions have tried to set up sniper programs and so far they have just been spinning their wheels. Unless there is someone really qualified to organize, set up, and conduct a sniper school starting with the very basic marksmanship principles, the program just falls away to nothing.

In this respect, an officer with a background in the shooting program would be a tremendous asset to the sniper instructor groups. I've seen officers from other divisions that were detailed to come here to the 9th to get a briefing on our program with the purpose in mind of returning to their units and starting a sniper school. Without pointing a finger at a particular unit, I've yet to brief a project officer from another division that was completely sold on the value of a sniper program. There is always some doubt as to how well a sniper can work in their particular area of operations. It is difficult to convince some of these people who have never seen a trained, highly skilled rifleman engage targets one shot at a time day and night. So, in answer to your question about an officer for each instructor group, I am definitely in favor of having one assigned to each group. I know officers with shooting experience are getting scarce and there may not be enough to go around.

(continued on page 155)

Long range firing was conducted at ranges of 800-1300 meters with the same equipment as used for mid-range firing.

Assisted in finalizing the SDR pertaining to a US Army Sniper Rifle (currently designated XM21).

USAMTU Support—The Infantry Board

Tested and provided data on six types of noise suppressors to determine their effect on accuracy at 100 and 300 meters.

USAMTU Support—U.S. Navy

Provided the Naval Weapons and Ammunition Center, Crane, Indiana with test data on noise suppressors for the M14 rifle as regards noise level and effect on accuracy.

Rebuilt to USAMTU standards, 40 National Match M14 rifles for the US Navy. Fabricated special fittings and installed telescope sights on the above rifles. The rifles were tested for accuracy and the telescopes zeroed. The rifles were then shipped directly to RVN for use on patrol boats.

Conducted accuracy tests on several lots of National Match ammunition for use by Navy rebuild shop and sniper teams.

Trained Navy personnel on the rebuild procedures used by the USAMTU to obtain required accuracy for the XM21 rifle.

USAMTU Support—Limited Warfare Laboratory, Aberdeen, Maryland

USAMTU fabricated the original mount for the Redfield self-ranging (Leatherwood) scope. Upon request by LWL, details and sample portions of this mount were furnished.

One M14 match rifle was built to USAMTU standards and furnished to LWL as a control weapon for test purposes.

Ten each National Match Sniper Rifles, with LWL Redfield self-ranging scopes, were completely built to USAMTU standards, tested in the accuracy cradle, zeroed at 300 meters, and tested at ranges of 300-600 and 700 meters. These rifles with Match 7.62mm ammunition were field-tested in Vietnam.

Tested ballistic ranging cam on the LWL self-ranging scope to ascertain if it would remain immobile during the firing of a series of shots. This resulted in the use of a locking device on the cam.

Tested large bore subsonic silenced rifle for accuracy and provided gunsmithing advice to improve accuracy (Winchester Model 70, .458 Magnum).

Accurized fifty-four M14 rifles to our specifications,

matched them with telescopes (ART), packaged and shipped them to the 9th Infantry Division Sniper School in RVN.

Tested, packaged, and shipped forty noise suppressors to RVN for the rifles mentioned above.

The above examples are indicative of USAMTU efforts to further the cause of U.S. sniping in Southeast Asia. The Vietnam-era U.S. Army Marksmanship Training Unit was commanded by Col. Robert F. Bayard, and later, Col. Robert M. Piper, who succeeded Bayard.

As the USAMTU defined it best, perhaps:

> No other single aspect of the military profession is so little understood as the necessity for accurate rifle shooting. All the patriotism, courage and determination in the world will never compensate for a thorough knowledge of how to use the rifle effectively in a combat situation.

However, when a division is just getting started with a sniper program this officer can get things done faster and sell the program better than a Senior NCO. After a program is off the pad and all the bugs are ironed out, then a Senior NCO could possibly handle the teams or groups under the guidance of the G-3.

—Maj. Willis L. Powell,
Commandant, Sniper School,
9th Infantry Division

CHAPTER 8

Noise Suppression: The Silent War

With the emergence of the M16 as the principal infantry arm of United States ground combat forces in South Vietnam, the major thrust of suppressor development was centered on the 5.56mm rifle. Except for isolated commercial development, the M14 was an orphan in this regard. The fielding of the Sionics M14SS-1 Noise and Flash Suppressor Assembly with the XM21 system was actually a spin-off of efforts to have the Army adopt Sionics' M16 suppressor design.

The USAMTU had been actively involved with suppressor testing during the course of Army evaluations. Consequently, suppressor evaluations and efforts to field satisfactory sniping equipment, although separate projects, paralleled each other, and the two (sniper rifles and suppressors) often came together at Ft. Benning during 1967 and 1968 in particular. When the accurized M14 sniper rifle took shape, it only followed as "logical" in some quarters that a suppressor be employed with this system as well.

So far as the AMTU was concerned, if there were certain benefits to be gained by field use of a suppressor-equipped M16 rifle, then fitting a similar device to an accurized sniper rifle "offered endless possibilities" for combat use in Vietnam. As events transpired, the USAMTU version of the M14 sniper rifle in combination with the Adjustable Ranging Telescope, the Starlight Scope, and the Sionics suppressor emerged as the most versatile sniping rifle fielded in South Vietnam.

To many combat veterans, the sight of an Army marksman armed

Patrolling in Vietnam. The M16 rifle is equipped with a noise suppressor, a part of the unconventional methods and hardware developed for use in Southeast Asia. Ground combat forces used suppressed M16s for various purposes, including long-range recon patrols, ambush situations, and special missions. Although various designs were evaluated during the late 1960s, the Sionics MAW-A1 model and the Army Human Engineering Laboratory (HEL) H4A suppressor were employed in Vietnam with the M16A1 rifle. Though difficult to see, the recon team member (left) displays a LRRP beret flash. Both men are wearing tiger stripe utilities; the M16 rifle has been camouflaged. (U.S. Army.)

with a suppressor-equipped M14 sniper rifle made a lasting impression. As one sergeant recalled, "I'd see these guys coming in from time to time just after first light, and I couldn't help thinking how damn glad I was they were on our side." Judging from the cumulative effect of suppressed sniper rifles and Army sniping in general, the VC and the NVA were, in their own way, no doubt, duly impressed as well.

Although suppressor-equipped M16 rifles mounting one telescopic sight or another were fielded in Vietnam, such measures were usually taken by enterprising units and/or individual riflemen acting on their own. Beyond official and quasi-official combat evaluations involving a limited number of weapons and personnel, telescopic sighted, suppressor-equipped M16 rifles were not fielded in conjunction with any organized sniper program in Southeast Asia.

However, conventional M16 rifles equipped with suppressors were employed for covert operations and by regular ground combat forces mainly for long-range recon patrols and ambush situations. At one time or another, the Army, Navy, Marine Corps, and Air Force were known to use rifle-mounted noise suppressors in Southeast Asia.

According to official documents generated during the war in Vietnam, the M16 suppressor program began in May 1966 when the United States Army, Vietnam (USARV) submitted an ENSURE request

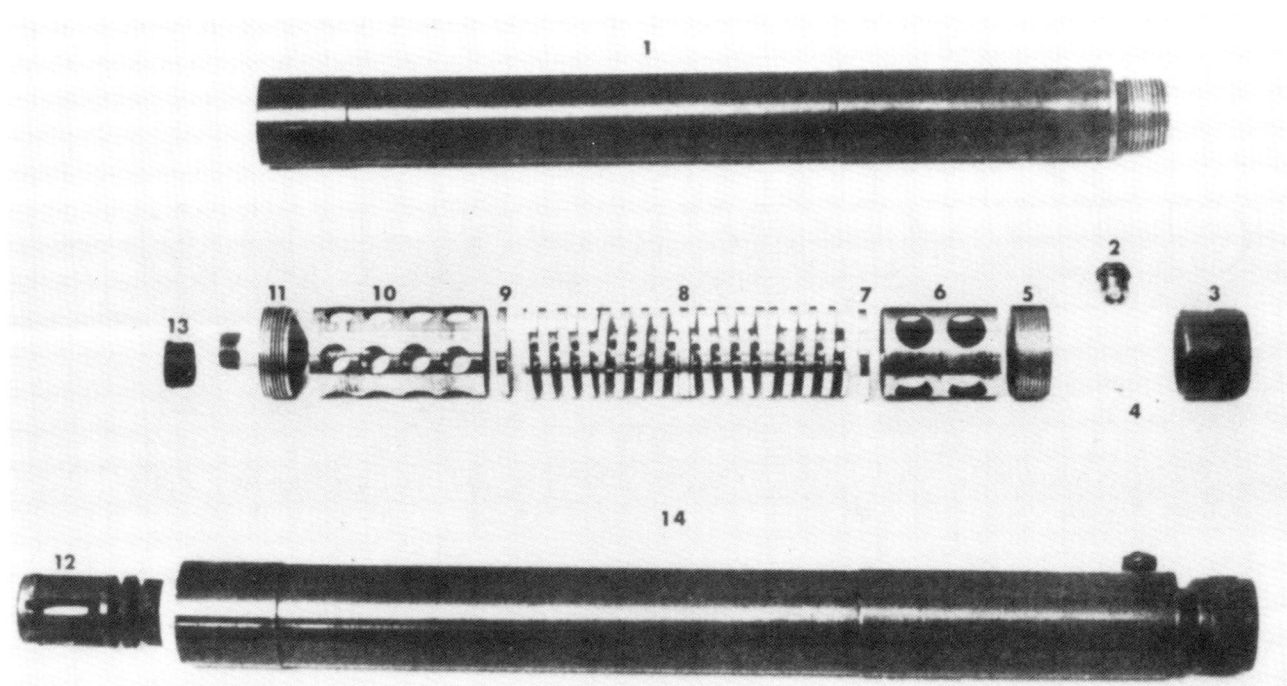

The Sionics M16A1 suppressor design referenced in the 1968 Army test report as the "Noise Suppressor Assembly S-1." The more conventional of the three Sionics variations then tested, the early version of the MAW-A1 was 13 inches in length (approximately 14.5 inches long with the M16 flash suppressor threaded to the end), and 1.235 inch in diameter. The outer casing was made of steel, the spiral suppressor rings were fabricated from aluminum alloy in this case. A synthetic collar bushing was used, and a spring-operated pressure relief valve was fitted to the body of the suppressor. With subsequent changes, the Sionics S-1 unit emerged as the production version of the MAW-A1 suppressor. (U.S. Army.)

for "silencers for the M16A1 Rifle" (ENSURE No. 77). Inexplicably, a considerable amount of time would pass before M16 suppressors were sent to South Vietnam for combat evaluations.

Apart from the design and development efforts of various government-funded research laboratories and civilian corporations involved with small arms silencers and suppressors for specific projects and/or purposes, it remained for the U.S. Army Human Engineering Laboratories, Frankford Arsenal, and Sionics, Inc. to furnish noise suppressors for consideration with the M16A1 rifle. The Army recorded the course of events as follows:

> In March and April 1968, the U.S. Army Infantry Board (USAIB) tested a noise suppressor (HEL-H4) designed by the Human Engineering Laboratories, Aberdeen Proving Ground, Maryland. This suppressor was found to have military potential, but was returned to the developer for correction of certain shortcomings.

NOTE: A small quantity of HEL-H4 suppressors (HEL-H4 suppressor assemblies were referenced as the HEL-M4 suppressor as well) were reportedly slated for testing in Vietnam in late 1967 or early 1968. An *Interim Operation and Maintenance Manual* was published for this purpose.

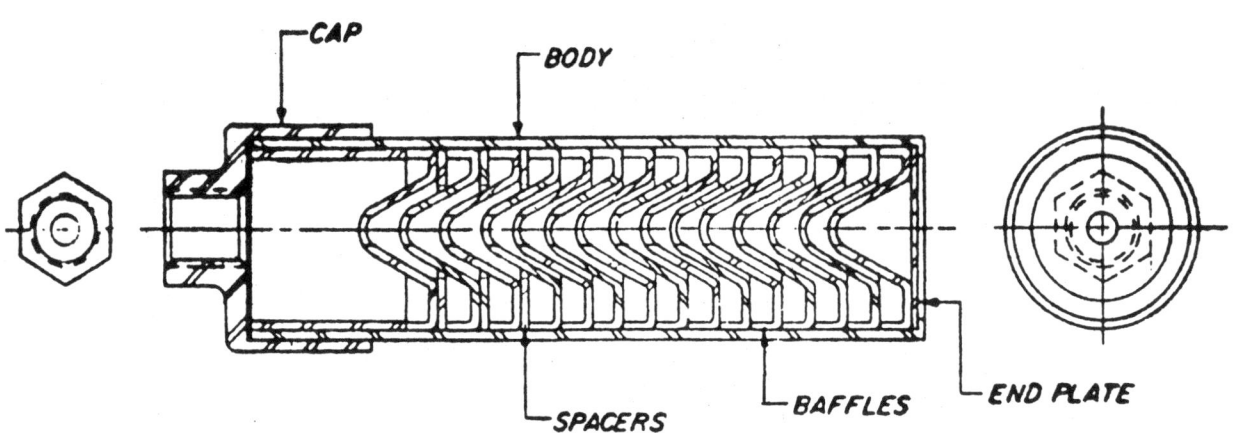

Sketch of Frankford Arsenal Noise Suppressor, FA-XM, from the "Military Potential Test of Noise Suppressors for M16A1 Rifle" (Final Report, September 1968). (U.S. Army.)

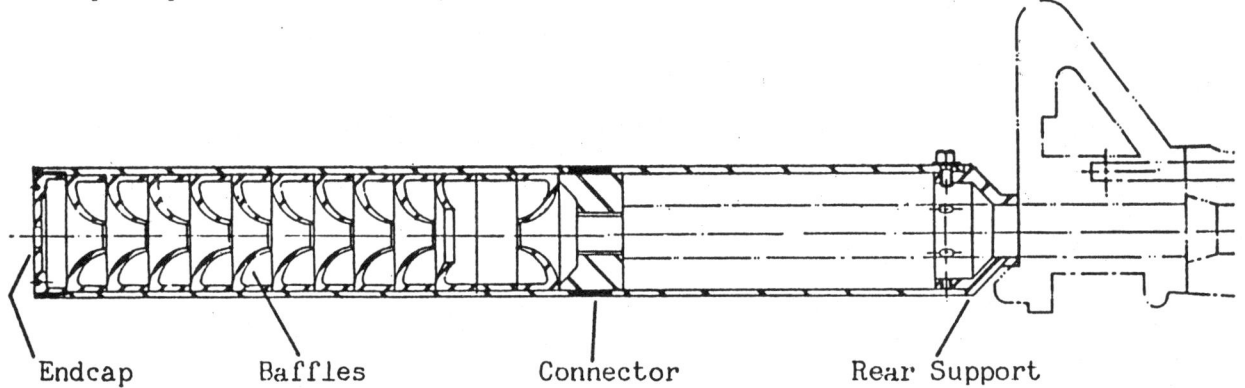

A cutaway sketch of a HEL-H4 noise suppressor for the 5.56mm, M16A1 rifle (the original system was referenced as the "M4" or the "H4" in Army documents dating from the Vietnam War). The HEL noise suppressor assembly consisted of a steel cylinder and a separate rear support with three mounting screws. The H4 model was 12 inches long; the H4A was 9.50 inches long. Both suppressors were 1.50 inches in diameter. The HEL H4 model required a specially modified bolt carrier; the H4A did not. The suppressors were phosphate-coated to protect them from the elements; there were no moving parts. Unlike the Sionics M16 suppressors, the HEL system required an alignment gage for installation. Although suppressor alignment was always a potential problem, the manner in which the HEL suppressors were fitted to the M16 barrel increased the chance of misalignment significantly. According to Army personnel involved in testing the system, it was not uncommon to see a HEL suppressor literally "shot from the end of an M16 barrel" and "travel down-range in the process." (U.S. Army.)

Various tests and reports pertaining to M16 suppressors were generated during 1968. The most notable of these, the "Military Potential Test of Noise Suppressors for the M16A1 Rifle," was conducted by the U.S. Army Infantry Board from 9 July to 26 August 1968, at Ft. Benning. The abstract for this test ("Final Report," September 1968), offered the following information:

> The purpose of this test was to evaluate the advantages and disadvantages of the test items with respect to such factors as: accuracy; position disclosing effects; system functioning; durability, reliability, and maintenance; and to select a device suitable for a Vietnam field evaluation and/or further develop-

Noise Suppression: The Silent War

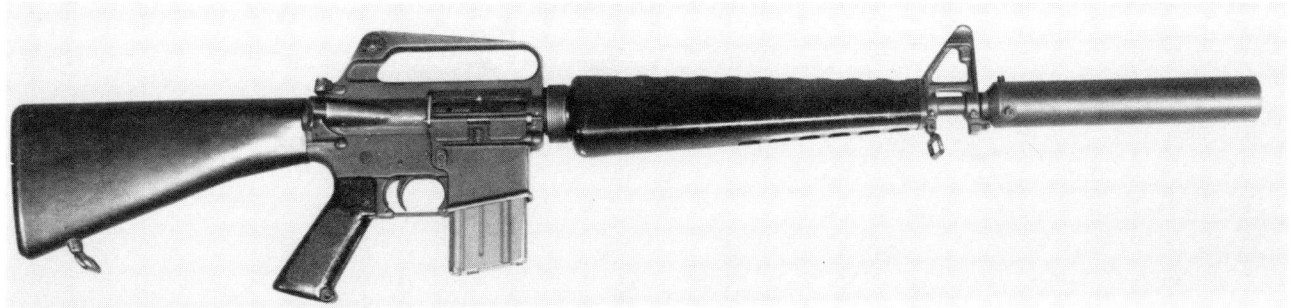

A combat veteran of the Vietnam War, an M16 rifle and a Human Engineering Laboratory (HEL) noise suppressor assembly employed by a 1st Cavalry Division sniper team. The 9.50-inch-long H4A suppressor was often referenced as the HEL "shorty" to distinguish it from the early 12-inch H4 model. Although HEL-H4 suppressors were reportedly evaluated in Southeast Asia, the H4A version was eventually issued for combat use. Inexplicably, surviving examples of the HEL production version (H4A) bear the markings "Noise Suppressor HEL E4A." (West Point Collection.)

A 9th Infantry Division LRP team during operations in the Mekong Delta region. The men are equipped with an M16 mounting a HEL H4A suppressor, a .30-caliber M1D sniper rifle with the telescope removed (center), and a Colt CAR-15 5.56mm submachine gun. Note the use of skin camouflage and tiger stripe utilities. The black beret was often seen on LRPs in Vietnam. A number of Army snipers were sent to the Reconnaissance/Commando (Recondo) School at Nha Trang for training, and many recon personnel were eventually trained as snipers. The ability to effectively eliminate the enemy at extended ranges provided an added dimension to a LRP team. (U.S. Army.)

Diagram from the Human Engineering Laboratories suppressor manual showing the effectiveness of a suppressor-equipped rifle in terms of the enemy's location to the weapon ("determining the location of an M16 rifleman equipped with the noise suppressor"). The area directly behind the firer was considered the "area of certain location." (U.S. Army.)

ment. Seven types of noise suppressors were tested: two designs by Human Engineering Laboratories (HEL), Aberdeen Proving Ground, Maryland; two designs by Frankford Arsenal (FA), Philadelphia, Pennsylvania; and three by a civilian corporation, Sionics, Inc. (S), Atlanta, Georgia.

[NOTE: Although Sionics had embarked on a separate development program for the M16A1 rifle in early 1967, their involvement in this case came as a result of an "unsolicited proposal" (no. S4-100), submitted to U.S. Army Weapons Command on 23 April 1968.]

Specific phases of testing under intermediate climatic conditions included physical characteristics, safety, signature effects, known distance accuracy, short exposure targets, durability and reliability, portability and aerial delivery, maintenance, human factors engineering, and value analysis.

There were two deficiencies: breakup of the FA noise

Noise Suppression: The Silent War

Marine Corps reconnaissance personnel (1st Recon. Bn.) shown posing with their weapons. The "Recons" performed duties similar to the other U.S. special mission groups. While primarily an intelligence-gathering unit, Marine Recons were also employed as raiders and CIDG advisors. The M16 rifle (center) is fitted with a HEL H4A suppressor; the trooper opposite carries a Swedish M45 9mm submachine gun. Note the camouflaged M16 rifle directly below. (U.S. Marine Corps.)

suppressors; and loss of component parts of the M16A1 rifle, i.e., sights, sling swivel, and handguards caused by the FA noise suppressors. Five shortcomings were noted: all of the test weapons produced gas blowback into the firer's eyes; all of the test weapons required additional cleaning when compared to the M16A1 rifle; the HEL and S test weapons produced a bright flash; the bushings of the S test items were not durable; and the pressure relief valves on the S test items failed to remain operative.

It was concluded that the noise suppressors did cause an appreciable decrease in the muzzle noise of the M16A1 rifle; that they all established a requirement for additional cleaning of the M16A1 rifle; and that of all the noise suppressors tested, the HEL-H4A has the most military potential.

The US Army Infantry Board recommended that in the event one of the noise suppressors must be selected, then the HEL-H4A be considered suitable for a Vietnam field evalua-

Members of an Army reconnaissance team prepare for a helicopter landing. Operating in enemy territory as they did, helicopters were frequently employed for insertion and extraction purposes. Even though recon personnel were well-prepared to act as "hunters," the patrols avoided contact with the enemy as much as possible. Their primary mission was to secure information rather than engage in combat. The men are carrying radio sets; the M16 is equipped with a noise suppressor. (U.S. Army.)

tion; the HEL-H4A noise suppressor be attached to the M16A1 rifle by the company armorer and maintained at company level; and that the user be made totally aware of the extra care and detailed cleaning that an M16A1 rifle with noise suppressor attached requires.

As a matter of reader interest, the "seven types of noise suppressors" cited in this report were described as follows:

In May 1968, noise suppressors from three developers were submitted to meet the ENSURE 77 requirement. They were: the HEL-H4 and a shorter version, the HEL-H4A; the FA-CM and FA-XM designed by Frankford Arsenal; and the S-1, S-2, and S-3, three versions designed by the Sionics corporation.

[NOTE: The noise suppressor assemblies listed as the S-1, S-2, and S-3 were referenced by Sionics, Inc. as the MAW-A1, MAW-A2 and the MAW-A3.]

Description of Materiel

The noise suppressor assembly, S-1, consists of a steel

Noise Suppression: The Silent War

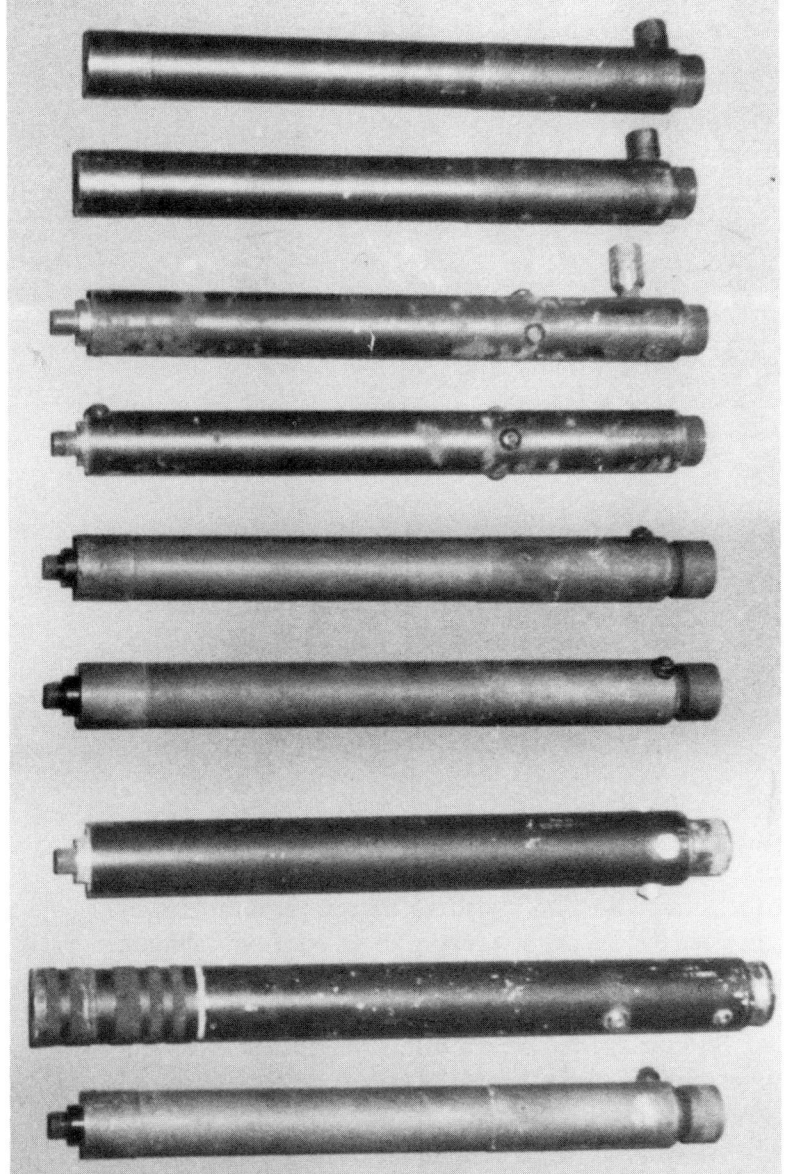

A variety of Sionics experimental M16 (5.56mm) noise suppressors dating from the late 1960s. The two models at the top are configured most closely to the final MAW-A1 design. The others display various design details, such as multiple pressure-relief valves and fore-ends threaded to accept the M16 flash suppressor. Note the model with an "auxiliary chamber" mounted to the front. Though later remedied, the barrel bushing and the pressure relief valve created the greatest problems of all the difficulties encountered during development. The bushing referenced as "plastic" (synthetic material) in the Army test reports (1968) would melt during sustained automatic fire, and the spring-operated pressure-relief valve would fail to remain operative. (Thomas Collection.)

cylinder with aluminum spiral suppressor rings, a plastic bushing under the rear retaining collar, and a spring-operated pressure relief valve on the body of the suppressor. The S-2 noise suppressor assembly is an all-titanium (stainless steel bore) modified version of the S-1 model. It has a 1-1/2-inch diameter compared to the 1-1/4-inch diameter of the S-1 model and is 2-1/2 inches shorter than the S-1 model. The S-3 noise suppressor assembly is an all-titanium (stainless steel bore) version exactly the same size as the S-1 model. All of the S models have a plastic bushing under the rear retaining collar and a spring-loaded pressure relief valve. None of the S test items require modifications to the M16A1 rifle except for the removal of the flash suppressor.

[NOTE: According to Sionics personnel then active,

An early Sionics suppressor fitted to an M16 for demonstration purposes in Vietnam. Note the wrench flats on the barrel collar, multiple pressure-relief valves, and M16 suppressor placed in front of the unit. (Thomas Collection.)

efforts to furnish the Army with an "extremely durable product" included fabricating test suppressors made from titanium. Though virtually indestructible, the titanium literally "ate the machine tools and drove everybody nuts in the process." In view of the difficulty and the expense, the special alloy was not used after the 1968 evaluations.]

The FA-XM noise suppressor assembly consists of a round, steel, outer body with internal baffles. It has two small holes drilled in the rear of the suppressor body, containing two screws which may be removed, if necessary, to maintain the proper cyclic rate. It has no moving parts. Attachment of the FA-XM suppressor requires no modifications to the M16A1 rifle, except that the flash suppressor must be removed from the rifle. The FA-CM noise suppressor assembly consists of a tube containing a cavity and a section of porous aluminum to absorb propellant gases following the projectile. It has no moving parts. It requires no modifications to the M16A1 rifle except that the flash suppressor must be removed. Due to its failure in the safety subtest, it was dropped from further testing.

The noise suppressor assembly, HEL-H4, consists of a steel cylinder with three mounting screws and a separate rear support. It has a series of internal baffles but no moving parts. In order to attach the HEL-H4 model to the M16A1, three modifications to the rifle are required: a third gas pressure relief port

The cover from a Sionics Operation and Maintenance Manual for the production version of the MAW-A1 M16 suppressor assembly. (Peter R. Senich.)

is needed in the bolt carrier to maintain the proper cyclic rate; a gas deflector was added to the charging handle of the weapon to deflect escaping gases from the firer's eyes; and the flash suppressor must be removed from the rifle. The noise suppressor assembly, HEL-H4A, is similar to the HEL-H4 model; however, it is 2 1/2 inches shorter than the HEL-H4 model and its attachment requires no modifications to the M16A1 rifle, except that the flash suppressor must be removed.

So far as it is known, the Army gave the Frankford Arsenal design (FA-XM) no further consideration. However, Frankford Arsenal later (1970) produced and fielded a variant "XM" noise suppressor for use by Air Force Combat Control Teams (CCTs) with the CAR-15 in South

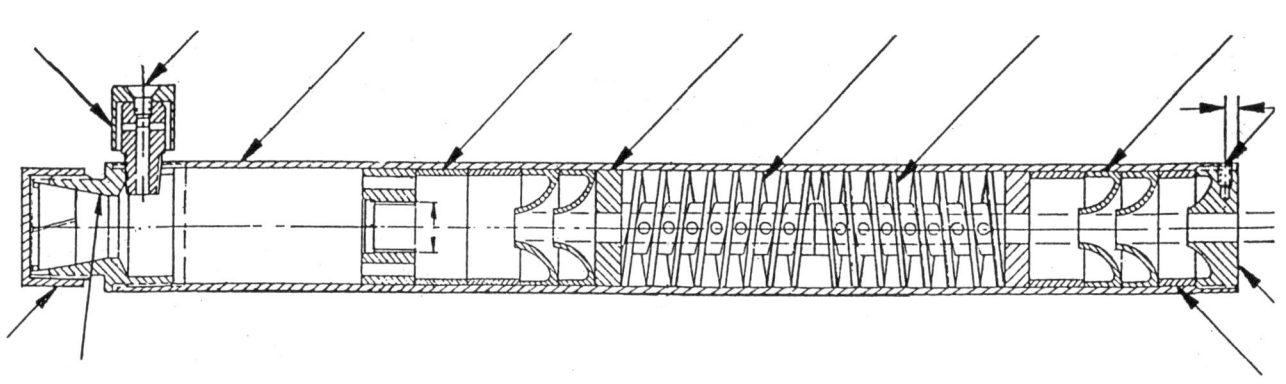

The Sionics Noise and Flash Suppressor Assembly MAW-A1 intended for use with the M16A1 rifle is 12.63 inches long, extends 9 inches past the muzzle, has a diameter of 1.235 inch, a bore of .302 inch, and a weight of 1.81 pounds. Primary internal components were made of stainless steel. The outer casing, rear retaining collar, spacers, and muzzle system were fabricated from steel. In final form, a special "Naval Brass" was employed for the collar bushing to withstand extreme temperatures during sustained automatic fire. External parts were protected by a black oxide coating. There were no moving parts. The illustration is part of an original Sionics engineering drawing. (Thomas Collection.)

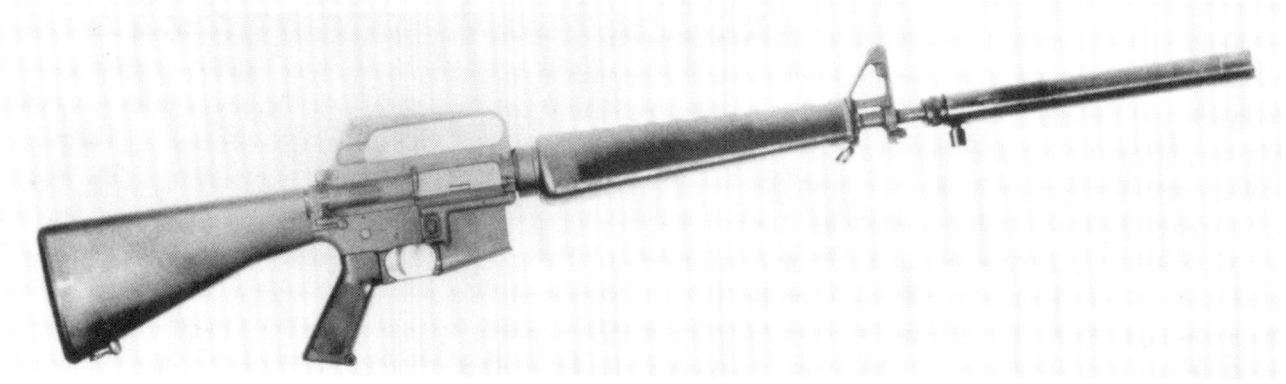

A 5.56mm M16 fitted with the "production version" of the Sionics MAW-A1 noise suppressor. Although specific quantities remain unknown, the Sionics attachment was procured by the U.S. military for combat purposes in RVN. However, it is important to emphasize that rifle suppressors in any form saw only limited use in Southeast Asia. (Thomas Collection.)

Vietnam. Special subsonic 5.56mm ammunition attributed to Frankford Arsenal was reportedly furnished as well, though this is unconfirmed.

In September 1968, the U.S. Army, enamored with the improved HEL-H4A system, made plans to manufacture and ship H4A suppressors to South Vietnam in quantity.

Major design changes were made to the Sionics system. The best features of the three variations tested during July and August 1968 were consolidated, and the improved version was eventually field-tested under combat conditions in Vietnam. According to pertinent Sionics information, the vastly improved MAW-A1 suppressors were engineered to "withstand any physical abuse imaginable." Judging from the success of this system in Southeast Asia, the Sionics statement proved true. By all accounts, the MAW-A1 suppressor was viewed as "dependable" by those tasked with its combat use.

In final form (Vietnam issue), the Sionics Noise and Flash Suppressor

Noise Suppression: The Silent War

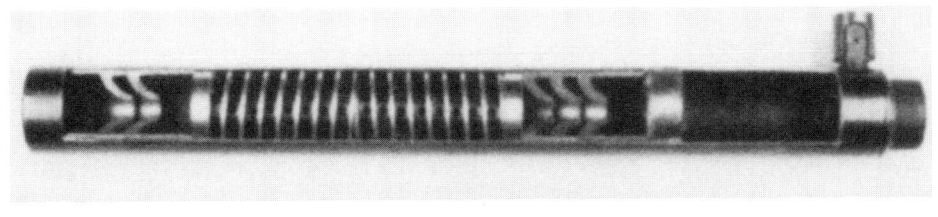

An illustration of a Sionics MAW-A1 Noise and Flash Suppressor Assembly for the 5.56mm M16A1 rifle as modified by Sionics, Inc. for sales and demonstration purposes. The "factory cutaway" was used to explain the workings of the Sionics system of sound suppression. A small quantity of M14 and M16 units were altered for this purpose. (Thomas Collection.)

An Army Special Forces trooper shown sighting an M16 rifle mounting a Sionics MAW-A1 noise and flash suppressor. (Thomas Collection.)

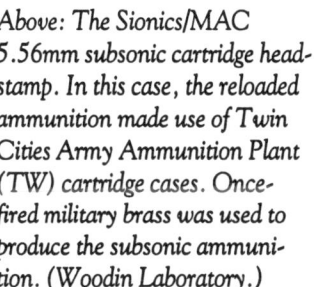

Above: The Sionics/MAC 5.56mm subsonic cartridge headstamp. In this case, the reloaded ammunition made use of Twin Cities Army Ammunition Plant (TW) cartridge cases. Once-fired military brass was used to produce the subsonic ammunition. (Woodin Laboratory.)

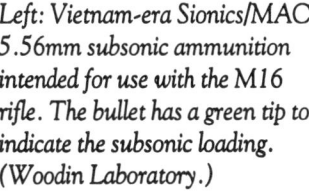

Left: Vietnam-era Sionics/MAC 5.56mm subsonic ammunition intended for use with the M16 rifle. The bullet has a green tip to indicate the subsonic loading. (Woodin Laboratory.)

Assembly MAW-AL, for use with the 5.56mm M16A1 rifle, was 12.63 inches in length (the suppressor extended approximately 9 inches beyond the muzzle), 1.25 inches in diameter, and weighed 1.81 pounds. The outer casing, internal spacers, rear retaining collar, and muzzle system were fabricated from 4130 steel. Internal components were made of 303 stainless steel. The bushing was "high-temperature-resistant Naval brass," and external parts were given a black oxide coating. There were no moving parts.

NOTE: In earlier form, the "plastic bushing" and the "spring-operated pressure-relief valve" cited in the Army report had been the source of major problems during the 1968 evaluations. The heat generated by sustained automatic firing had literally destroyed the bushing and rendered the relief valve spring inoperative. The new bushing was made from brass instead of synthetic material, and the valve assembly (gas relief port) was redesigned to eliminate the spring. The use of a special bushing in this case was based on the automatic-fire capability of the M16A1 rifle. A

Above: Special Forces Capt. Robert K. Brown firing an M16 equipped with a 3-power Colt/Realist scope and Sionics suppressor in Vietnam. (Thomas Collection.)

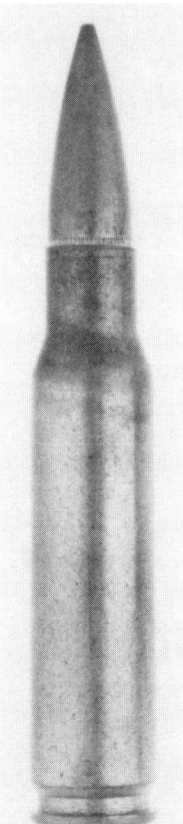

Left: 7.62mm subsonic ammunition as manufactured and marketed by Sionics/MAC during the Vietnam War. (Woodin Laboratory.)

Below: Sionics/MAC 7.62mm subsonic cartridge headstamp. The "circle and cross" is a NATO standardization mark, the case was made by Winchester Repeating Arms Co. (WRA). Rather than a green bullet tip, though barely visible, the base of the cartridge was colored green in this case. (Woodin Laboratory.)

Teflon bushing was furnished with the Sionics M14SS-1 suppressor employed with the semiautomatic XM21 sniping rifle.

Even though the HEL-H4, H4A, and Sionics M14SS-1 and MAW-A1 noise suppressors were known to have seen field use in Southeast Asia, with proper regard to the tentative plans and preproduction estimates cited in contemporary offerings, the specific quantities and/or actual number of Human Engineering Laboratories and Sionics suppressors sent to South Vietnam remain unsubstantiated.

Of further interest in this matter, though most M16 suppressors fielded in South Vietnam were employed with standard 5.56mm ammunition, many of the special mission groups (Rangers, Special Forces, SEALs, Recons, LRPs) had either experimented with or employed subsonic rifle ammunition as a matter of course. Though difficult to obtain in most cases, subsonic ammunition was procured in small quantities directly from civilian sources or the government

Noise Suppression: The Silent War 171

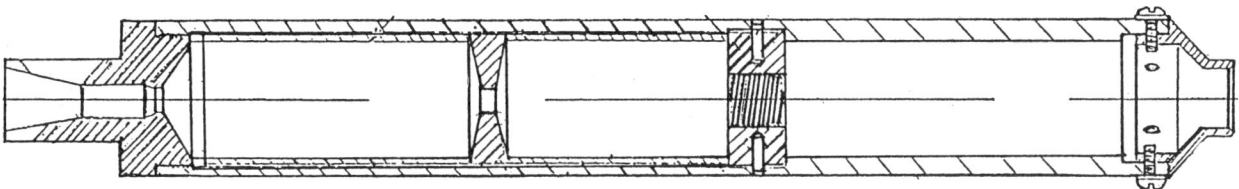

A U.S. Navy illustration of an M16 "blast suppressor" developed by the Naval Ordnance Laboratory for UDT and SEAL teams operating in South Vietnam. The Navy suppressor was designed to work with both the M16 and M16A1 rifles. (U.S. Navy.)

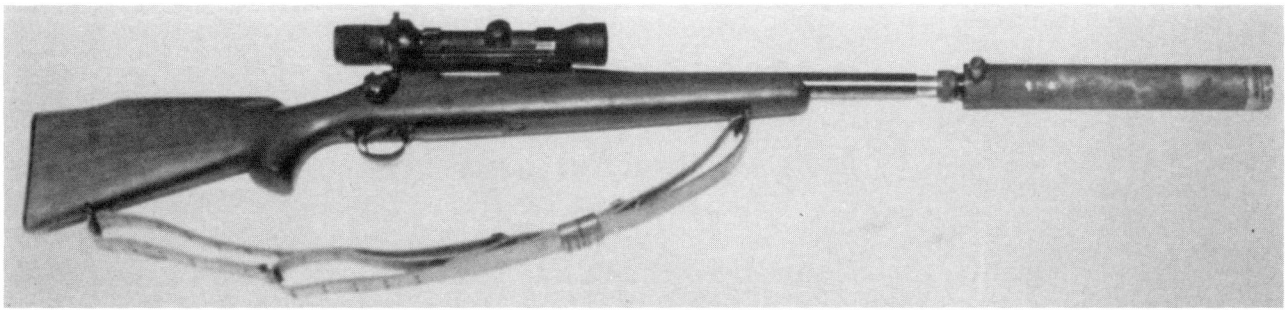

A Remington Model 700 sniper rifle with a 7.62mm Sionics suppressor dating from the Vietnam War. The telescope is a 1.5X-4.5X Leatherwood/Realist Adjustable Ranging Telescope; note the barrel machined and threaded to accommodate the noise suppressor. The 7.62mm Sionics suppressors fitted to the bolt-action rifles were the same as the standard M14 units. The weapon illustrated was modified for suppressor use by the Sionics firm. Though unsuccessful, Sionics had attempted to interest the Marine Corps in its 7.62mm and 5.56mm suppressors for sniping and general combat use in Vietnam. (Thomas Collection.)

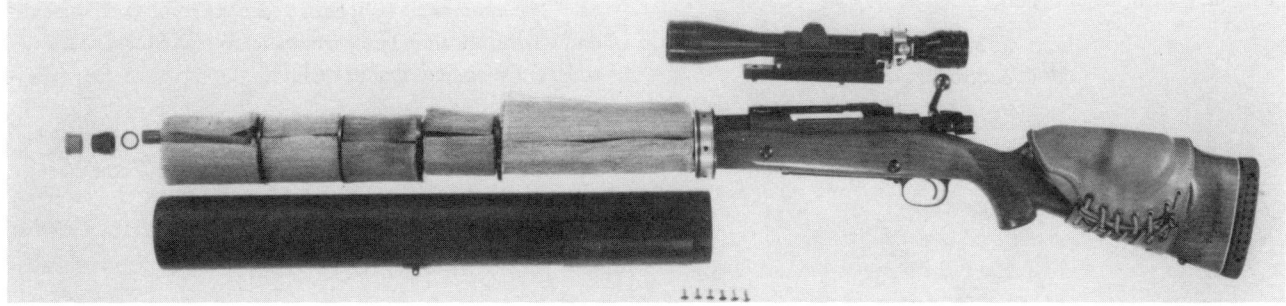

An early version of the .458 Magnum cartridge silent sniper system. The Winchester Model 70 bolt-action rifle was fitted with an integral noise suppressor. The sighting system was based on a 3X-9X variable-power Redfield scope reconfigured to ART specifications; a special ballistic cam was developed for the modified cartridge. The ammunition was specifically loaded for subsonic velocity. The wire mesh encircled the vented barrel, the suppressor casing ("canister") covered the assembly; a leather cheek pad was fitted to the Winchester stock. (Alley Collection.)

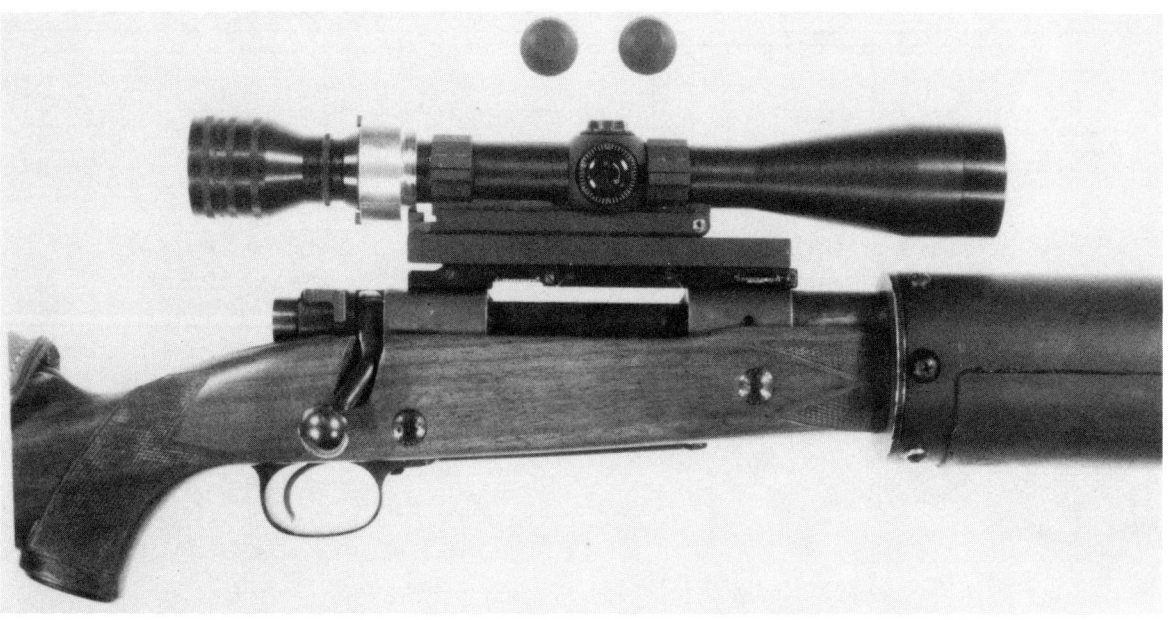

A close view of the developmental .458 Magnum cartridge silent sniper system. The telescope is a second-generation Redfield 3X-9X variable-power model; the special ART mounting was fitted to a Williams commercial receiver base. Note the scope rings shaped the same as those used with the early LWL ART system. This Winchester Model 70 (serial no. 862746) was manufactured in 1967. (Alley Collection.)

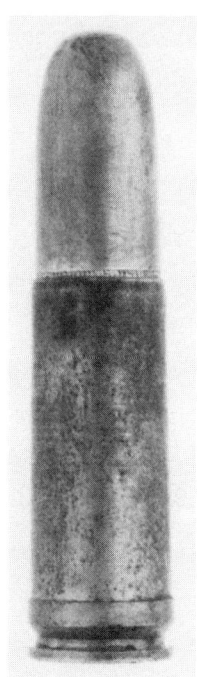

Far Left: The special .458-caliber subsonic round developed for use with the silent sniper system in Vietnam. As then stated, "The ammunition is specially loaded for subsonic velocity and is a modification of the commercial .458 Magnum cartridge." (Woodin Laboratory.)

Left: The .458-caliber subsonic cartridge headstamp showing the Winchester-Western (W-W) markings. (Woodin Laboratory.)

agencies tasked with furnishing "special purpose" arms and ammunition for covert operations.

An example of this activity was recorded by Gary Douglas Ford, in his work, *4/4: A LRP's Narrative* (Ivy Books: New York, NY, 1993).

> Most of our equipment was standard, but there were a couple of specialty items. A number of British Mk II-S Sten guns, World War II standard submachine guns with silencers, were acquired and issued to the team leaders. Test firing revealed that the 9mm rounds they fired were almost totally silent. In turn, I let Crowe carry my M16 with its suppressor. We had a number of 5.56mm rounds bootlegged, using low velocity powder and soft lead bullets that did make the suppressor quite effective ... The lead bul-

Noise Suppression: The Silent War

Winchester Model 70 .458 Magnum cartridge silent sniper system as fielded for evaluation purposes in Vietnam. In addition to changes to the sighting system, and the suppressor, a "straight stock" replaced the sporter version on the weapons tested by the 23d Infantry Division (AMERICAL) Sniper School in 1971. The XM21 sniper rifle was deemed "far superior" to the silent sniper system in all respects except noise suppression. The noise suppressor capability was considered its best feature. (U.S. Army.)

lets worked fine, except for one drawback, you had to hand-cycle each round. Their power was too weak to work the action of the rifles. The Sten would fire full auto with its standard ball ammo. We were prepared to assassinate anyone who stumbled over us and not let the whole countryside know we had come a callin'.

NOTE: As a matter of interest, while an occasional subsonic round would "work the action" of an M14 or M16 rifle, in most cases it was necessary to operate the action manually to chamber and extract each cartridge (hand-cycle each round). With a less-than-standard powder loading, the subsonic ammunition did not possess enough "power" for normal functioning.

Even though the technology necessary to produce subsonic rifle ammunition rested well within the capabilities of any number of commercial cartridge companies, government agencies, and competent "hand-loaders," for that matter, the problems associated with developing satisfactory subsonic ammunition for a given application or specific purpose while remaining within the parameters necessary for subsonic performance proved to be extremely vexing in many cases.

Drawing from his experience as a Sionics associate during the company's halcyon days, respected military historian and silencer authority Donald G. Thomas provided the following insight on the difficulties Sionics encountered while developing special subsonic cartridges for its suppressor line:

> A concerted effort was made to develop suitable subsonic ammunition. However, a major problem came as a result of the reduced powder loading.
>
> When the M16 cartridge was down-loaded to the point that it became subsonic, there was only a small amount of powder left in the case. When the weapon was angled downward,

RIFLE & AMMUNITION MARINE M-40 #6257338   SUPPRESSOR #983-B
M-118 MATCH LC 12073   300 METERS   17 FEB 1970

RIFLE NR.	TYPE WPN	TYPE AMMUNITION	ROUNDS THRU BARREL	1ST GROUP V	1ST GROUP H	1ST GROUP ES	2ND GROUP V	2ND GROUP H	2ND GROUP ES	3RD GROUP V	3RD GROUP H	3RD GROUP ES	SHOOTER	ES
	M-40	M-118 W/SUPPRESSOR	?	6.9	4.9	7.4	6.9	4.8	6.9	6	6.4	6.5	BOUTIN	
				3	6.1	6.1	7.5	4.5	7.5	5	7	7.5	ORTON	
	M-40	M-118 W/O SUPPRESSOR	?	5.2	5.7	5.9	5.2	6.8	7.5				BOUTIN	
				4.9	6.2	7							ORTON	

WEATHER OVERCAST   LIGHT DULL   REMARKS SAND BAG REST FROM BENCH
TEMP 50°   WIND N/A   DIRECTION N/A
FT B (TUSAMTU) FORM 22 (10 DEC 59)

NOTE: LC 12073 AVERAGED 6" EXTREME SPREAD FROM THREE TEST BARRELS (5 GROUPS OF 10 RDS FROM EACH)

*The U.S. Army Marksmanship Training Unit was continuously evaluating telescopic sights, rifles, ammunition, and noise suppressors in its quest for the optimum sniping system. In this case, the weapon testing involved a Marine Corps M40 sniper rifle (serial no. 6257338) fitted with a Sionics 7.62mm suppressor (no. 983B) at Ft. Benning on 17 February 1970. Testing such as this frequently involved one or more weapons on loan from one branch to another. Even though the weapon serial number would tend to suggest a previously unknown serial number range for the Vietnam-era USMC M700/M40 sniper rifles, for the sake of clarification, according to Remington information, the "first" Model 700 serial number series began at 1000 in 1962 and ended with the 1968 model year at or near 387000. The second block began on or about 26 November 1968 at 6200000. The "second series" (rifle serial numbering) began as a result of the 1968 Federal Gun Control Act. A small quantity of M40 sniper rifles with serial numbering in the early "second series" was, in fact, procured from Remington for USMC test and evaluation purposes following the difficulties encountered with the system in Vietnam. Except for the rifles mentioned, it is important to emphasize that all but a few of the Model 700 Remington sniper rifles furnished to the Marine Corps were assembled and shipped before 1969, and these, of course, will bear "six-digit" serial numbering. The Vietnam-era USMC M700/M40 sniper rifles with seven-digit serial numbers are categorized as being part of the "product improvement series." (**NOTE:** In the interest of historical accuracy, without the benefit of Remington or Marine Corps verification in this case, it is not known if this weapon [serial no. 6257338] was loaned to the USAMTU by Sionics Inc. or the Marine Corps. However, Marine Corps ordnance documents from this era do list rifles used for evaluation purposes with seven-digit serial numbers.) (U.S. Army.)*

the powder showed the tendency to move forward in the case, away from the primer and ignition was either irregular or nonexistent.

It was necessary to employ a filler on top of the powder charge. Numerous substances such as oatmeal, cream-of-wheat, and cotton were tried; all with disastrous results. After firing a few rounds, the rifle gas port and the suppressor became clogged with the inert filler. This did solve the ignition problem, but the mess created by the various fillers was something to behold.

Nitrated paper and nitrated cotton were also tried and while this did work much better than the inert fillers, it seemed there was always enough unburned paper or cotton left to foul the gas port and the suppressor port as well. The ultimate solu-

Noise Suppression: The Silent War

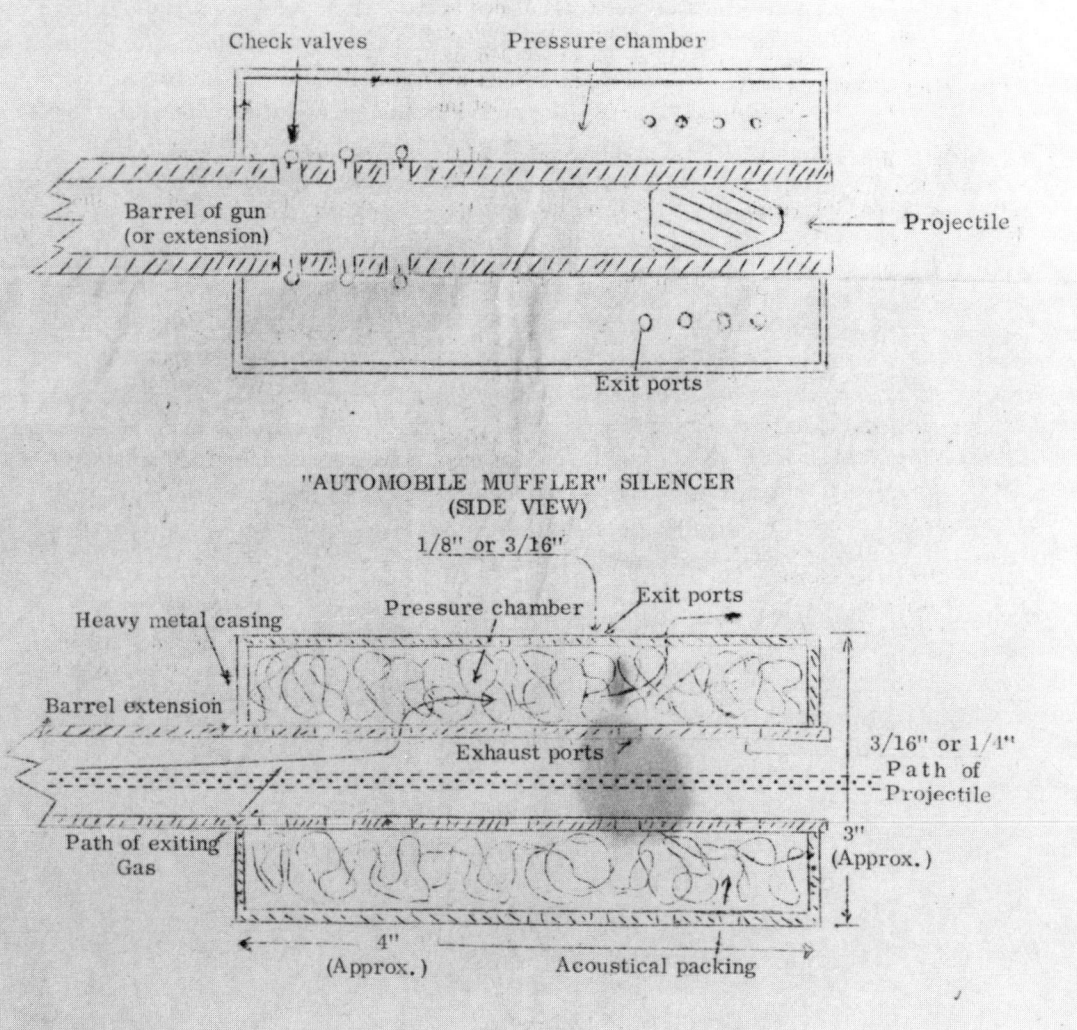

SILENCERS....   - 3

RESUME: Thus far we have learned that the silenced firearm is preferably of large bore and low velocity, closed-breech design (such as an automatic pistol or rifle); it has the longest possible barrel; the cartridge is best if as heavy as possible, and loaded to velocities less than 1140 f.p.s.; a fast-burning powder is preferable in order to lessen the length of barrel necessary for complete burning. The following schematic diagrams illustrate the principles involved in the various silencers, and show how effective silencers are built by authorized, competent gunsmiths:

"BLEED-OFF" SILENCER, SCHEMATIC

"AUTOMOBILE MUFFLER" SILENCER
(SIDE VIEW)

An excerpt from a four-page dissertation on silencers used to fabricate prototype silencers for the Winchester Model 70 sniper rifle. A part of the early efforts in Vietnam, Maj. Robert A. Russell, Commanding Officer of the 3rd Marine Division sniper program, had two prototype silencers made by Force Logistics on Okinawa for field testing in Vietnam with the Model 70. According to Russell, however, "the silencers were dismal failures; they just wouldn't function properly." Despite claims to the contrary, there were no 3rd Marine Division snipers qualified with silencers or suppressor-equipped M70 rifles in Vietnam. (Russell Collection.)

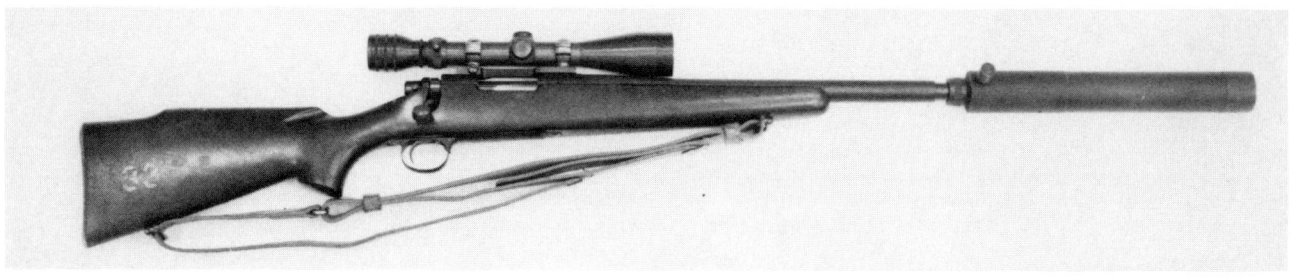

Suppressor-equipped Model 700 (M40) 7.62mm sniper rifle. According to Remington records, "rifle no. 6257227 was manufactured and shipped to Sionics, Inc. in December 1969." The telescope is an "un-numbered" (no serial number) 3X-9X Redfield (green anodized finish) variable-power scope fitted with the early version of the Shepherd range-finder reticle. The Sionics M14SS-1 suppressor (M14 Sound Suppressor Type 1) is serial-numbered 992D; there are no other markings. (Bruce Nelson.)

tion rested with the use of epoxy. The case was partially filled with epoxy and allowed to harden. The epoxy was inserted into the case in such a way that a small central cavity for the powder remained after the epoxy had dried. While successful, this method was time consuming and extremely expensive.

Early experimental and special loadings had no specific markings on the cartridge casing or bullets. Once fired military brass was normally used to fabricate the subsonic ammunition. Special markings were applied after the ammunition was fully developed. The bullet tips were dipped in green paint and the 20 round cardboard boxes had labels identifying the cartridges as being subsonic.

[NOTE: The green paint served to identify the cartridges as intended for silencer/suppressor use. Using green markings to denote silencer ammunition had been a universal practice for many years.]

The subsonic cartridges were developed with the help of skilled ammunition reloaders in the Atlanta area. Their assistance was invaluable. In spite of the fact that the Sionics subsonic cartridges worked extremely well, no significant quantities were ever sold.

Adding to our perspective on the Vietnam-era subsonic rifle cartridges, Lt. Col. Frank Conway related the following regarding his involvement with the USAMTU 7.62mm subsonic ammunition sent to RVN for 9th Infantry Division sniper use in late 1968:

We saw a definite need for subsonic ammo, but with the low velocities needed and the 12-inch twist barrel of the M14, we had some problems.

For ambush work with the suppressor we wanted bullet stability out to 100 meters in order to hit a man-sized target, or preferably the head, at that distance.

Even though the velocity of a subsonic round is normally listed as 1080 fps at sea level, other factors such as temperature

Noise Suppression: The Silent War

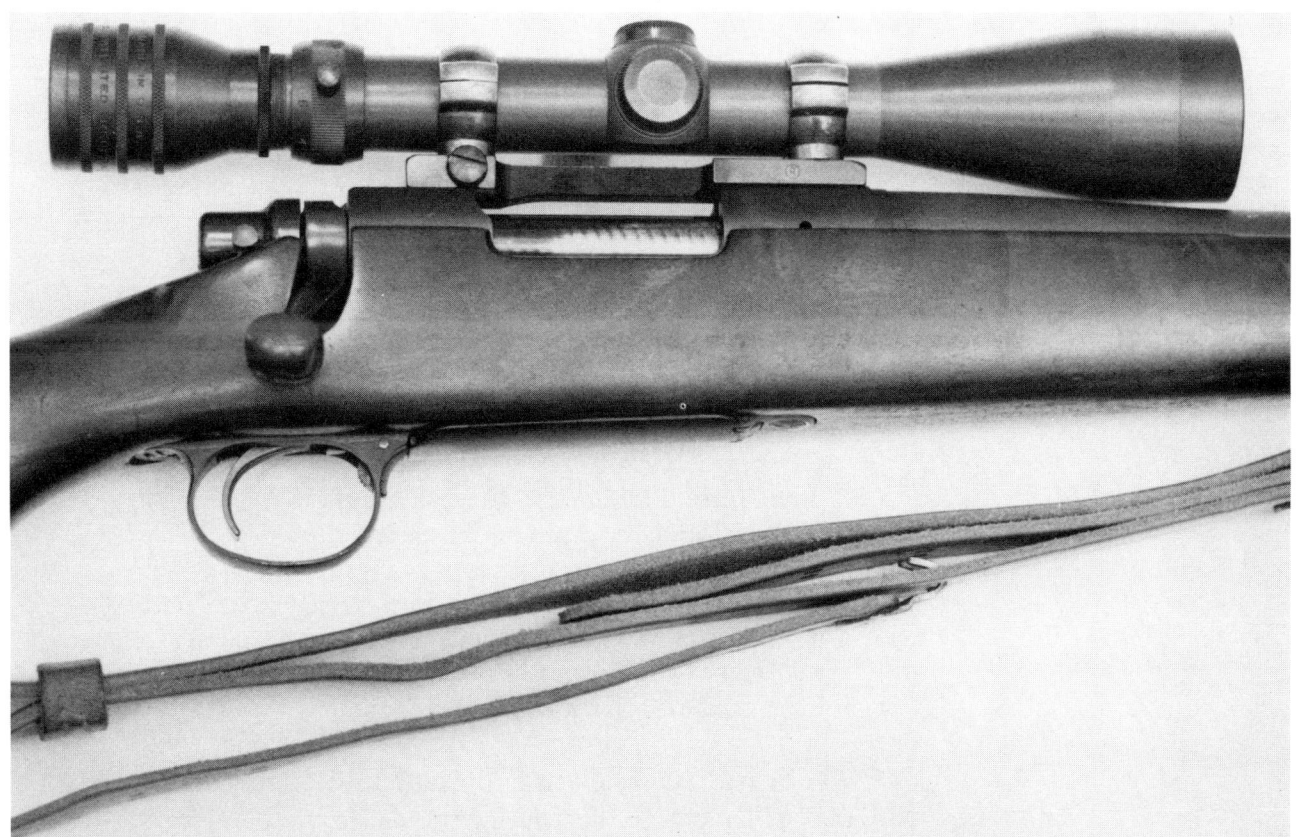

A close view of the Remington Model 700 no. 6257227. The rifle is finished and marked the same as the Vietnam-era USMC sniping issue. The Redfield "Junior" telescope mounting base is a later ("rounded-end") version. According to Dan Shepherd, the inventor of the unique Shepherd Scope and reticle system, the range-finder reticle was offered to Redfield during the late 1970s, "without much success." A limited number of 3X-9X variable-power sights was subsequently fitted with the Shepherd reticle and submitted to the Marine Corps for test and evaluation without the benefit of explanation and/or instructions for proper use. As Shepherd added, "It was much the same as a 'here, try these' kind of situation," with less-than-satisfactory results. As a matter of interest, even though this unique weapon is considered authentic, there is no known connection with the Marine Corps. (Bruce Nelson.)

A close view of the Sionics noise suppressor fitted to the Model 700 (M40) sniper rifle (no. 6257227). The unit is a standard 7.62mm M14 suppressor (M14SS-1) typical of those issued with the Army XM21 sniper rifle in Vietnam. The pressure-relief valve (valve assembly) at the back of the suppressor is clearly visible. (Bruce Nelson.)

A relatively unknown example of suppressor development. A late-war "silencer for the M16A1 rifle" as submitted to Rock Island Arsenal for test and evaluation by Firearms Research Corp. in 1971. (U.S. Army.)

and humidity affect performance as well. All things considered, we felt that 1000 fps here in the states would also work in Vietnam, but we found that our 150-grain bullets would not stabilize to 100 meters. While thinking of going to the 108-grain 30-carbine bullet, I tried some 150-grain bullets made by Dominion Arms in Canada and they stabilized just fine.

During testing in Vietnam, however, with the marked increase in temperature and humidity, about one round in four would make a ballistic crack so we dropped the velocity to 950 fps on the next batch and these did the job.

NOTE: Although subsonic rifle ammunition saw only limited use with the M14 and M16 rifles during the war in Vietnam, for a time (late 1968), the question of employing either noise suppressors with standard and/or subsonic ammunition or .22-caliber silent rifles for combat use, was seriously considered. Though "silent .22 Rimfire rifles" were fielded, the suppressor-equipped M16 rifle was deemed "far more practical" for general field use. At the time, this was stated as follows:

> Caliber .22 Rimfire rifles and ammunition have the potential advantage of subsonic velocities and can be effectively silenced, but the small 40-grain projectile at such low velocities has very low incapacitation potential. Ideally, a "silent" weapon for close-range operations should utilize a projectile with subsonic velocity, but with sufficient mass to possess good incapacitation characteristics. The experimental use of silencer-equipped Australian 9mm and US M3 submachine guns are examples of this approach. If the choice is to be made between the "noise-suppressed" M16A1 rifle with its inherent ballistic "crack" and a caliber .22 Rimfire rifle with its inherent low lethality, it is believed that the user would be far more satisfied with the M16 in the long run.

A relatively unknown facet of suppressor development during the war in Southeast Asia involved U.S. Navy efforts (1968–1969) to develop a separate M16 suppressor for Underwater Demolition Teams (UDTs) and SEAL teams operating in South Vietnam. This is described as follows:

> Under the Swimmer Weapons System Program a project

Noise Suppression: The Silent War

A member of a recon team is shown moving through the high grass; a suppressor is attached to his rifle. Should any period stand as the Golden Age of Silencers, it would certainly be the era of U.S. military involvement in Southeast Asia when a variety of silencer- and suppressor-equipped weapons were employed by "regular and covertly regular U.S. military personnel" for special operations in Laos, Vietnam, and Cambodia. (U.S. Army.)

was established to develop a blast suppressor for use with the M16A1 rifle. The Mechanical Systems Material Division of the Underwater Mechanical Engineering Department of the Naval Ordnance Laboratory was given the design responsibility for this device. The Mechanical Evaluation Division of the Underwater Evaluation Department planned and executed the evaluation program for this device. The suppressor is described by the Naval Ordnance Systems Command Parts List 2493260. The production specification is WS-13098. The suppressor will work with both M16 and M16A1 rifles. Tests were conducted with both weapons.

180 — THE LONG-RANGE WAR: SNIPING IN VIETNAM

Navy SEAL team member circa 1991. The Colt 5.56mm M16A2 (M4) carbine is fitted with a contemporary sound suppression device, an OPS Inc. "muzzle brake suppressor" (MBS) developed and patented by O.P. (Phil) Seberger Jr. The stainless steel suppressor is 1 1/2 inches in diameter, 9 7/8 inches long, and weighs 23.9 ounces. OPS Inc. "muzzle devices" are currently in use by U.S. special operations groups. (Max Crace.)

Noise Suppression: The Silent War

Silencer-equipped M3 .45-caliber submachine gun ("grease gun") employed by a 1st Cavalry Division sniper team in Vietnam. Though unmarked, the silencer is either one of the original units developed by Bell Laboratories for the Office of Strategic Services during World War II or a close copy. The special mission groups in Southeast Asia fielded a variety of silencer-equipped submachine guns. (West Point Collection.)

The U.S. Navy Suppressor, Blast, M16 Rifle, Mk 2, MOD reached operational status, though the extent of combat exposure in Southeast Asia remains unknown. In any case, a variety of silencer- and suppressor-equipped pistols, submachine guns, and rifles were employed by Navy special missions personnel during this era.

By some estimates, the most imaginative effort to field sniping rifles in Vietnam involved a telescopic sighted, silencer-equipped Model 70 Winchester bolt-action rifle firing specially prepared subsonic ammunition.

On 18 August 1967, the U.S. Army Limited Warfare Laboratory (USALWL) initiated a program to develop a Silent Sniper System for use by sniper teams in South Vietnam. The scope of this task was described as follows in miscellaneous USALWL documents:

> Develop a sniping weapon system which combines a long-range, first-round hit capability and reduced noise level. Noise level reduction through decreased bullet velocity necessitates increased bullet weight to maintain casuality-producing capability at long range. Investigation will be directed toward use of a low velocity, large-caliber bullet and a rifle which is modified to reduce muzzle blast. This weapon will be used with an optical sighting system for long-range accuracy.

In the interest of comparing this method of noise suppression with the XM21 system, excerpts from "Technical Report No. 71-13," by Elmer K. Landis, Chief, Munitions Branch, U.S. Army Land Warfare Laboratory, are presented as follows:

> The design, development and fabrication of feasibility prototype weapons were performed on a development contract

with the AAI Corporation. During this contract, a commercial .458-caliber rifle (Winchester) was chosen as the basic weapon system. The sound level of the weapon was reduced by venting the barrel and adding an expansion chamber. The standard caliber .458 cartridge was modified by reducing the case length and propellant volume to provide consistent ballistic pressures and reduce the velocity spread. The bolt action was modified only in the magazine area to accommodate the modified ammunition. Two prototype weapons and two thousand rounds of modified ammunition were delivered at the completion of the contract.

Two sniper weapons were submitted to the Materiel Testing Directorate (MTD) of Aberdeen Proving Ground for testing in November 1968. Early tests revealed several problem areas which needed correction before the tests could continue. Some preliminary accuracy, sound and velocity-versus-range testing with cupronickel bullets without water-proofing sealant was initiated. This testing was suspended until improvements could be made to the weapons to improve accuracy as well as the durability of the mount and muzzle bracket of the sound suppressor. Metallic fouling of the bore by the cupronickel bullets was eliminated by using steel-jacketed bullets clad with gilding metal. The new ammunition was also provided with a water-proofing sealant. Because of other mechanical problems, including noise suppressor mounting, these tests were stopped until improvements could be made.

A supplement was added to the original contract with the AAI Corporation to improve the ballistic and firing signature characteristics of this weapon system and ammunition, and to fabricate an evaluation quantity of six weapons and 9000 rounds of ammunition for OCONUS evaluation. This supplement resulted in an improved weapon with the following basic changes: A straight stock (minimum drop at the heel) to improve the firer's ability to hold the weapon on target. Baffles which allow the barrel to vibrate in its normal mode. A heavy, vented barrel replacing the heavyweight barrel. A one in fourteen inch twist of the rifling as opposed to a steeper twist since the change in twist gave no significant accuracy improvement.
Weapon Description

The Silent Sniper System was comprised of three elements, including: the weapon, the sighting system, and a specially loaded subsonic ammunition.

The weapon is a heavy, bolt-action rifle with an integral noise suppressor. The sighting system is based on a 3X to 9X variable power range-finding telescope which is retained in a flexible mount. A ballistic cam, physically attached to the telescope power adjusting ring, automatically provides the proper superelevation for a given range. This is the same sighting system as the LWL-developed Adjustable Ranging Telescope used as an element of the XM21 Sniper System. The ammunition is specially loaded for subsonic velocity and is a modification of the commercial .458 Magnum Cartridge. The case has been purposely shortened to prevent inadvertent loading and firing of the standard cartridge for safety reasons. Capability for night operations is supplied by the use of a Starlight Scope mount base adaptor which will accept the AN/PVS-1 and the AN/PVS-2 Starlight Scopes.

In February 1971, Mr. Franklin Owens of the USALWL accompanied five .458 magnum silent sniper rifle systems to the 23d Infantry Division (AMERICAL) Sniper School in Vietnam for evaluation purposes. The sniper school cadre and division snipers tested and evaluated the rifles during March, April, and May on the sniper range near Chu Lai. Two rifles were sent to the field with snipers who volunteered to evaluate the weapons during missions under combat conditions.

The following information was contained in the LWL final report for the Silent Sniper System (November 1971):

Results of Test and Evaluation Training

There were no problems encountered in training the personnel to assure reliable and competent use in combat situations. Trained snipers required only one day of training to adapt to the silent sniper system.

Maintenance

Some problems were encountered in maintenance of the equipment and could not be completely corrected by the armorer. The telescope mounts did not fit flush or solidly on the receiver because of the difference in the angle of their surfaces. Recoil constantly caused the mount screws to work loose, changing the zero of the system. This was partially solved by fiberglassing the screws in place for the test. The difficult task of removing the cannister of the noise suppressor for cleaning and removal of carbon build-up could only be accomplished by the armorer. The problem was compounded because cleaning of the noise suppressor was necessary after each day of shooting and disassembly necessitated rezeroing the system before use.

Performance

The system continually changed or shifted zero for no apparent reason. During firing the armorer continually tried to alleviate this problem and even re-glass bedded two rifles, but could not completely eliminate the shifting of zero. No accuracy tests were conducted as such. However, testing personnel could not consistently group on a fifteen by thirty-inch silhouette target beyond 250 meters.

Difficulty was encountered with the ART telescope by all who participated in the evaluation. It was virtually impossible to cam the telescope (change distance) accurately enough to obtain a first round hit at any range. Any system employing a heavy bullet and low muzzle velocity requires the bullet to have a high angle of trajectory in order to hit the target. Since this system had these characteristics, the lobbing effect of the heavy 500-grain bullet made the target very difficult to hit. Any error in camming caused the firer to miss the target, and the error became more critical as the distance to the target increased.

The slow moving, heavy bullet proved to be very wind sensitive even at short range. Thus, during windy conditions, the capability of the system to obtain a first round hit was further decreased.

The noise suppressor capability of the system was considered its best feature. The noise heard down range was so adequately dispersed that the location of the firer and the direction from which it came was impossible to locate.

Suitability

Because of the relative inaccuracy and limited effective range of the system, only experienced volunteer snipers were allowed to evaluate the rifle in the field. Extreme caution and maximum security during employment was stressed. Snipers in the field said the rifle was too heavy and bulky to carry on operations. They had very little confidence in the system and were reluctant to fire at a target over 250 meters unless they were very secure.

Recommendations

Although subsonic ammunition and a silent-type sniper system has merit for some type of operations, it is recommended this system not be adopted or included in the small arms inventory for the reasons listed.

A. The system is not accurate enough to consistently hit a man sized target beyond 250 meters.

B. The rifle must be zeroed for the specific range of respective targets at ranges short of 250 meters in order to insure a first round hit.

C. The camming device on the ART telescope is not accurate enough to insure first round hits after it is changed (cammed).

D. The bullet is too wind sensitive and therefore adds to the inaccuracy of the system.

E. The system is too heavy for the already weighted down sniper to carry in the field.

F. The XM21 sniper rifle is far superior to the .458 magnum silent sniper system in all respects except noise suppression.

Interestingly, even though a fair number of Winchester and Remington rifles were employed by Army and Marine marksmen, the use of sound-suppression devices with bolt-action sniper rifles did not reach practical proportions in Southeast Asia.

Unlike the M14 or the M16, which simply required removing the standard flash suppressor and installing a noise suppressor in its place, a bolt-action rifle necessitated machining and threading the end of the barrel to attach a contemporary silencing device. Consequently, aside from the handful of suppressor-equipped bolt-action sniper rifles that made it to Vietnam for test and evaluation purposes, there was little official interest in modifying the weapons already in country or those destined for combat use.

Even though the Marine Corps was known to evaluate silencing devices made by White Laboratory and Sionics, Inc., its combat use of silencer- or suppressor-equipped sniper rifles, if any, remains obscure.

While it was aware of the trend of suppressor development and use by the Army, the Marine Corps was less than enthusiastic about employing hardware such as this. For that matter, many Army and Marine snipers were wary of what they considered "unnecessary equipment" and wanted absolutely nothing to do with noise suppressors.

As some men viewed the situation, "a 10- or 12-inch piece of tubing hanging from the end of the barrel was just something more to fuck with." In this regard, one successful Marine marksman's statement, "The best sniping was based on the principle of the further the better," expressed a view shared by many sniper veterans of the war in Vietnam.

CHAPTER 9

The Marine Corps Model: The Green Scope

The Redfield 3X-9X variable-power rifle sight was introduced in 1962. The constantly centered nonmagnifying reticle, variable power, and range-finding capability offered with the highly rated scope proved to be exactly what the Marine Corps was seeking for sniper use in South Vietnam.

NOTE: When the Marine Corps deemed it necessary to replace the Model 70 Winchester/8-power Unertl combination with a lighter rifle and a scope that would aid the sniper in getting off a "quick first round," in December 1965, Headquarters, USMC directed that the Weapons Training Battalion (Marksmanship Training Unit) at Quantico, Virginia, "recommend for procurement a rifle and telescopic sight suitable for use by Marine Corps snipers." Due to the urgency for an early recommendation, the MTU conducted comparative testing of "off the shelf" commercial weapons and rifle scopes in December 1965 and January 1966. It concluded that the Remington Model 700-40X and the Redfield 3X-9X variable-power Accu-Range telescope were "superior" to items then in use. Acting accordingly, the Marine Corps adopted both the rifle and the telescope, and, as part of the planning process, the Assistant Chief of Staff drafted a formal "Letter of Adoption and Initiation of Procurement of Equipment for Scout Sniper Rifles" to the Quartermaster General of the Marine Corps (7 April 1966) detailing the planning, budgeting, procurement, and funding phases for the Remington rifle and the Redfield telescope. According to the Marine Corps, the new sniping system utilized "regu-

One of the earliest known illustrations of a Vietnam-era USMC M700 sniper rifle. This is a Remington Arms Co. photo (May 1966) of rifle serial no. 168346 as it emerged from the Custom Shop. Officially referenced as the "Rifle, 7.62mm, Sniper Remington, M700" in original form, the Vietnam-era USMC sniper rifles were produced at the Remington Custom Shop at Ilion, New York. Although procurement activity had begun earlier in the year, the Marine Corps formally adopted the M700/Redfield system on 7 April 1966. (Remington Arms Co.)

An alternate view of the early USMC Remington Model 700 sniper rifle (serial no. 168346). The telescope is a first-generation commercial finish (black gloss) Redfield 3X-9X variable power model. Note the soft plastic lens caps and the leather sling. The lens caps would serve as issue items with the USMC/Redfield contract sights; "leather or web slings" were furnished with the sniper rifles. It was common practice for arms manufacturers to photograph (record) one or more rifles during the initial or early stages of production. The weapon shown represents one of the first USMC M700 sniper rifles made for Marine Corps use in Vietnam. (Remington Arms Co.)

lar production components" and had "no unique specifications, just the right combination of parts."

With range estimation as big a problem as it was for the average sniper, the Accu-Range system Redfield offered was considered essential for effective sniping in Vietnam.

NOTE: The Accu-Range reticle was offered as an option beginning in 1965. Redfield referenced this as "the first built-in distance finder in a telescopic sight."

As Redfield then stated, "The Accu-Range feature provides an accurate means of determining the distance from the shooter to the target." The power selector ring located in front of the eyepiece controlled the power of magnification and the range-finder functions of the scope. Though later detailed in the Vietnam-era Marine Corps sniper training manual *FMFM 1-3B, Sniping* (5 August 1969), the range-finding system was explained by Redfield Gun Sight Co. in the instruction booklets it furnished to the Marine Corps (USMC procurement documents reference this booklet as the "Manual, Commercial Type").

The Marine Corps Model: The Green Scope

A Marine Corps M700 sniper rifle mounting a 3X-9X variable power Accu-Range USMC/Redfield contract sight. An original "matched assembly" in this case, the telescope and receiver base are engraved with the rifle serial number (no. 224353). The barrel and receiver are parkerized, the bolt assembly was given a black oxide finish. The aluminum trigger guard and floorplate were "colored black." The Redfield sight was anodized (olive green) to match the barrel and receiver; telescope mounting hardware was finished in black. (Otte Collection.)

The three related elements in a Redfield Accu-Range Variable are the "stadia" wires, located near the top of the sight picture, a power selector ring for enlarging or reducing the image, and a range scale located in the lower righthand quadrant, marked in yard increments.

To find the range to a target, position the target between the upper parallel (stadia) wires and begin to turn the power selector ring. Continue to turn the power selector ring until the stadia wires bracket the target from shoulder to belt. Read the number at the bottom of the range indicator scale—this is the distance from you to the target. Once the range is known, you determine the holdover necessary for an accurate shot with the weapon and the load you are using.

NOTE: The term "holdover" is the procedure used to hit a target at ranges other than the range for which the rifle is zeroed. The correct use of "holds and leads" enabled the sniper to hit his target without holding his sights directly on the target.

According to Marine Corps "Supply Contract" NOm-73565, dated 17 May 1966, a total of 700 Redfield 3X-9X variable-power Accu-Range rifle scopes ("Scope, Special USMC Model"), along with Redfield JR (junior) 1-inch split-rings (low), and Redfield "Base, Special, JR 40X" were ordered from the Redfield Gun Sight Company, Denver, Colorado, for use with the Remington M700 Rifle.

A close view of another matching number USMC M700/Redfield sniper rifle produced during the Vietnam War. The rifle serial number (322764) was applied to the left side of the receiver mounting base and the telescope tube directly behind the objective bell. The numbering was done with a "hand-held engraving tool" (electric pencil) when the weapon passed final inspection. The rifle serial number was also placed on the underside of the bolt. A review of Vietnam-era USMC M700/M40 rifles and sights indicates that the numbering was consistent in form and artfully applied. Remington met its obligations by serial numbering the sight assemblies, but with telescope mounting hardware toleranced and manufactured as it was (i.e., the use of interchangeable components) and as long as the rifle and scope were both in working order and zeroed properly, it made little difference if the parts were numbered or not. When problems beset the weapon system in Vietnam, the rifles and scopes were "switched" on a routine basis in an effort to keep sniping equipment in the field. Few of the remaining matching number ("factory matched assembly") Remington/Redfield sniper rifles were ever subjected to combat use in Southeast Asia. (Scott Collection.)

Of further interest in this matter, the contract specified that shipment of the telescope and mounting hardware be made as follows:

- 29 each of the telescope, rings and instruction booklet were to be sent to Marine Corps Supply Center, Albany, Georgia.

- 121 each of the same items were consigned to the Marine Corps Supply Center, Barstow, California.

- 550 each of the telescope and rings, and 700 of the Redfield base and instruction booklet were to be shipped directly to the Remington Arms Company, Ilion, New York.

The contract also stated that shipments were scheduled to begin on or before 20 June 1966, with final shipment on or before 29 August 1966.

In addition to the Redfield order, Headquarters, USMC placed a parallel contract with the Remington Arms Company, Bridgeport,

The Marine Corps Model: The Green Scope

A typical first-generation 3X-9X variable power Redfield Accu-Range rifle scope issued with the USMC M700/M40 sniper rifle during the Vietnam War. The scope was colored green (anodized) to match the parkerized finish of the rifle. The power selector ring (numbered 3 to 9) located in front of the eyepiece assembly controlled the power of magnification and the range finder functions of the scope. The elevation and windage adjustment turrets were identical in appearance and movement; the turret caps tighten against small rubber rings to form a moisture seal. Commercial markings appear on the eyepiece, a factory serial number beneath the turret housing. According to Redfield, "Except for the green finish, the Marine Corps rifle scopes were the same as the standard model available in sporting goods stores." The sights were not marked to indicate military service. Marine Corps contract specifications defined the telescope and mounting hardware as, "Scope Special USMC Model, Item. No. 112035, w/Jr 1" Low Ring, pr Item No. 523503" and the receiver base "Base, Special, JR 40x, Item No. 511153." (Peter R. Senich.)

Connecticut ("Supply Contract" N0m-73566, 17 May 1966), for the Rifle, 7.62mm, Sniper, Remington M700 with requirements as follows:

- 550 each, Redfield scope and base installed, calibrated and test fired.

- 150 each, Redfield base only installed.

In accordance with the contract specifications, in this case, shipments were to be made as follows:

- 123 of the rifles with telescopic sights and 29 without the sights (base only), were consigned to Marine Corps Supply Center, Albany, Georgia.

- 427 of the rifles with telescopic sights and 121 without the sights (base only) were destined for shipment to Marine Corps Supply Center, Barstow, California.

The time of delivery for both the telescope and the rifle was coordinated through 29 August 1966 in the contract as well.

When it came to bringing the rifle and telescope together, Ludwig P. (Paul) Gogol, the Remington design engineer and custom shop foreman when the USMC M700 sniper rifles were manufactured, offered the following:

> Ordnance inspectors witnessed all operations including targeting, final inspection and packing procedures. The rifles were sighted-in and targeted at the Ilion Fish and Game Club range facilities. After targeting and acceptance, the rifles were placed in a hard case with their accessories, packed in card-

The flip-up lens covers ("flip-open covers") originally fielded with the USMC/Redfield contract sight as a remedial measure were made by the E.D. Vissing Co. (so marked). The cover is pictured on the ocular end of a Marine Corps telescope. The illustration also provides a good view of the Redfield power selector ring; the ring is positioned at 3 power. (Peter R. Senich.)

board containers, and palletized for shipment.

NOTE: The USMC contract requirements specified the following, in part: "The rifle, scope and base shall be identified with matching numbers utilizing the rifle serial number." This procedure took place following targeting and final acceptance of the rifle and scope as a "matched assembly." So far as it is known, the rifles shipped from Remington without telescopic sights did not have the serial number engraved on the receiver base.

As Gogol added, "The rifles left Remington as a complete package, ready for use."

NOTE: Even though Remington production records indicate a total of 995 7.62mm Model 700 sniper rifles were manufactured from 1966 to 1971, Remington completed the 1966 Marine Corps order for 700 of them that same year (550 rifles with telescopic sights, 150 rifles without telescopes). In addition to *a small quantity* of rifles the Marine Corps obtained for combat and subsequent development purposes following the initial order, the U.S. Navy and the Air Force reportedly obtained an unknown number of the Vietnam-era Remington sniper rifles as well. In any event, by 1973, as official documents attest, there were only 425 ("total density") Remington M700/M40 sniper rifles remaining in the Marine Corps on a worldwide basis.

Although USMC/Redfield telescopic sights were made and finished to Marine Corps specifications, there were no unique features, characteristics, or markings to indicate military service in this case. Except for their green anodized finish (simply referenced as a "military finish" by the Marine Corps), the sights were essentially the same as the commercial models sold over the counter.

Rather than an attempt to "camouflage" the scope, according to Redfield records, "the external finish was matted and colored to match the parkerized finish of the Remington M700 rifles on which they were mounted." Fabricated from aluminum alloy as they were, the sights

The Marine Corps Model: The Green Scope

E.D. Vissing lens cover fitted to the objective end of the Marine Corps sniper sight. The cover is shown in the open position in this case. An effective means of protecting the lens, the plastic covers were developed and patented by E.D. Vissing as an accessory item for commercial use. (Peter R. Senich.)

were "anodized" to protect them from the elements.

CAI Technologies, the company responsible for anodizing and color-finishing the original USMC/Redfield contract sights (and which still provides the anodizing and finish work for the Redfield line) provided the following insight on the process used with this system:

> The coloring of aluminum anodized components is achieved in much the same manner as that of dyeing an Easter egg. The clear anodized finish is put on first, electrolytically, then the parts are immersed in a hot bath of the desired color organic dye. The anodized coating is very porous and absorbs the dye... The coating is then chemically sealed to prevent the dye from leaching back out.

A radical departure from most telescopic sights of the day with their typical black finish, the "green" rifle scopes were considered unique in appearance when first issued. Furthermore, following extended field use in Southeast Asia, many of the USMC/Redfield scopes took on an unusual hue, which CAI Technologies attributed to "prolonged exposure to sunlight." As CAI explained further:

> The nature of organic dyes is such that they are sensitive to degradation by ultraviolet radiation. Prolonged exposure to sunlight causes damage to the dyes. This often results in the dye color changing from one color to another. For example, as a brown dye is damaged, it turns pink, and as a black finish degrades it often turns blue or purple. The burnished copper or bronze look was a degradation process on the green scopes.

In addition to concerns regarding the finish, exposure to the rigors of combat, Marine snipers, and the weather extremes in South Vietnam

A close comparison between the elevation and windage adjustment turret housing on the first-generation (top) and the second-generation 3X-9X variable power USMC/Redfield rifle telescopes. The entire assembly was redesigned, as Redfield stated, "to improve adjustments." Note the change from "Redfield 1″ Tube" to an updated version of "Redfield." The "3X-9X" model designation remained the same. As a matter of interest, the small markings on the turret housing (bottom) served as reference points for elevation and windage adjustments. The practice was known as "marking the sights" to many Marine marksmen, with either nail polish or paint used for this purpose. (Peter R. Senich.)

The Marine Corps Model: The Green Scope

A typical second-generation 3X-9X variable power Redfield Accu-Range rifle scope. The most obvious differences between this and the first-generation Redfield sights were the turret housing and the power selector ring. The early USMC scopes were colored green; the newer model has a black satin finish in this case. Even though second-generation Redfield sights were available during the later stages of Marine Corps involvement in South Vietnam, the extent of combat use, if any, remains unknown at present. Although combat use has not been confirmed, second-generation sights of this type were in fact purchased by the Marine Corps for use with the M700/M40 sniper rifle as a replacement for first-generation USMC sights that were lost in combat or beyond repair. (Peter R. Senich.)

resulted in a number of problems with the Redfield system. The scenario was all too familiar. Though more than adequate for general field use in the hands of a civilian rifleman, when commercial rifle scopes were pressed into military service in an "as manufactured" state, they rarely held up in a combat environment.

Although a number of Redfield 3X-9X variable-power telescopic sights fielded in Vietnam were rendered inoperative for one reason or another, many were still in service when the last Marine combat units left Southeast Asia. According to one Marine veteran, an armorer with firsthand experience in RVN, "It was a lot like buying a new car. It seemed you either got a good one or you didn't."

In deference to the Redfield system, even though most of the problems encountered in Vietnam were rightfully attributed to "design inadequacies" exacerbated by combat use, an untold quantity of Redfield sights were literally beat to hell due to negligent and/or careless handling. In some cases, their length of field service was hardly more than a matter of time in the hands of some Marines.

However, concurrent with difficulties affecting both the rifle and the telescopic sight, Marine Corps ordnance documents summarized the Redfield situation as follows:

> The scope is easily damaged, subject to fogging and inadequately sealed against moisture.
>
> The body of the sight cracks under the variable-power adjustment ring. [NOTE: a lateral opening or slot in the tube, (approximately 180 degrees) beneath the power selector ring was necessary for the "power-ring" to move the erector lenses to change magnification. As such, there was a tendency for "cracks" to form when the tube was stressed.]
>
> The range scale melts. Rays of the sun are reflected through the objective lens and are magnified, thereby causing the range finder to melt and/or lose adhesiveness which in turn results in the scale dropping into the tube rendering the scope less effective. [NOTE: The range scale was held to the internal lens sur-

An original Marine Corps issue M700/M40 sniper rifle mounting a post-Vietnam 3X-9X variable power Redfield Accu-Range sight. Although Vietnam-era M700/M40 rifles were reconfigured eventually (M40A1), the Redfield scopes remained in service until replaced by the Unertl 10-power Sniper Scope in the early 1980s. (Peter R. Senich.)

face with a "clear mastic adhesive." The sunlight, magnified as it was entering the tube at certain angles, caused the adhesive to melt and the range scale would then slip out of place, if it didn't melt in the process. Even though the scope remained functional, the Accu-Range feature was useless. Many Marine snipers referred to this as "losing the reticle."]

The lens covers provided with the sight loosen in the heat and fall off. [NOTE: Redfield furnished soft (pliable) plastic lens covers with each sight assembly. Though intended for field use, the plastic covers were more effective protecting the telescopes in transit than in the field. When subjected to elevated temperatures or direct sunlight, the lens covers softened and simply fell from the tube. The plastic lens caps were part of the original equipment package. As a matter of interest, the same type was later issued with the Army AR TEL sighting system with the same results. Separate telescope carrying cases or covers were not furnished with the USMC M700/Redfield system in Vietnam.]

Though rarely noted, it was not uncommon for the "point of impact" to shift significantly when power settings were changed in the variable-power sights. Whenever possible, Marine snipers were known to "pick through" whatever sights were available "to find one that worked properly." Marine snipers were taught to replace damaged reticles (crosshairs) and perform routine maintenance and basic repairs on the Unertl target scopes during early combat activity in RVN. But as complex as the Redfield variable-power system was by comparison, there were practical

The Marine Corps Model: The Green Scope

limits to the repairs a Marine sniper or a trained armorer could make, even under the best conditions.

Because the Redfield was a first-generation variable-power sight, only basic design improvements separated the Marine Corps model from those introduced to the commercial market a few years earlier. An "improved" 3X-9X variable-power sight described by Redfield as a "beefed up" version was available in 1968. However, except for a "limited quantity" of this version reportedly sent to Southeast Asia for evaluation during the final months of Marine Corps combat involvement, most, if not all, of the M700/M40 sniper rifles Marine snipers employed during this era made use of the first-generation 3X-9X variable-power Redfield sights commonly known as "the green scopes."

When it came to remedial measures taken in response to problems encountered with the Redfield sighting system during stateside sniper training and combat use in South Vietnam, one of the most effective solutions was the procurement and issuance of "flip-up" lens covers to counter the problem with sun-damaged range scales. An accessory item originally intended for commercial use, the lens cover protected both ends of the telescope and popped open instantly when the sight was needed.

NOTE: For the sake of clarification, even though they have been mentioned elsewhere as having been made and furnished by the Redfield firm, for the record, the flip-up lens covers ("flip-open covers") originally fielded with the USMC/Redfield contract sight as a remedial measure were made (and so marked) by the E.D. Vissing Company, a plastics firm based in Idaho Falls, Idaho. As a Redfield supplier, in addition to eventually producing the Redfield "Supreme" flip-up covers, Vissing also made the soft plastic lens caps furnished with the Vietnam-era USMC and Army Redfield sights. The Vissing firm was sold to the Butler Creek Corporation in 1974.

The following admonition was eventually added to the instruction booklet furnished with the Redfield Accu-Range sights:

> IMPORTANT: Avoid letting the sun shine directly into the objective lens. This lens can act as a "burning glass," causing deterioration of the Accu-Range scale.

When it came to the improved model, whether significant changes to the Redfield 3X-9X variable-power sight came as a result of the Marine Corps problems in Vietnam or were scheduled improvements has not been substantiated. In any case, what Redfield then referred to as "improving the line" emerged as a redesigned second-generation 3X-9X variable-power sight.

Even though the two models appeared similar at first glance, the improved version displayed some notable differences. The turret housing, adjustment turrets, and caps were completely redesigned, as Redfield stated, "to make adjustments easier." (The scale on each turret [elevation-windage] was changed from 33 to 48 index lines. The graduation adjustment values [1/2-minute of movement] remained the same.) The tube was reinforced at the opening beneath the power selector ring, and the ring itself was reconfigured. Instead of a "jointed tube" (screwed together), the objective bell and the main tube were eventually formed from a single piece of aluminum alloy. While this was essentially a "one-piece tube," the eyepiece assembly still threaded to the end (this design change was noted in 1968 USAMTU and LWL documents as a significant improvement). The eyepiece assembly was enlarged, and the field and ocular lenses were resized accordingly. The range scale (Accu-Range reticle) yard markings and divisions were also changed.

NOTE: A random sampling of "green" 3X-9X variable-power Redfield sights issued with the Vietnam-era USMC Remington M700/M40 sniper rifles indicates some use of range scales normally found in the second-generation scopes. Whether these represent sights "rebuilt" by Redfield (as many of the original issue scopes subsequently were) or manufactured as such remains unknown.

Commercial sights were available with a black gloss or black satin anodized finish. Though few in actual number, the variable-power telescopes procured as replacements for first-generation sights that were lost in combat or beyond repair made use of the satin finish. Both first- and second-generation 3X-9X variable-power Accu-Range telescopic sights (green-black) remained in Marine Corps service during the 1970s.

While it seems that the Marine Corps experienced considerable difficulty with the Redfield system while the Army apparently did not, as an Army spokesman summarized the matter in retrospect, "The improvements made to the Redfield sighting system [1968] did make a significant difference in their reliability."

NOTE: According to Marine Corps information, in keeping with its contractual obligations, the Redfield firm absorbed the expense of repairing any telescopic sight with defects relating to design flaws or the manufacturing process.

Whereas the USMC/Redfield contract sights were first-generation variable-power scopes, the adjustable ranging telescopes fielded by the Army, beginning with those sent to the 9th Infantry Division in late 1968, were based on the improved second-generation model.

As a matter of historical interest, the Limited Warfare Laboratory Adjustable Ranging Telescopes evaluated by ACTIV during 1967 were based on first-generation 3X-9X variable-power Redfield sights. The Adjustable Ranging Telescopes sent to South Vietnam as part of the emerging 9th Infantry Division sniper program were second-generation 3X-9X variable-power sights reconfigured to ART specifications by the LWL. The

The Marine Corps Model: The Green Scope

U.S. Army AR TEL Adjustable Ranging Telescopes considered "production sights" were also based on second-generation Redfield 3X-9X variable-power sights. In this case, however, the Army scopes were manufactured as such at the Redfield plant (1969) to ART specifications.

In one form or another, the Redfield 3X-9X variable-power telescope served as the principal Army and Marine Corps sniper sight during the war in Vietnam.

CHAPTER 10

Silencers and Suppressors: The Sionics Legacy

When the nature of the war in South Vietnam made it clear that different combinations of silencer-equipped small arms would be necessary, in addition to the research and development conducted by military and government agencies, various civilian firms turned their attention to designing silencers and noise suppressors for combat use in Southeast Asia.

Although some of these commercial organizations were branches or divisions of major corporations with ordnance ties to the government, small, independent firms intent on gaining their share of a potentially large market carried out a considerable amount of development work.

The most notable of these, perhaps, was Sionics, Inc. (Studies in Operational Negation of Insurgency and Counter Subversion), founded by Mitchell Livingston WerBell III for the express purpose of designing, developing, and marketing silencers and noise suppressors for military and quasi-military operations in Southeast Asia.

Having served during World War II as an officer with the fabled OSS, the forerunner of Central Intelligence Agency (CIA), Mitch WerBell had gained considerable insight into and experience in the combat application of silenced small arms. Though many considered WerBell an outright rogue, the Vice President and Director of Research and Development of Sionics, Inc. was well-known in military and political circles as a dauntless anti-Communist.

With the pressing need that existed among regular and covertly regular U.S. military personnel in Southeast Asia for silencer-equipped

Mitchell L. WerBell III, the Vice President and Director of Research and Development of Sionics, Inc., is shown with a telescopic sighted M16 rifle mounting a Sionics 5.56mm MAW-A1 noise and flash suppressor. The guiding force behind Sionics during the war in Vietnam, WerBell spent a considerable amount of time in RVN, generating interest in his firm's silencers, suppressors, and military hardware. This unique photograph was made during WerBell's promotional tour of South Vietnam during late 1968 and early 1969. (Thomas Collection.)

weapons, the Sionics organization was guided by the basic marketing philosophy often stated by WerBell: "If the military buys a silencer, I want them to buy it from us." In many respects, Sionics came close to achieving this goal.

As the war in Vietnam escalated, it became obvious that the greatest potential for sound-suppressing devices rested with the 5.56mm M16 rifle. By 1967, the major thrust of Sionics development activity was directed toward perfecting an optimum suppressor design for this weapon system. While the emergence of the Sionics 7.62mm suppressor for the M14 proved to be a residual benefit, the primary focus remained developing a satisfactory suppressor for the M16 rifle.

According to company records, "Intensive research and development on the M16A1 suppressor began in early 1967. Approximately 75 experimental models were eventually fabricated and tested." Of all the

Silencers and Suppressors: The Sionics Legacy

South Vietnamese and U.S. Army personnel during a test-firing session with Mitch WerBell (right). The rifle is an M16 equipped with a 3-power Colt/Realist scope and Sionics suppressor. Note the Sionics corporate logo on WerBell's bush hat. (Thomas Collection.)

silencers and noise suppressors Sionics developed during this era, the final version of the MAW-A1 Noise and Flash Suppressor Assembly for the M16A1 rifle evolved as the principal suppressor.

In addition to noise suppressors for the M14 (M14SS-1) and M16 (MAW-A1) rifles, both of which the Army procured for use in Vietnam under ENSURE authority, Sionics also developed and marketed a wide range of silencers, suppressors, and subsonic ammunition for pistols, submachine guns, and rifles to the U.S. military, law enforcement agencies, and friendly free-world governments.

From the late 1960s through the early 1970s (the name Sionics, Inc. was changed to Military Armament Corporation, or MAC, in 1970), the Sionics/MAC product line ranged from a diminutive .22-caliber "handheld firing device" to special suppressors for 7.62mm miniguns (multiple-barrel [6], belt-fed, electrically driven machine guns) mounted on helicopters and aircraft in Southeast Asia. The broad-based line of specialized military hardware and counterinsurgency equipment included the Ingram submachine guns, the Atchisson subcaliber conversion device for the M16 rifle, and various long-range and intermediate-range telescopic sighted suppressor- and silencer-equipped rifles and carbines for sniping and countersniping.

A South Vietnamese Army officer test-firing a 9mm Sionics Sniper Carbine at the ARVN Infantry School. The Sionics "silent sniper carbine" developed during the late 1960s was based on the Spanish "Destroyer Carbine," a magazine-fed, bolt-action, carbine-sized weapon once employed by police and military units in Spain, although full- and sporter-stocked models were fabricated early on. The weapon demonstrated by Mitch WerBell in Vietnam made use of a collapsible "wire stock" with a pistol grip, special Sionics silencer with an "auxiliary front chamber," and a side-mounted Mossberg 4-power telescopic sight originally intended for a small-bore rifle. (Thomas Collection.)

A part of the early Sionics 9mm sniper carbine development series. A sporter-stock version of the Spanish Destroyer Carbine fitted with a barrel- mounted M14 supressor, the versatile M14 suppressors were frequently employed by the Sionics firm for test and development purposes with different weapons. (Thomas Collection.)

Silencers and Suppressors: The Sionics Legacy

The Commanding Officer of I Field Force, Vietnam (I FFV), Lt. Gen. William R. Peers, USA, is pictured with Mitch WerBell during one of the ordnance demonstrations WerBell conducted in Vietnam. As impressed with the Sionics sniper carbine as he was, General Peers was instrumental in having the Army place an order for "ten Destroyer Carbines with silencers and telescopic sights" for evaluation purposes, although substantial quantities of the Spanish carbine had been imported by arms dealers during the early 1960s. The supply had dried up by the time Sionics decided to use the weapon as the basis for its 9mm sniper carbine. Ironically, when the order came through, there were no weapons available for conversion purposes. Despite efforts to withdraw from the contract, the Army, in no uncertain terms, directed Sionics, Inc. to "find a suitable substitute." (Thomas Collection.)

At the peak of its activity, Georgia-based Military Armament Corp. employed 75 people. Although Sionics, Inc. had maintained corporate offices in Atlanta, it carried out design, development, manufacturing, and testing at the WerBell family compound ("The Farm") in Powder Springs. During its final years of operation as Military Armament Corporation, the firm was based in Marietta, Georgia.

Military Armament Corp. suspended all operations in 1975, and Mitchell L. WerBell III passed away in 1983. The Sionics/MAC legacy to small arms research, particularly as it applied to silencers and suppressors during the Vietnam War, will be long remembered.

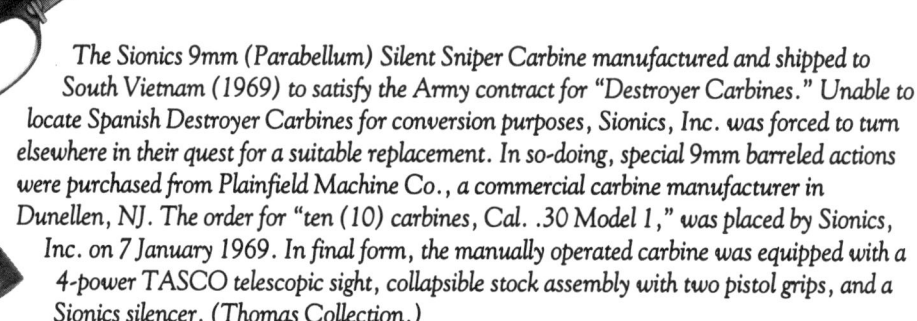

The Sionics 9mm (Parabellum) Silent Sniper Carbine manufactured and shipped to South Vietnam (1969) to satisfy the Army contract for "Destroyer Carbines." Unable to locate Spanish Destroyer Carbines for conversion purposes, Sionics, Inc. was forced to turn elsewhere in their quest for a suitable replacement. In so-doing, special 9mm barreled actions were purchased from Plainfield Machine Co., a commercial carbine manufacturer in Dunellen, NJ. The order for "ten (10) carbines, Cal. .30 Model 1," was placed by Sionics, Inc. on 7 January 1969. In final form, the manually operated carbine was equipped with a 4-power TASCO telescopic sight, collapsible stock assembly with two pistol grips, and a Sionics silencer. (Thomas Collection.)

The Vietnam-era Sionics Silent Sniper Carbine shown disassembled. Note the silencer unit separated from the special 9mm vented barrel, operating rod (slide assembly) altered for manual operation, and 13-round Browning High Power pistol magazine modified to fit the carbine receiver. The weapons were assembled by Sionics, Inc. and test-fired prior to shipment. In addition to the 10 carbines ordered by the Army, an internal company memo dated 17 February 1969 noted that four 9mm silenced carbines were included with a variety of silenced weapons and miscellaneous equipment ordered by the 9th Infantry Division. At this juncture, there is nothing to indicate that Sionics produced more than 14 9mm silenced carbines in this configuration. Although details surrounding their subsequent field use have not been disclosed, the 9mm Sionics carbines are known to have seen limited use by MACV/SOG personnel in Southeast Asia. (Thomas Collection.)

A Remington Model 788 bolt-action rifle reconfigured as a 9mm (Parabellum) carbine. The action was fitted with a 9mm barrel and Sionics silencer; the original stock was modified accordingly. The detachable clip magazine assembly was altered to take an 8 round P-38 pistol magazine, and a 4-power TASCO telescope was mounted directly over the receiver. The silencer is marked "SIONICS U.S.A. 9mm"; the receiver and the silencer were both numbered "X1028." A West Point Museum piece in this case, the 9mm carbine was obtained from Rock Island Arsenal (RIA) in 1973. Unfortunately, there is no way of determining if this weapon type was developed by Sionics as a part of an ongoing program or, as some contend, as a replacement system for the improvised 9mm Army contract carbines sent to Vietnam in 1969. In any event, however, Military Armament Corp. was known to send hardware to RIA for comparative testing during the course of the war. (West Point Collection.)

A February 1970 Aberdeen Proving Ground photograph of a Remington Model 788 bolt-action rifle as reconfigured by Sionics, Inc. for Army evaluations. In this case, however, the weapon was simply referenced as a "Carbine, 9mm parabellum (modified)." In addition to Sionics markings, this companion to the West Point Museum piece is numbered "X1029," although the numbering is barely visible. Details concerning this system remain obscure, but Sionics is known to have produced at least four weapons of this type. (Alley Collection.)

Silencers and Suppressors: The Sionics Legacy

Mitch WerBell shown attaching a Sionics suppressor to a Remington Model 788 (.243 caliber) rifle during preparations for a Special Forces weapons demonstration. (Thomas Collection.)

Special Forces sergeant test-firing the Remington Model 788 bolt-action rifle. The telescope is a 3X-9X variable power Redfield model; the special suppressor was made for the Remington .243 Win.-caliber rifle (6.16 x 51mm) in this case. The rifle and suppressor were the "only one of their kind" fielded by Sionics. (Thomas Collection.)

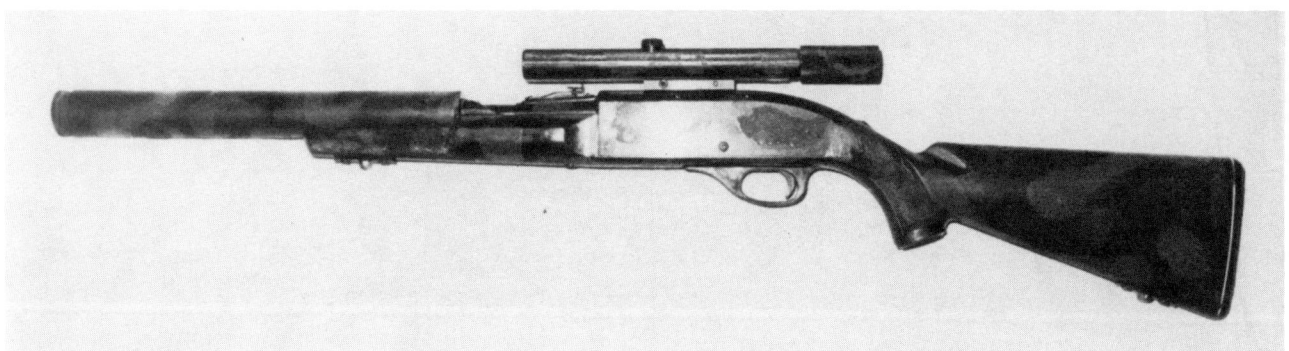

Remington Nylon 66 .22-caliber rifle with 4-power Bushnell telescope and Sionics silencer. The semiautomatic small-bore rifle was furnished by Sionics, Inc. for U.S. military use in Southeast Asia during the late 1960s. Though effective, the Nylon 66 (nylon stock) proved difficult to disassemble and clean. The military was also less than enthusiastic about the tubular magazine feeding through the stock as it did. The rifle was considered "difficult to load." From a conversion standpoint, both the barrel and stock required extensive modifications to adapt the silencer. The weapon weighed 4 pounds with the silencer and rifle scope. Standard velocity Caliber .22 Ball, Long Rifle (jacketed bullet) cartridges were recommended. Army contract specifications listed the effective range as 100 meters (110 yards). The Remington Nylon 66 was superseded by the Ruger 10/22 carbine, also in .22 caliber. Although special .22 caliber weapons were popular in Vietnam, the availability of suitable ammunition proved to be a problem in many cases. As a matter of interest, the use of silenced .22-caliber rifles came as a result of requests from combat units in RVN. According to Army information, "The silenced .22 caliber rifles were intended as supplemental weapons for long range patrols, ambush situations and 'snatch missions' when specific individuals were captured in a clandestine manner." (Thomas Collection.)

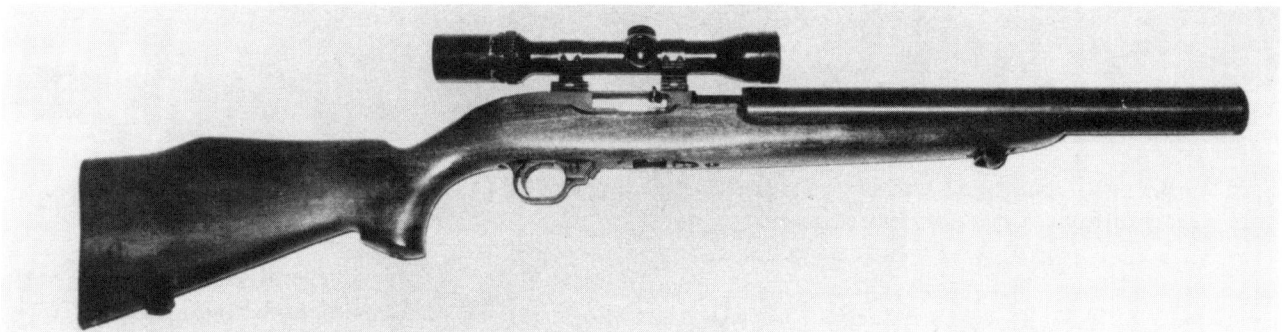

The Ruger Model 10/22 semiautomatic rifle emerged as the principal .22-caliber Sionics/Military Armament Corp. "Special Mission" weapon beginning about 1970. As then described, "This weapon was designed for ranges of 0 to 175 yards. It is equipped with a silencer which lowers the noise level to that of a quiet air gun." The Ruger 10/22 was well suited for conversion purposes. It was easy to maintain, and the 10-shot detachable rotary magazine made loading uncomplicated. The rifles were available with Realist 1.5X-4.5X variable power or auto-ranging telescopic sights. In addition to the full-stocked version, a folding stock was eventually offered as well, even though a "bolt-latch" device (for optimum single-shot quiet firing) was developed and tested with the Remington and Ruger rifles during the course of Sionics development. This feature was not available on the "production rifles." The weapon illustrated is fitted with a 1.5X-4.5X variable power Realist sight. The Sionics/MAC silencer was 15.37 inches long; the weapon weighed 6 pounds. (Thomas Collection.)

Military Armament Corp. (MAC) Ruger 10/22 .22 caliber "autoloader" complete with Realist variable power scope, Sionics silencer, and folding stock with pistol grip. When military sales ended, the manufacturer changed the focus and the weapon was marketed to law enforcement agencies as the "MAC 10/22 Silent Counter Sniper System." In addition to the silenced .22-caliber hardware generated by Sionics/Military Armament Corp., a variety of special purpose, silencer-equipped .22-caliber weapons developed elsewhere (Winchester, AMF corp., et al) were evaluated at Rock Island Arsenal during the late 1960s and early 1970s. Although many different types of silencer- and suppressor-equipped weapon combinations were employed in Southeast Asia., silenced .22 caiber pistols and rifles were among the most effective. (Thomas Collection.)

Armalite AR-7 .22 caliber survival rifle fitted with a Sionics silencer and Bushnell telescopic sight. In original form, the weapon was intended to be used by downed airmen for hunting small game. The commercial version of the Air Force survival rifle was marketed as the "Explorer." Though few in actual number, silencer-equipped Armalite AR-7 rifles were also sold to the Army for use in Vietnam, their primary purpose being to "eliminate people" at relatively short ranges while remaining undetected. At least one other silenced version of the AR-7 from another source was tested at Rock Island Arsenal. (Thomas Collection.)

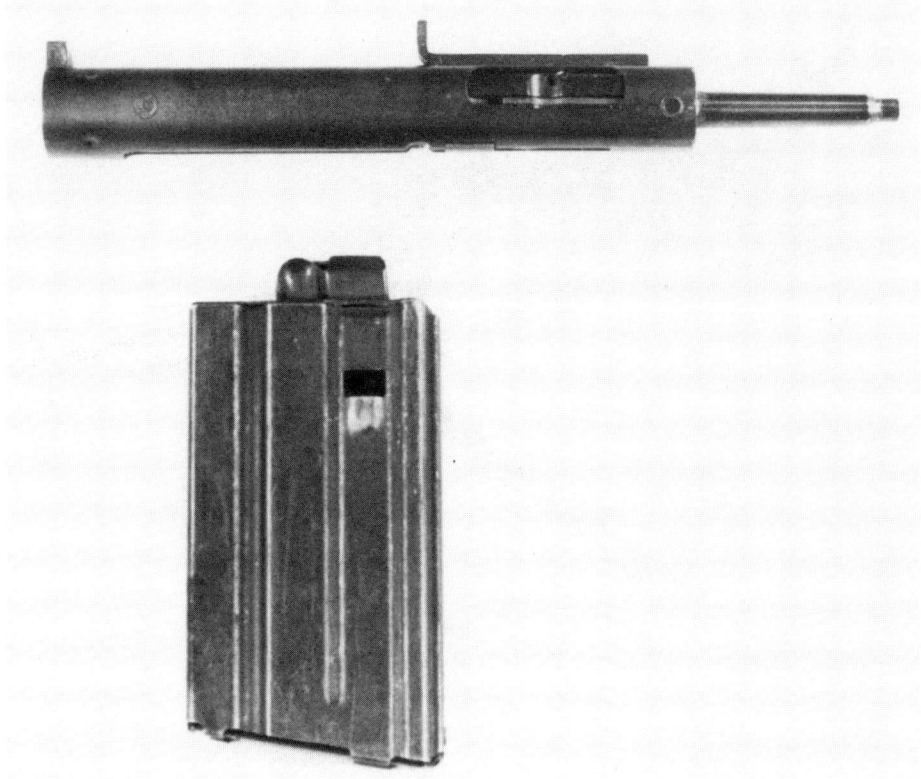

An Atchisson AR15/M16 .22 Long Rifle Conversion Device as manufactured by Military Armament Corporation beginning in 1971. The subcaliber device allowed the use of regular .22-caliber ammunition for training purposes. The ".22 Rimfire Conversion Package" was designed and developed by Maxwell G. Atchisson in 1970. The original version was manufactured and marketed under license by Military Armament Corp. for approximately two years. A complete package included the replacement bolt assembly, special 16-round magazine designed for .22 rimfire ammunition, and a pouch for storing the kit or the standard M16 bolt. Installing the unit took less than a minute. The assembly illustrated was the "first production unit" and bears the serial no. "1." A Sionics logo and Military Armament Corp. markings appear on the bolt and the magazine. Had the Atchisson conversion package been available at the height of U.S. combat involvement in Southeast Asia, experts believe that special operations personnel could have used a standard M16 fitted with a conversion device and noise suppressor on an as-needed basis rather than employing separate silencer-equipped .22-caliber rifles and carbines. (Thomas Collection.)

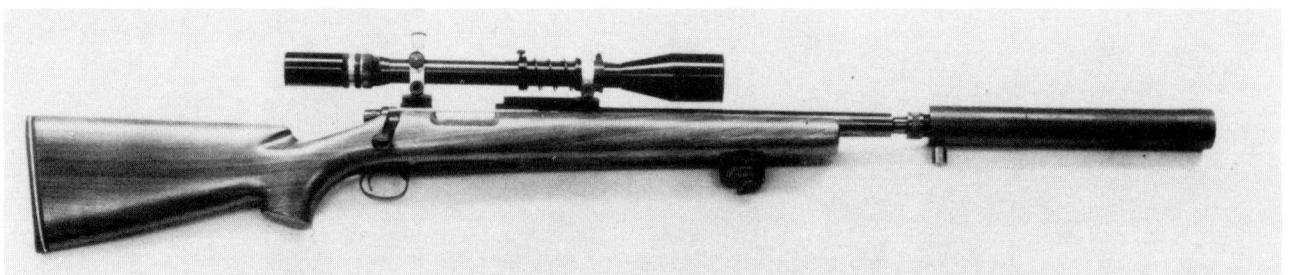

Remington Model 40-XB 7.62mm target rifle fitted with a Unertl BV-20 telescopic sight and a Sionics suppressor (1972). Although post-Vietnam efforts to market bolt-action sniping and countersniping rifles by Military Armament Corp. were centered on 7.62mm (.308) and 5.56mm (.223) versions of the Remington Model 700, heavy-barrel target rifles were equipped with telescopic sights and suppressors for law enforcement sales during the early 1970s as well. At one point, the Remington target rifle was referenced as the "MAC Model 73." (Donald G. Thomas - John Foote.)

Silencers and Suppressors: The Sionics Legacy

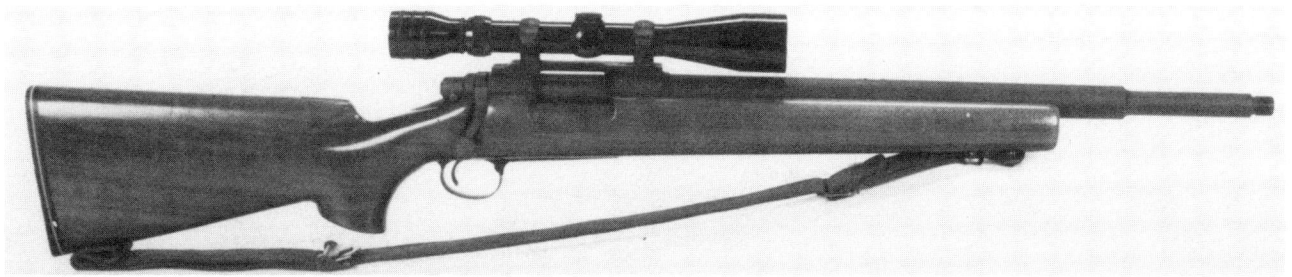

Remington Model 40-XB 7.62mm target rifle with the barrel modified for suppressor use. According to Remington records, the rifle was shipped to Military Armament Corporation in February 1973. The telescope is a standard Redfield 3X-9X variable power model. (Glover Collection.)

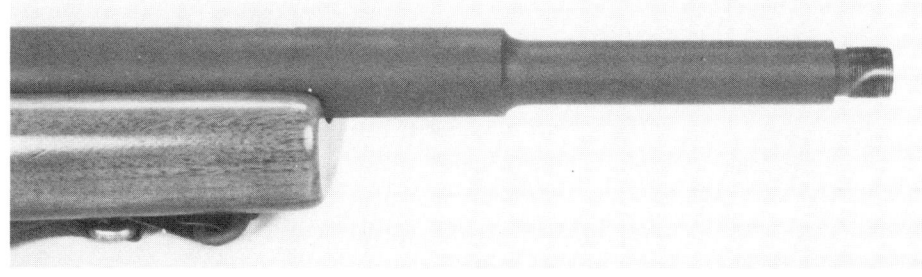

A close view of the Remington target rifle showing the machined suppressor mounting area of the barrel. The muzzle threads engaged the "retaining ring" inside the 7.62mm suppressor. Note the large radius at the juncture of the machined section and the original barrel. Although sales of M14 suppressors had all but ended when American troops began redeploying to the United States, the 7.62mm suppressors were offered with the MAC sniper rifles following the war in Vietnam. (Glover Collection.)

Max Atchisson sighting a Military Armament Corp. "Counter Sniping System" intended for sales to law enforcement agencies. The MAC Model 72 sniping rifle was based on the bolt-action Remington Model 700. The system was offered as a 7.62mm long-range model and a 5.56mm intermediate-range version. The rifles were glass-bedded and were available with a 3X-9X Leatherwood automatic ranging telescope (LART), straight-line thumb hole stock, and the appropriate noise suppressor. The suppressors furnished with this system were essentially standard M14 and M16 units. Although MAC product information (circa 1970) had listed the M14 and M16 suppressors as the "MAC Mk III M-40 7.62/5.56mm Suppressors," equipment designations were changed frequently, and this reference does not appear to have been used in sales literature for the Counter Sniper System. (Thomas Collection.)

Mounted on the M-14 Rifle

leatherwood automatic ranging telescope

The LART and Suppressor Mounted on the M-16 Rifle

An advertisement for the Leatherwood automatic ranging telescope (LART) as referenced and marketed by MAC and the Cromwell Corporation circa 1972. A 3X-9X auto-ranging scope is pictured with an M14; a 1.5X-4.5X version is mounted on the M16. At that point, the Leatherwood/Realist ART system was offered with the M14, M16, and the MAC countersniper rifles. (Thomas Collection.)

The LART comes in two models. Your selection of the model is dependent on the calibre and range capability of your own counter sniper weapon. For most common law enforcement situations, the .223 with effective ranges up to 450 meters is optimal. For extreme ranges, the 7.62 NATO (Win. 308) system with ranges up to 900 meters is recommended.

Intermediate Range LART
for .223 (5.56)
Available in two configurations: A 1.5 x 4.5 Adjustable with automatic ranging to 450 meters. Or a 3x9 Adjustable with a delayed-rise cam which allows increase of magnification up to 6 power before the cam actuates the ranging feature to 450 meters.

Long Range LART
for 7.62 (.308)
3 x 9 Adjustable with automatic ranging from 325 meters to 900 meters.

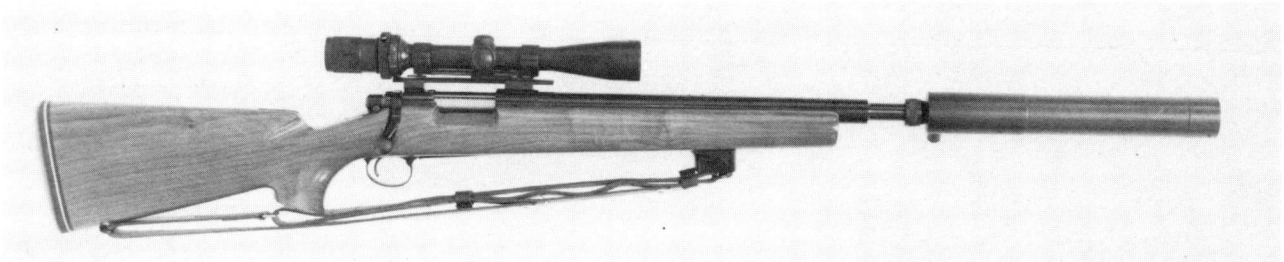

A military Armament Corp. "countersniper system" (Model 73) based on the 7.62mm Remington 40-XB rifle. The sight is a Leatherwood/Realist 3X-9X variable power Adjustable Ranging Telescope (ART). Note the difference in the barrel machining between the MAC-modified Remington target rifles pictured in this chapter. (Thomas Collection.)

Silencers and Suppressors: The Sionics Legacy

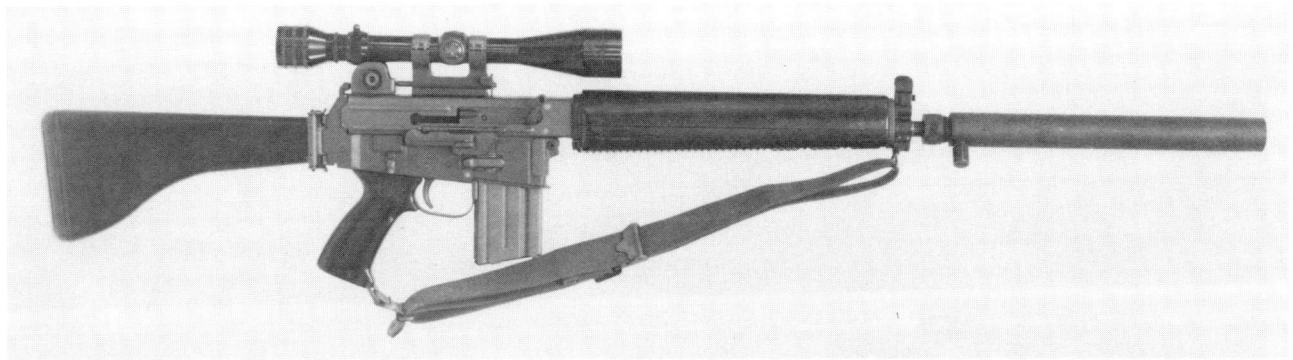

Sionics suppressors were mounted on a wide variety of weapon systems to demonstrate their versatility and to generate sales. In this case, an Armalite AR-18 5.56mm assault rifle was fitted with a standard MAW-A1 suppressor. The telescope mounting was an accessory item offered by Armalite. The telescope is a 3X-9X variable power Redfield commercial sight; the adjustment turret caps are removed. (Thomas Collection.)

A Stoner 63A 5.56mm assault rifle manufactured by Cadillac Gage Company fitted with a Sionics noise suppressor. Notes generated by Mitch WerBell during his ordnance demonstrations in Vietnam (1968/1969) indicated that the Royal Thai Army and MACV/SOG personnel were "extremely interested" in the Stoner weapon system. (Thomas Collection.)

Mitchell L. WerBell IV ("Mitch Four") with a suppressor-equipped Stoner 63A assault rifle. The sons of the founder of Sionics/MAC (Mitchell WerBell III), Mitch Four and Geoffrey, were involved with the day-to-day operations of the company and were also directly responsible for various silencer/suppressor design improvements. Photographs such as this were used in the maintenance and operation manuals for the Sionics suppressor line. (Thomas Collection.)

Above: An experimental Sionics suppressor developed for the 5.56mm CAR-15. As popular as the Colt submachine gun was with the special mission groups operating in Southeast Asia, Sionics had considered manufacturing component parts for the system in addition to noise suppressors. Though similar in appearance to the standard Sionics M16 suppressor (the MAW-A1), the CAR-15 unit was different in that its barrel length determined the physical characteristics of the suppressor (length and diameter). The CAR-15 unit was different than the standard Sionics M16 suppressor. Although various firms and government agencies were reportedly involved with CAR-15 suppressor development, so far as it is known, the only device considered operational was the Frankford Arsenal CAR-15 suppressor made for the Air Force. (Thomas Collection.)

Donald G. Thomas, noted silencer authority and associate of Sionics/Military Armament Corp. during its halcyon days, is shown firing a suppressor-equipped Ingram 9mm Model 10 (MAC-10) submachine gun at the WerBell range circa 1971. Of all the specialized military equipment manufactured and marketed by Sionics/MAC during the late 1960s and early 1970s, the suppressor-equipped Ingram submachine gun emerged as the principal product line, followed by the MAW-A1 5.56mm suppressor. (J. David Truby.)

Silencers and Suppressors: The Sionics Legacy

217

An early 1970s photograph of John Foote (left), Gordon Ingram, and Max Atchisson (right), following an afternoon "shoot" at the WerBell compound ("The Farm") in Powder Springs, Georgia. Military Armament Corporation boasted a unique blend of small-arms design talent and shooting experience. In addition to those pictured, Jim Leatherwood, Franklin Owens, and Burt Waldron, the Army's premier sharpshooter, were all involved with various aspects of small-arms research and development at the firm. (Thomas Collection.)

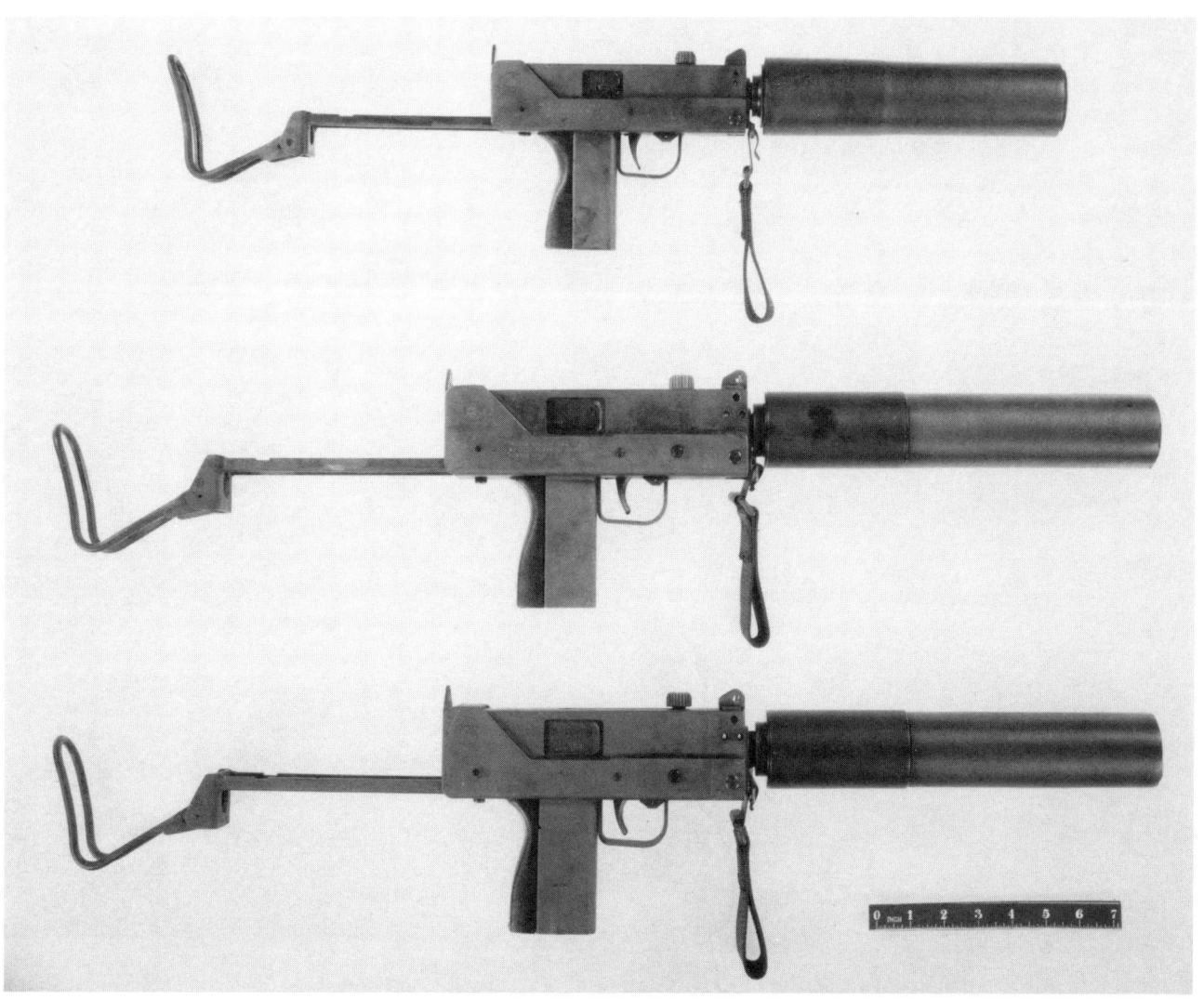

Aberdeen Proving Ground photograph (1970) of the MAC Ingram Model 11 submachine gun caliber 9mm Short (.380) and the Model 10 in 9mm Parabellum (center) and .45 caliber (Model 10) directly below. The stocks are extended; the suppressors have the early foam rubber covering. Grasping the strap beneath the barrel served to counteract the tendency of the weapon to recoil toward the right. As the system was then described, "The Ingram-Sionics Model 10 and 11 submachine guns are small, easily concealable pistol-caliber weapons capable of delivering high volume full automatic fire at moderate ranges . . . Originally designed for clandestine operations in urban environments, these weapons are of optimum value in any situation where ease of concealment, high fire-power, and lack of detection through sound suppression are of importance." (Alley Collection.)

Ingram submachine guns in storage racks at the Military Armament Corp. plant in Marietta, Georgia (approximately 30 miles northwest of Atlanta). The weapons have been test-fired and are ready for cleaning and packaging. The Ingram/MAC submachine guns saw limited use by U.S. Navy SEALs and various other special mission groups during the final stages of the war in Vietnam. (Thomas Collection.)

Partial view of the "Glover Street" production facilities at the Military Armament Corp. plant in Marietta, circa 1974. Faced with one financial crisis after another, MAC declared bankruptcy in 1975. The remaining assets were liquidated the following year. (Thomas Collection.)

A snake (Cobra) encircling the world with a stylized "S" to signify Sionics' global sales served as the Sionics, Inc. and Military Armament Corp. logo during the course of their business activity. After Sionics became Military Armament in 1970 (the name was acquired by agreement from Donald G. Thomas, a Sionics associate and owner of a small military and law enforcement equipment supply business operating under that name), the weapons and hardware MAC manufactured carried the original Sionics logo, the corporate name, and either a Powder Springs or Marietta, Georgia, location.

CHAPTER 11

Night Vision Sights: A Definite Edge

Following the Korean War, the military continued development of weapon-mounted infrared units, with primary efforts directed at improving the effective range as well as eliminating the cumbersome power pack. By the late 1950s, satisfactory devices meeting both criteria were developed for use with the M1 Garand rifle.

An improved variant, designated T-1, Infrared Weapon Sight, was issued in limited quantities for the Ml Garand (Special) and its successor, the 7.62mm M14 rifle, in the early 1960s. Such units consisted of an infrared light source, the image-forming telescope, and—unquestionably the most significant aspect of the new devices—an integral, miniaturized high-voltage power unit that obviated the need for an awkward knapsack-carried power source. The operator could now easily carry power, supplied by a rechargeable 6 VDC Nicad battery, by affixing it to his cartridge belt.

Unlike the M1 Garand, which necessitated a special receiver mounting, the M14 ordnance design had provided for ready attachment of accessory devices such as infrared and telescopic weapon sights by incorporating a bracket-mounting groove and screw recess on the left side of the receiver. As compared to the 28- to 30-pound Korean War variants, the new Infrared Weapon Sight was vastly improved from this standpoint alone.

Beginning in 1961, the U.S. Army's prime contractors, Varo Inc., of Garland, Texas, and Polan Industries, Inc., of Huntington, West Virginia, furnished it with the improved Infrared Weapon Sights. The sights were known as Models 9903 and P-155, respectively.

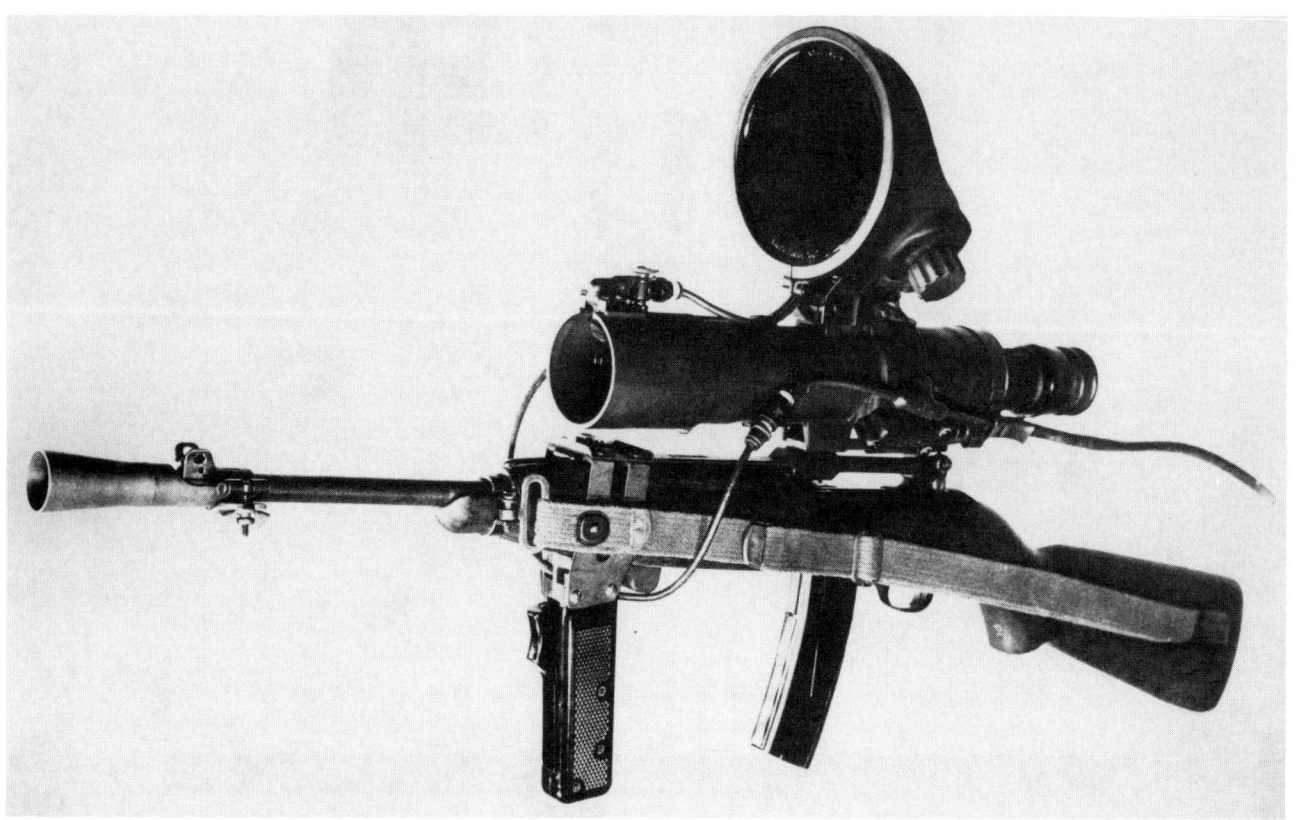

The last of the carbine-mounted infrared units, the M3 Sniperscope. Officially designated "Sniperscope Infrared Set No. 1, 20,000 volts," the M3 was manufactured by the American Optical Co. and Capehart-Farnsworth circa 1950–51. South Vietnamese troops (ARVN) employed limited numbers of M3 units, despite their vintage, during early action against the Vietcong. (Sam Bases.)

Subsequent combat use of the infrared weapon sights by U.S. Special Forces units in Southeast Asia during the early 1960s revealed that reflections from foliage, grass, and branches restricted ranges significantly. Effective coverage up to 250 meters was achieved over river surfaces and up to 150 meters over rice paddies. However, in grassy areas, where blades of grass and weeds partly obstructed the view, range was limited to only 100 meters (interestingly, this was the basis for original complaints registered during early infrared combat use in the South Pacific in World War II).

Combat reports generated in South Vietnam indicated that infrared use was most effective on clear, dark nights. Soft natural light, such as twilight, dawn, bright moonlight, or starlight, caused a hazy glow in the electronic telescope, thereby reducing image clarity. Although ambient light did not render an infrared device useless, the unit would not perform as well as it could in complete darkness, for example.

By this time, Russian development, use, and supply of night-vision equipment to Communist Bloc allies was well known to the U.S. military. U.S. combat personnel tasked with using infrared equipment knew that enemy soldiers also equipped with infrared weapon sights or detection viewers could pick up the beams projected by their light sources and

Night Vision Sights: A Definite Edge

The AN/PAS-4 Infrared Weapon Sight produced by Varo, Inc. (9903) and Polan Industries (P-155), as used by South Vietnamese (ARVN), U.S. Army, and Marine Corps troops in Vietnam. Utilized primarily with the M14 rifle, the sight could be adapted to the M16 with a special mount. Though later replaced by Starlight Scopes for combat purposes, infrared weapon sights saw continued use in a training capacity. (Sam Bases.)

A typical Vietnam-era AN/PAS-4 Infrared Weapon Sight. As then described, "The weapon sight is a battery-operated sight and aiming device consisting of an infrared light source, an infrared sensitive image-forming telescope [4.5-power] with integral miniaturized high voltage power supply, and a light source power supply [a belt-mounted 6 VDC rechargeable nickel-cadmium battery]." The telescope assembly was 13 inches long; the telescope and light source were approximately 14 inches high. The entire system weighed slightly over 12 pounds. The Infrared Weapon Sight and supporting equipment were issued with a carrying case. The AN/PAS-4 was the last infrared weapon sight U.S. forces employed. References for the infrared system included TM 5-1090-200-15 and TM 5-1090-25P, and Operation, Maintenance and Overhaul Manual, Model P-155, by Polan Industries. (Excalibur Enterprises.)

accurately pinpoint their location. Even though they were instructed how to avoid possible detection, this fact caused considerable concern among ground combat forces in Vietnam during operations involving the infrared sights.

The system fielded for use in Southeast Asia was referenced as the AN/PAS-4 Infrared Weapon Sight. The workings of the AN/PAS-4, an "Active-Infrared Type," were summarized as follows by Excalibur

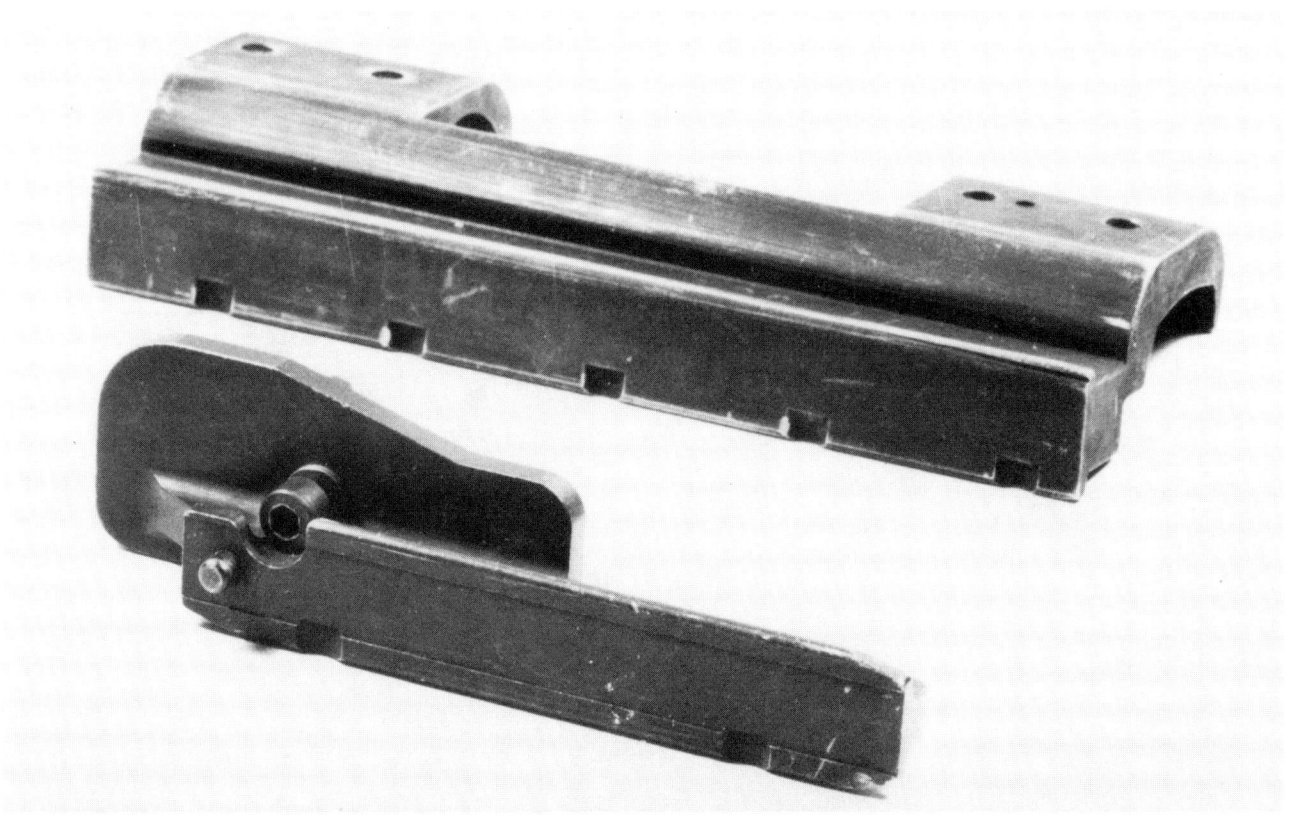

A special aluminum mount (top) fabricated by the USAMTU to permit use of the Starlight Scope with the Model 70 Winchester. The MTU mount was designed to fit directly on top of the M70 receiver with the Starlight Scope offset to the left. The "one-of-a-kind" mounting was made by the MTU at the request of the Limited Warfare Laboratory. The late M.Sgt. Robert Walsh performed the necessary machine work. A standard M14 night vision sight adapter bracket is also shown. (Lt. Col. F.B. Conway, Ret.)

Enterprises, a firm many in in the civilian and military establishment acknowledge as the "night-vision equipment specialists":

> The active night weapon sight possesses its own light source, providing its user with the advantage of being able to see, even in total darkness, if necessary, at the flick of a switch. Most active type units utilize light sources of the infrared type, since infrared rays are invisible to the naked eye. Looking through the electronic telescope that is part of the device, one can, however, readily see the object of surveillance because the telescope electronically converts infrared rays reflected from the object back into visible light.
>
> The effective viewing range of an infrared or IR unit, as it is called, depends on a number of things. First, the IR functions exactly as does a spotlight, only with light rays that are invisible to the naked eye. Hence, the same things that influence visible light rays also influence IR rays. For example, vegetation in the light beam between the unit and the object of surveillance causes glare to be reflected and reduces the ability to see beyond the vegetation in proportion to the magnitude of the glare, exactly as it does with a regular spotlight.
>
> Other natural conditions that influence IR performance are a

Night Vision Sights: A Definite Edge

An early U.S. Army public information (press release) photograph of the original "Starlight Scope, Small Hand-Held or Individual Weapons Mounted Model No. 6060," from the U.S. Army Mobility Equipment Research and Development Center, Ft. Belvoir, Virginia. As then stated, "The Starlight Scope is designed for employment on the M14, M14A2, and XM16E1 rifles, M60 machinegun, 40mm grenade launcher M70, 90mm recoilless rifle, M67, and the 66mm high explosive antitank rocket M72." The unit is pictured with an early version of the 5.56mm M16 rifle. (U.S. Army.)

high level of ambient light, fog and rain. Even though the IR unit will function under the conditions described, the efficiency of the unit is affected by those conditions to whatever degree of magnitude those conditions prevail.

Though eventually replaced by the Starlight Scope, the AN/PAS-4 infrared sight saw extended use by U.S. and ARVN troops, primarily for training purposes, in acclimating combat personnel to night-vision equipment. Such devices were to be both the principal and the last in the long series of small-arms-mounted infrared units utilized by U.S. forces.

With full cognizance of infrared limitations long before the conflict in Vietnam, in 1955 Army Warfare Vision personnel began developing light-amplifying tubes that would enable combat troops to fight more effectively

TC 23-11

DEPARTMENT OF THE ARMY TRAINING CIRCULAR

STARLIGHT SCOPE
SMALL HAND-HELD OR
INDIVIDUAL WEAPONS MOUNTED
MODEL NO. 6060

HEADQUARTERS, DEPARTMENT OF THE ARMY
NOVEMBER 1966

Department of the Army training circular TC 23-11 for the Model No. 6060 Starlight Scope (November 1966). The technical manual for the system (TM 11-1090-268-15) was packed with the sight and accessories in a metal carrying case. The first-generation Model No. 6060 was later adopted as the AN/PVS-1 (Army-Navy/Portable Visible-Light Detection Series Number 1). This system was the first Starlight Scope fielded for combat use in Southeast Asia. (U.S. Army.)

at night with a passive system that the enemy could not detect.

Night-vision scientists produced and successfully demonstrated a two-stage cascade image-intensifier tube in 1957. As a result, the military allocated funds to enable them to continue their efforts. U.S. Special Forces, anti-guerrilla warfare advisors, and Department of Defense studies further emphasized the need for passive night-observation devices in 1961. A special presidential advisory committee identified the lack of night-fighting capability as a serious shortcoming in the Army's preparedness for limited warfare.

Based on tests of a feasibility model built in-house at the Night Vision Laboratory following acceleration of the night-vision program, a contract for engineer design models was awarded to the Bell & Howell Company in June 1962. Production contracts for an Individual Weapons Night Vision Sight (Small Starlight Scope) were awarded to Electro-Optical Systems Inc. (a subsidiary of Xerox) in September 1964. In November 1965, the program was transferred from the Army Engineer Research and Development Laboratories and became a major element of the Army Electronics Command (ECOM) Combat Surveillance, Night Vision and Target Acquisition Laboratories complex.

At the same time, the Army Materiel Command, parent organization of ECOM, created a night-vision project manager's office at Ft. Belvoir,

Night Vision Sights: A Definite Edge

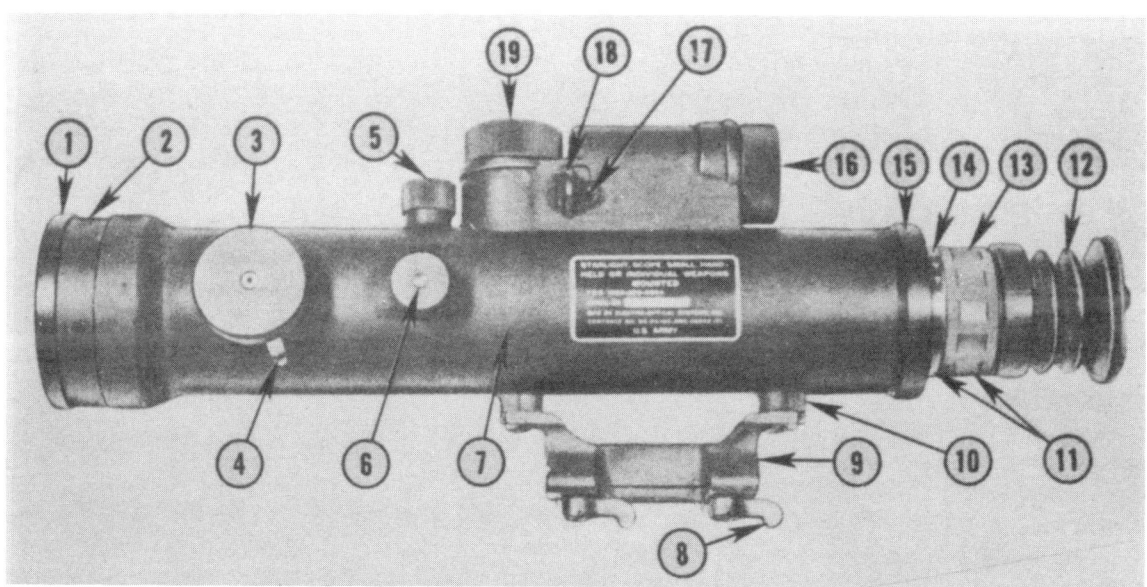

Vietnam-era Department of the Army illustration of the AN/PVS-1 Starlight Scope (1966). The 4-power night vision sight was 18.50 inches long and 3.375 inches wide, and weighed 6 pounds. The telescope was fitted with a conventional mount assembly. The two "locking knobs" at the bottom of the mount rotated to the rear to lock the scope on the rail. (U.S. Army.) Principal components: (1) Lens cap; (2) Objective lens assembly; (3) Focusing knob; (4) Locking lever; (5) Elevation adjustment knob; (6) Azimuth adjustment knob; (7) Main housing; (8) Lock knob (2); (9) Telescope mount assembly; (10) Mounting stud (2); (11) Eyepiece assembly; (12) Rubber eyeshield; (13) Eyepiece focus ring; (14) Diopter scale; (15) Eyepiece retainer nut; (16) Battery cap; (17) Control switch; (18) Switch guard; (19) Oscillator cap.

The AN/PVS-1 Starlight Scope is a portable, battery-operated, electro-optical instrument for passive visual observation and surveillance at night. It uses natural light, moonlight, or starlight for target illumination. This device uses a 25mm, 3-stage cascade image-intensifier tube and has built-in reticle adjustments for windage and elevation. (Excalibur Enterprises.)

The findings of a USAIS representative during a CONARC liaison visit to South Vietnam (7–22 September 1970) included the following information on field use of the Starlight Scope:

Units reporting on use of the AN/PVS-2 indicate that it is used in the hand held mode predominantly. Generally, the mounted scopes are used by snipers for point targets and the unmounted scopes are used by sentries to scan an area. The unmounted scopes are relatively ineffective because of the difficulty of coordinating the unmounted scope and effective fire. Aside from the fact that mounts are in short supply, the individual soldier is reluctant to mount the scope because of the time necessary to bore sight the scope and the extra weight added to the weapon. The mounted scope is ideal for an observation post or a sniper role but has drawbacks in a general purpose mission.

A unique post-Vietnam photograph by Excalibur Enterprises, the "Night Vision Equipment Specialists," showing two men posing as Vietcong. The simulation provides a representative view of the VC as they would have appeared through a Starlight Scope during the war in Vietnam. (Excalibur Enterprises.)

Virginia, to speed production of night-vision equipment as warranted. As a result of increased military activity in Southeast Asia, Varo, Inc., received additional production contracts for Starlight Scope manufacture in June 1967.

The heart of the new night-vision systems, the image-intensifier tube, consisted of three modular sections, which were mechanically and optically coupled to form a three-stage intensifier. The three modules with the multiplier sections of the high-voltage power supply were completely encapsulated, and a recessed connector was provided for plug-in of the power-supply oscillator assembly.

The original 25-millimeter image-intensifier tube used in the Small Starlight Scope and the Crew Served Weapon Sight was approximately 7 inches in length and 2 3/4 inches in diameter. Contractors engaged in production of the first-generation image-intensification tubes were Machlett, RCA, ITT, and Varo.

Basically, such equipment permitted viewing at night without the aid of any light source other than the dim glow of the moon and stars, or even faint sky glow. When light from the night sky struck the end of the objective tube, a "fiberoptic" (a bundle of individual glass fibers) trapped the light, bringing it into the tube where it struck a photoemissive surface. The tube then discharged electrons into a vacuum. These electrons,

Night Vision Sights: A Definite Edge

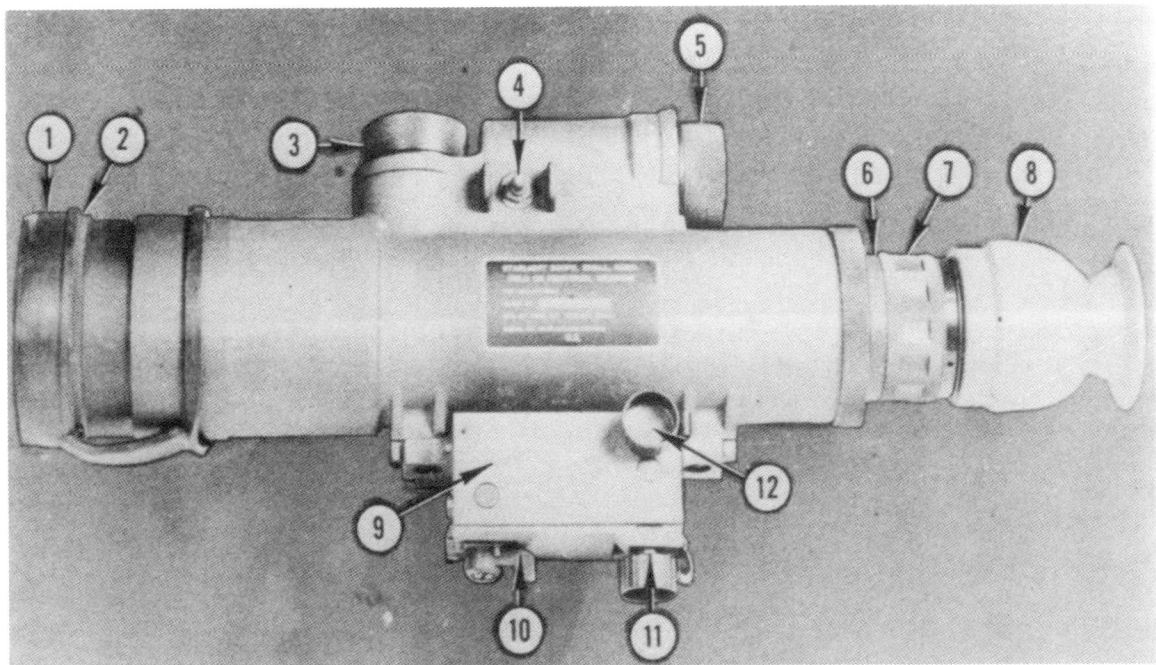

The second in the series of Starlight Scopes fielded for combat use in Southeast Asia. The AN/PVS-2 is pictured in an Army illustration dating from the war in Vietnam (1969). The 4-power sight was 17.50 inches in length and 3.50 inches wide and weighed 6 pounds. Though similar in appearance to the AN/PVS-1, the improved model offered better focusing characteristics and a clearer reticle. The new system came with a mount assembly for "boresighting" the sight to the rifle. Army TM 11-5855-203-10 served as the Vietnam-era technical manual for the AN/PVS-2 night vision sight. (U.S. Army.)
(1) Lens cap; (2) Range focusing ring; (3) Oscillator cap; (4) Power switch; (5) Battery cap; (6) Diopter scale; (7) Eyepiece focusing ring; (8) Rubber eyeshield; (9) Boresight mount assembly; (10) Mount lock knobs (2); (11) Elevation adjustment knob; (12) Azimuth adjustment knob.

energized by 15,000 volts of electricity, struck a screen similar to a television picture tube, giving off light. This process was repeated twice so that the electrons were energized to the point that when they struck the final screen near the eyepiece, the image was 40,000 times brighter than when it entered the tube.

The Small Starlight Scope could be hand-held for visual observation or, in conjunction with appropriate weapon adapter brackets, mounted on the M14 and M16 rifles. The larger-sized scope was used on crew-served weapons such as machine guns and recoilless rifles.

The function of the Starlight Scope was to provide an efficient viewing capability during night-combat operations. While the sight would not afford the clarity of daylight vision, a trained operator could see well enough to detect and fire on enemy targets while remaining free from detection by visual or electronic means. The Starlight Scope, however, was not without limitations. Depending as it did on ambient light from the night sky, the unit would not function properly under absolute darkness. Optimum performance could only be expected on bright, moonlit nights. When the sky was overcast or the ambient light level low, the use of flares or illuminating shells on the flank or to the rear, as circumstances warranted, greatly increased the viewing capabilities of the Starlight Scope.

A 9th Infantry Division sniper shown mounting an AN/PVS-2 Starlight Scope on his XM21 rifle. The alternate use of the Adjustable Ranging Telescope, a Starlight Scope, and the Sionics noise suppressor with the semiautomatic XM21 rifle provided the Army with an extremely versatile sniping system in Vietnam. (U.S. Army.)

Night Vision Sights: A Definite Edge

Light gain for The AN/PVS-2 Starlight Scope is 75,000 times or more. The system was fielded as the AN/PVS-2, AN/PVS-2A, and AN/PVS-2B. According to information provided by the Army, "An automatic brightness control (ABC) is included in the AN/PVS-2B. This feature automatically varies the brightness of the image intensifier assembly for varying levels of light. The AN/PVS-2 and AN/PVS-2A do not have this feature, but the image intensifier assembly will cut off completely if the surrounding light level is too bright." The AN/PVS-2 Starlight Scope saw extensive combat use in Southeast Asia. (Excalibur Enterprises.)

Fog, smoke, dust, and rain had an adverse effect on the instrument's viewing capability, decreasing both the range and resolution. Eye fatigue became a serious consideration when the scope was employed for extended periods. A point of instruction specified graduated periods of exposure beginning with 10 minutes, followed by a rest period of approximately 15 minutes. After several periods of viewing, the time limit was extended.

The greatest sensitivity of the Starlight Scope rested with its susceptibility to damage from exposure of the objective lens to bright light such as direct sunlight. It was mandatory to have the lens cover in position during daylight hours. When inadvertently exposed to bright light during night operations, the sight would automatically switch itself off to prevent damage to the operator's eye and to the image-intensifier tube. When traversed to a darker area, the sight would automatically turn on, allowing normal operation to be resumed.

Of all the post-Vietnam accounts relating to actual field use of the Starlight Scope, among the most descriptive is the following narrative of David Donovan, an Army officer with combat time in RVN, in his work, *Once a Warrior King* (McGraw-Hill, 1985):

> Eventually, it was my turn to keep the "Starlight" watch. In 1969 the Starlight Scope was still a classified instrument.

Although various methods were used to zero a Starlight Scope, in this case, sections of 1-inch-thick armor plate were employed. When viewed at night through the Starlight Scope, the impact of the bullet against the plate produced a very bright light or flash. According to the Vietnam-era technical manuals, "The recommended nominal distance for zeroing the night-vision sight, in daylight or at night, is 150 meters when mounted on the M14 and M16 rifles." (U.S. Army.)

Using special light-intensifying technology, the scope gave the user a see-in-the-night capability far beyond normal human limits. One could squint through the single ocular of the scope and see the surrounding darkness illuminated by an eerie green glow. Since the scope used the light from the moon and stars to operate, the brighter the night the better the scope worked. On pitch black nights, the scopes weren't much good at all.

We had only one scope on our patrol, so each man was assigned an hour to be on watch with it. The man with the scope was responsible for watching the tree lines, the front of the brick house behind us, and the canal in front of us. Any suspicious movement was to be reported to the patrol leader. One of the things we had been taught about using the scope was that one should never allow something to so startle him that he gives in to the urge to remove his eye from the scope and try to see what is going on with both naked eyes. Not only was it unlikely that anyone would see better without the scope than with it, but in moving his head and having to readjust his eyes to the darkness, the watchman would probably lose whatever it was he had in the

Night Vision Sights: A Definite Edge

An infantryman aims an M16 rifle equipped with an AN/PVS-2 Starlight Scope. Despite some use by the Army and Marine Corps with the M14, the vast majority of rifle-mounted Starlight Scopes employed in Vietnam were mounted on the M16. However, by some estimates, Starlight Scopes were most commonly used as "hand-held units" in Southeast Asia. Both carrying straps and cases, or "bags," as some were referenced, made transporting the scope a relatively simple task, as any man having used a Starlight Scope in the field will attest to. It was far easier to hand-carry or strap the scope to a pack than to carry one mounted on a rifle. (U.S. Army.)

field of the scope in the first place. I had been taught that lesson, but I hadn't learned it very well.

Rather than watch the canal, our assigned ambush zone, I kept a closer watch on the jungle around us and on the abandoned house behind us. The moon had gone down, but the clear and starry night gave enough light for the scope to work very well. I kept my eye glued to the ocular and watched the surroundings with nervous anticipation. I expected to see a platoon of Viet Cong come creeping up on us at any moment. I would occasionally sweep the canal with the scope, but I had given up on our staging a successful ambush. I was more worried about surviving the attack that I was sure was coming. I moved the scope slowly as I watched the jungle through its pale green glow, and my view moved over the canal bank to the right as far as I could see. Nothing there.

I swung the scope back to the extreme left to view the jungle and the canal bank on that side of our position. I had my eye to the scope as I swung it rapidly from my right back to my left. I wasn't really paying any attention to the rippling green water in the scope's field of view; I was more interested in the trees. A form in the water moved rapidly across the scope's field. I was mechanically moving the scope back to the right to check on it before I realized that what I had seen was probably a person.

A small unit moves into the bush just before sundown. The Army sniper (foreground) is armed with an XM21 mounting an AN/PVS-2 Starlight Scope. (U.S. Army.)

Suddenly, there he was again. An icy clutch squeezed my chest.

A Vietnamese man was standing there in waist-deep water! He was directly in front of me, craning his neck to try and see over the canal bank. An ammo belt was slung across his chest.

I couldn't believe it! I was so shocked at actually finding something out there that I just froze stiff. I was probably fixed for only a second, but at the time it seemed like an hour of indecision. When I did move, my reaction was to jerk the scope away from my disbelieving eye to try and confirm the sighting by using two eyes. Predictably, I saw nothing in the darkness. I was only halfway through the motion of removing the scope when I knew I had made a mistake. I quickly put the scope back up and looked out at the canal. I saw only a widening circle of ripples where I was sure I had seen a man seconds before. Desperately, I scanned the water, the opposite bank, and the jungle that approached the bank. At the same time, I was cursing myself for my stupidity. Now I didn't know if I had really seen a man or if it was just a figment of my imagination.

Night Vision Sights: A Definite Edge

Silhouetted against the evening sky, a Starlight Scope-equipped Army marksman prepares for night operations in the Delta. With the Communist insurgents moving and fighting as much as they did under the cover of darkness, it was said that "the night belonged to the Vietcong" during early combat activity in South Vietnam. However, with the buildup of American forces and the expanded use of efficient night vision equipment, the VC could no longer use darkness with impunity. (U.S. Army.)

Despite careful and extensive instruction to destroy the Starlight Scope by small-arms fire, fragmentation, or thermite grenades when capture or loss was imminent, Vietcong and North Vietnamese combatants captured a number of night vision sights and redirected them against U.S. forces. As it was then stated, "In 1967, in particular, a new Starlight Scope might well have been the most valuable piece of equipment the VC could have captured."

Although all branches of U.S. forces in Southeast Asia utilized Starlight Scope variants in myriad applications, mounting such devices on special sniping rifles provided an excellent means of achieving first-round hits during periods of darkness. The 9th Infantry Division, considered a trendsetter in Army sniper use and deployment in Vietnam, included night-firing instruction in its sniping syllabus. In addition to becoming proficient with the telescopic sight, each candidate learned to engage targets with the Starlight Scope at ranges of 150, 300, and 600 meters.

The Infrared Weapon Sight, prior to its gradual replacement by the Starlight Scope, had been employed to some extent in early, loosely organized sniping operations. However, not until an effective sniping program was finally instituted in South Vietnam in the late 1960s was the practical significance of night-vision sighting in this capacity fully realized. Concurrent with organized sniper use and deployment, the improved AN/PVS-2 Starlight Scope became the principal night-vision instrument utilized by both Army and Marine Corps marksmen, with telling effect.

The business end of an AN/PVS-2 Starlight Scope-equipped M16 rifle during field exercises held at Ft. Hood, Texas, in October 1970. The AN/PVS-1 and the AN/PVS-2 Starlight Scopes were categorized as "first-generation" individual-served weapon sights. (U.S. Army.)

Though generally well received, early versions of the AN/PVS-2 were to experience various problems, including difficulties involving reticle adjustment, range focusing, diopter settings, and inconsistent reticle illumination. Of further interest in this case, according to ordnance documents dating from this era, from a standpoint of sniper use, inasmuch as the specialists were trained to use the "spotweld" firing technique (i.e., the right cheek pressed against the rifle stock to provide adequate support while sighting), with the telescopic sight positioned directly over the receiver and the Starlight Scope mounted high and to the left, viewing through the AN/PVS-2 required use of the left eye (in order to have the right cheek touch the stock). While hardly an insurmountable problem, depending on a man's physical stature, viewing through the night vision sight required a "stretch of the neck" and was considered extremely awkward by many of the men, particularly when firing from the prone position. By all accounts, the right eye was used for day firing with the telescopic sight and the left eye at night with the Starlight Scope.

Night Vision Sights: A Definite Edge

An AN/PVS-2 Starlight Scope "assembled and mounted on an M16 rifle for an airborne combat test" at Ft. Bragg, North Carolina, (82nd Airborne), November 1971. (U.S. Army.)

Below Left: A relatively unknown Starlight Scope fielded in Vietnam, the "Night Vision Sight, Miniaturized AN/PVS-3" was developed for use with the M14 and M16 rifles. Though well-received because of its extremely light weight (3 pounds), the system had operational problems that prevented widespread use in Southeast Asia. The diminutive 4-power night vision sight was 13.50 inches in length, 3.50 inches in width, and only 5.75 inches in height, complete with the "boresight" mount assembly. A carrying case and accessories were issued with the unit. The early technical manual (operator's manual) for the system, TM 11-5855-209-10, was dated 28 December 1967. (Excalibur Enterprises.)

An Army photograph of an M16-mounted AN/PVS-3, circa 1971. When introduced, the miniaturized night vision sight was touted as the "smallest and lightest starlight scope produced for the military services." The first-generation device made use of an 18mm, 3-stage cascade image intensifier with a light gain of 60,000 times or more. The image tube had a built-in automatic brightness control, which adjusted tube brightness to compensate for different levels of ambient light. Though later improved as the AN/PVS-3A, the compact night vision sight saw only limited combat use before the war ended in Vietnam. (U.S. Army.)

The following information, furnished by Excalibur Enterprises, Emmaus, Pennsylvania, provides a brief description of the "Passive Starlight Types" and the principal difference between the first- and second-generation Starlight Scopes:

> The passive night-sight electronically amplifies ambient light such as moonlight, starlight or sky glow to the level that the scene viewed through the telescope appears much brighter than with the naked eye. Since it has no light source of its own, it is dependent upon ambient light to function. So, understandably, the more ambient light, the better the unit performs. This is the direct opposite of the active type infrared system.

Night Vision Sights: A Definite Edge

A 9th Infantry Division private with a .50-caliber Browning machine gun fitted with the AN/TVS-2 night vision sight, August 1968. Although improved versions of the crew-served weapon sight proved effective in Vietnam, the early units were easily damaged by the recoil of the heavy machine gun. Further, the muzzle flash would cause the sight to be saturated with light and literally shut down as a result. When first issued, the AN/TVS-2 was intended for use with the .50-caliber HB M2 machine gun and the M40A1 106mm recoilless rifle. The early system was detailed in Department of the Army technical manual TM 11-1090-269-15. (U.S. Army.)

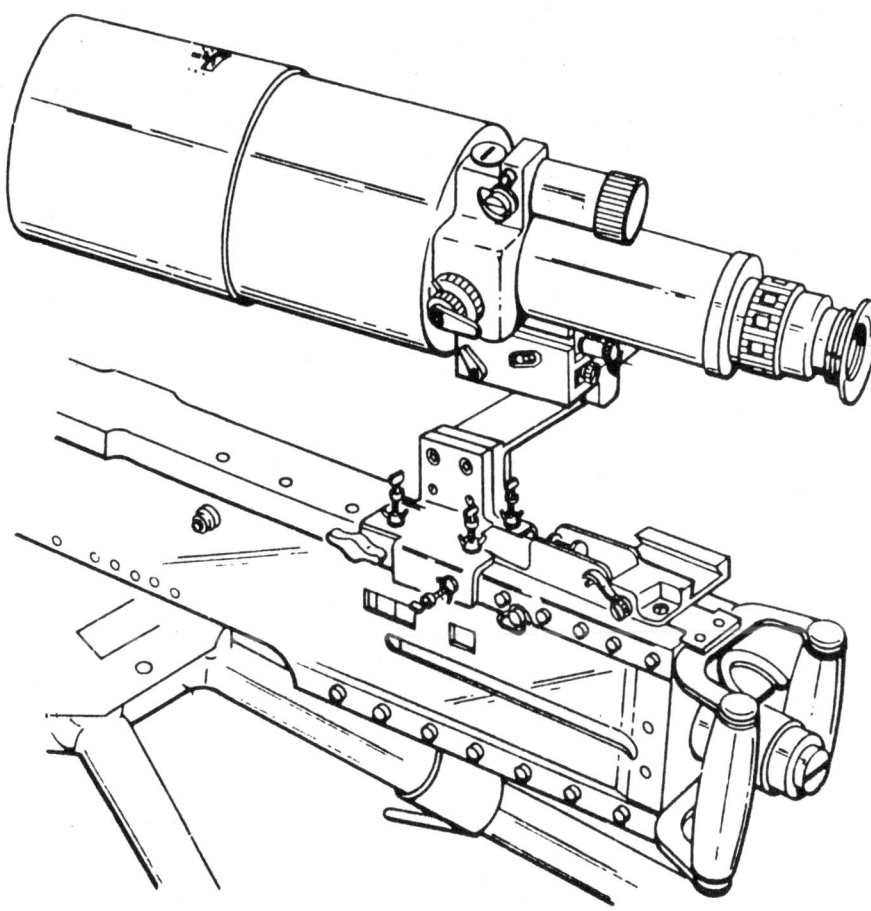

A Vietnam-era Army manual illustration of the AN/TVS-2 crew-served weapon sight with the adapter bracket for the Browning machine gun. The 7-power night vision sight was 24.50 inches in length and 6.50 inches wide, and weighed 16 pounds. Although principal combat use of an optical sighting system with the .50-caliber machine gun in Southeast Asia rested with the Starlight Scope, the Marine Corps made some use of target telescopes with the "Big Browning" in Vietnam, as it had in Korea. (U.S. Army.)

The tripod-mounted Night Observation Device (NOD) units were first used for observation purposes along the Ho Chi Minh Trail, the main infiltration route into South Vietnam. In this case, an infantryman is shown "scanning the area for enemy movement" near Khe Sahn, June 1969. (U.S. Army.)

Starlight type viewers and weapon sights are manufactured using two different generations of image intensifier tubes. Both are current military issue worldwide.

First generation devices use an image intensifier module consisting of three first generation stages coupled together in to one unit. Each stage has a light gain of approximately 40,000 times, but in coupling them together some gain is lost. The end result of a 25mm first generation module is approximately 75,000 to 85,000 times light gain over ambient light being viewed. This is 1/3 higher light gain than devices using second generation image intensifiers. First generation modules have a high degree of resolution (ability to resolve distant objects) and clarity of image. They are also very rugged and can withstand a 75G shock. However, a first generation device, when viewing bright lights, will bloom (a large saturated bright spot on the image tube screen) or will shut itself off, if the light is bright enough, until the unit is aimed in another direction. Another drawback of first generation devices is a certain amount of distortion on the edges of the viewing screen.

Second generation devices use an image intensifier consisting of a single stage, which utilizes a MCP (micro channel plate).

Night Vision Sights: A Definite Edge

An Army spotter team directing artillery fire with an AN/TVS-4 NOD at Dong Tam, March 1967. The long-range passive night vision sights were intended primarily for surveillance, target acquisition, and adjustment of direct and indirect fire during periods of darkness. (U.S. Army.)

The MCP acts as a current limiting device and reduces blooming. Second generation intensifiers are considerably smaller and lighter than the first generation type because they only use one stage. However, light gain is approximately 1/3 less on a 25mm second generation intensifier than on a 25mm first generation intensifier. Also, the resolution and output screen brightness is less than on the first generation units. Overall, second generation devices are best suited for use in cities or other scenarios when the user would encounter frequent bright lights.

In summary, first and second generation units have both advantages and disadvantages. First generation devices have a high light gain and will operate at much lower light levels with much better resolution. Second generation devices are small, have less edge distortion and do not bloom when aimed at bright lights.

[NOTE: For the sake of clarification, the Vietnam-era AN/PVS-1, AN/PVS-2, and AN/PVS-3 were categorized as "first-generation" passive night-vision sights. The AN/PVS-4, for example, was the first in the ongoing series of "second-generation" Starlight Scopes subsequently employed by U.S. military forces.

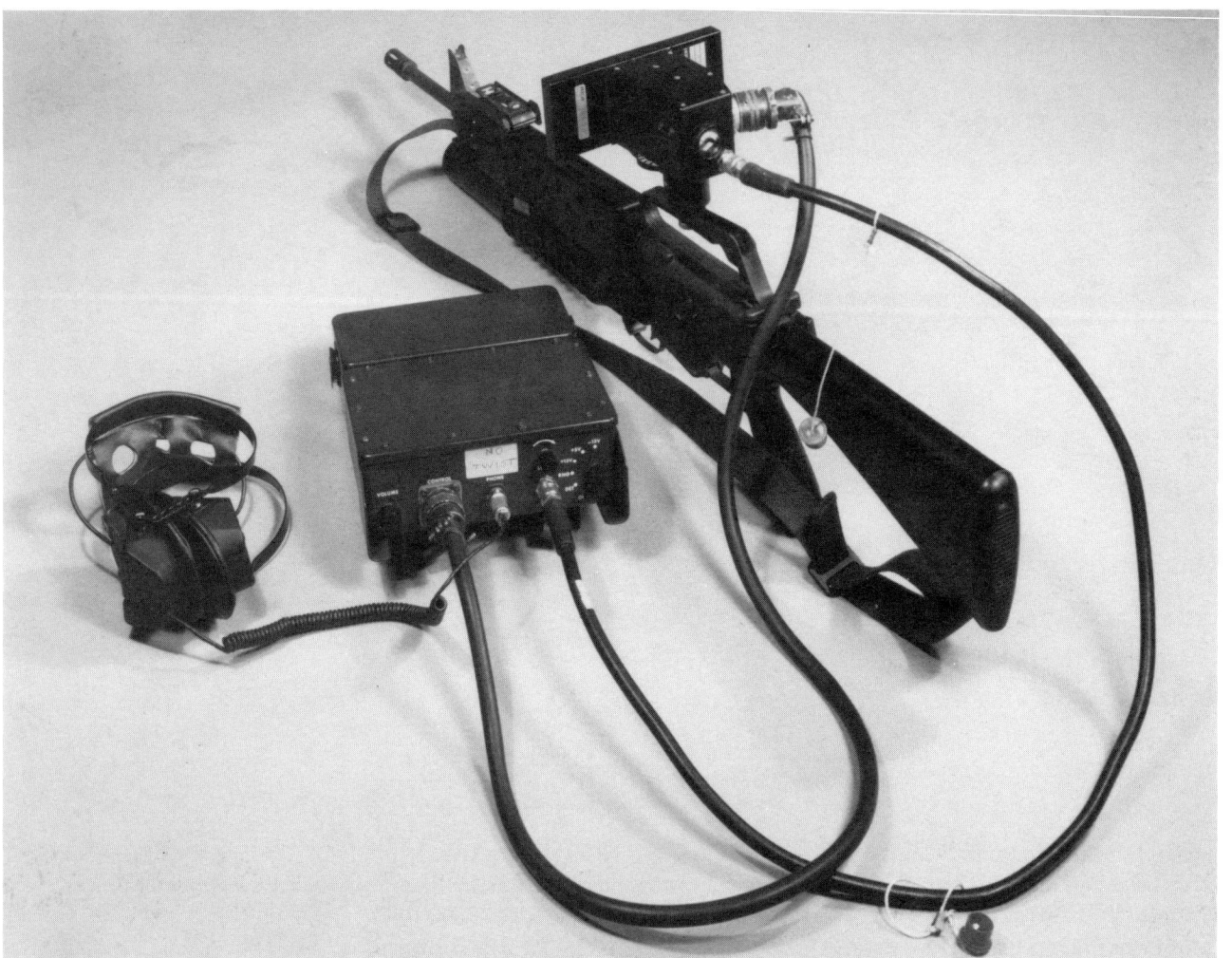

A variety of night vision equipment intended for small arms was developed and tested during the Vietnam War. In this case, an experimental Novel Electronic Weapon Sight (NEWS) was fitted to an M16 with an M203 grenade launcher for evaluation at Rock Island Arsenal (July 1971). (U.S. Army.)

With a wide and impressive range of night vision equipment at the disposal of the Army, Navy, Marine Corps, and Air Force in the years following the war in Southeast Asia, the U.S. military had an overwhelming edge in night-vision technology. That edge prompted the following statement (5 January 1990) by Chief of Staff Carl E. Vuono, a U.S. Army general, in commenting on Operation Just Cause, America's high-tech invasion of Panama]:

Early on 20 December 1989, Army forces supported by sister services initiated Operation JUST CAUSE . . . JUST CAUSE is the most complex contingency deployment and employment of U.S. forces undertaken since World War II . . . The ability of our joint forces to project overwhelming combat power at the points of decision resulted in the early success with minimum losses . . . Fighting at night gave us a significant advantage . . . It is evident that with our training and equipment, we own the night . . .

Night Vision Sights: A Definite Edge

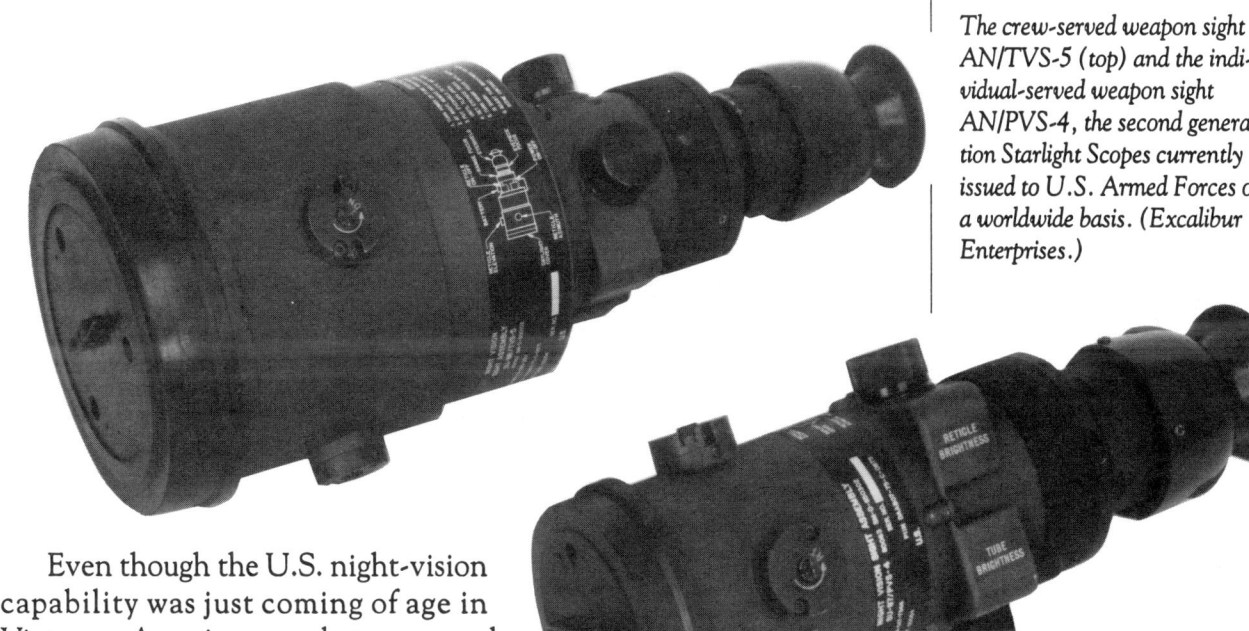

The crew-served weapon sight AN/TVS-5 (top) and the individual-served weapon sight AN/PVS-4, the second generation Starlight Scopes currently issued to U.S. Armed Forces on a worldwide basis. (Excalibur Enterprises.)

Even though the U.S. night-vision capability was just coming of age in Vietnam, American combat personnel held a decided edge in this regard. Consequently, the statement "we own the night" was as applicable during the conflict in Vietnam as it was more than 20 years later in Operation Just Cause and, in particular, Desert Storm.

In 1970, based on the results of its extensive night sniping, the Army requested development of a "match-grade thermoluminescent 7.62mm round" for use in conjunction with the Starlight Scope. The special cartridge, to be visible only when viewed through the Starlight Scope, would in concept permit observation of the round in flight and adjustments to the point of impact should a second or third round be required. Though the request was seriously considered, subsequent development or field use, if any, remains obscure.

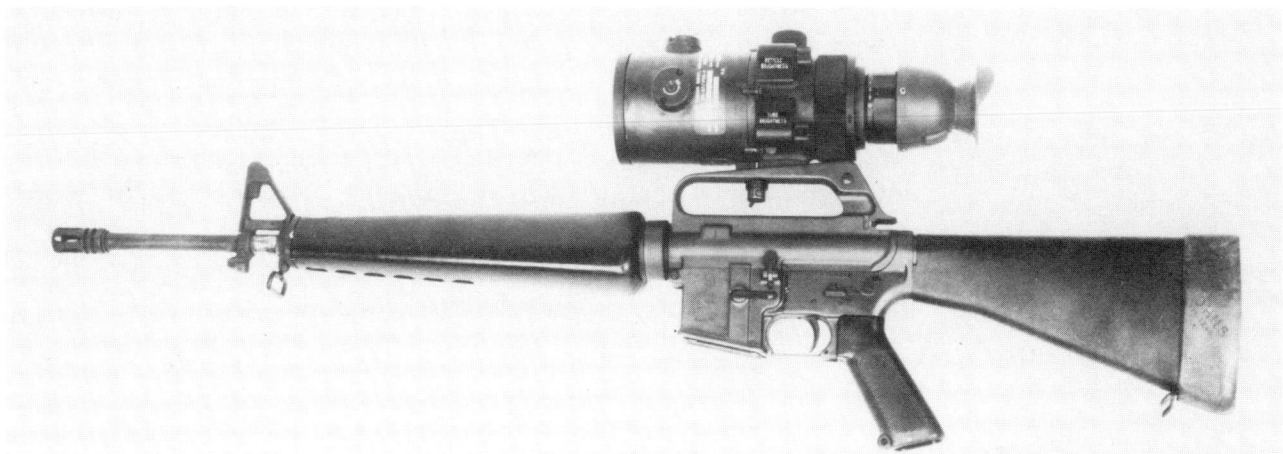

The AN/PVS-4 Starlight Scope mounted on the M16 rifle. The 4-power sight is 9.50 inches in length and 4.50 inches wide, and weighs 3.8 pounds. Even though development work on the second generation Starlight Scopes began during the war in Vietnam, the vastly improved night vision sights were not produced in appreciable quantity until after the conflict had ended. (Excalibur Enterprises.)

A close view of the AN/PVS-4 Starlight Scope fitted to an M16 rifle. A variety of special mounting brackets enable the sight to be used with the M14 and M16 rifles, M67 recoilless rifle, M60 machine gun, M79 and M16/M203 grenade launchers, and the M72A1 rocket launcher. In addition to being mounted on a weapon, the unit may be hand-held for night reconnaissance. (Excalibur Enterprises.)

Use of the specially prepared M14 rifle (XM21) for sniping purposes was to provide the Army with a highly efficient night sniping instrument as well. Marine Corps snipers, on the other hand, utilizing the 7.62mm M700/M40 bolt-action rifle (Remington) as their primary sniping arm, were, by necessity, to employ regular-issue M14 and M16 rifles for mounting the Starlight Scope during sniper deployment. Although active pursuance of a satisfactory bracket to permit Starlight Scope mounting to the Remington sniper rifle was specifically mentioned in Marine Corps documents as early as 1967, Marine sniper rifles would not possess a night-vision capability during the war in Vietnam.

Night Vision Sights: A Definite Edge

A 10th Special Forces Group (Airborne) marksman zeroing an AN/PVS-4 Starlight Scope (Ft. Devens, Massachusetts, 1992). The M25 sniper rifle is fitted with a Brookfield Precision Tool (BPT) M14 telescope mounting and AN/PVS-4 adapter. Note the "Daylight Cover" in place on the scope. (Mitchell E. Mateiko.)

An alternate view of an M25 sniper rifle (Ft. Devens, Massachusetts). In this case, a rifleman makes use of AN/PVS-7 night vision goggles (NVGs) with an infrared (IR) laser mounted on a Brookfield Precision Tool laser base and M14 mount assembly. When boresighted to the weapon, the operator simply places the aiming light (beam) on the target and fires. Accelerated development of head-mounted night vision devices began during the Vietnam War. Developmental versions of the NVGs and rifle-mounted aiming lights were employed by MACV/SOG and Special Forces personnel during the closing stages of the war. (Mitchell E. Mateiko.)

CHAPTER 12

The M21: A System in Transition

In the months following the end of U.S. combat involvement in South Vietnam, so far as sniping was concerned, apart from an official "Sniper Capability Study" generated by the Army's Infantry Agency and intended to "authorize snipers for Infantry Battalions throughout the Army," the sniper program slipped into a state of lethargy until 1973. At that point, as the Army recorded, "due to a great number of requests for marksmanship assistance" primarily from law-enforcement agencies, the U.S. Army Marksmanship Unit (USAMU) reinstated the marksmanship aspect of the school at Ft. Benning.

NOTE: In retrospect, the USAMTU had, as a matter of course, rendered support to governmental agencies and police departments in regard to countersniping equipment and activity. For example, a comprehensive 28-page *Counter Sniper Guide* was published and circulated by the USAMTU under date of 13 July 1970. The manual, authored by Lt. Col. F.B. Conway, USAMTU, was intended to advise law enforcement agencies in the "selection of equipment, training, and employment of the countersniper." Of further interest in this case, in May 1971, Major Powell and the AMTU Sniper Instructor Group were tasked with training U.S. Secret Service personnel in pertinent countersniping measures and the effective use of the XM21 weapon system. The examples cited are indicative of USAMTU involvement with governmental and law enforcement agencies.

According to USAMU information dating from that time, in conjunction with efforts to maintain a suitable sniper/countersniper training

An M21 fitted with a Vietnam-era Redfield Adjustable Ranging Telescope (ART). The Army sniper rifle served as the "control item" for the evaluations held at Aberdeen Proving Ground in 1977. The photographs in this series were made from weapons used in the tests. (U.S. Army.)

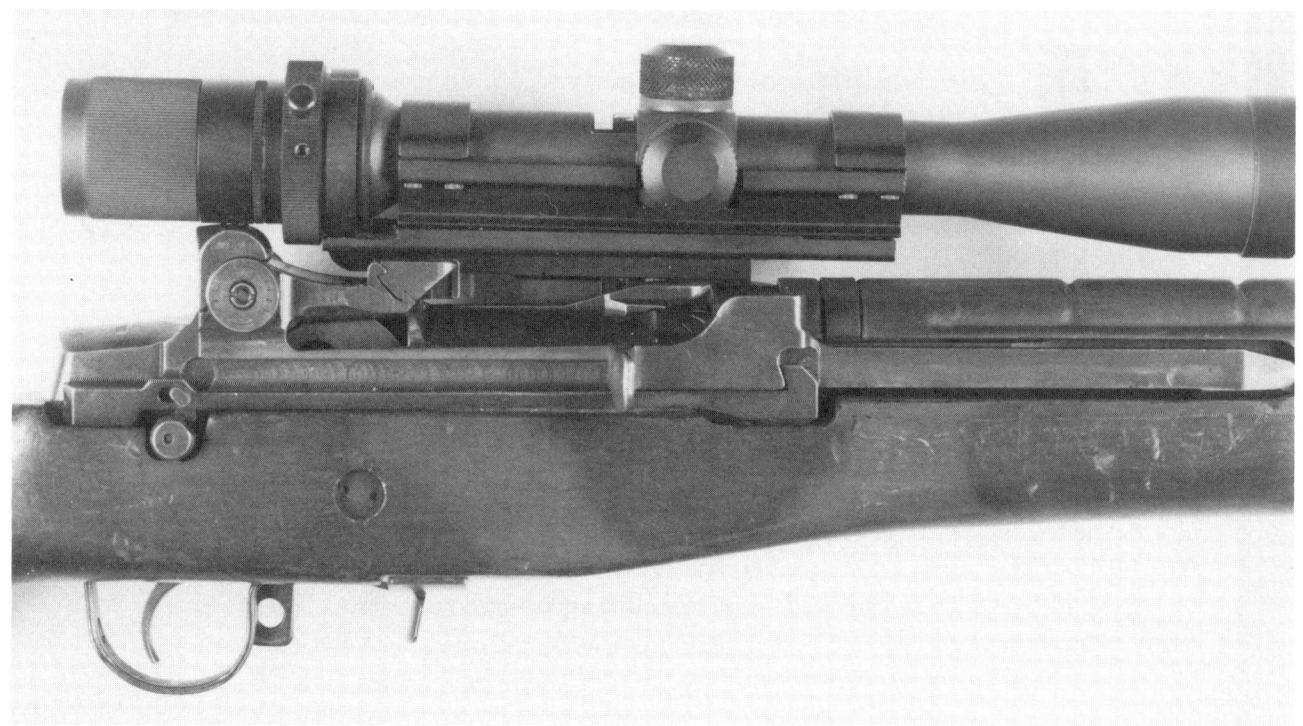

The Army M21 sniper rifle mounting a Leatherwood Bros. Adjustable Ranging Telescope (ART). Though intended primarily as a test of sniper rifle candidates, both Redfield and Leatherwood telescopic sights were employed as "accessory equipment" during the evaluations. (U.S. Army.)

The M21: A System in Transition 249

An example of the "prone position setup" at APG. This test, by the Materiel Testing Directorate at Aberdeen Proving Ground from 1 May 1977 to 30 December 1977, was done to evaluate the performance of various weapons to determine their potential for use as sniper rifles. (U.S. Army.)

syllabus, the USAMU and its three marksmanship units (MTUs) conducted more than 40 two-week instructional classes and had plans to increase the number in future months. Before graduating, each student was required to achieve first-round hits at ranges from 200 to 900 meters.

Though USAMU efforts were geared primarily toward training "sharpshooters" for law enforcement purposes, by the end of 1975, in response to the USAMU program, the Army began to show interest in training active sniper units, as the following U.S. Army information demonstrates:

> There has been a rising interest in sniper training in Active Army units as a result of the demonstrations put on by USAMU members. In fact, plans are now underway to equip selected commands with sniper weapon systems. Hopefully, the question, "Is there still a need?" has been answered by the large number of requests for sniper and countersniper clinics which have been received at AMU and the MTUs.

Without question, the most significant post-Vietnam effort to train and equip Army snipers took shape during early 1976 under the aegis of Lt. Gen. Henry Emerson, commanding general of the XVIII Airborne

The special M14 Rock Island Arsenal/Rodman Laboratory test rifle made use of a heavy barrel, laminated target stock, and modified gas system. The telescope is a Leatherwood ART. The Leatherwood telescopic sights employed with the 1977 Army test rifles were early versions of the second generation adjustable ranging telescope eventually sold to the Army as the Leatherwood 3X-9X variable-power ART II sighting system. By some estimates, the exposure of the Leatherwood system at Aberdeen Proving Ground had served as the impetus for subsequent adoption by the U.S. Army. (U.S. Army.)

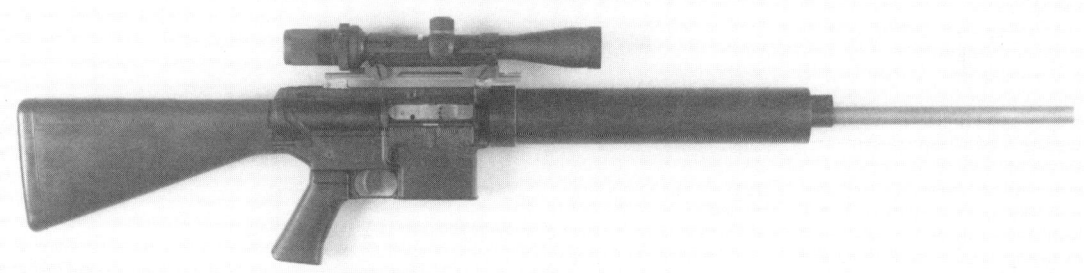

An overall view (right) of the rifle described in the Aberdeen Proving Ground report (1977) as the "Rodman Laboratory, modified Armalite AR10." (U.S. Army.)

Corps, headquartered at Ft. Bragg, North Carolina.

A USAMU program was launched at Ft. Benning to rebuild 342 M21 sniper rifles for use by the XVIII Airborne Corps. During this rebuilding process, the MTU trained unit armorers from the 82nd Airborne Division, the 101st Airborne Division, and the John F. Kennedy Special Warfare Center to support these weapons properly.

In addition to providing information on project details, the USAMU monthly newsletter, *The Marksman* (March 1976), offered the following:

The M21: A System in Transition

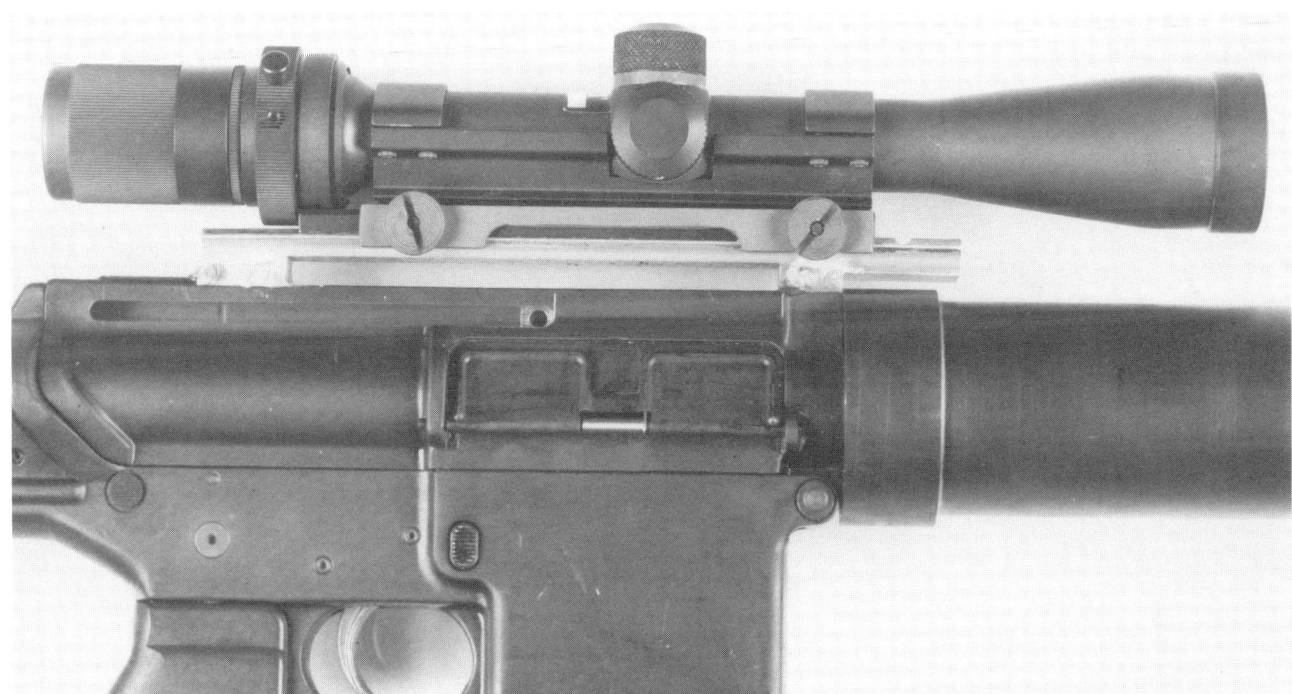

An example of the 7.62mm Rodman-Laboratory-modified Armalite AR-10 rifle. According to the APG report, "Modifications made to convert this item to a sniper rifle include a heavier barrel free of any stock attachments. The handguard is a metal tube, secured to the receiver. The carrying handle on the upper receiver has been removed to allow for mounting the telescopic sight. Originally, the charging handle was on top of the upper receiver inside the carrying handle. Since the handle has been removed to allow for telescope mounting, provision was made to charge the bolt from the right side by welding a charging lug on the bolt carrier. A clearance slot was cut on the right side of the upper receiver to allow the charging handle to engage the lug." The Leatherwood ART was fitted to the rifle using a "Quick-Detachable" (QD) mounting. The AR-10 rifles used for the Army testing were originally made in Holland. (U.S. Army.)

The Aberdeen Proving Ground "benchrest and velocity instrumentation setup" employed for the 1977 sniper rifle evaluations. As then stated, "The testing started with a comprehensive weapon inspection, followed by a benchrest accuracy test at 200 yards (184 meters). A 10-shot group was fired in each rifle every day for a total of 10 days. The rifles of each model with the largest and smallest mean radius (MR) were used in a machine-rest accuracy test." (U.S. Army.)

Winchester Model 70 match rifle with Leatherwood scope and mount, "free-floating" heavy barrel, and target stock. (U.S. Army.)

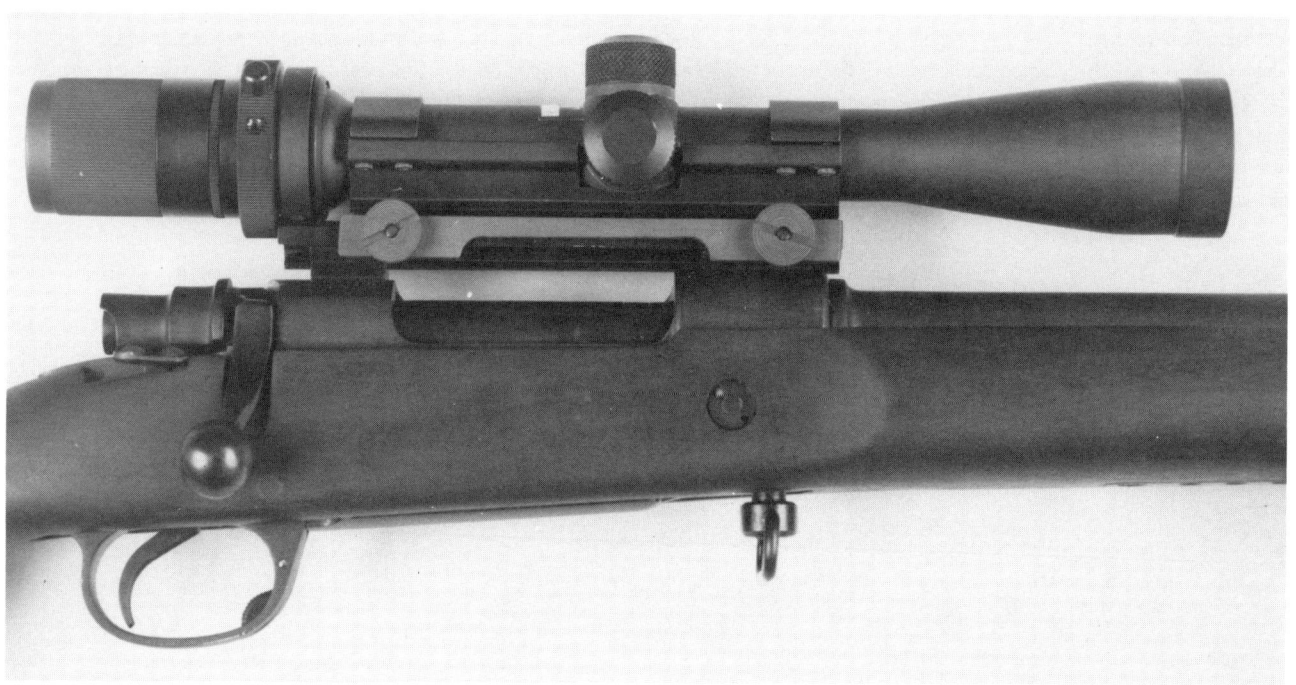

Parker-Hale 1200 TX (Canadian Army C3), limited-production sniper rifle. The telescope is a Leatherwood model. (U.S. Army.)

The Army Marksmanship Unit conducts numerous sniper clinics for all branches of the Department of Defense and various law enforcement agencies. Members of the XVIII Airborne Corps who have completed the sniper clinic will conduct their own clinics once the rebuilt M21s have been delivered to Fort Bragg.

The M21: A System in Transition 253

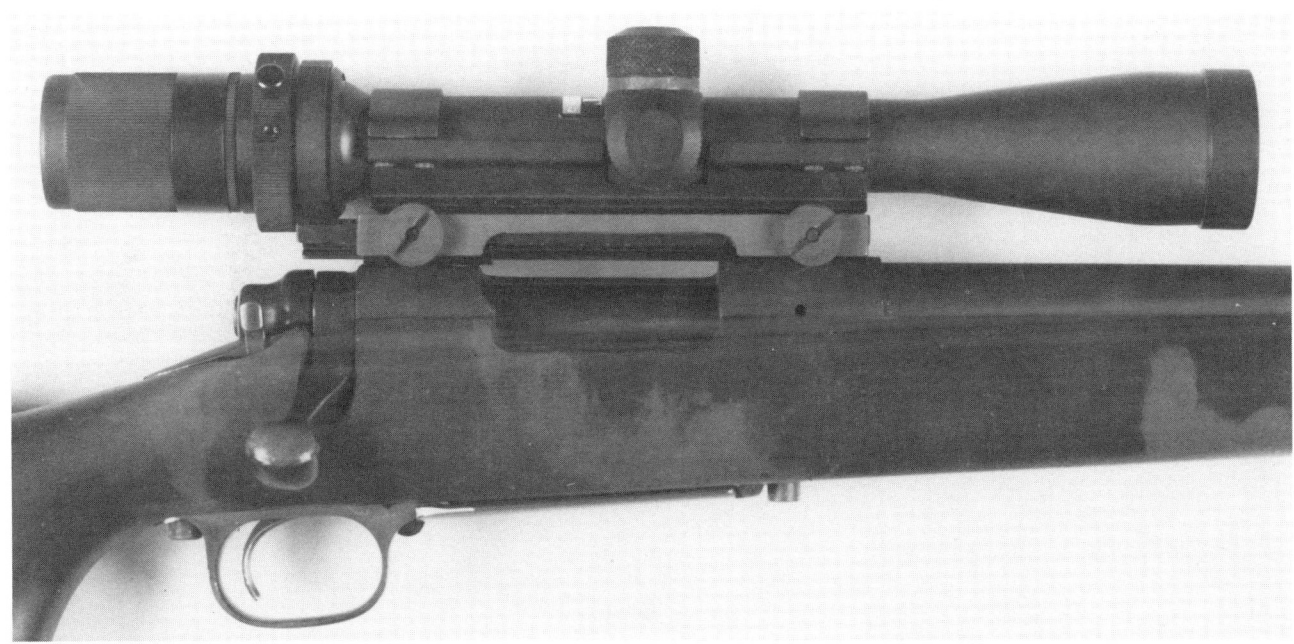

Marine Corps M40A1 sniper rifle circa 1977. The weapons furnished to the Army for testing purposes were fitted with stainless steel barrels and fiberglass stocks. The reconfigured Remington Model 700 (M40) sniper rifles were originally fielded during the Vietnam War. The weapon pictured is an early version of the then-emerging M40A1 sniper rifle. At this juncture, the Marine Corps was still using the 3X-9X variable-power Redfield Accu-Range scopes with its sniping issue. The Leatherwood sights were mounted on the USMC rifles at Aberdeen Proving Ground. (U.S. Army.)

The Aberdeen Proving Ground "machine-rest" setup. In this test, according to the U.S. Army, "The targets were reportedly set at 300, 600, 800, and 1000 yards (274, 549, 732, and 914 meters) and shot simultaneously in five 10-shot groups. The third rifle underwent a 50-round rapid-fire test as part of the final inspection to check functioning under hard use. The final inspection on all rifles was a check on mechanical integrity." (U.S. Army.)

French FR-F1 7.62mm sniper rifle (French National Arsenal). The APX-804 telescopic sight is a 3.8 fixed-power model made in France. The French rifle was only used for comparison purposes; it was not considered a candidate weapon. (U.S. Army.)

NOTE: As then followed (April 1976), sniper training activity at Ft. Bragg was officially referenced as the "XVIII Abn Corps & Ft. Bragg AMTU Sniper Training Course."

Renewed interest in sniper rifles and their employment led to efforts in the Army to satisfy its current sniper needs and to consider its future sniper rifle requirements.

In line with these efforts, as noted in the *Infantry News*:

> Five candidate 7.62mm sniper rifles were selected for testing by the Infantry Board. Three of the candidate rifles were bolt-action rifles, one was semiautomatic, and one was both semiautomatic and automatic. The accuracy of the candidate sniper rifles was compared with that of the M21 sniper rifle that is now classified by the Army as Standard B. The telescopes used on the candidate rifles were essentially the same as the telescope used on the M21.
>
> During the testing period, six master riflemen from the Army's Marksmanship Training Unit, several of whom had been snipers in combat, fired over a modified Palma Match Course and over a combat accuracy test course. The firing was designed to measure the effects of various firing conditions

The M21: A System in Transition

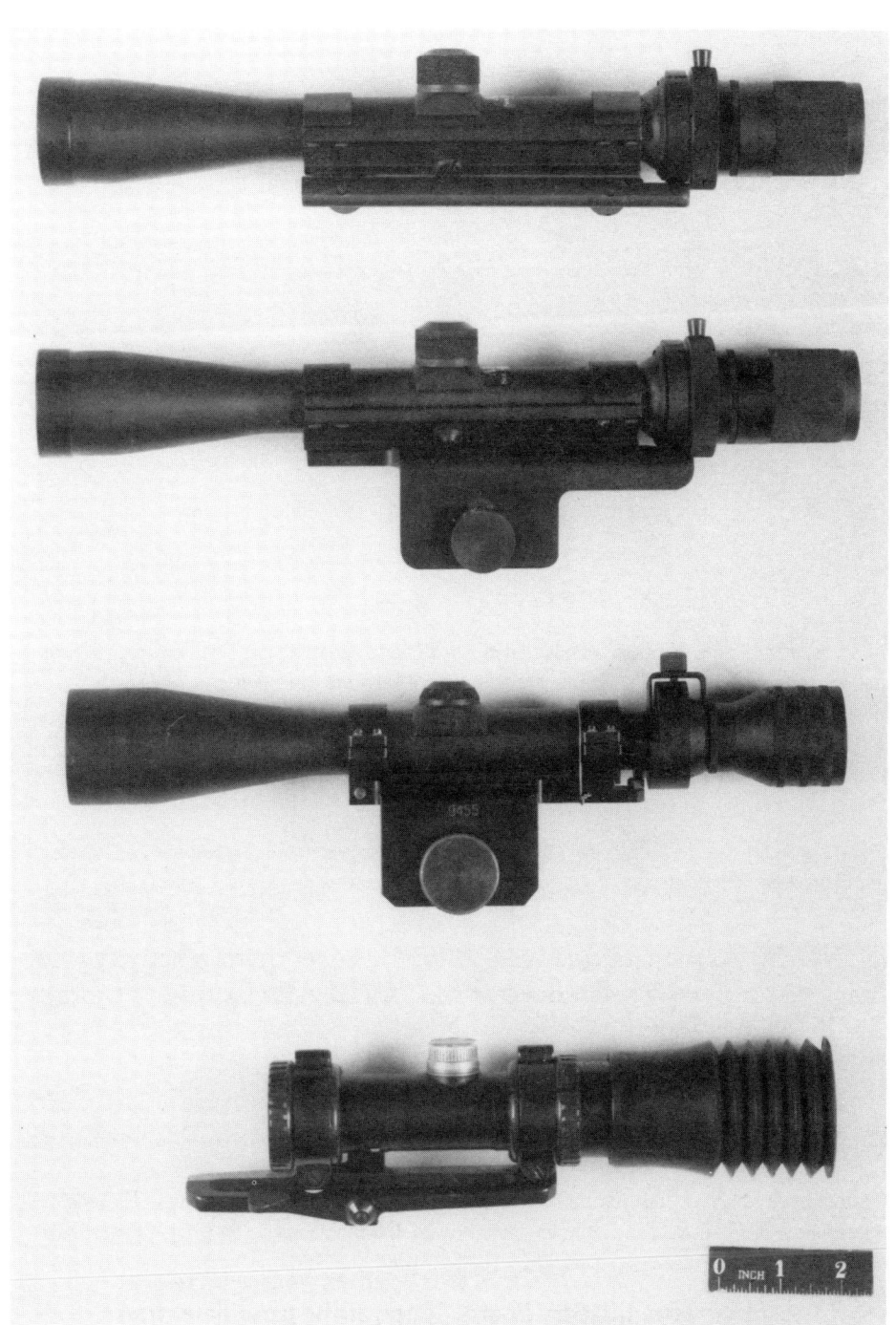

The telescopes and mounts used for the 1977 APG sniper rifle evaluations. From top to bottom: Leatherwood Bros. Adjustable Ranging Telescope with a quick-detachable mount, a Leatherwood ART and M14 mounting, Redfield AR TEL as fielded with the XM21 system in Vietnam, and the French 3.8-power APX-804 telescopic sight. (U.S. Army.)

(cold bore, fouled bore, dry bore, oiled bore, and heat generated by rapid fire) on accuracy, changes in the center of impact, and functioning.

Accuracy data from the various firings were collected, evaluated, and compared for significant differences between the types of rifle systems. Safety data was also collected and evaluated. Structured interviews were conducted to determine firer observations and opinions.

The results of the test indicated that there were no significant differences between the test items and the stan-

A significant part of an official "product improved M14 rifle program" conducted at Rock Island Arsenal, the Test Fixture 7.62mm Semi-Automatic Sniper Rifle was intended to "squeeze every possible degree of performance from the M14 action." The highly modified system featured an M14 action, a massive stainless steel barrel and gas cylinder, laminated thumbhold stock, and set trigger. The first in a series of unique rifles developed at RIA, the special M14 is equipped with a Redfield Adjustable Ranging Telescope and a bipod. Robert E. Snodgrass, the program director, is shown with the system (26 October 1970). (U.S. Army.)

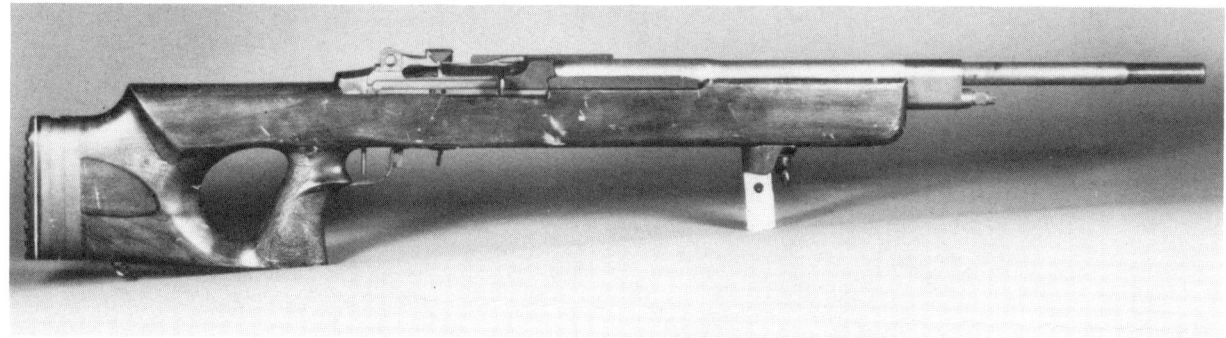

The Rock Island Arsenal/Rodman Laboratory 7.62mm "test fixture" pictured in a 1982 photograph. According to RIA technical information, in original form, the 13-pound rifle was 43 inches in length with a 24 1/2-inch barrel. The unique system was based on a Springfield Armory M14 National Match receiver (so marked). (U.S. Army.)

dard M21 from an accuracy standpoint. The test soldiers unanimously reported that they preferred a semiautomatic sniper rifle with externally loaded magazines.

According to the U.S. Army Test Evaluation Command "Final Letter Report: Engineer Design Test of Sniper Rifle Candidates" by George B. Niewenhous (Aberdeen Proving Ground, February 1978):

This test, by the Materiel Testing Directorate at US Army Aberdeen Proving Ground (APG), Maryland, from 1 May 1977 to 30 December 1977 was done to evaluate the perfor-

The M21: A System in Transition

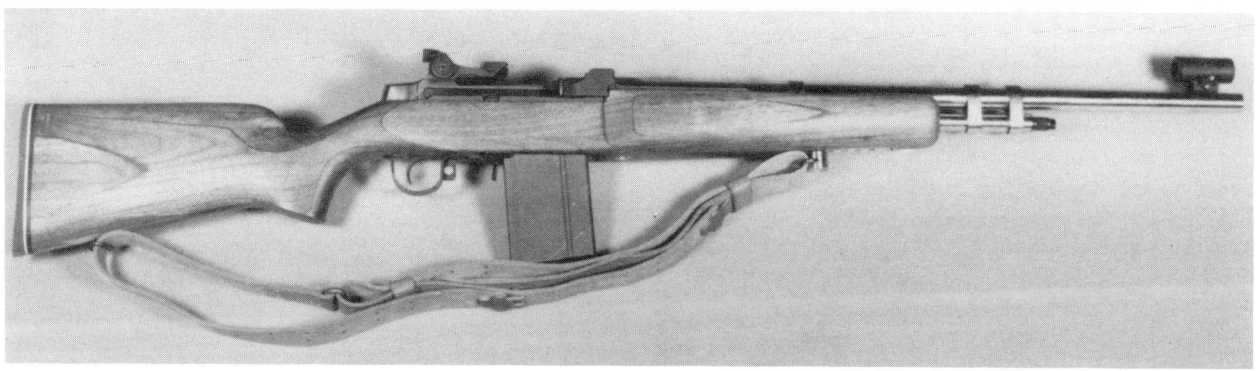

The "first prototype" of the Rock Island Arsenal M14 National Match Product Improved Rifle (6 May 1975). (U.S. Army.)

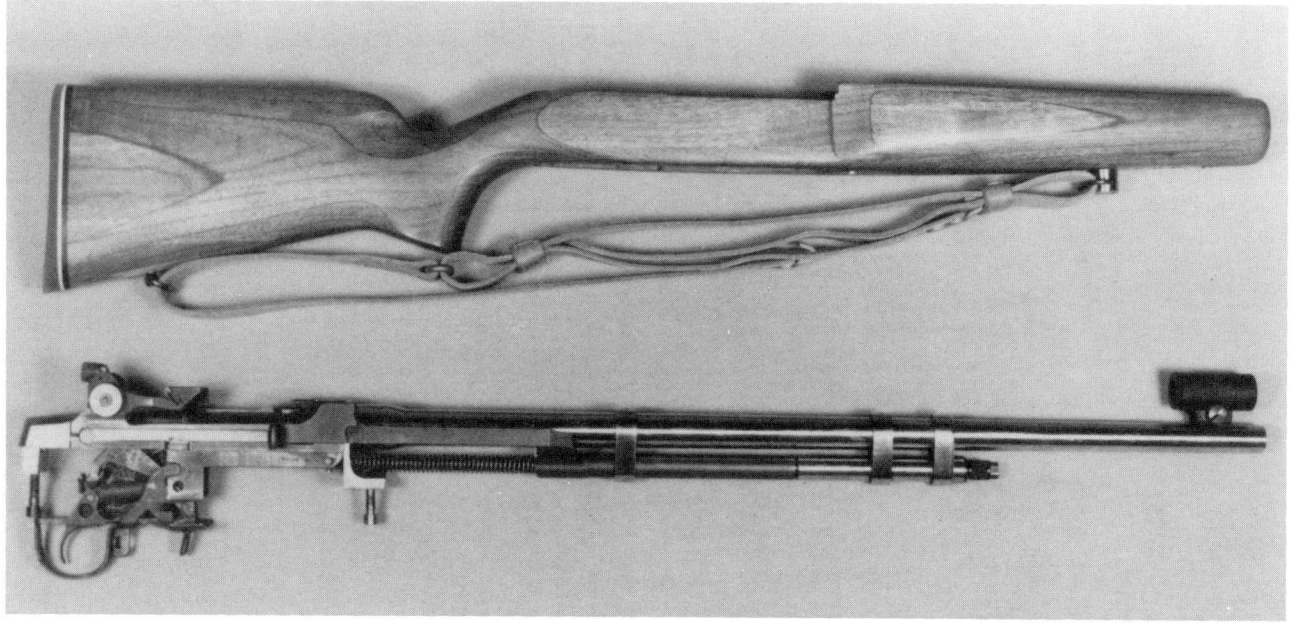

A view of the first prototype M14 rifle with the action removed from the stock. The 10.5-pound rifle was 43 1/2 inches in length with a 24-inch free-floating stainless steel barrel. The telescope-mounting area of the receiver remained unchanged. A Redfield front sight was used with the National Match rear sight assembly. A "two-point" stock mounting was used to secure the action to the lamination stock (6 May 1975). (U.S. Army.)

mance of seven types of rifles to determine their potential for use as sniper rifles.

NOTE: The U.S. Army Marksmanship Training Unit and the U.S. Army Infantry Board conducted a follow-on operational evaluation using the same rifles at Ft. Benning.

As further stated, "The candidate sniper rifles represented weapons requiring minimum development for Army use." The rifles then tested consisted of "three each" of the following models:

    M21   Rock Island Arsenal

A Vietnam-era Rock Island Arsenal photograph (June 1967) of a typical "accuracy and targeting fixture." According to RIA information, "In this firing fixture, the weapon is positioned on a cushion locator at the rear bottom of stock and on a V-Block near front end of stock to the rear of sling swivel. Two steel jaws lined with rubber cushions are pneumatically operated to rigidly clamp and hold the weapon in position for firing. The weapon recoils in firing fixture, under spring tension, and returns to its original position ready to fire the next round." The standard machine rest was also used to accuracy-check National Match rifles. (U.S. Army.)

M14M	Rodman Laboratory, modified M14
AR10M	Rodman Laboratory, modified Armalite AR10
M70	Winchester, minor modification by APG
C-3	Parker-Hale, limited production for Canadian Army
M40A1	Remington 700, modified by USMC Development Center
FR-F1	French National Arsenal

The Army M21 sniper rifle served as the "control item," and all rifles fired 7.62mm M118 match ammunition. The FR-F1 (French National

The M21: A System in Transition

Rock Island Arsenal "Prototype No. 2" of the M14 National Match Product Improved Rifle series (18 June 1975). (U.S. Army.)

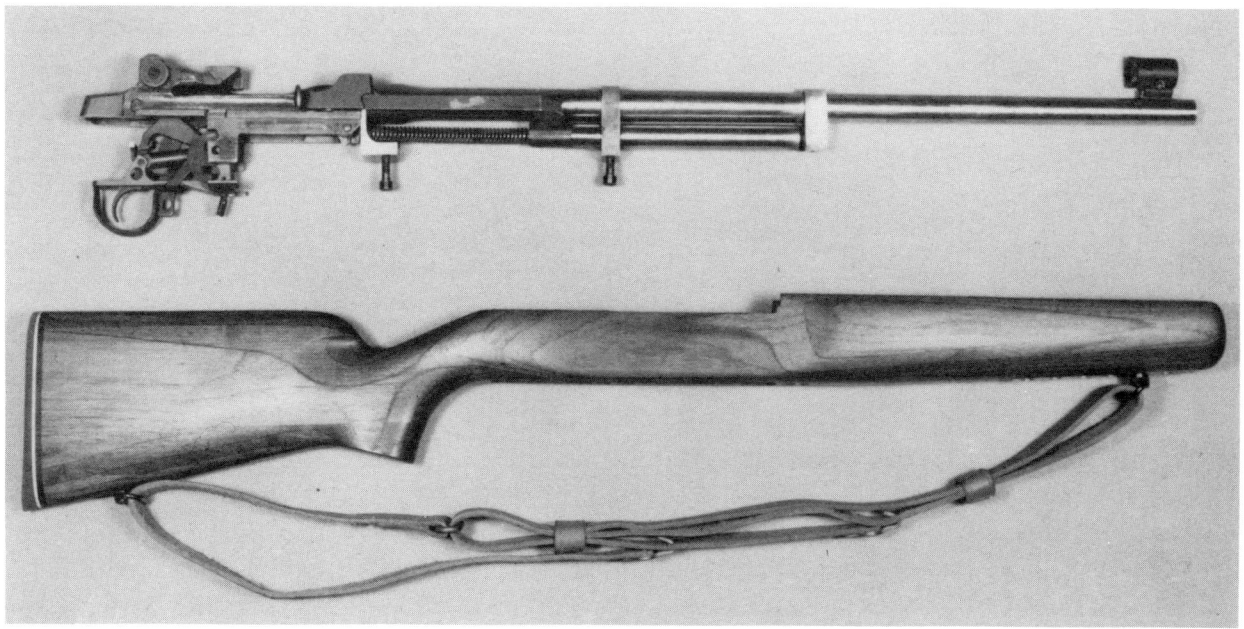

The RIA "Prototype No. 2" M14 rifle with the action removed from the stock (18 June 1975). (U.S. Army.)

Arsenal) bolt-action rifle mounting a French APX-804 telescopic sight was "tested for comparison purposes only." Though intended primarily as a test of sniper rifle candidates, Redfield and Leatherwood Adjustable Ranging Telescopes served as "accessory equipment."

NOTE: The Leatherwood Bros. telescopic sight referenced in the Aberdeen Proving Ground report (February 1978) was based on an evolving version of the Leatherwood/Realist 3X-9X variable-power ART design tested by the Army during the Vietnam War. While similar to the earlier model, the second-generation Leatherwood ART had been improved significantly. The Redfield sight was the final production version of the ART system (AR TEL) made for the Army in 1969. For the sake of clarification, although Redfield and Leatherwood ARTs were employed for the evaluations, The Vietnam-era Redfield sights were only used with the M21 sniper rifles.

Even though the Army had challenged the M14's long-term suitability

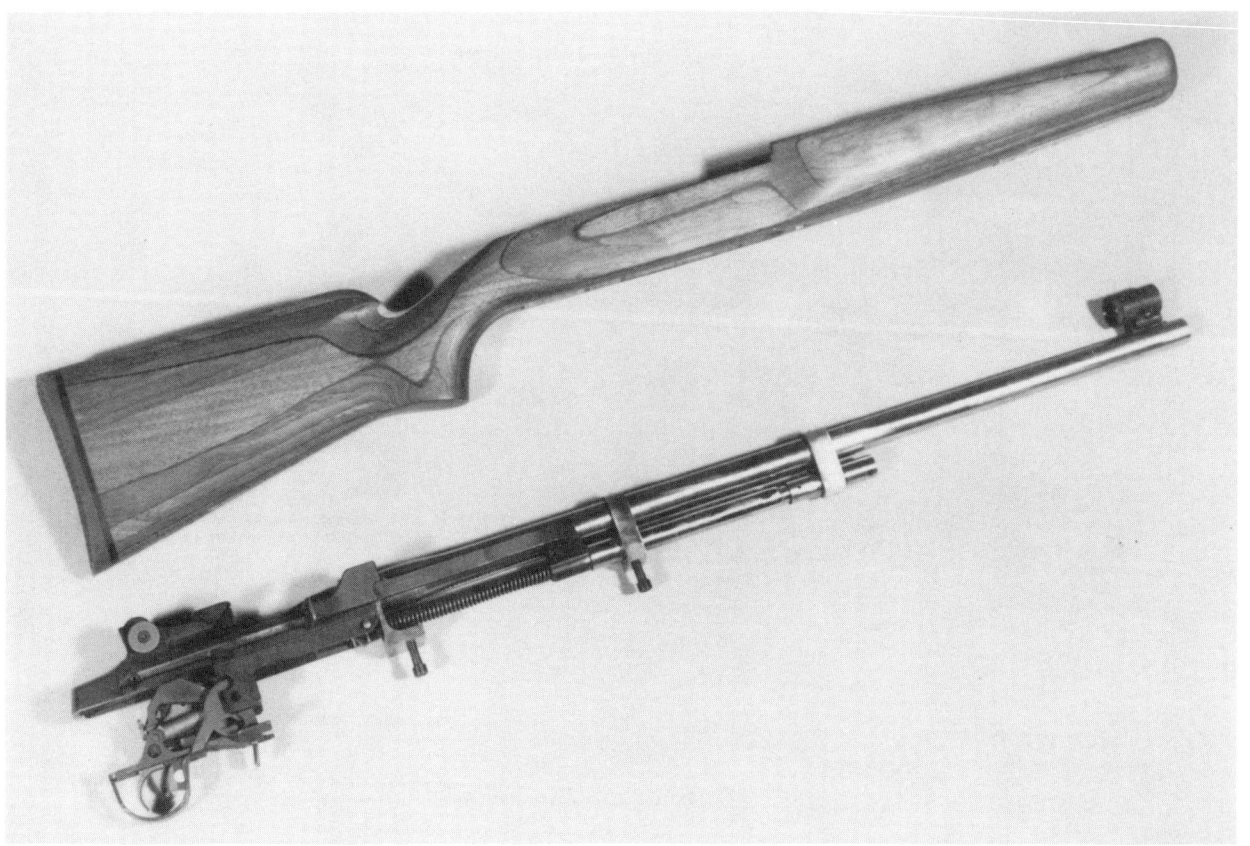

Rock Island Arsenal "Prototype No. 3" M14 rifle with the action removed from the stock. The overall length, weight, and barrel length were essentially the same for RIA M14 prototype series (16 September 1975). (U.S. Army.)

as a sniper rifle time and again, when the results of the testing indicated a preference for a "semiautomatic sniper rifle with an externally loaded magazine" and "no significant difference" between weapons from an accuracy standpoint, the evaluations conducted during 1977 effectively added another 10 years to the life span of the M21 as an Army sniper rifle.

As a matter of historical interest, the M14M noted earlier as modified by the Rodman Laboratory in the list of APG "candidate sniper rifles" was one of a series of unique prototype rifles dating from the early 1970s.

The special M14 was part of an erstwhile project intended to maximize the level of M14 accuracy and performance under the banner of "product improvement." The rifles were developed at Rock Island under the direction of Robert E. Snodgrass, a civilian employed at the arsenal (Army Weapons Command).

NOTE: An accomplished marksman and respected authority on small arms research and development, R.E. Snodgrass was counted among the "ordnance heavyweights" of the day.

Even though the M14 prototype rifles would reportedly attain accuracy levels previously unheard of, with the war in Vietnam over, the reassessment of priorities and funding brought an end to the project in

The M21: A System in Transition 261

A contemporary illustration of an Army sniper during a training exercise. The rifle is an M21 mounting an ART I (Vietnam-era AR TEL) adjustable ranging telescope. The sniper is wearing a Ghillie Suit, an elaborate form of individual camouflage intended to provide optimum concealment. (U.S. Army.)

1975. Snodgrass summarized the accuracy of the M14 rifles as follows:

> All concepts have produced less than two minutes of angle dispersion at 100 yards using M118 match ammunition. This represents approximately 100% improvement over the current acceptance standard of the M14 NM specifications.

Even with the M14 firmly entrenched as the Army sniper rifle in the years following the war, as time passed and the difficulty associated with maintaining the Vietnam-era weapon system increased, in addition to most of the original M21 rifles being rebuilt, standard M14s were accurized on an as-needed basis.

However, with continued use of the ART I (AR TEL) and the ART II past the point of practicality, by the mid-to-late 1980s, various sighting systems were considered as an "interim replacement" for the adjustable ranging telescope. In an effort to upgrade the system, the combat units maintaining an active sniper/sniper training program went so far as to procure small quantities of contemporary telescopic sights (fixed-power) and mounts for their M14 rifles.

Members of the 519th Military Police Battalion, Ft. Meade, Maryland (January 1984) during a base "counter-terrorist exercise." The rifle is an M21 with an Adjustable Ranging Telescope (AR TEL). Note the towel wrapped around the rifle stock, a simple means of easing the effects of a cold stock during extended firing. (U.S. Army.)

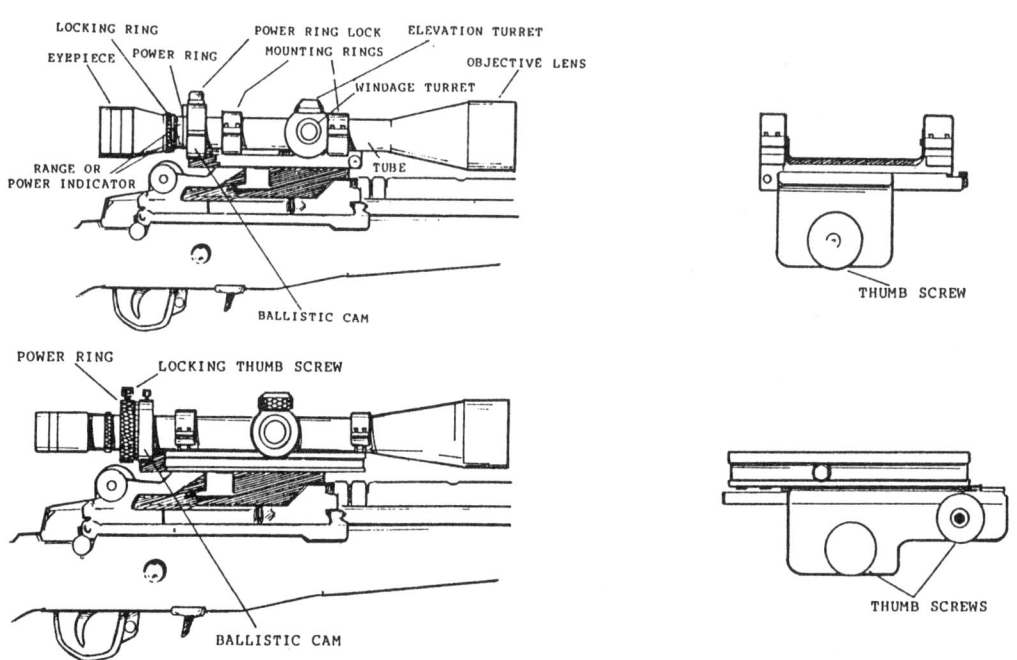

A composite illustration from TC 23-14, "Sniping Training and Employment," 14 June 1989 (this publication superseded the 27 October 1969 edition of TC 23-14, the Vietnam-era Army sniper manual) provided an effective comparison between the ART I, the ART II, and their respective mountings. The revised manual also provided operation and maintenance information for the Remington M24 Sniper Weapon System (SWS). When the Army decided to purchase the ART II Leatherwood sighting system in 1980 for sniper use, the Vietnam-era ART (AR TEL) was referenced as the ART I to avoid confusion. Even though many of the AR TEL production sights were sold off at surplus auctions (Defense Property Disposal) in the years following the conflict in Southeast Asia (some were rebuilt one or more times), a number of vintage ARTs remained in Army service more than 20 years after the last combat units left Vietnam. (U.S. Army.)

The M21: A System in Transition 263

A U.S. Army photograph with caption that reads, "A sniper and his spotter from 4th Bn., 22nd Inf., 25th Infantry Division (Light), and two Thai soldiers during a combined Thai/U.S. exercise" (Thailand, May 1990). The camouflaged Army marksman (right) is armed with an M21 mounting a Leatherwood ART II sighting system. (U.S. Army.)

M24 Sniper Weapon System (SWS) manufactured by Remington Arms Co. for the U.S. Army. The bolt-action 7.62mm (.308 Win.) rifle was fielded as a replacement for the M21 (M14) sniper rifle in 1988. The telescope is a 10-power Leupold ULTRA M3 model. (Remington Arms Co.)

264 THE LONG-RANGE WAR: SNIPING IN VIETNAM

U.S. Navy (SEAL) sniper takes aim at front-line Iraqi forces near Kuwait City (Operation Desert Storm, February 1991). The weapon is an M25 ("product improved M21") sniper rifle with a Bausch & Lomb 10-power "Tactical Riflescope," Brookfield Precision Tool (BPT) M14 telescope mounting, fiberglass stock, and bipod assembly. By all accounts, the 7.62mm M14 rifle was the SEAL weapon of choice during the Persian Gulf War. (Max Crace.)

The M21: A System in Transition

A match-conditioned M14 rifle with a "low-profile" magazine, Leupold ULTRA M2 10-power (fixed-power) telescopic sight, and ARMS (Atlantic Research Marketing Systems) M21 scope mount. The flip-up lens covers are made by Butler-Creek. The weapon is typical of the M14 sniper rifles fielded by various Army combat units during the late 1980s. Both Leupold & Stevens and Bausch & Lomb fixed-power rifle scopes have seen combat use with the M14 rifle in recent years. (Landies Collection.)

A photograph of an M25 (M14) sniper rifle taken in the 3/5th SFG (A) "armsroom" at King Khalid Military City (KKMC) in Saudi Arabia following the Persian Gulf War. The M25 system was originally developed by the 10th Special Forces Group (Airborne) based at Ft. Devens. The rifles fielded during Operation Desert Storm were attributed to the Naval Weapons Support Center, Crane, Indiana. The Navy version of the M25 was issued in an aluminum hard case with spare magazines and cleaning equipment. (U.S. Army.)

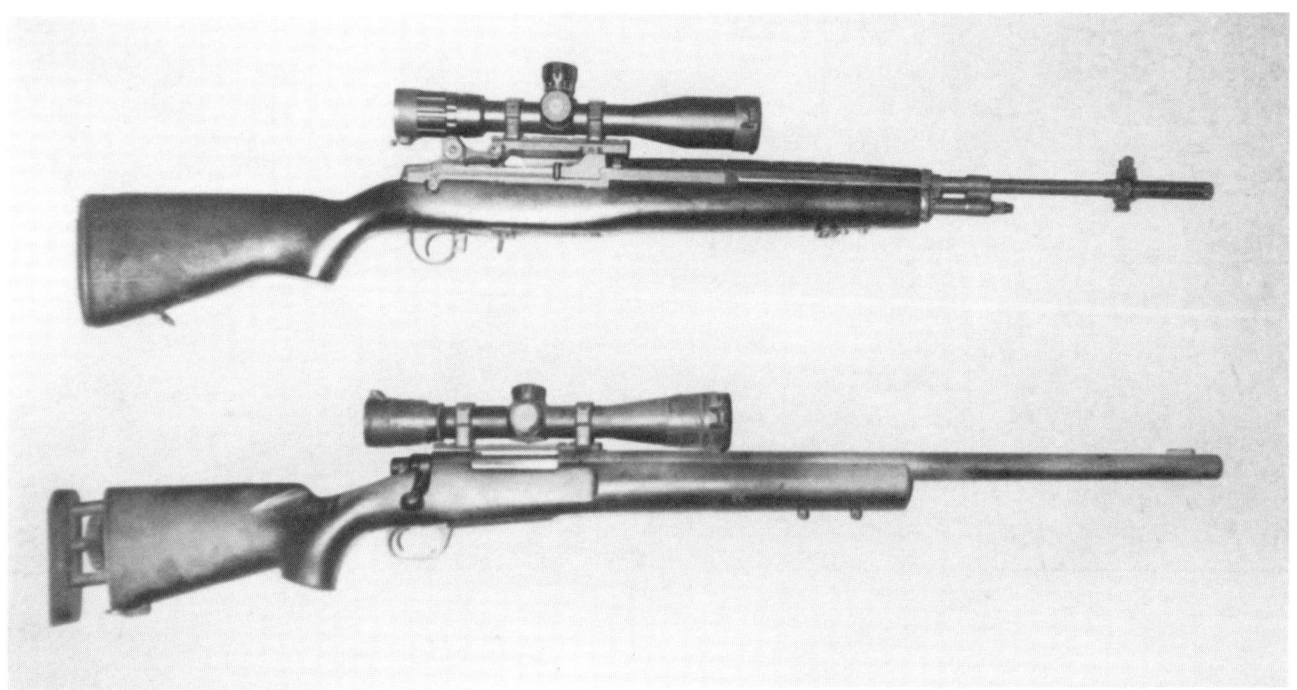

A 3/5th SFG (A) armsroom photograph provides a direct comparison between a semiautomatic M25 (top) and a bolt-action M24 sniper rifle. (U.S. Army.)

Army marksman and spotter circa 1992 (Ft. Campbell, Kentucky). The rifle is a "transitional weapon system," a 7.62mm M25 sniper rifle mounting a 10-power Bausch & Lomb telescopic sight. (U.S. Army.)

The M21: A System in Transition

5th Special Forces (Airborne) personnel during a live-fire training exercise at Ft. Campbell (1992). Their weapons are M24 bolt-action sniper rifles. The M16A2 (background) is fitted with a 4-power Hensoldt & Sohne, BLITS rifle scope (Beta Lighted Infantry Telescope System), one of a variety of telescopic sights currently in use by the military with the M16A2 rifle. (U.S. Army.)

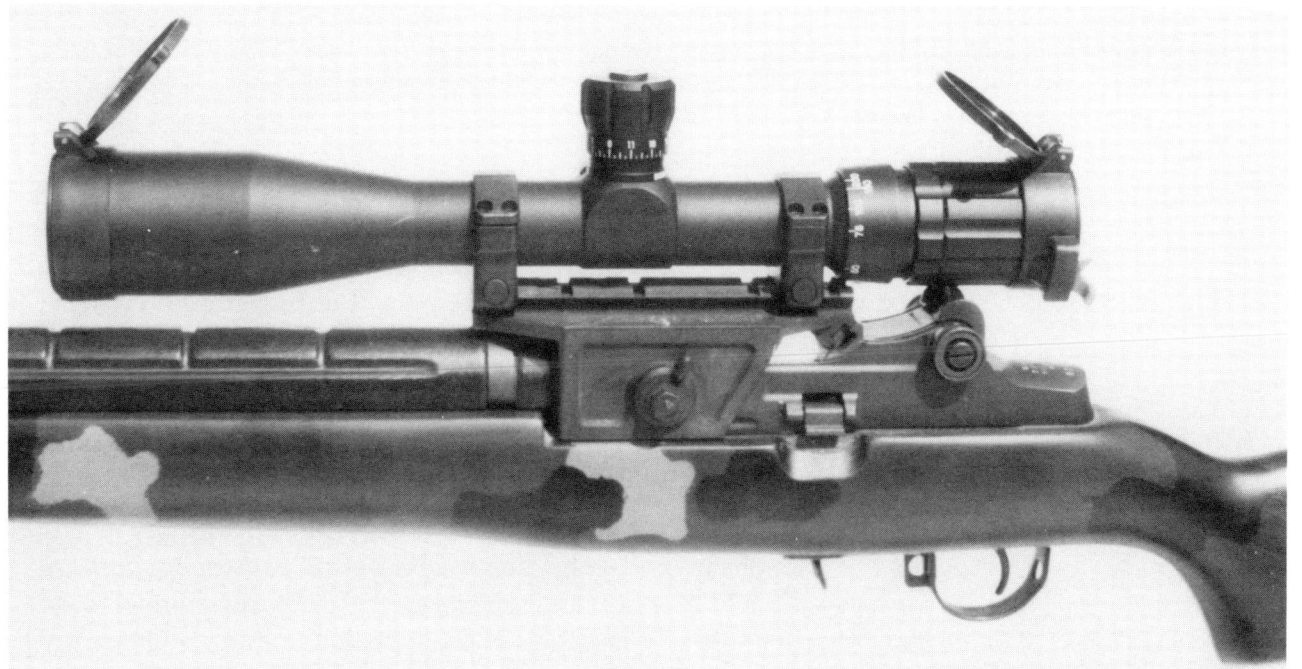

A close view of the Navy version of the M25 sniper rifle circa 1991. The sight is a 10-power Bausch & Lomb Tactical Riflescope in a BPT Advanced Scope Mounting System. The rifle makes use of a McMillan Fiberglass stock and a Harris bipod assembly. A BPT stock liner, special gas piston, and NM spring guide are part of the system as well. The "M25 sniper rifle" has been referenced as both the XM25 and M25 in contemporary Army and Navy ordnance documents. The weapon is still considered a "transitional system" at present. (Mitchell E. Mateiko.)

10th Special Forces Group (Airborne) SOTIC instructor Sfc. Thomas E. Kapp is shown "firing at 900 meters" with the "Army version" of the XM25 (Ft. Devens). The M14 sniper rifle is fitted with a Leupold ULTRA M3 10-power sight, BPT scope mounting, McMillan fiberglass stock, Harris bipod, and OPS Inc. noise suppressor. The system was developed by 10th SFG(A) in response to a requirement for a match-grade M14 for Special Forces sniper teams. By all accounts, Sergeant Kapp was instrumental in "breathing new life" into the M14 as a sniper rifle. According to a U.S. Special Operations Command (USSOCOM) letter of appreciation," 7 May 1991: "Sergeant Kapp played an integral role in the design and development of the USSOCOM Light Sniper Rifle . . . He has earned our sincere appreciation and respect." (Mitchell E. Mateiko.)

Though the M14 was succeeded eventually by the bolt-action 7.62mm M24 Sniper Weapon System (SWS), the Army did not turn loose of it as a sniper rifle. Listed in one Army "Operational Requirements" document or another as a "Product Improved M21," "Light Sniper Rifle," or "Sniper Security System," for example, the "match-grade M14" was still viewed as a potential sniping weapon for use in a limited, specialized capacity.

In spite of the fact that the M24 was adopted as a replacement for the aging M21 system, the bolt-action Remington rifle did not meet the expectations of the Army. Consequently, with the U.S. military redefining the roles of the "bolt-guns" and the "gas-guns" for sniping purposes, various-caliber bolt-action and semiautomatic rifles, in addition to special .50-caliber rifles, became part of the apparently never-ending evaluation process the U.S. Army conducted in its quest for suitable equipment for special operations and conventional sniper use.

At this juncture, the M14 rifle is still a viable candidate.